CHET ATKINS

MUSIC OF THE AMERICAN SOUTH SERIES

CHET ATKINS
MR. GUITAR

Don Cusic

The University of Georgia Press ∽ Athens

Athens, Georgia 30602
www.ugapress.org

Designed by Erin Kirk
Set in Miller Text
Printed and bound by Sheridan Books, Inc.

The paper in this book meets the guidelines for permanence and durability of the Committee on Production Guidelines for Book Longevity of the Council on Library Resources.

Most University of Georgia Press titles are available from popular e-book vendors.

Printed in the United States of America
29 28 27 26 25 C 5 4 3 2 1

Library of Congress Cataloging-in-Publication Data

Names: Cusic, Don, author.
Title: Chet Atkins : Mr. Guitar / Don Cusic.
Description: Athens : University of Georgia Press, 2025. | Series: Music of the American South | Includes bibliographical references and index.
Identifiers: LCCN 2024051352 (print) | LCCN 2024051353 (ebook) | ISBN 9780820373393 (hardback) | ISBN 9780820373409 (epub) | ISBN 9780820373416 (pdf)
Subjects: LCSH: Atkins, Chet. | Country musicians—United States—Biography. | Guitarists—United States—Biography. | Sound recording executives and producers—United States—Biography.
Classification: LCC ML419.A83 C87 2025 (print) | LCC ML419.A83 (ebook) | DDC 787.87/1642092 [B]—dc23/eng/20241029
LC record available at https://lccn.loc.gov/2024051352
LC ebook record available at https://lccn.loc.gov/2024051353

EU Authorized Representative
Easy Access System Europe—Mustamäe tee 50, 10621 Tallinn, Estonia, *gpsr.requests@easproject.com*

Contents

Introduction

This is a story of a young boy who fell in love with the guitar. He obtained an old Silvertone and spent hours sitting alone, hunched over his guitar until it seemed like his body was shaped into the guitar. The young boy was poor and did not have many toys, but he had a ferocious ambition and aspired to become a world-famous guitar player, so he practiced and practiced and practiced. In East Tennessee, where he was born to a broken family, he heard other musicians play and watched their fingers, movements he mimicked until he could play what he heard.

He was a sickly boy with asthma so bad his mother feared for his life. He could not attend school or lay down to sleep, so he sat in a chair and practiced his guitar.

As a teenager he heard the great thumbpicker Merle Travis on the radio and longed to emulate his style, so he practiced but didn't quite master the technique. Instead, he developed a unique form of fingerpicking.

He dreamed of playing on the radio and first did so in Knoxville, Tennessee, then went on to other stations and eventually the Grand Ole Opry.

The boy's name was Chester Atkins, but after a radio station employee called him "Chet," the name stuck. He wanted to be different, to play his own way, and so he practiced. His ambition for fame pushed him on.

Chet's big break came when he joined the Carter Family, backing them on their radio shows and live performances. He learned from them and continued to practice. In Nashville with the Carter Family he began backing country artists; his distinct talent led to work producing records for a wide variety of artists. Before long he joined RCA Records as an artist and record producer and later as an executive.

Chet kept practicing as his name became known in music circles and then amongst the public, eventually renowned as the most famous guitarist in the world. He had a knack for perfect timing in his career and kept practicing.

During his lifetime Chet Atkins became known as one of the architects of the Nashville Sound, a key figure in transforming Nashville into Music City U.S.A. He played for Hank Williams and other country stars, then on early recordings of Elvis Presley and the Everly Brothers at the birth of rock and roll. When the Beatles came to the United States in February 1964, lead guitarist George Harrison played a Chet Atkins model Gretsch on their *Ed Sullivan Show* debut before 73 million TV viewers.

By the end of his life, Chet Atkins had recorded over a hundred solo albums, won fourteen Grammys, including one for Lifetime Achievement, won nine Country Music Association Instrumentalist awards, and was enshrined in the Country Music Hall of Fame. Countless trade magazines and organizations also honored his musical career.

At the height of his fame, when known simply as "Mr. Guitar," Chet Atkins still practiced. This is the story of that young boy who fell in love with the guitar and practiced alone for hours.

CHET ATKINS

CHAPTER 1

During the 1920s and 1930s, Luttrell, Tennessee, was bound together by music. The main street general store served as an informal community center; people sat around and played and sang. Visitors would bring an instrument—fiddle, guitar, banjo—and play. Music glued the community together.

Luttrell sits about twenty miles northeast of Knoxville in the Clinch Mountains. Chet's great-grandfather bought a fifty-acre farm in Luttrell, where the family grew tobacco and corn and raised horses and cows. Chet's grandfather, Sylvester "Wes" Atkins, a Unionist during the Civil War, built and played fiddles. Chet Atkins's father, James Arlie Atkins, taught music, tuned pianos, and traveled with evangelists, leading the worship.

James Arlie and Ella Archer Atkins grew up and wed in Luttrell. Arlie's two brothers had moved to south-central Nebraska, so Arlie and Ella followed them. Their first child, James Cornet Atkins, was born there in 1912. Ella contracted tuberculosis and died in 1915, so Arlie and his young son moved back to Luttrell, where they moved in with his aging parents. Ida Sharp served as caretaker for the elderly couple and had a daughter, Willard, when she was fifteen. Ida, called "Idie," married Arlie after giving birth to their daughter, Niona.

Following Arlie's parents' death in 1917, Arlie and Ida moved to Cincinnati, where Arlie worked for the railroad and attended the Cincinnati Conservatory of Music and Ida worked as a live-in maid. After they returned to their farm in Luttrell around 1920, the couple gave birth to a son, Lowell, in 1921, and then to Chester Burton Atkins on June 20, 1924.

His name came from the C. B. Atkins Moving Company; "Burton" derived from Senator Burton K. Wheeler, but the "Chester" was always a mystery; later Chet surmised that "maybe it was the first name he thought of that started with 'C.'"[1]

During most evenings the family sat around playing music and singing. In 1924 Arlie bought Jim, who was twelve years older than

Chester and Chester's idol, a Washburn guitar. Chester "touched [the guitar] a lot, rubbed my fingers lightly over the top, savoring the silky varnish, and picking the strings ever so lightly." Those steel strings "felt cold and magical" to his fingers.[2]

Chester experienced his first strong memory at about four or five. A friend had left behind a ukulele, and Chet used wire from their screen door to string the instrument. One day he was playing by the stream near their house when his mother told him to "go to the spring and get me some water." When young Chester didn't do it right away, his mom cracked him on the head with the ukulele and "busted it up."[3]

Chester's father often traveled with evangelists to revivals, tent meetings, and other church gatherings. Arlie was a difficult man: "I don't think he could have gotten along with anybody since he wanted everybody to be perfect. He was a man of conflicting ideals, an enigma. He was a believer, in an odd sort of way. I think he believed in God, but his was a mechanical belief—a strange concept for an evangelistic singer."[4] Chester was never close to his father. "I minded him because I was scared to death of him," he remembered. "And the rest of the time I just stayed out of his way."[5]

Arlie and Idie struggled in their relationship; Chester "hated the sounds that came from their room."[6] They reached the point in 1930, when Chester was six, that Arlie announced he was leaving. Dressed in a blue serge suit with a straw hat and carrying a cardboard suitcase, Arlie told the children: "Well, goodbye, kiddies. I'm leaving. I won't be back for awhile." Arlie walked off whistling while Idie cried.[7]

The next time Chester saw his father was when he visited the family from his new home in Tuscaloosa, Alabama, where he had remarried and had a child, Jeannie. Arlie brought along a guitar for Lowell. Chet asked for a fiddle, and his dad promised he would get one for him on his next visit; however, Arlie brought Niona a mandolin. On another visit a year later, Arlie brought along a fiddle and promised it to Chester, but then Arlie took it with him when he left. The disappointment of not getting that fiddle hurt Chester deeply; he remembered the experience vividly his entire life. Arlie and Idie's love had transformed into a deep hatred, and whenever his name came up at home Idie had nothing positive to say. She also resented the fact that he never supported them financially.

During the first six years of Chet's childhood he was part of a traditional family with his father as the breadwinner. The next five years were spent in deep poverty with a single mom trying to support three children during the Great Depression. The family was proud to have never accepted a handout. The children received one pair of shoes each winter, and depending on how well the tobacco crop did they might receive a pair of gym shoes in the spring. They largely went barefoot the rest of the year. Their house lacked electricity, indoor plumbing, and running water, but it was filled with music.[8] Many years later, enjoying success and wealth, Chet told a friend, "The poor and the rich will never understand each other." He could have been talking about his own life.[9]

Chester's musical epiphany occurred around 1930, at the age of six, when his mother took him to Knoxville. "I saw a blind man playing a guitar on the street," Atkins recalled, noting that even late in life "I can still see him, with that old, beat-up guitar and a tin cup tied close to the pegs. I can even hear the coins drop into the cup."[10] Chester was captivated by the singer and his beat-up guitar: "It hit me like a bolt of lightning, I was spellbound by it. My mother had to drag me away. I think that's when I knew I wanted to be—had to be—a musician."[11]

In the fall of 1932, Idie married Willie Strevel, who lived a few miles away. Chester, Lowell, and Niona now had a stepfather, who played music but also drank a lot of moonshine.

Willie owned a Model T Ford, which he traded for fifteen dollars and an old Silvertone, his second guitar. Chet eventually bartered with Willie for the Silvertone, which became his constant companion: "I would lean on it for the love I never seemed to have enough of and depend on it for the friendships I didn't always find."[12]

"I never had many toys," said Chet. "But the guitar was different. It was not a toy. It was life itself to me. I dreamed of someday becoming a great star, though using it to make money never crossed my mind. I couldn't imagine getting paid for anything as wonderful as playing the guitar for people. I would have paid to play on the radio—if I had had the money."[13]

Although that first guitar was treasured, it had major problems. "It had a pretty good spruce top, but the neck had been broken on it, pulled away from the back, and someone had run a big screw into it to try and repair it," remembered Chet. "As soon as you got away from the nut, the action was about a half-inch high, so it was hard to play . . . [but] it helped strengthen my left hand." Chester made a new bridge out of walnut but lacked the proper tools, so when he "put the weight down on it, the bridge slipped and I didn't notice it, so it got glued on crooked." Whenever guitars were swapped and someone ended up with the Silvertone "they always wanted to trade back right away," said Chet. "Those heavy old strings and that warped neck were hard on fingers, too."[14] By the time Chester was eight, he could play most of the major and minor chords. "When I heard a lick I liked, I stole it," he said.[15]

In 1932, when Chester was eight, an eleven-year-old boy, Buster Devault, moved into the Victorian house owned by his grandmother. Chet's home was nearby, down in a "holler" below, and the two boys became close friends. "We used to build crystal radio sets and we had a lot of fun," said Buster. The radio allowed Chester to hear radio shows on NBC and CBS, which featured big band music. Many of the songs Chet later recorded date back to the songs of that era. The first "country" music Chet heard on the radio was the Sons of the Pioneers, whose transcription discs were played on WNOX as the "JFC Coffee Boys." Chester later claimed the Sons of the Pioneers as a major influence, especially guitarist Karl Farr and fiddler Hugh Farr, "real jazz players."[16]

Willie and Idie Strevel remained on the farm owned by Arlie for a few years but then had to move because Arlie retained ownership in the divorce.

During the 1920s and early 1930s, the fiddle was the most popular instrument for rural, country folks. Fiddlers—judged by how many tunes they could play—would play for dances and other social gatherings. Chester got his first fiddle from his Uncle Joe Atkins. Since that fiddle had no bow, Chester refurbished an old bow with hair from their horse's tail.

Nearly every Saturday night the rugs would be rolled back, the furniture moved, and neighbors came over to dance while Chester, Lowell, and Willie played. It quickly became known that the Atkins boys had musical talent, so they were invited to play at others' homes and the general store. A teacher asked Chester and Lowell to play for a school assembly; Chester was "shaking like a leaf, but, for some reason—I don't know why—I liked it. We played 'Wildwood Flower' and the kids cheered." Chester was only ten years old at the time but knew "this was where I had to be: out on some stage, or any place in front of people, playing the fiddle or picking the guitar. The applause gave me more confidence in myself than anything ever had."[17]

Chester saved his money and bought a crystal radio set from one of his schoolmates; each evening he sat with his radio, his connection to the outside world. Whenever he heard music he liked, he grabbed his guitar or fiddle and, with dogged determination, learned to play it.

Chester practiced and improved on both the guitar and the fiddle, playing the gospel music that was a staple of their community as well as old British folk songs. Chester learned songs from the radio—Knoxville stations like WNOX could be heard in Luttrell—and from those who had traveled to Knoxville or elsewhere and learned songs. There were also records—Willie Strevel had a record by Blind Lemon Jefferson and Chet's friend, Buster Devault, had three Jimmie Rodgers records, *T for Texas*, *Yodeling My Way Back Home*, and *Waiting for a Train*. Chester had played "Wildwood Flower" before he heard the Carter Family's version on a record that his teacher played in school.

Chet Atkins was born at the right time. In 1923 the first commercially successful country music recording was made by Fiddlin' John Carson in Atlanta. That success led recording companies to record rural talent throughout the South. In 1927, Victor's Ralph Peer recorded the Carter Family and Jimmie Rodgers in Bristol, Tennessee, not far from where Chet was born. Country music was played on radio "barn dances," variety shows aimed at rural audiences. In April 1924 the National Barn Dance, broadcast on WLS in Chicago, went on the air; WSM in Nashville began broadcasting in October 1925 and the following month began a barn dance that came to be known as the Grand Ole Opry by 1927.

In 1934 the Atkins family enjoyed a bumper tobacco crop, but the winter of 1934–1935 was wet and caused Chester's asthma to worsen; Idie wondered if he would even survive. Sometimes the asthma was so bad Chester "couldn't eat anything or go to bed for days at a time. If I did either, I wouldn't be able to breathe. I would sit up straight in a chair and pick the guitar all day, practicing and feeling sorry for myself."[18]

Idie wrote to Arlie, who was living on a two-hundred-acre farm in Hamilton, Georgia, asking him to take Chester to Georgia in hopes of assuaging his asthma. Arlie agreed. His Model A Ford could go only thirty-five miles an hour, so it was ten thirty at night when they arrived in Hamilton and were met by a "beautiful woman."[19]

Arlie, forty-seven, had married yet again; his fourth wife, Tommie, was just twenty-two years old. Tommie was a good stepmother to eleven-year-old Chester and treated him like her own. Chester had been in Georgia only a few days when Tommie took him to an African American church; Chet had never seen a Black person before. “We were in a Model A Ford outside looking in the window,” he remembered. “They’d preach, the women would faint, and I’d hear these spirituals.”[20]

After three days in Georgia Chester wanted to go home, but his father refused: “You’re not going home. You’re here, you’re going to school here and you’re going to be here. And you might as well like it.” Chet’s father “was kind of authoritarian,” said Chet. “There was no backtalk. You did what he said; if you didn’t you’d find yourself on the ground. I wasn’t used to that. I was real scared of him at first.”[21]

The second phase of Chet’s childhood was more comfortable than the poverty he endured in East Tennessee. He lived on a large farm, his father earned a steady income, and central Georgia was lush and green with good topsoil. Chet was fortunate to attend Mountain Hill School, which featured electricity and indoor plumbing at a time when much of the rural South did not. Chester entered fourth grade a year older than most of his classmates because of the year of schooling he missed due to asthma.

Arlie taught music at Mountain Hill during the day and grew tobacco on his farm. A dramatic difference between East Tennessee and central Georgia was the dearth of music in Georgia. Even so, Chester continued to practice his guitar and fiddle and could pick up more radio stations in Georgia (the mountains of East Tennessee hindered radio reception). He also began corresponding with his brother Jim.

In 1937, after Chester had been in Georgia for a year and a half, Arlie ordered him and his sister to return to Luttrell. When Chester and Niona arrived back home, things had changed. “Willie had gotten used to us not being around and he treated us like intruders,” said Chet. “It was an odd feeling. Mother was loving, but she was busy raising my new half sister, Billie Rose.”[22] Shortly thereafter Niona got married and Chester moved in with her and her husband. Before long he returned to Georgia to live with his father. Although he returned to Luttrell for visits, he never lived there again.

In 1938, Chester was living with his father in Fortson, near Hamilton, Georgia, where Arlie had leased a thousand acres and acquired three hundred steers; Chester helped care for the cattle. Always thirsty for knowledge, Chester returned to school and at home read his father’s

Book of Knowledge Encyclopedia cover to cover. He enjoyed school, where the teachers occasionally asked him to play music, and convinced his dad to purchase the complete works of Mark Twain. He brought his guitar to school every day and during lunch and recess played in the bathroom. His musical talent stood out in Georgia; many residents of East Tennessee played an instrument, but that was not the case in Georgia.

"The people around me at the time thought I was guitar crazy, and they were right," said Chet. "I was obsessed with the guitar, and with improving my ability to play it. . . . I wanted to be famous, and I knew I had to be good to achieve that, so I really dedicated myself to it."[23]

Chet listened to popular radio shows like *Amos 'n' Andy*, *Fibber McGee and Molly*, and *The Shadow*. This connection helped Chester feel more worldly and less isolated. Listening to Broadway songs or the Grand Ole Opry, he felt part of a larger world outside rural Georgia. He dreamed of traveling to faraway places and seeing his name on marquees.

CHAPTER 2

After Jim Atkins moved to Central City, Nebraska, in 1929, his Uncle Joe took him to radio station WIND to audition, and they hired him. In 1935 Jim auditioned for George Bigger with WLS in Chicago and was hired and billed as Tommy Tanner, a name owned by the station. On WLS's National Barn Dance Jim was a member of the Hilltoppers, with Ernie Newton and Don Wilson. During the early 1930s Newton played bass for the Texas Ramblers, sang on Carson Robinson's "Going Back to Texas," then joined Mac and Bob, the popular blind duo on WLS in Chicago. Newton was a staff musician on WLS and played with the Hoosier Hot Shots. That was where he met Jim Atkins.[1]

Jim did not want to be identified as a country singer because "everybody looked down their noses at hillbillies," he said. "But the odd thing about it was the country music boys were making the money! And the modern boys were eating hamburgers, when and if they could buy one."[2]

One night at WLS Jim met Lester Polsfuss, who was performing on the National Barn Dance as Rhubarb Red. During the winter of 1934 Joe Wolverton and Les joined CBS's Chicago affiliate WBBM, where they were billed as the Ozark Apple Knockers. In Chicago Les first heard records by Art Tatum, an innovative jazz pianist, and Belgian Gypsy guitarist Django Reinhardt. Astounded by Reinhardt's playing, Les learned songs Django performed with the Hot Club of France, like "Avalon," "Tiger Rag," "Smoke Rings," "Nagasaki," and "Nuages." By the mid-1930s Lester Polsfuss had become Les Paul and earned a comfortable living playing on WJJD as Rhubarb Red and jazz guitar on WIND as Les Paul.

Jim Atkins and Les Paul sought to branch out from country music, so they formed a trio with Ernie Newton on bass; Jim played rhythm and sang with a voice reminiscent of Bing Crosby. The trio convinced WLS to book them on a National Barn Dance road show that passed through Upstate New York. They first auditioned in New York City but failed to get hired.

Fred Waring was a popular big band leader who hosted national shows. He had the Pennsylvanians, featuring a band, a singing chorus, and a variety of talent. A chance encounter between the Les Paul Trio and Waring led to an impromptu audition, and Waring hired them. Waring had signed with NBC for a live radio show on Saturday nights. On June 19, 1939, *Chesterfield Pleasure Time* debuted, broadcast live. Before long the Les Paul Trio was one of the most popular acts on Waring's show.

Chester had heard his brother play on the National Barn Dance on WLS. "I think I cried, I was so proud of him," he remembered. "It inspired me to work that much harder at learning to play because, by this time, I had already made up my mind that I was going to be a guitar player. I wanted to be a famous guitar player, that was my goal but I told myself, even if I don't achieve fame, playing guitar is still what I'm going to do."[3]

Listening to WLW in Cincinnati one night in 1939, Chester heard Merle Travis. "His guitar style was closer to that sound I had been searching for than anything I had ever heard," said Chet. "The clever way he played melody and rhythm at the same time knocked me over. I knew he was finger picking, but I didn't know how he was doing it. I would pick up WLW and Merle about once a month when conditions were right. When I couldn't pick him up on the radio, I would try to invent things that sounded like him. If I'd heard him more often I would have wound up playing exactly like him."[4]

Merle Travis grew up in the coal mining region of eastern Kentucky and developed a thumbpicking style of guitar, influenced by others in the region, such as Mose Rager and Ike Everly. Thumbpicking, where the guitarist wears a thumbpick and plays the bass strings with the thumb while picking out the melody on the high strings with the other fingers, has its roots in western Kentucky. There remains a pervasive myth that the style was first developed by Arnold Shultz, an African American musician who lived near Rosine, Kentucky, the hometown of Bill Monroe. However, the true originator of thumbpicking is likely Kennedy Jones, whose thumb was reportedly swollen and sore after a night of playing. He went to a music store in 1918 and found a box of thumbpicks, which were used by musicians playing lap guitar.

According to music historian Mike Seeger, whose account was quoted by Erika Brady, Jones put on a thumbpick, grabbed a guitar in the store, "and I started pickin' with it. . . . Just a thumb and finger, that's all I used. I couldn't do a good job with it to start with, but in about a week or two, I was really rockin'."[5]

Brady interviewed Paul Yandell, Atkins's longtime accompanist, who told her "Kennedy Jones is the father of it all. . . . Jones was the first guy that started playing with a thumbpick, which was a major, major advancement because you take somebody that plays thumb-style and take their thumbpick off, you sound *completely* different."[6] Mose Rager and Ike Everly were thumbpickers who influenced Merle Travis, who became the first to make the thumbpicking style nationally known.

Willie Strevel had used his fingers playing guitar when he tried to copy the licks from a Blind Lemon Jefferson record he owned and "once in a while I'd hear someone who was using the fingers of their right hand in some way or other, and I would always be drawn to it," said Chet. "I liked the way finger rolls sounded on the banjo, and it wasn't hard to figure out how to do simple versions of that on the guitar. I liked it because it sounded different, more like the way a piano is played."[7]

It was hearing Merle Travis on the radio that crystalized Atkins's desire to develop a fingerpicking style. "From Merle Travis I added a lot of songs to my repertoire," said Atkins. "He certainly stimulated my imagination as to what could be done with a guitar. His strong thumb and fingerstyle playing gave me the focus I had been needing. It wasn't just the notes he played, it was the intensity of his playing that got through to me. It sounded full and complete, like he was in total command of the instrument. I loved it, but I couldn't figure out how he was doing it so I had to invent my own way." Chester developed a style that involved playing with his thumb and three fingers. "I was lucky that although I was a Merle Travis fan, I hadn't had the opportunity to listen to him enough to copy him," said Chet. "I play an alternate bass and he played a thump, almost like a four/four. I always played with my fingers. I'd take a toothbrush made of celluloid, heat it up and cut off a piece with a pocket knife. Then I'd put it in hot water and fit it around my thumb to make my own thumb pick."[8]

Merle Travis played with his thumb and one finger, with the thumb playing the bass notes—in the key of C this would either be the C or

G note. Chet developed his style with the thumb playing the A string, then D string, then E string, then D string. In the key of C it would be C, E (on the D string), then G (on the E string), then E (on the D string). Chet likened this sound to a "stride piano." He also credited the classical music magazines that his father received "which described classical guitar techniques."[9]

The secret of thumbpicking is not in the left hand, which forms the chords and fingers the notes, but in the right hand, which gives a song a heart and a beat. The soul of a fingerpicker comes through in the right hand, which controls the feel of a song. Thumbpicking gives a song a driving beat, while fingerpicking softens the sound.

Chet also heard George Barnes, "a single-string player" who was "just magnificent. He was like a damn machine." Barnes was on the *Plantation Party* radio show in Chicago "kind of an uptown music show," remembered Atkins. "It wasn't country but Barnes played country songs like 'Turkey in the Straw.' He'd jazz them up and just play wonderful arrangements," said Chet.[10]

Every morning in Georgia, Chester got up at five o'clock, chopped wood for the stove, and listened to the radio before school. Between chores and school he practiced. "I wouldn't give up one minute of practice," he remembered. "I was determined to find my sound—a sound that would take me where I wanted to go: on a stage any place where people would applaud my music and come back for more."[11] He often stayed up until midnight, listening to the radio and practicing his guitar and fiddle.

CHAPTER 3

In the spring of 1941 Chester was hired by the National Youth Administration, one of President Franklin Roosevelt's New Deal initiatives, to help build a new gym at Mountain Hill School. He had read about converting an acoustic guitar into an electric guitar in *Popular Mechanics*, so he purchased a coil, magnetic pickup, and amplifier from Allied Radio (later known as Radio Shack) and assembled the parts. The pickup could be attached to the bridge of his flattop Silvertone guitar.

Now he had an electric guitar—but his home had no electricity—so he played at school during recess and lunch and at church, where his father directed the choir. "My music was developing so that I was beginning to find my own licks," he said. "Because of the radio, I had finally realized that there was a strong link between hillbilly music and jazz. I had been listening to a lot of jazz; the freedom and spontaneity of it appealed to me. When I tried the jazz licks on the guitar, they sounded good so I felt sure that my day was near."

On December 7, 1941, Chester heard on the radio that the Japanese had bombed Pearl Harbor, and a few weeks later his father told him that he was moving to Cincinnati to work for the war effort. Chester needed to return to East Tennessee.[1]

Chester had not planned to return to Tennessee, but Arlie's decision forced him to drop out of school in the tenth grade. He caught a Greyhound bus in Columbus with two suitcases, one for his clothes and the other for his books and radio. Chester was uncertain of his future, but there was a bright light in the distance.

By the time he left Georgia, seventeen-year-old Chester Atkins had mastered his fingerpicking style and sounded like Chet Atkins.

It was late at night when Chester arrived in Knoxville, so he spent the night in the bus station. The next morning he caught the bus to Luttrell. Chester did not enroll in school in Tennessee, a decision that he regretted; he always felt undereducated and was intimidated by well-educated people, yet he felt he had made the right decision to pursue music as a career.

Chester spent the first few weeks back in Tennessee at home, helping with the chores and practicing his guitar and fiddle. After he reassembled his radio, he listened to WNOX in Knoxville, which had started a noon show, *The Midday Merry-Go-Round.* WNOX had two "hillbilly" shows; Archie Campbell, known as Grandpappy, had a fifteen-minute late afternoon program, and Roy Acuff and the Crazy Tennesseans performed a daily lunchtime show from twelve fifteen to one o'clock. Acuff and his group moved to WROL a few months later, and the noon show was renamed *The Merry-Go-Round.* In May 1936 an extended version of the show was held on Saturday nights at Market Hall and known as the WNOX *Carnival.* In addition to the noon broadcast, the Stringdusters (featuring Jethro Burns on mandolin, Homer Haynes on guitar, and Bill Carlisle) were added. In 1942 the evening show was renamed the *Tennessee Barn Dance.*

In early 1942 a local friend told Atkins about a songwriter in Knoxville. Atkins took his fiddle (his guitar was "too beat up" to take) and caught a bus to Knoxville. Atkins found the house, knocked on the door, and, when a man answered, stammered, "I'm Chester Atkins and I . . . write songs."

"Lissen, kid, the place is alive with songwriters," replied the man. "C'mon in."[2]

Mel Foree and Tommy Covington of WNOX were in the house when Atkins arrived. Impressed with Chester's fiddling, Foree asked how he could reach Chester, but Atkins could tell him only where he lived because there was no phone in his home in Luttrell. Three days later a man visited and told Chester, "Mel Foree asked me to stop by and tell you that they had a job for you over at the radio station if you want it. Playin' fiddle." Chester was on the next bus to Knoxville.

Foree was not at the station when Chester arrived but had left word for him to speak with Bill Carlisle or Archie Campbell, who needed a fiddle player for their next show. Campbell introduced himself, Carlisle, and station manager Lowell Blanchard to Chester. Nervous to the point that he couldn't remember his name, Chester said that he was Jim Atkins's brother. Blanchard replied, "Play something for us, and we'll see if it runs in the family." Chester played "Sally Goodin'" on his fiddle and was hired on the spot.

Atkins was told that he would receive three dollars a night for the shows and found himself, forty minutes later, frozen in stage fright, playing the fiddle tune "Bile Them Cabbage Down" on air. They then decided he would play "Wildwood Flower," "Foggy Mountain Top," and "Spanish Two-Step" the next day.[3]

Chester's first road performance came in Rockwood, about fifty miles west of Knoxville. The show, in a movie theater before an audience of around a hundred people, began with the performers behind a curtain; as they began their opening number, the curtain opened. After a few numbers, Archie Campbell left the stage to change into a costume for his comedy routine while Chester played "When You and I Were Young, Maggie" on the fiddle. "My hands were sweaty and my heart was beating fast," remembered Chet. "But everything was fine when I heard that applause."[4] Chester continued to tour with Archie Campbell and Bill Carlisle for three dollars per gig. At one point Chet asked Campbell, "Why do you and Bill just pay me three dollars a night when we work?" Archie replied, "'Cause you're a bad fiddle player! You're no damn good!"

On their way back to Knoxville after one of their performances, Chet was in the car's backseat with Carlisle's Martin guitar. "I got to picking it sitting back there," said Chet. Lowell Blanchard asked how many tunes he knew, to which Chester answered "two," although "I probably knew four." "Great," said Blanchard, "you're our new guitar soloist. Can you learn a few more tunes?" Chet replied "I'll surely try."[5]

Chester Atkins was now in the country music business, playing on the radio to attract offers from civic groups, churches, and organizations to come for a performance. Radio was essential for a group to attract performance invitations. Musicians generally made their money through live performances, although some acts enjoyed sponsors and would receive a cut of each sale. The best job for a musician was to be on staff at a radio station, backing up a number of other acts and performing solo.

"Being a staff guitarist on a city radio station was my idea of making it in the big leagues," remembered Chet. "That was my number one goal when I was a teenager." Chester wasn't yet a staff guitarist, but an important door had been opened.[6]

When Chet began on WNOX, he played his Silvertone guitar until Jim lent him a Martin archtop guitar. Making three dollars a night, Chet couldn't afford to buy a good guitar until bass player Aytchie Burns agreed to sign a note for him. Chet bought a small Gibson—probably an L-25—and returned the Martin archtop to his brother. He was going to discard his old Silvertone, but his mother insisted on him keeping it; thankfully, the guitar has been preserved.

Chet's first quality guitar was a Gibson L-10 that Les Paul had custom built around 1938 or 1939. Paul traded it to Jim, who gave it to Chet sometime around 1942 or 1943. On WNOX Chester joined Tommy Covington's band, The Victory Boys, a name inspired by the "victory" slogans of World War II. Covington played "chimes" on his steel guitar. "Tommy used his right ring finger laid across the strings lightly at an angle, and then struck the strings with his thumb, causing the harmonic or 'Chime,'" said Chet. "Tommy says that he did it a little differently from most players, in that he would also strike an adjoining string that sounded without the harmonic and it resulted in two strings together, one harmonic and the other without the harmonic."[7] Chester spent three years in Knoxville on WNOX and found a major influence: Django Reinhardt.

Born in Belgium, Django was the son of a musician and part of a family of Gypsies close to Paris. He was a professional musician by fifteen and made his first recordings in 1928 at eighteen. A fire in the caravan nearly killed him. He managed to get his wife and himself out of the fire but suffered first- and second-degree burns over half his body. His right leg was paralyzed, and the third and fourth fingers on his left hand were paralyzed from extensive burns. Reinhardt learned to walk and play the guitar with only three fingers—his thumb, index finger, and middle finger—on his left hand.

Django lived a hand-to-mouth existence from 1925 until 1933, but in 1934 he began performing with violinist Stephane Grappelli as part of the Hot Club of France. Reinhardt was a pioneer in making the guitar the lead instrument in a jazz group. During the mid-1930s he acquired a Selmer, an acoustic guitar that became his main instrument. (The guitar is also known as a Selmer-Maccaferri or simply as a Maccaferri.)

During World War II the Nazis rounded up Jews and Gypsies and sent them to concentration camps. Although Django was rounded up, a jazz-loving Nazi released him. He tried to escape to Switzerland but was returned to France. He miraculously survived the war, and his song "Nuages" became an unofficial anthem in Paris for citizens longing for liberation.

In 1935, Decca released three records of the Hot Club of France in the United States. "I first heard Django when I became a so-called professional when I had a job at WNOX in Knoxville," remembered Chet. "I played rhythm guitar and once in a while a solo with the Dixieland Swingsters on WNOX, with Buck Houchens on clarinet and Dave Durham on trumpet and Jerry Collins on piano and Clifford Stier and Herbie Cooper on drums. They told me, 'You gotta hear this Django Reinhardt, you gotta hear this Charlie Christian' and I'd never heard of any of those people. So they dug out a record and played it for me. I guess it was an orchestra or something and Django just played a few notes and a chorus and I was impressed by his drive and the fact that he was so on the beat and played with so much excitement and that's about all I thought about it. Then later I heard 'Limehouse Blues' and 'Sweet Georgia Brown' and some of those great records and I fell in love with his stuff at that time and started trying to copy them. My brother, Jim, of course, was with Fred Waring so he told me all the time about Reinhardt and [how] Les Paul copied Reinhardt and played all his choruses so that got me interested too because I loved Les' playing and, at the time, Les did sound a lot like Reinhardt and played acoustic guitar and everything."[8]

Listening to Django Reinhardt records showed him how a guitarist "could really execute fast scales. Reinhardt just had a great banjo-type technique. He could play chromatic runs, right on the beat and every note would be right on the damned button!" said Chet.[9]

At WNOX, Chet had to learn a new song every day. In addition to constant practice, he listened to records in the station's library of recordings that included transcription discs. "I would copy choruses of people like George Barnes and people like that who were on the transcriptions." Guitarists often slowed records down to learn the notes, "but I don't think I had to slow them down," said Chet. "I may have played some of Reinhardt's things on the transcription turntable, but I doubt it. I don't think I ever slowed down his records and tried to learn them. I could just listen and tell what he was playing generally and I could tell the string. With experience you can tell if he's playing on the first, second, third, or fourth or fifth string. So I had that ability but he did a couple of things that I never did learn to do, and I never heard anyone do those chromatic runs that go from the ground to the sky and vice versa. I never heard anybody else do that. I can do it accidentally once in a while but he was so good at playing chromatic 32nd notes or whatever they were and ending right on the right increment of the beat on a certain note. He did a run on 'Some of These

Days' that I've never been able to do. Hank Garland and I used to try to figure out what he was doing and you could figure out the notes, but we couldn't play it. We couldn't figure out what position he was in, and you know, he had [the use of] two fingers, so there's no telling how he did it."[10]

In the latter half of 1943 or early 1944 Chet Atkins was filmed while he performed with the Tennessee Hillbillies. During this same period he made his first recordings in the WNOX studio. With a piano player Chet recorded two songs, "Why Don't You Leave Me Alone" and "Empty Slippers," singing lead and playing a solo guitar break. Chet's first recording session came in 1944 when he went to Atlanta and played on a session for Wally Fowler and Pappy Gube Beaver, who recorded "Propaganda Papa" for Ken Nelson and Capitol Records. His next session was in 1945 for the Carlisles.

During one of his shows, Chet looked up from the bandstand and saw his father standing in the back. He went to say hello and noticed tears in his father's eyes. "My Dad wasn't like that," said Chet. "He was real tough and had been trained that grown men don't cry. He didn't say anything and I didn't either, but I think they were happy tears. I think he realized I might amount to something after all and I think he was kind of proud of me. And maybe he saw in me something he had wished to do and hadn't."[11]

Knoxville's WNOX held a talent audition in 1932, and both Henry Haynes and Jethro Burns attended. They struck up a conversation and quickly discovered common interests—Django Reinhardt and jazz performer Fats Waller. When Lowell Blanchard heard them play he immediately disqualified them from the talent show, insisting they couldn't be amateurs because they were too good. However, Blanchard hired them to perform on the radio station and gave them their name, "Homer and Jethro," when he began an introduction but couldn't remember their names.[12]

Henry "Homer" Haynes and Kenneth "Jethro" Burns were born in the same year, 1920, and both grew up in Knoxville. Jethro was only six when he picked up the smallest instrument in the house—a mandolin—and, after a brother showed him some basic chords, became a self-taught musician.

By 1935 the duo worked full-time at WNOX. In addition to backing station acts, they formed their own band, the String Dusters, with guitarist Charlie Hagaman and Jethro's older brother Aytchie (for H. E.) who played bass. The String Dusters were a jazz/swing group who did comedy skits and sang pop songs in an exaggerated, nasal, "country" voice. While their comedy went over well, their music was not a hit with Tennessee audiences. By 1939, the group disbanded.

By 1945 Chester had spent three years at WNOX, and Lowell Blanchard encouraged him to move on to better himself; although Chester was surprised, Blanchard assured him that he would "always have a job as long as I'm at WNOX."

Chester's first choice was the Grand Ole Opry in Nashville, but he heard that WLW in Cincinnati was looking for country performers. Chester contacted his brother Jim, who knew the program director for WLW. Chester was invited for an audition but suffered doubts, worries, and fear.

On his way to Cincinnati, Chester got off the bus in Mount Vernon, Kentucky, and hitchhiked to Renfro Valley, where he played an audition for John Lair. Impressed with Chet's unique playing, Lair offered him a job for fifty dollars a week. Chester told him he needed a few days to think about the offer then, boosted by the encouragement, continued on to Cincinnati.[13]

Chester arrived in Cincinnati at two in the morning, obtained a room at the YMCA, and the next day saw Mr. Chamberlain at WLW, who hired him after hearing a few songs. The following day Chester appeared on a morning show with the Trailblazers; he earned fifty dollars a week but had to arise at three thirty each morning. Always a worrier, Chester fretted and doubted himself. "I became shy and introverted again," he remembered. "I smoked more than ever, my hands were always cold, and I played badly. I became so nervous that I scratched my face, developing big sores all over it."[14]

There was a bright spot when he met the Johnson twins, Fern and Laverne, who sang on WLW. Intrigued, Chester asked band member Louie Innis the name of the shorter twin, Fern, and was told it was Leona. Too shy and reserved to speak, he practiced his guitar until one day Leona approached him and asked, "Why don't we have a Coke?"

"I was smitten immediately," said Chet. "Leona was so pretty and I was so ugly." The couple went to movies, picnics, and other dates.[15] But soon Chester caught the mumps and was hospitalized for three weeks: "The only person they permitted to visit me was Leona. She brought me food and presents." After his release Chester suffered severe depression, which didn't lift until he met Merle Travis for the first time. Travis, who lived in Los Angeles, came by to visit friends at WLW. "Merle was so nice to me, and he even asked me to play the guitar for him," said Chet. "He praised my style for the rest of the evening, putting himself down. He said such things as, 'I can't play the guitar. Not like you can, Chester.'"

After that evening, his confidence bolstered, "things began to happen quickly . . . [and] I started doing a lot of network shows." Chester was heard from coast to coast but had walled himself off from others, particularly station management, so when a directive came down to eliminate some staff musicians, Chester was among the first let go, on Christmas Eve 1945.[16] Chester had to seek work but did not want to leave Leona, so he decided to call Johnny Wright and Kitty Wells, musicians at WPTV in Raleigh, North Carolina.

CHAPTER 4

In June 1942 Johnnie and Jack joined the Mid-Day Merry-Go-Round on WNOX, where they met and became friends with Chester Atkins. Wright's wife, Muriel Deason, was popular on the station, which prompted Lowell Blanchard to tell Johnnie that she needed a stage name because Muriel was too hard to pronounce. Johnnie loved an old ballad, "Kitty Wells," so Muriel Deason became Kitty Wells.

In late 1944 Wright was offered a radio show on WPTV in Raleigh. Southern musicians moved fairly often; they would obtain a spot on a radio station and build a following so they could tour local venues, where fans paid to see them perform. Once the local market had been exhausted, they moved on. The money earned from their performances was minimal, so artists sold pictures and sometimes song books to supplement their incomes. Johnnie Wright helped found the Carolina Barn Dance in Raleigh and one day received a phone call from Chester Atkins, asking if there was an opening for a guitarist. Wright confirmed there was, so Chet headed to Raleigh. "I was unhappy all the time," said Chester.[1] Chester stayed there only two months before his asthma flared up.

In Nashville Roy Acuff, frustrated because he made more on Saturday night personal appearances around the country than performing at the Opry, decided to quit as host of the *Prince Albert Show* on the NBC network portion of the Opry. Chester heard that Red Foley was poised to succeed Acuff, so he gave his notice and caught a bus to Chicago, where he hoped to meet and audition for Foley.

Chester informed Leona that she should wait for him because with Red Foley he would "make enough money to come back here and do something drastic." "Like what?" she asked. "Just wait, that's all."[2]

By 1945 Red Foley was a major star. Programming for the National Barn Dance on WLS was headed by John Lair, who organized the Cumberland Ridge Runners, which featured Foley on bass and singing. In March 1934, when the National Barn Dance was first broadcast over the NBC network, Foley was part of the show. In March 1941 Red recorded ten songs; one was "Old Shep," a song he wrote about Hoover, his boyhood German Shepherd. The song enjoyed massive success and launched Foley's career.

In December 1945, right at the end of World War II, the Grand Ole Opry had the acts that would define the future direction of country music. Roy Acuff, host of the NBC network segment *Prince Albert Show*, presented a "mountaineer" image and string-band-based country music; Lester Flatt and Earl Scruggs joined Bill Monroe's band, and Scruggs's three-finger style of banjo playing came to define the sound of bluegrass music. Ernest Tubb, in cowboy hat and boots, had the honky-tonk sound that was later called "traditional" country music. There were no singing cowboys, although a number of acts wore western outfits. The smooth-voiced Eddy Arnold emerged as the music vacillated between smooth and rough.

The Grand Ole Opry became the top show in country music because producers hired the best talent and had a fifty-thousand-watt clear channel signal that blanketed the United States east of the Rockies. The show also received increased exposure on the West Coast through transcriptions of its shows and boasted a sponsor, Prince Albert Tobacco, which remained with them until 1960. The National Barn Dance lost its sponsor, Alka Seltzer, and then its network connection after Foley left.

When Roy Acuff left the Opry, WSM management went outside their star-studded lineup for Acuff's replacement. They sought a smooth-voiced singer with network experience who could reach Middle America, and executives at the Esty Agency, which held the Prince Albert account, wanted Foley.[3]

Chester's plan was to obtain a job with WLS, where Foley could hear him and hopefully hire him, but the station turned him down. Instead he auditioned for the CBS affiliate, WBBM, which offered him a job but informed him that he had to play in clubs for six months before he could join the union, a requirement for musicians on a network show. Chester landed a job at a club on Madison Street for $150 a week, but after one week playing for a rowdy bar crowd he collected his check and never returned.

Chester sought the assistance of Bill Ellsworth, a booking agent for country talent in Chicago. "I came all the way to Chicago to get a job so that Red Foley would notice me," said Chester, who was surprised to discover that Foley was also in Ellsworth's office. "Red smiled and said, 'Play something for me, Ches,'" remembered Atkins. "I played several songs, and then we spent a lot of time talking. Finally, Red said the magic words: 'Ches, how would you like to go to Nashville with me?' I closed my eyes and said, 'Yes, sir. I sure would.'"[4]

In March 1946 Foley appeared as a guest performer on the Opry, an audition for his new role. The Esty Agency was satisfied, so on April 13, 1946, Chet Atkins stood on the Grand Ole Opry stage at Ryman Auditorium. After Foley sang "Old Shep" and just before a commercial break, Foley introduced Atkins: "And now folks, Chester Atkins will play 'Maggie' on the acoustic guitar."

Chester was received well; when he met Ernest Tubb, the Texas singer was warm and gracious. After Foley finished his portion of the show, Minnie Pearl went to Chet and kissed him on the cheek, telling him, "You're a great musician, and you're just what we have been needing around here." Minnie said "everything you are supposed to say to make someone feel good" remembered Chet.[5]

As he watched the show, Chester "just sat there in a half-daze, half-dream," he said. "Somehow it had all seemed worth it—working the roadshows, selling songbooks, sleeping in the train station. I was now a regular on the Grand Ole Opry."[6]

The Opry had established a booking agency, the WSM Artists Bureau, and during the week the agency booked Opry artists on package tours. Red Foley, with Chet Atkins, performed on shows with Minnie Pearl, Ernest Tubb, and Eddy Arnold during the week, then headed back to Nashville for Opry appearances on Saturday night. Chester hoped the Opry gig would allow him to stay home more because he hated to travel, but he was expected to perform on package shows. Further, as Foley became established on the Opry, the demand for his appearances increased.

In July Chet was in New York for a recording session with Foley. Although not invited to play on the first two songs, he was part of a vocal trio with Foley and his wife, Eva (known professionally as Judy Martin), on "Till the End of Time." On the third song, "Foggy River," written by Fred Rose, the recording seemed to be missing something so Foley suggested, "How about Chester over there? Let's use him for a solo after the bridge." The producer asked, "Can you play a few bars of this?" and Chester replied, "That's what I'm here fer." On the next song, "Lay Down Your Soul," Chet sang in a vocal trio. Chester was disappointed; he yearned to be a session guitar player but hadn't been given much of a chance.

In Nashville, Chester lived at the YMCA and hung out at the Clarkston Hotel, a popular hangout for musicians. When he had the opportunity, Chet caught the train to visit Leona in Cincinnati, where, on June 3, 1946, they were married. "It was so illogical it made sense," said Atkins.[7]

When Chet Atkins arrived in the spring of 1946, Nashville was a small, thriving city, with six major banks and 180 insurance companies as well as three hundred manufacturers. There were twenty-seven publishers, many specializing in religious books, and 358 churches representing twenty-three denominations. There were two daily papers—the *Tennessean* and the *Banner*—one Sunday paper, four weeklies, a newspaper for African Americans, the *Nashville Globe and Independent*, and a magazine, *Progressive Journal of the New South*.

When the Japanese surrendered in August 1945, Nashville did not have a single professional recording studio or record label, but that would soon change.

Eddy Arnold had recorded his first records for RCA Victor in December 1944 in the WSM Studios. That was the first studio recording by a major label in Nashville. Three WSM engineers, Aaron Shelton, Carl Jenkins, and George Reynolds, began recording singers in the WSM radio studios in the National Life and Accident Building. They set up Castle Recording Laboratories, named for the WSM logo, "The Air Castle of the South," at the Tulane Hotel on Church Street. By early 1946 this was the first professional recording studio in Nashville.

In November 1945 booking agent and former WSM announcer Jim Bulleit (pronounced "Boo-lay") and Wally Fowler discussed starting a record label with C. V. Hitchcock, owner of Hermitage Music. Fowler proposed recording his group, the Georgia Clodhoppers, in addition to other WSM performers. By the end of the year Bulleit had agreed to start Bullet Records with Hitchcock as a partner.

Bullet Records, seeking to cover all the markets, established a series for pop, R&B, Black gospel, white gospel, and country music. The first record in the country series, "Wave to Me, My Lady" (vocal by Joe Carroll) and "Zeb's Mountain Boogie" by Brad Brady and his Tennesseans, a pseudonym for Owen Bradley, was issued in January 1946. On the second pressing, the billing was changed to Owen Bradley and His Tennesseans. That release was followed by "Guitar Reel" and "No One Will Ever Know" by the Turner Brothers (Zeb and Zeke).

During the summer of 1946, Bullet released a line of "hillbilly" records. Grand Ole Opry artists Bradley Kincaid, Minnie Pearl, and Pee Wee King, backed by King's band, the Golden West Cowboys, were recorded in the WSM studios by J. L. Frank, King's manager, who sold the recordings to Bullet. The backing band comprised Cowboy Copas on rhythm guitar, Chuck Wiggins on bass, and Don Davis on steel guitar. Minnie Pearl's first single was "Jealous Hearted Me," which Minnie performed live in a loud, off-key manner. Other artists on Bullet's country roster included Clyde Moody and Ford Rush, Pete Pyle, the York Brothers, the Turner Brothers (Zeke and Zeb), the Texas Troubadours, Tommy Scott, and Bunny Biggs & Lee Davis "Honey" Wilds, who performed as the blackface duo Jam-Up and Honey.[8]

During that spring Bullet recorded Chet Atkins playing "Guitar Blues (Pickin' the Blues)" and "Brown Eyes A-Cryin' in the Rain," which featured a vocal by Jack Shook, staff guitarist for WSM. Accompanying Chet on the recordings were Louie Innis on rhythm guitar, Roy Lanham on guitar, Jack Shook on guitar and vocal, Ernie Newton on bass, and Dutch McMillan on clarinet.

On that session, produced by Owen Bradley, Chet probably played his Gibson L-10. The record was released as *Chester Atkins and the All-Star-Hillbillies* but received little traction. Though this first professional solo release was not a hit, the single earned Chet twenty-two dollars in royalties.

During his time with the Opry Chet met guitarist Harold Bradley. "I was backstage at the Opry," said Bradley. "I was working with Eddy Arnold and Bradley Kincaid. This was 1947. I remember sitting backstage playing 'Blue Skies' all by myself and this tall skinny guy walks up and says, 'That's pretty good. Have you ever thought of playing it this way?' He started playing this moving bass line. I said, 'No, I never thought of playing it that way.' He introduced himself and that was the first time we met each other."[9]

Chester appeared on the Grand Ole Opry for six months before the William Esty Agency decided that his featured solo was unnecessary. Chester was insulted and decided to quit. "I didn't want to be a sideman; I wanted to be a soloist," said Chet.[10] Also, Foley wanted Chet to remain exclusively as his band member and not do sessions with other artists. Foley tried to talk him out of quitting, but Chester's mind was made up.

Out of a job, Atkins decided to return to Knoxville and WNOX but received a call from Sunshine Sue with the Old Dominion Barn Dance on WRVA in Richmond, Virginia. She had lost her guitarist, Joe Maphis, to army service. With no other prospects, Chester and Leona loaded their belongings into her 1941 Ford and moved to Richmond, where as a soloist he earned fifty dollars a week, matching his Grand Ole Opry wages.

On the Old Dominion Barn Dance, Sue introduced Chester Atkins as "the world's greatest guitar player." Unfortunately his asthma roared back, forcing him to miss a number of shows. Compared to the energetic and entertaining Joe Maphis, Chet, distant and aloof, lacked showmanship, so Sunshine Sue fired him.[11] Chester and Leona decided that she would return to Ohio to live with her parents while he went to Chicago to look for work. Before he dropped her off at her parents' home, the couple discovered that Leona was pregnant.

In Chicago, Chester called Karl Davis of the Karl and Harty duo, popular acts on the National Barn Dance. Karl invited Chester to stay with him while he sought work at WLS, WMMB, and WJJD, to no avail. "I lost some of my drive," remembered Chet. "When I did audition, it was with so little enthusiasm that nobody in his right mind would have given me a job. I became convinced that everybody hated my music." For the next month, Chester hung around Karl's home and practiced guitar, then Louie Innis called about an opening at KWTO in Springfield, Missouri. Chester drove down to Springfield, listening to KWTO: "I had never heard so many hillbillies in my life, and I wondered how my mixture of country and pop music would go over."

Before he left Chicago Chet saw Django Reinhardt perform live on tour with Duke Ellington's group. "I got a ticket and went down and I was in the very back of the Civic Opera House," said Chet. "He played, and then I went around and got his autograph after the show (the only autograph I've ever gotten) and people were bothering him. There were guys back from the war, and they were saying, 'Remember when I saw you in Paris and we played together and then we went and got a drink?' and he'd say yes or 'oui, oui' since he didn't speak English, and so I waited until everybody left and I stuck a piece of paper in his face and he didn't have a pencil so he said, 'You have a penceel?' or something and signed 'D. Reinhardt,' which I learned later was all he could write. I wanted to play a tune for him. I thought, 'Boy, if I could play a tune for him, he'd really love it,' but I was too shy to ask him to listen, and he seemed to be in a hurry to leave."

"I remember it so well," continued Chet. "I remember the Black members of Duke Ellington's band yelling. When he played a lick they liked they'd yell. They loved him! He played that 'Improvisation #3' that he wrote and then played some tunes with the band. Everybody loved Django. You can't overestimate his importance because he taught the world. You know, before he came along, there was only Eddie Lang, who played with chords and didn't play single lines much. He was a good guitarist who played with Bing Crosby as an accompanist but he didn't have the drive of Django and he died at about thirty. Then there was Lonnie Johnson, a Black blues player. Lonnie was a good single string picker, but he just played blues. Then Django came along and he was light years ahead of everybody else. He played all over the guitar and played all kinds of arpeggios and exciting licks, and no one had ever done that before and unless you were alive at that time you tend to not realize that and not to be cognizant of it, but he taught the world!"[12]

CHAPTER 5

In 1933, Ralph Foster and Jerry Hall founded KWTO ("Keep Watching the Ozarks") in Springfield, Missouri. Foster's assistant, Ely E. "Si" Siman, first came into KWTO while still in high school. Simon, with Foster, Lester Cox, and John Mahafffey, formed RadiOzark Enterprises to produce radio shows, which they syndicated to other stations. They recorded the shows on sixteen-inch transcription discs that could hold fifteen minutes of music; the tapes were "open ended," with space left for local stations to add messages or ads, and were shipped to stations across the country.[1]

When Atkins arrived at KWTO, Siman matched him with Slim Wilson and the Tall Timbers Trio, a group patterned after the Sons of the Pioneers; within several weeks Atkins received his own show.

Atkins sent for Leona, and they moved into a two-room cottage off Route 66, where their daughter, Merle, was born on March 10, 1947. Si Siman took an interest in Chester and began calling him "Chet," which Atkins liked and adopted.

KWTO's show "Korn's-a-Krackin'" was filled with corny humor. Siman put Chet on the show, and he began doing personal appearances.[2] RCA had a "custom" division that pressed records and transcription discs for outside companies. The "Korn's-a-Krackin'" transcription discs were sent to Chicago, where, under the supervision of Al Hindle, discs was pressed and sent to radio stations. Hindle sent a disc to Steve Sholes, head of RCA Victor's country recordings, because "he thought I might be interested in some of the material on there," said Sholes. On that disc was Chet playing "Canned Heat."[3]

During World War II, Steve Sholes had helped manage the V-Disk program, selecting the songs that were sent to military personnel overseas. The strike by the Musicians Union, called by James Petrillo in 1942, was in force, but the Armed Forces received permission to record acts for their V-Disk series. After he left the service, Sholes returned to RCA, where he had worked before the war. He was "a company man" with a sense of duty, inherent honesty, and selflessness.

Jean and Julian Aberbach were Jewish brothers from Austria who had escaped Hitler's Nazi Reich. Jean had worked for Chappell Music in New York, managing and promoting copyrights, and Sholes and Jean met through their involvement in the music business.[4] In December 1944 Sholes signed the Sons of the Pioneers to RCA Victor and Jean and Julian Aberbach formed Hill and Range Publishing. The Aberbachs pioneered publishing agreements where the artist owned half the publishing company while the Aberbachs kept the other half.[5]

In addition to his work as Sholes's studio assistant, control room technician, and music arranger, Charles Grean was tasked with screening the singers and songs submitted to RCA Victor. When the transcription disk of Chet Atkins playing "Canned Heat" came to RCA, Grean was so impressed that he played the disk repeatedly. As a musician himself, Grean recognized that Atkins was a unique talent and a true original.

Steve Sholes listened to the disc and "when I got to this thing called 'Canned Heat' played by Chet Atkins, I was so knocked out by the finger-style guitar that Chet played and I'd never heard before, that I thought I'd like to take a chance with this guitar player."[6]

The Atkins disk arrived in the spring of 1947. As a record company executive, Sholes was well aware that Merle Travis, a thumbpicking guitarist and hit vocal artist on Capitol Records, had a number-one hit in 1946 with "Divorce Me C.O.D." That was followed by two other Travis hits, "Cincinnati Lou" and "No Vacancy." Sholes was also aware of the success of guitarist Les Paul and sought a similar act for RCA. Marketing an instrumentalist was risky because, unlike fiddle or brass or woodwind players who stood in front of a band to lead it, guitarists tended to play sitting down, hunched over, head bowed, and barely moving. Sholes did not want to take that risk alone, so he contacted Jean Aberbach.

Back in Springfield, Si Siman went on an extended vacation, and during his time away the station manager fired Atkins. Out of work again, Chet wired his brother Jim for a loan, and Zed Dennis, a singer in the Tall Timbers Trio, took him to Denver and introduced him to Shorty Thompson, who had a cowboy band. With this band Chet would have to wear western clothes for the first time.

Chet and Leona moved into the Thompsons' guest house in Kennison, a suburb of Denver. The Thompsons' young son Wayne, who later became a well-known songwriter under the name Wayne

Carson, remembered looking through the screen door and seeing Chet "sitting at the table and playing the guitar. He would take a bite of food and then he'd play the guitar."[7]

One day Chet received a phone call from Aberbach, who told him that Steve Sholes with RCA and he both liked the transcription sent by Si Siman. Aberbach asked if Chet was interested in recording for RCA and if he could sing, with Chet responding in the affirmative to both. Chet had a lifelong desire—which he rarely admitted publicly—to be a singer. Although Chet genuinely loved the guitar, it was his lack of singing ability that became a factor in him dedicating himself to becoming a great guitarist. Finally, Aberbach asked him if he wrote songs, with Chet answering, "Sure, I do." Sholes followed up with the contract, signing Atkins to RCA's roster.

Chet's answers may have been slightly misleading; he sang on the radio but was not talented as a singer, never considered a lead vocalist. And most of the songs he performed had been written by others. Aberbach told Chet to be in Chicago the next week for a recording session. The next day Chet asked Shorty Thompson for a few days off so he could record. "I told him everything Jean had said to me," remembered Chet. "He said, 'Well, you'll need a singer. You can't sing.' Chet replied, 'Sure I can. At least I'm going to try.'"

The next day Shorty went to Chet's house and told him, "Listen, Chester, I've been doing some thinking, and I've decided that we won't be needing you in the band anymore. So there's no use for you even to come back from Chicago."[8] Shorty Thompson had seen the offer from Aberbach to Chet as a major opportunity for himself and expected Chet to open the door to a recording career. That would not happen, so once again Chet was jobless when he headed to Chicago for his recording session.

There is another side to the story. According to Wayne Thompson Carson, when Chet was onstage "he looked like he was sleeping." Chet needed "to be more of a showman," but he "wouldn't go out there and smile, talk to the crowd or jump around a little bit. He wasn't an out front person."[9]

Songwriter Cy Coben first heard of Chet Atkins when Coben was pitching songs to Steve Sholes in New York, just after Sholes had signed Chet. "Steve, along with his right hand man, Charles Grean, and I were listening to a new acetate demo by a hot new guitar player," said Coben. "Those guys are great!" Steve responded, "What do you mean?" Coben said, "Well, there's got to be two of them." Steve retorted, "No, there is only one!" Coben and Grean offered to bet Sholes that there was more than one guy playing. "I'll take the bet," answered Sholes. "I know it is one guy. I just signed him to the label!"[10]

In early August 1947, Chet and Leona arrived in Chicago, where they stayed at Karl Davis's home. The next day Chet went to the Knickerbocker Hotel, where he first met Steve Sholes, who "greeted me warmly." Jean Aberbach was there too. In his phone conversations with Sholes Chet had told him he wanted a strong backing group of musicians, and when they met "Steve told me that he had gotten me the best rhythm guitar player he could get." When Sholes dropped the name George Barnes, Chet was stunned. Steve asked, "Don't you want George Barnes?" Chet replied, "Want him? He's just one of my idols, that's all. I just don't know if I can play with George Barnes around."[11]

The session was set for the following day, August 11, 1947, at RCA's Studio C. In addition to George Barnes, on rhythm guitar behind Chet's soloing, musicians included Augie Klein, an accordionist who was a staff musician at WLS and worked on the National Barn Dance, fiddler Charles Hurta, and bassist Harold Siegel. Playing the Gibson L-10 acoustic that his brother Jim had given him, Chet recorded "Ain'tcha Tired of Makin' Me Blue," "I'm Gonna Get Tight," "Canned Heat," and "Standing Room Only." After a break he recorded "Don't Hand Me That Line," "Bug Dance," "(I Know My Baby Loves Me) In Her Own Peculiar Way," and "The Nashville Jump." Chet wrote the instrumentals "Canned Heat" and "Bug Dance" and, with Lowell Tennis, "The Nashville Jump." Since RCA saw Chet as their answer to Merle Travis, Atkins sang five songs. RCA Victor released the records under the name "Chet Atkins and His Colorado Mountain Boys."

"That first session was a good one, but I really did have trouble playing solos with George Barnes around," remembered Chet. After the session, "I decided that I had better try to write some songs—after all, I had said I was a writer. I labored over two or three little songs and finally came up with one that wasn't too bad—'I May Be Color Blind But I Know When I'm Blue.' Unfortunately, it never got very far."[12]

Ironically, on the same day that Chet made his first recordings for RCA Victor, an important recording session was taking place in Nashville. Ernest Tubb was a major record seller for Decca, and Paul Cohen, head of Decca's country division, suggested that Tubb record in Nashville at Castle, which could handle professional recordings. In early 1947 Nashville had its first million-selling record, *Near You*, by Francis Craig. It was on the chart when Cohen made the suggestion. Tubb agreed to record in Nashville, opening the door for the city to become a major recording center. "If Tubb had said no," said Owen Bradley, Nashville as a recording center "would not have happened."[13] They recorded Decca artists Ernest Tubb, Red Foley, and Milton Estes led by musician Owen Bradley. The first of two days of sessions was August 11, 1947, when Chet Atkins made his first recordings for RCA.

Steve Sholes was impressed by Chet's playing and saw his potential as a studio musician. In late 1947, Sholes brought Chet to New York to back RCA Victor artists for a number of recordings because James Petrillo, head of the American Federation of Musicians, had called a musician strike beginning on January 1, 1948. Labels needed to stockpile recordings so they could release new music the coming year. Chet played guitar on recordings by Elton Britt and Texas Jim Roberts and noted, "It was the first time I had ever worked with New York musicians. . . . They were good musicians but a different breed from the country musicians I had been used to. The fiddle players sounded like Jascha Heifetz."[14] Chet had recently purchased a Gibson L-7 electric, which he used on those two sessions.

Charles Grean supervised a session on Chet on November 11, 1947, at RCA Studio 1 in New York, where Chet was backed by his brother Jim on guitar, Buck Lambert on fiddle, Joe Bivano on accordion, and Grean on bass. Chet recorded "My Guitar Is My Sweetheart" and three songs that he had written, "I'm Pickin' the Blues" (written with brother Jim), "Gone, Gone, Gone," and "Barnyard Shuffle." The same musical lineup returned to the studio eight days later and recorded four songs written by Chet: "Save Your Money" (written with brother Jim), "(I May Be Color Blind But) I Know When I'm Blue," "I've Been Working on the Guitar," and "Dizzy Strings." "I've Been Working on the Guitar" was Chet's new arrangement of the old song "I've Been Working on the Railroad." He had played the tune as an arrangement of "The Eyes of Texas Are Upon You" during his time with Shorty Thompson; both songs had the same melody. On "Dizzy Strings," Chet used "banjo-style rolls that consist of multiple hammer-ons and pull-offs," like Earl Scruggs was doing on the banjo with Bill Monroe's band.[15]

Chet had not given up hope of having a hit as a singer; he sang "My Guitar Is My Sweetheart," "I'm Pickin' the Blues," "Gone, Gone, Gone," "Save Your Money," "(I May Be Color Blind But) I Know When I'm

Blue," and "Barnyard Shuffle," yet the two instrumentals, "I've Been Working on the Guitar" and "Dizzy Strings," stole the show.

While in New York Chet met songwriter Cy Coben. "He was in New York to play on some country sessions that Steve Sholes was producing," remembered Coben. Chet told Cy, "I want to go down to the Greenwich Village area, there is a man I've been corresponding with that makes guitars named D'Angelico. I would like to meet him." Coben volunteered to go along "and on the way back, we stopped by Chet's hotel room and wrote a song named 'Dobro.'"[16]

After the sessions in New York Chet found himself once again unemployed. He remembered the promise from Lowell Blanchard that he could always come back to WNOX, so he called Blanchard, who was true to his word. Chet drove to Cincinnati, picked up Leona, and then continued on to Knoxville. In a little over a year, Chet had gone from being on the Grand Ole Opry on fifty-thousand-watt clear channel WSM and performing on the NBC network segment to a local ten-thousand-watt station in Knoxville, where Blanchard offered him a pep talk: "Listen, Chester, you've got a pretty big name around here, and you'll do well. You can get your own band together and make a lot of money."

"It was one of the lowest periods of my life," said Chet.[17] Chet thought about quitting music, going so far as to buy a set of piano-tuning tools and taking lessons in the craft. It looked like he might follow in his father's footsteps. Since Chet had told Jean Aberbach that he wrote songs, he contacted his old friend, Mel Foree, and went over to his house on Sundays to write songs. One song, "Heartbreak Avenue," was recorded after publisher Fred Rose rewrote it.

When Chet returned Homer and Jethro were on WNOX. The three musicians teamed up to create a stage act, the Colorado Mountain Boys, and became regulars on the Tennessee Barn Dance on Saturday nights. Jethro—Kenneth Burns—had married Leona's sister, and they moved in next door to the Atkins. The group featured Homer playing rhythm guitar, Jethro on mandolin, and Jethro's brother Aytchie on bass. Homer and Jethro were billed as a comedy team, but the duo usually played some light jazz before their comedy routine.

The problem with Homer and Jethro was that their audiences were not musically sophisticated but wanted to be entertained with comedy, which Homer and Jethro excelled at. Being jazz musicians, the duo wanted to perform challenging jazz instrumentals, while the audience wanted simple country entertainment. Chet Atkins, Homer Haynes, and Jethro Burns shared a common musical foundation; all three idolized Django Reinhardt. Haynes and Burns developed into a formidable instrumental team who knew many of the pop and swing tunes Chet also loved. On their road shows, in order to attract a crowd, they began staging an amateur contest where the winner appeared with the group on Saturday night at the Tennessee Barn Dance. To supplement their incomes, Leona and her sister Lois began singing on Knoxville station WKGN.[18]

CHAPTER 6

The Carter Family—A. P., Sarah, and Maybelle—were founding acts, with Jimmie Rodgers, of commercial country music. Beginning with their first recording session in Bristol, Tennessee, in 1927, they supplied the world of country music with a number of songs, generally credited to A. P. Carter, that became standards. They rarely performed live and were not a traveling act; royalties from their records provided a comfortable income.

A. P. Carter was often gone on long "song hunting" trips, leaving his wife Sara to fall in love with Coy Bays, a neighbor and cousin to A. P. When A. P. discovered the affair, he and Sara divorced and Coy and his mother moved to California. Sara and Coy wrote to each other, but their letters were intercepted by family members, so they spent years without hearing from one another.

Dr. John Romulus Brinkley made a financially lucrative offer to the Carters to sing on XERA, in Mexico just across from Del Rio, Texas. Sara was reluctant to perform with A. P., although they had continued to record together, but she finally accepted the offer.

One night on XERA—eight years after Coy left the Carters' home in Maces Springs, Virginia, and with no contact between Sara and Coy during that time—Sara leaned into the microphone before singing "I'm Thinking Tonight of My Blue Eyes" and said she was dedicating the song to Coy Bays in California. Coy was listening and told his mother, "I'm gonna go get Sara."[1] He traveled to Del Rio, where the two reunited and married.

Maybelle wanted Sara and Coy to return to Maces Springs, but Coy would not hear of it; instead, Sara left her home and children and moved to Greenville, California, with Bays. After the split, Mother Maybelle and the Carter Family re-formed as Maybelle and her three daughters, Helen, Anita, and June. In 1946 they performed on the Old Dominion Barn Dance with Sunshine Sue.[2]

In 1948 the Carters left WRVA and went back to their home in Maces Springs, where they farmed. Lowell Blanchard learned of this and wanted them on WNOX. The Carters had heard the Midday Merry-Go-Round and were aware of the station, so by late summer 1948 they joined WNOX. On their first trip to the radio station, the Carters met Chet Atkins and Homer and Jethro.

"When I heard Chester and Homer and Jethro start playing, my mouth dropped about ten miles," said Anita. "There was no better group in the world. Jethro was such a great mandolin player, he just scared me. And they had Aytchie Burns, Jethro's brother, playing with them, the best bass player I ever heard." June remembered, "We sat at their feet, especially Chester's."[3]

Eck Carter, Maybelle's husband and the girls' father, booked the group, and the five of them shared the money equally. Impressed by Chet Atkins's guitar playing and committed to the Carter Family's success, Eck decided that the addition of Chet to the show would be a boon to the family. Chet remembered that Eck "sat down beside me one day and said: 'Chet, we've been talking, me and the girls and Maybelle, and we think we need another instrument in our group. You sound good, and we'd like to have you join us if you're interested.'" It didn't take Chet long to say yes. Then Eck said, "We'll cut you in for one-sixth of what we make. That's equal shares for each of us." "Bingo!," remembered Chet. "I had never expected that much. He was talking about a lot more money than I had ever made."[4]

There were good reasons for the Carters not to hire Chet. Maybelle's rhythm guitar playing was solid and fit the Carters' songs, which were musically simpler than Chet's jazz-influenced playing. Chet had an electric guitar and amplifier to carry, and the car, Eck's Frasier, would have to hold six people instead of five. Also, June, a vivacious extrovert, was a born comedienne, while Chet was a quiet introvert. Yet Chet agreed to join, and on their first road trip Eck stayed home. Unfortunately, the car had a flat tire that Chet had to quickly learn to repair. Chet later referred to that night as the time he "taught those girls how to cuss."[5]

The Carters' show with Chet Atkins raised their performances musically. The Carter girls performed some pop tunes, and Chet's guitar fit perfectly. On the traditional Carter songs Chet added some musical flourishes to enliven them. Chet also performed instrumental numbers that added variety to the show. Audiences loved the Carters' singing, and now they were astounded and entertained with the jazzy guitar runs of Chet Atkins. They were billed as "The Carter Sisters and Mother Maybelle, Chet Atkins and His Famous Guitar." Helen's accordion playing and Anita's bass playing became better under the influence of Atkins. They had now become a self-contained act with Maybelle's singing, Chet's playing, and June's comedy antics.

June Carter was a cutup who used Chet as a foil for her comedy; Chet grew into his role to enhance June's comedy. They performed with a primitive sound system, just two speakers and one microphone.

Their theme song was "The Blue Ridge Mountains of Virginia," which opened the show, then June sang an up-tempo humorous or novelty number, followed by a pop song, and then Maybelle sang one of the Carter Family songs. A solo by Chet followed, then Anita offered a love song. Except for the few opening numbers, they performed with no set list, playing what their audience wanted to hear. Chet played the fiddle while Maybelle played banjo if the audience wanted bluegrass, or they might perform mostly hymns and spirituals on a Sunday. Chet Atkins learned to listen to the audience while performing with the Carters. "Pleasing the audience remained Maybelle's single focus," noted authors Mark Zwonitzer and Charles Hirshberg in their biography of the Carters. "She never acted as if the effort deserved special reward; the way she saw it, it was her privilege to be given the chance to perform."[6]

"It was the first time I ever took stock of the people to whom we were playing for or what our music was saying to them," remembered Chet. "The Carter name certainly had a tremendous drawing power because the original Carter Family was still remembered."[7]

The group performed each Saturday night on WNOX's Tennessee Barn Dance, then headed off to an engagement somewhere and were back on Monday for the Midday Merry-Go-Round at noon. After that show it was back on the road for another engagement, returning by noon the next day. It was a physically demanding life, but the Carters and Chet thrived—they learned new songs, worked out harmonies, and even wrote songs.

At the end of January 1949, RCA Victor held sessions at the Fox Theatre in Atlanta to record a number of their southern artists. Portable recording equipment was installed in an upstairs room, with the sessions supervised by Steve Sholes and Charles Grean.

On February 3, Chet was in the makeshift Atlanta studio on Peachtree Street with his half sister, Billy Rose, along with Homer and

Jethro and Charles Grean. Their first session was all vocals, with Chet and Billy Rose singing "Guitar Waltz" (written by Zeke Clements) and "Wednesday Night Waltz." Chet sang "Telling My Troubles to My Old Guitar," which Shorty Thompson used to sing and recorded on a transcription when Chet was with him. "Money, Marbles and Talk" was a ballad sung by Chet, who was joined by Billie Rose, Homer, and Jethro on the chorus. During their second session, Chet recorded four instrumentals, "Dance of the Goldenrod," which was part of Merle Travis's repertoire, and three songs written by Chet, "Galloping on the Guitar" (later changed to "Gallopin' on the Guitar"), "Barber Shop Rag," and "Centipede Boogie."

Chet played his Gibson L-10 acoustic with a removable DeArmond pickup, creating an electric guitar sound. This was the first time Chet recorded with Homer and Jethro, and the influence of Django Reinhardt shone through their instrumentals.

A turning point in Chet Atkins's life came from his conversations with Aytchie Burns. "Aytchie Burns was my shrink for a long time," remembered Chet. "Lying on the back seat of his car headed for a personal appearance, I used to pour out my problems to him. He gave me good country philosophy, which is as good as any philosophy if you just take the time to listen."

One night, as they drove to Asheville, Chet asked Aytchie, "Why don't people like me, Aytchie?" Aytchie replied, "Well, Chester, all your problems are because of your shyness and your complexes. That's it—complexes. It comes across like you detest people, like you're antisocial or something." "I knew he was right," said Chet. "It was because of my attitude that I got fired all the time. I never had made any effort to make friends—I felt everybody hated me because I was ugly and retarded. There was no question in my mind that my bosses didn't like me because I was just plain stupid."

Chet complained, "I get fired all the time," but Aytchie reminded him that he always landed another job. Discussing how he came by his style of playing the guitar, Chet told him he'd first heard the fingerpicking style on an old 78 by Charlie Stump but that Merle Travis was his major influence. Aytchie replied, "You did it on your own. Nobody led you by the hand. Damn it, Chester, stop waitin' for somebody to come along now and lead you around." Aytchie then added, "Stand right up there, eye-to-eye with people, and talk to them and let them know you're interested in them."

Chet remembered that "I tried Aytchie's Dale Carnegie course and it was amazing therapy. People started liking me and talking to me. I realized that these were people just like me—no better, no worse. I had gone through a long period of thinking that I was the only one who ever had it hard, and I hated the world for it. I realize now, of course, that my life wasn't a great deal different from a lot of people who came up through country music."

"If I simply said, 'Mornin','" continued Chet, "and went on with my head down as I usually did, he would stop me and say, 'What did you say? I couldn't hear you' I would hold my head up, look him in the eye, and say: 'Good morning, Aytchie. How are you this morning? Fine day out, isn't it? How's the wife and kids? You're looking well. We should have a cup of coffee together one of these mornings. Nice to see you, Aytchie. Good day.'"

Aytchie provided good therapy; Chet found himself friendly to and connecting with others. "The applause I got from the large audiences had built up my confidence to what was probably the highest point in my life," said Chet. "Aytchie's short course rounded out my personality, and I think it showed in my playing. I relaxed more onstage, knowing I was projecting a much warmer feeling."[8]

Steve Sholes signed the Carters to RCA Victor Records, and they recorded for the label in early 1949; their first single was "The Kneeling Drunkard's Prayer," which they wrote in the car while traveling. Sholes signed June Carter to a solo recording contract; she recorded "Baby, It's Cold Outside" with Homer and Jethro, with Chet on guitar. The single was released in August 1949 and reached the pop chart.

During his time at WNOX, Chet recorded several sessions with the Carters. On October 12, 1949, the group went to Chicago, where they recorded with Homer Haynes on rhythm guitar, Jethro Burns on mandolin, and Anita Carter on bass, with vocals by Helen and Anita. The group performed "Under the Hickory Nut Tree" (written by Anita, Helen, and June), "I Was Bitten by the Same Bug Twice" (written by Helen), "One More Chance," and "The Old Buck Dance" (written by Chet), which sounded like the old song "Buck and Wing." Chet, Homer, and Jethro sang the lead vocals in unison, with Helen and Anita on harmony. The next day, with the same musical lineup, they recorded two songs written by Chet, "Boogie Man Boogie" and "Main Street Breakdown."

During the fall of 1949 the Carters were offered a job with KWTO in Springfield, Missouri; Eck accepted. Chet Atkins returned to Springfield, where he and Leona moved into a home on Pacific Avenue. Homer and Jethro had already joined KWTO, so Leona and her sister had gone ahead and found a place to live. Before he left Knoxville, Chet bought a 1947 Ford. In Springfield Eck traded his Frasier for a Lincoln, which the Carters and Chet traveled in when they weren't performing on the radio.

Each week on KWTO there were 150 live programs, which Si Siman syndicated through RadiOzark. The shows were fifteen minutes long, and the Carters, with Chet, recorded about forty. The recordings were made direct to acetate disk (recordings on tape were not yet popular), so they had to record the entire fifteen-minute show with no mistakes. If something went wrong, Chet—a perfectionist—would stop the recording and they would all begin again. Maybelle "never complained, even when it took an hour to record a single fifteen-minute show. She was always happy for the chance to get it right," said Chet.[9]

The group recorded over two hundred songs for the transcriptions, including Chet's songs "Dizzy Strings," "Canned Heat," and "There'll Be Some Changes Made." On "Whistlin' Rufus," "Dill Pickle Rag," and "Turkey in the Straw," he played the fiddle. The songs Chet sang were mostly comic numbers, like "You Made Toothpicks of the Timber of My Heart" and "My Little Pup with the Patent-Leather Nose and the Wiggily-Waggily Tail."

Red Star Flour sponsored the group. Sometimes June would find a young girl in the audience and try to convince her to marry Chet: "Chester wasn't much to look at; was, in fact, ugly as fifteen miles of bad road. But still, he needed a wife and since the girl wasn't already married, she couldn't be choosy. Problem was, Chester didn't know how to do anything except play the guitar, so they'd never have any money" and "he'll probably put you to work playing the bass."

"You sure will have to get Red Star Flour and use it for a lotta things," June would say. "You can use it on your face for powder; in fact, girl, you could use some on your face right now. If Chester still don't like you the way you look, you can mix up some of that flour with water in a little mug and you've got a great beauty mask, but you gotta be sure it's Red Star Flour—the other kind don't work."[10]

The group was soon performing nearly every night. Chet was

making fifty dollars for each show and was able to open a savings account, his first. The group usually performed in auditoriums, whose crowds "liked what we were playing," remembered Chet. "If they didn't, we would switch to bluegrass or whatever it took, but we were determined never to let an audience leave unhappy. I even added pop and jazz when I thought it necessary."

"You learn that your business is to entertain people, no matter where you are and no matter how many people are in your audience," said Chet. "And you do it at their level. If you go into a schoolhouse and play the greatest classical guitar in the world and put everybody to sleep, you are not an entertainer. But if you go in there and give those same people bluegrass because that's what they paid their admission price for, and they cheer and stomp their feet, you have performed a service. That service is called entertainment, and you can leave with a warm feeling because you have made people happy. Often these people have no other outlet for entertainment; if you fail them, you have failed all of show business."[11]

The Opry invited the Carters to Nashville for a guest appearance, which was well received; June's high-energy comedy went over well, and Chet played several solos on his electric Gibson L-7. Before long, executives at WSM contacted Eck Carter with an offer to join the Grand Ole Opry, sponsored by Martha White, but there was a catch—the offer extended only to the Carters, not Atkins. If the Carters accepted the offer, they could not bring Chet. Eck declined and was told that Chet could not be included because the Musicians Union did not want another guitar player in Nashville, especially one as talented as Chet. The Opry refused to believe that the Carters would decline their offer and continued to sweeten the deal with more money, but Eck remained adamant that Chet had to be included.

KWTO, aware of the interest from the Opry, offered Chet a raise to seventy-five dollars per week if he stayed, but he elected to remain with the Carters.

Musicians could join the Opry only if they were sponsored by a union member; eventually George Morgan's steel guitar player Don Davis agreed to sponsor Chet, but he could not perform on any recording sessions for six months after joining. Chet was hesitant but called Fred Rose in Nashville and asked his advice. "Come on to Nashville, Chet," said Rose, "and I'll use you on some recording sessions."[12] Rose was recording Hank Williams and other acts for MGM.

It had been six months of wrangling with the Opry before an agreement was reached. In 1950, the Carter Family with Chet Atkins debuted on the Saturday night Grand Ole Opry at the Ryman Auditorium. The Carter Family and Chet Atkins were paid $825 a week for a minimum of four shows: the Grand Ole Opry at eight o'clock on Saturday nights, an evening show held prior to their Opry performance for the Veterans' Hospital, Noontime Neighbors on weekdays, and a gospel program on Sunday mornings. Chet was eternally grateful. "I owe everything to the Carters," he said. "I don't know what the hell would have happened to me if I hadn't run into 'em."[13]

In June, Chet and Leona loaded up their 1947 Ford and drove to Nashville, where they stayed with Don Davis until they moved into their own apartment. "The Carters and I began writing some of our own songs for the show," said Chet. "One of them, 'Someone Else, Not Me' was recorded by Red Foley."[14]

CHAPTER 7

In June 1950 Chet, Leona, and Merle Atkins moved to Nashville. That same year Dave Cobb, a disc jockey at WSM, introduced Red Foley's network show, "From Music City USA, Nashville, Tennessee, the National Broadcasting Company brings you the Red Foley Show!" WSM program manager Jack Stapp called Cobb into his office after hearing the introduction: "That's the greatest thing I ever heard." He encouraged Cobb to continue using "Music City USA" on the air, giving Nashville an identity that continues.

In 1950 Ernest Tubb, Red Foley, Eddy Arnold, and Hank Snow all had number-one records with Foley's "Chattanoogie Shoeshine Boy" on the pop and country chart at the beginning of the year. The year ended with a Nashville published song, "Tennessee Waltz" by Patti Page, in the number-one pop position. Both songs were published by Fred Rose's firm, Acuff-Rose Publishing. "Tennessee Waltz" was important for Nashville because it alerted record producers in New York, particularly Mitch Miller, that Nashville was a rich source for pop hits.

In early 1950 RCA Victor sent out their newsletter, *The Spotlight*, with the headline "Victor Considers Him 'Greatest Guitarist.'" In the article Chet explained that his development of playing lead, harmony, and a kind of accompaniment simultaneously came because he had "nobody to play duets or trios with," so during his years in Georgia "I tried making my playing sound like two guitars, and after awhile—it worked."[1]

Chet had met Fred Rose in 1946 when he first came to Nashville with Red Foley. One day Fred invited Chet to his house on Rainbow Trail. "I remember we went up in his attic and he had a disc cutter of some kind. We made a demo or two." After moving back to Nashville, Chet hung out with Rose, a great editor and "song doctor" who improved other songwriters' works without taking credit. Chet watched Rose toil on a Hank Williams song and "fixed up" "Half as Much," written by Curley Williams. "He said, 'you can't rush it. You just sit and the lines will come to you,'" remembered Chet. "Just wait and they'll come."

Chet and Fred were discussing Jenny Lou Carson when Fred told him, "Don't mention her name around my wife" or else "she'll shoot me. I think he'd been carrying on a little with her," said Chet. "He'd been writing her songs, I know," and Chet named "Jealous Heart" and "Let Me Go, Lover" as songs that Rose "probably had something to do with." Rose "fixed some up for me," said Chet, who had written a song, "Heartbreak Avenue," with Mel Foree. "When he got through with it, I didn't even know it. A different song." Chet was sure that he fixed up "No One Will Ever Know" for Tommy Covington and Mel Foree as well as the Davis Sisters hit, "I Forgot More Than You'll Ever Know About Him," for Cecil Null, who "never wrote another hit." Fred also wrote the middle section of "Cattle Call" by Tex Owen, which was a hit for Eddy Arnold.

Fred Rose "was always helping people," remembered Chet. "He'd read about somebody in the paper that needed help or something and he'd do it and not let anybody know, so I've heard. He told me that once." Chet said that Rose helped him "once in a while. He'd buy me things. Said, 'But you've got to be careful when you're good to people. You don't want to make a bum out of them. If you're too nice, then they'll keep coming back for more.'" Rose told Chet that he made $60,000 a year and would "spend every damn cent of it!"

Chet stated that Rose "hated the word 'hillbilly.' He thought it was degrading." He remembered hearing Fred say back in the 1940s, "We've got to stop these magazines from calling country music 'hillbilly music.'"[2]

The National Labor Relations Act (known as the Wagner Act) established the National Labor Relations Board and led to the formation of a number of unions, including one to represent radio broadcast engineers. Since the lines between radio (and later television) broadcast engineers and recording engineers was "blurry," those unions came to represent studio engineers associated with RCA and CBS. RCA's contract with the unions required that all recording sessions be done by RCA engineers, so the label could not record at the Castle studio. Instead, the earliest RCA Victor recordings in Nashville were done at Brown Radio Productions studio, located at 240 ½ Fourth Avenue North, with RCA engineers and equipment brought in from New York. Steve Sholes began recording RCA Victor acts in Nashville there in 1950.

On March 27, 1950, in likely the first RCA recording in the Brown Brothers studio, Sholes produced a Johnnie and Jack session where they recorded "Poison Love," which became their first hit. Sholes continued to record RCA acts at the facility. After Chet arrived, Sholes used him to call musicians and arrange sessions.

"Steve would call me before leaving New York to advise me of the number of sessions he wanted to do and what type of band he required for each artist," remembered Chet. "I got on the phone and booked musicians; many times I was included. When Steve arrived in Nashville, we would make about three sessions a day for a week or so. Between sessions or after we were through for the day, Steve and I would talk about the business. He frequently mentioned his desire to set up a permanent RCA studio in Nashville, and I was to run it."[3]

On Sunday, August 20, Chet Atkins played on his first session for Eddy Arnold, produced by Steve Sholes at Brown Radio Productions. Other musicians on the session included Jack Shook and Guy Willis on guitars, Little Roy Wiggins on steel, Chuck Wright on bass, Skeeter Willis on fiddle, Vic Willis on piano, and Anita Kerr on organ. They recorded two songs, "If I Never Get to Heaven" and "The Lovebug Itch," which reached number two on the country chart.

That was Chet's first Nashville session for RCA and the first time he worked with Anita Kerr, just twenty-three. She was born Anita Jean Grilli in 1927 in Memphis and was leading the Grilli Sisters by the time she was fourteen, writing arrangements, playing piano, and singing with them as well as working as a keyboardist and vocalist on a regular show on WREC. She began teaching herself to write orchestra arrangements, which eventually led her to Nashville in 1948.

In Nashville she found work playing and singing in clubs and at dances, then became the staff pianist at WMAK. She organized a quartet that sang on WLAC—for free. Jack Stapp, program director at WSM, heard about the quartet and hired her to direct the eight-voice choir that was on the network show, "Sunday Down South," starring Snookey Lanson.

WSM, which owned the Grand Ole Opry, was essentially the headquarters for the Nashville music industry, an active hub of musical activity. Paul Cohen had been coming to Nashville regularly since 1947 to record Decca acts Ernest Tubb, Red Foley, and others at Castle Studio. Cohen wanted a choir for a religious song, "Our Lady of Fatima," which Foley was scheduled to record, so he approached

Kerr. That led to her performing regularly with a singing group on the "Prince Albert Show," backing Opry singers. She signed with Decca, with Cohen naming them the Anita Kerr Singers.[4] During the 1950s, her group sang on up to twenty sessions a week.

Chet first recorded in Nashville as an RCA artist on August 22. Accompanied by Harold Bradley on guitar, Ernie Newton on bass, and Anita Kerr on organ, Billie Rose Atkins, Chet's half sister, sang "Confusin'," written by Louie Innis, while Helen Carter wrote "Music in My Heart." The next day he recorded "Indian Love Call" and "Birth of the Blues," accompanied by Ernie Newton on bass and Poppa (sometimes known as Papa) John Gordy on piano. On "Indian Love Call," Chet used "harmonics," created by lightly touching a string with the left hand at a specified fret and plucking the string with the right hand, producing a chiming sound. Chet popularized this chiming sound of harmonics among country guitarists.

Chet's recordings began to receive radio airplay, so he was expected to make personal appearances. Chet disliked traveling and wanted to remain in Nashville and play on recording sessions, but "WSM certainly wouldn't stand for any artist to sit back in Nashville and record," said Chet. "I liked the Nashville scene, and I knew that I wanted to be a star there. I had spent eight years making personal appearances; now I wanted to settle down to work in one spot—and what a spot the Opry was."[5]

WSM program director Jack Stapp defended Chet when Jim Denny wanted to fire him for not touring. In addition to saving his job with the Opry, Stapp hired Chet to perform regularly as a "guest" for a hundred dollars a show on "Sunday Down South," a show that WSM fed to the NBC network. Stapp was also the producer of the "Prince Albert Show" on the Opry, which was broadcast on NBC, and hired Chet for a hundred dollars a week to play a song that could be shortened or lengthened, depending on whether the show was running short or long.[6]

In the fall of 1950, Chet, Leona, and Merle rented a house on Caldwell Avenue, near the WSM TV antenna. On WSM and on the Opry he worked with the Carters and performed on his own. He did extensive session work as a sideman, aside from his own RCA Victor sessions.

Chet had met legendary handcrafted guitar maker John D'Angelico during a visit to his small shop in Brooklyn before he moved to

Nashville. D'Angelico began as a violin maker before concentrating on guitars. "I'd had the chance to play a few D'Angelico guitars and had recognized that they truly were superior instruments," stated Chet. "D'Angelico had learned about the sustain and tone of violins and applied that to the acoustics of his guitars."[7]

Chet enlisted his brother Jim's help to approach D'Angelico about making Chet a custom guitar. D'Angelico made two models at that time, the New Yorker, eighteen inches wide, and the Excel, seventeen inches. Chet ordered the Excel because it was less expensive. D'Angelico made acoustic guitars, so "when I indicated I was probably going to electrify it, he wasn't too pleased, but he agreed to put sound posts in it for me," stated Chet. "When I was younger, I had preferred a narrow neck because it was easier to finger certain chords, but I realized after a while that the narrow neck produced a lot of buzzes from unintended contact with the strings. A wider neck gives you more space between the strings and makes for cleaner, stronger playing."[8]

Chet received his D'Angelico in August 1950 and "got it out of its case and just looked at it, turning it every which way to inspect every detail. It was shiny and beautiful," remembered Chet. "I tuned it up and played it for hours, all over the neck and in every key, like a kid with a new toy." Chet admitted that there was "a certain status symbol value attached" to the guitar, "the equivalent of getting a Rolls Royce. It was the ultimate in archtop guitars, and the fact that I was able to afford one was a way of saying I'd arrived as a guitarist."[9]

Chet always tinkered with his guitars, adjusting them to suit his needs. On his D'Angelico he put in a metal bridge for better sustain and worked on the nut so the string height would be perfect and installed his Vibrola. No one was installing electric pickups, so Chet had to do that himself. He didn't have the proper tools, but he "drilled a small hole in the top, then took a keyhole saw and cut small sections out to allow for the pickups and wiring." He mounted his Gibson P-90 pickup near the bridge, a metal Bigsby under the end of the neck, a Gibson volume control for each pickup, and a cord jack.

Chet was "fairly pleased" with the result, although he had no tone controls, adjusting the tone and overall volume on the amp after he mixed the volume levels of the two pickups. It worked "but it made changing tonality during a song almost impossible." He then acquired a three-position switch from a radio broadcast console and placed it on a small strip of metal in the treble f-hole, which allowed him to play either pickup or both at once. Doing that makes the pickups out of phase, but Atkins didn't realize that until Ray Butts pointed it out several years later.[10]

Just before Christmas, on the evening of December 21, Chet played electric guitar on a Hank Williams session at Castle Studio. Sammy Preutt and Hank also played guitars, while Drifting Cowboys band members Jerry Rivers and Don Helms played fiddle and steel guitar. Either Ernie Newton or Howard Watts (who went by the name Cedric Rainwater) played bass. On piano was either Owen Bradley or Fred Rose. The songs they recorded included "Cold Cold Heart," "Dear John," "Just Waitin,'" and "Men With Broken Hearts." The last three formed part of Hank's "Luke the Drifter" recordings.

CHAPTER 8

Country singers were generally backed by their road bands during early recording sessions in Nashville, and between 1950 and 1955 there was a corps of excellent studio musicians. At the time of Chet's arrival, the top guitarist was left-handed Jerry Shook, who played a right-handed guitar. He was also a talented singer. After a stint in New York, he settled in Nashville as a staff musician at WSM.

Red Foley's band was often considered the best. In August 1947 Foley was backed by Zeke Turner on electric guitar, Louie Innis on rhythm, Jerry Byrd on Hawaiian guitar, Farris Coursey on drums, Tommy Jackson on fiddle, Bronson "Barefoot Brownie" Reynolds on bass, and WSM bandleader Beasley Smith on piano. Around 1948, Innis, Tommy Jackson, Jerry Byrd, and the Turner brothers, frustrated with their income at WSM, left Nashville for Cincinnati and WLW's "Midwestern Hayride" as well as appearances on a number of the station's TV and radio programs. Fred Rose brought Hank Williams to Cincinnati for a December 1948 session with Jackson, Byrd, Turner, and Innis to record Hank's first big hit, "Lovesick Blues." By 1952 the musicians had returned to Nashville.

Hank Williams had a great band with Sammy Pruett (guitar), Don Helms (steel), and Jerry Rivers (fiddle) forming the core. On Hank's last sessions, Ernie Newton or Howard Watts played bass, with Owen Bradley or Fred Rose on piano and Chet on guitar. Eddy Arnold's band included the Willis brothers, Guy (guitar), Skeeter (fiddle), and Vic (accordion) with Chuck "The Indian" Wright on bass. The Willis brothers debuted on the Grand Ole Opry in June 1946, recorded for Sterling Records, and backed Hank Williams on his first recording sessions. They and steel guitarist Roy Wiggins formed Eddy Arnold's band in late 1948.

Musicians who formed the dream team for Nashville recording sessions included Grady Martin, who led the Slewfoot Five, a jazz-based group; Farris Coursey, the WSM staff drummer who performed with Owen Bradley's big band; Hank Garland, who wrote "Sugarfoot

Rag" while with Red Foley's band; Billy Byrd, lead guitarist for Ernest Tubb; Harold Bradley, who began accompanying Eddy Arnold and Ernest Tubb on the Grand Ole Opry; Velma Williams, who became the first female guitarist to play on sessions in Nashville and was part of Roy Acuff's band; Smilin' Eddie Hill, who became part of the Louvin Brothers group; rhythm guitarist Ray Edenton; steel guitarist Don Davis; and steel guitarist Jerry Byrd, who injected the Hawaiian sound into country music.

Tommy Jackson and Dale Potter were pioneers in playing two strings at once on the fiddle, known as "double-stop" fiddling. They often recorded twin fiddles on sessions. Ernie Newton had played in the Les Paul Trio, which included Chet's brother Jim, and was the first bass player to use a drumhead mounted on his bass for a rhythmic effect; Bassist Floyd "Lightnin'" Chance also played clarinet, saxophone, and bass horn; Poppa John Gordy was a Dixieland and ragtime piano player who was the major pianist with the WSM radio orchestra. Marvin Hughes was a pianist in WSM's staff band and, Owen Bradley, who became music director at WSM in 1942, served as a music arranger for Paul Cohen and Decca Records and helped set up and guide the sessions.

Drums were usually not included on country recording sessions during the 1940s and early 1950s, but the top Nashville session drummer from the mid-1950s on was Murrey Mizell "Buddy" Harman Jr., who became the staff drummer at the Grand Ole Opry in 1959. Other musicians who played on recordings that Chet either played on or produced include Charles Grean (Steve Sholes's assistant, who often came to Nashville and played bass on sessions), Dutch McMillan (clarinet), Anita Carter (bass), and Howard Watts (bass).

Chet Atkins did not stand apart from those early session musicians in terms of his radio background or love of jazz, but his guitar playing was notable. He also stood apart as a recording artist with a major label and not just a session musician. Also, he had caught the eye and ear of Steve Sholes, who would mentor him to success outside the studio and support him as an artist.

Boudleaux Bryant grew up in Moultrie, Georgia, and studied classical violin; he was a member of the Atlanta Philharmonic during 1937–1938 before he joined Hank Penny's Radio Cowboys on WSB in Atlanta. Chet first heard him on WSB while living in Georgia; Bryant played fiddle infused with a touch of Stephane Grappelli–inspired jazz. In 1940, during the "ASCAP War," when radio stations boycotted ASCAP songs, radio performers had to perform works in the public domain, and on those old songs "Boudleaux would play the melody on a tune such as 'Jeannie With the Light Brown Hair' and then he would play a chorus in a light swing fashion," said Chet. "This was brand new to my ears and nearly blew my mind."[1]

Chet first met Boudleaux in 1944 when Bryant was playing fiddle nightly at the Gibson Hotel in Cincinnati. Homer and Jethro took Chet to Bryant's home: "It was just a thrill to meet somebody with that amount of talent," said Chet. "I don't think I'd ever run into anybody before who knew everything there is to know about playing a guitar or fiddle."[2]

In the summer of 1945, while on tour with a jazz group, Boudleaux met Felice Scaduto in Milwaukee; they married in September. Felice loved to write poetry and soon Boudleaux began adding melodies to her poems. In 1948 Fred Rose heard their song "Country Boy" and gave the song to Little Jimmy Dickens and it became a hit. Rose persuaded the Bryants to move to Nashville in 1950, the same year Chet moved to town, and they became the first full-time songwriters in Nashville. Rose did not sign songwriters to exclusive contracts—except for Hank Williams—instead signing only the songs he felt he could get recorded. Rose had first choice of their songs for Acuff-Rose Publishing, and the Bryants soon became popular as songwriters. Jimmie Dickens recorded "I'm Little But I'm Loud," "Take Me as I Am," "Out Behind the Barn," and "Hole in My Pocket," while Carl Smith recorded "Hey, Joe," "Back Up, Buddy," and "It's a Lovely, Lovely World."

After he moved to Nashville, Chet and Boudleaux began writing songs together, including advertising jingles for Martha White. "It wasn't long before I was hanging out with him a lot," said Chet. Bryant taught him "a lot about classical music because he knew almost every classical piece that had been written. He would teach me the melody, and I would make up my own arrangements."[3]

Red Foley recorded "Midnight," written by Chet and Boudleaux, which became a number-one country hit in 1952. Chet remembered that he got the melody for "Midnight" from a blues phrase that Jethro Burns taught him from "Floyd's Guitar Blues" that was popular with Andy Kirk and His Twelve Clouds of Joy, a Kansas City swing band.

The most enduring song that Boudleaux and Chet wrote was "How's the World Treating You." The melody came to Chet while he was in New York for an appearance with the Carters. Atkins was in his hotel room, alone and lonely, when he "wrote the lonesomest melody I could think of." "What's New" was a pop song that Chet liked "so I stole a line from it and titled my song 'How's the World Treating You?'" When he returned to Nashville, he went to Boudleaux's house and played him the melody. Boudleaux said, "I like it. You got a name for it?" "How's the World Treating You?" replied Chet. A couple of hours later, Boudleaux "came up with some of the most beautiful lyrics I have ever heard."[4] Eddy Arnold was the first to record it.

"Boudleaux taught me a lot about writing a song," said Chet. "You have to begin with an idea. . . . From that point, it's like painting a picture. You write it, and you go over it time after time."[5]

On January 31, 1951, at the Brown Brothers Radio Studio, accompanied by Jack Shook on guitar, Ernie Newton on bass, and Marvin Hughes on piano and organ, Chet recorded three instrumentals he wrote, "Mountain Melody," "Hybrid Corn," and "My Crazy Heart" (written with Helen Carter), and a Stuart Hamblen song, "You're Always Brand New," which featured a vocal by Danny Dill. Chet believed that those were the first songs that he recorded on his D'Angelico guitar. On April 23, at RCA Studio 1 in New York, Chet recorded "Jitterbug Waltz," written by Fats Waller, with Chet on both guitar and bass, through the process of overdubbing—adding instruments by playing the initial track over to a second recorder while adding a new part. That method of recording had been pioneered by Les Paul. Three days later, also in New York, Chet recorded "One Man Boogie" and "Crazy Rhythm." Three days later Chet recorded "One Man Boogie," an adaptation of the Tommy Dorsey big band hit "Boogie Woogie," and "Crazy Love."

Chet recorded four instrumentals on September 25 in New York at RCA's Studio 2. Accompanied by his brother Jim, with Frank Carroll on bass, Chet recorded "Rainbow," "Rustic Dance," the Glenn Miller hit "In the Mood," and "Spanish Fandango." "Rainbow" had been a hit in 1908 and was released with "Good-bye Blues," which became a hit for the Mills Brothers in 1932. Chet recorded "Good-bye Blues" accompanied by Jerry Byrd on rhythm, Ernie Newton on bass, Marvin

Hughes piano, and the Beasley Singers chorus. By this time, it appeared that RCA had abandoned the idea of Chet as a singer/guitarist like Merle Travis and concentrated on him as an instrumentalist. The record was billed as "Chet Atkins—Playing All Instruments." Two days later, Chet recorded two songs he and Boudleaux Bryant wrote, "Midnight" and "Sweet Bunch of Daisies," and a song written solely by Boudleaux, "Your Mean Little Heart."

During 1951 Chet released the singles "In the Mood" / "Sweet Bunch of Daisies," "Rainbow" / "Good-bye Blues," "Spanish Fandango" / "You Mean Little Heart," and "The Wall Flower Waltz" / "Fiddlin' Fool."

CHAPTER 9

By 1952 Chet was performing daily with the Carters on their early morning show. "I arose at five a.m., lit a cigarette, got dressed and drove my new Oldsmobile to WSM, arriving about 15 minutes before the show began," said Chet.[1] On the Noontime Neighbors show Chet performed solos.

Chet first met guitarist Hank Garland in 1946 when he came to the Opry with Red Foley. Only fifteen, Garland was already a phenomenal guitarist who, like Chet, practiced constantly. Whenever they met they jammed. "We used to swap choruses," remembered Chet. "I would play rhythm and Grady Martin would play the chorus; then we would switch around, Hank Garland would play rhythm and Billy Byrd, who was a good jazz guitarist, would play a chorus or two . . . everybody was trying to outdo the other person, and there were some fantastic licks floating around."[2]

"I was beginning to do more work in the recording studios," said Chet, "cutting some records as a sideman, and some as the leader. Royalties were beginning to come in but the Carters' act at WSM was beginning to come apart. June had married Carl Smith, and Anita was married to Dale Potter. We didn't rehearse as much as we had in the beginning because the girls had lost a lot of interest in the show. E. J. and Maybelle were unhappy about the act falling apart. To make matters worse, Jim Denny again tried to get the flour company to fire me. He was still unhappy because I wasn't working the road. I had to go in and plead for my job: 'Man, I just want to make a living. The girls are married, but I'm still interested in staying at WSM.' Jack Stapp again came to my rescue."

Fred Rose was a great supporter who "was one of the most important people in my life because he showed confidence in me when a lot of others didn't," said Chet.[3] Rose and other producers began using Chet on sessions, many yielding major hits. He played for Faron Young on "Goin' Steady," "If You Ain't Lovin'," and "I've Got Five Dollars (And It's Saturday Night)" as well as Webb Pierce's "There Stands the Glass" and "I'm Walking the Dog." Rose used Chet to play dead-string guitar (muting the strings with his right hand for a stronger rhythm) on the Hank Williams sessions done at Castle Studio. The Carlisles' 1953 hit "No Help Wanted" was at least partly defined by Chet's playing because every guitarist who worked with the band had to copy or approximate Atkins's fingerstyle licks to create the group's defining sound.

Chet worked with the Louvin Brothers on their MGM and Capitol recordings between 1951 and 1955. According to Louvin authority Charles Wolfe, Fred Rose, who produced the Louvins for MGM, built the band around Chet's guitar. He appeared on all the Louvins' early Capitol gospel sides produced by Ken Nelson as well as their hit "When I Stop Dreaming."[4]

On May 16, at Brown's Radio Studio, Chet recorded a song he and Boudleaux Bryant wrote, "Blue Gypsy," as well as "The Third Man Theme," "St. Louis Blues," "Nobody's Sweetheart," and "Lover Come Back to Me." "The Third Man Theme" came from the 1949 British film. The track was released in 1953 on his eight-song ten-inch album, *Chet Atkins and His Galloping Guitar*. During this period, labels released Broadway musicals and classical music on twelve-inch albums, while pop releases appeared on ten-inch albums.

Chet first met Hank Williams in 1949 while "Lovesick Blues" was a hit. In 1950, after Chet had moved to Nashville, he met Hank again. "Hank walked into one of the dressing rooms at the Opry and introduced himself," said Chet. "He was very skinny and looked like he was in bad health. In fact, as Sid Harkreader, one of the early members of the Opry commented, 'Hank was so skinny his ass rattled like a box of carpenter's tools.' I remember being amazed at the color of his eyes. They were almost black. But he was very open and friendly," said Chet.

"I hear you write songs," Hank said to Chet. "Yeah" was the only word Chet Atkins could say. Hank nodded. "Then we'll get together sometime and try to knock one out." Chet was floored but gave Hank his phone number. Hank called and they set up a time to meet. "I went out to Hank's house and we tried," said Chet. "But I just couldn't write with him. I was so in awe of the man that I choked."[5]

"We tried to write songs together a couple of times, and he always smelled very strong of bourbon," remembered Chet. "He was a funny guy. I think people think of him as a sad, melancholy sort of guy, but he was very funny, always speaking his mind, hurting somebody's feelings. But he could be very nice, too. Hank didn't have too much education and he was ignorant in a lot of ways, but he was very bright and clever."[6]

Chet said Hank was always writing. "He wasn't one of those guys who sets aside a time to be creative, writes his song and goes on about his day. Every time you'd see him, he'd just finished a tune. Hank would come up to you and say, 'I got a new one for you, Hoss.' Then he'd get right up in your face and sing it. . . . Then he'd play something like 'Mansion on a Hill' or one of those unbelievably great songs. He'd say, 'How do you like it?' I'd say I liked it fine, but if somebody like Ernest Tubb or Hank Snow was standing around, and they'd say, 'I'd like to record that, Hank!' Hank would narrow his eyes and say, 'No, it's too good for you. I'm gonna record it myself.' I think they were his test runs. If Ernest Tubb and Hank Snow wanted the song, Hank knew it was a hit."[7]

During a tour with the Carter Family Chet received insight into Hank: "I remember seeing him buy a stack of comic books at night and take 'em up to his room to read," said Chet. "That was his reading material. I often wondered if that's where he got his ideas for songs."[8]

Chet played on his first Hank Williams session at Castle Studio in December 1950. Chet backed Hank on the Opry a number of times and said the magic of a Hank Williams performance came mainly from "the way Hank moved. It was mesmerizing to watch his body language when he sang. It wasn't anything all that rhythmic, but more like the wind blowing a limb in rhythm with the music."[9]

Chet did not record with Hank Williams again until June 13, 1952, at Castle Studio. Hank was usually backed by his band, but his guitarist, Sammy Pruett, had joined Carl Smith's band, the Tunesmiths, so Fred Rose called Chet to play on the session. Jerry Rivers (fiddle) and Don Helms (steel guitar) were in Hank's band and on the session. Jack Shook played rhythm guitar and Willis Brothers member Charles Wright was on bass. The first song on the session was "Window Shopping," written by Marcel Joseph, a New York journalist. "Jambalaya" had been recorded as a vocal/guitar demo by Hank before it was recorded with a full band. Although Hank is listed as the only songwriter on "Jambalaya," it was cowritten with Moon Mullican, known as the king of the hillbilly piano players. Moon had been in Jimmie Davis's band on KWKH in Shreveport before he formed his own band in 1945. In 1951 Hank brought him to the Opry, where they wrote "Jambalaya." Mullican was paid royalties under the table.[10]

The third song on the session was "Settin' the Woods on Fire," written by Fred Rose and Ed Nelson, and the final song, "I'll Never Get Out of This World Alive," was credited to Hank and Fred Rose. The title came from a phrase popularized by comedian W. C. Fields. Although the title seems to foretell Hank's death, less than six months later—the song was on the country chart when Hank died—the subject is actually humorous. Years later, Chet remembered, "We recorded 'I'll Never Get Out of This World Alive' [and] after each take, he'd sit down in a chair. I remember thinking, 'Hoss, you're not just jivin' because he was so weak and all he could do was just sing a few lines, and then just fall in the chair."[11]

Chet was in the Castle Studio with Hank for a two-hour session again on Friday, July 11, the same day that Hank's divorce from his wife Audrey became final. With Chet were Jerry Rivers, Don Helms, Ernie Newton, and Jack Shook. They first recorded "You Win Again," originally titled "I Lose Again" before Fred Rose convinced Hank to change it. The next song was "I Won't Be Home No More," written by Hank, and then "Be Careful of Stones That You Throw," by steel guitarist Bonnie Dodd. Hank recorded it as Luke the Drifter. The final song on the session was "Why Don't You Make Up Your Mind," which Jimmy Dickens had recorded as "I Wish You Didn't Love Me So Much" before Hank rewrote and renamed it. It is a bitter, vengeful song aimed at Audrey.

The next day Hank performed "Jambalaya" and "Honky Tonkin'" on the Opry, then went to West Grove, Pennsylvania, where he performed, then went on a drinking binge. Back in Nashville, Hank was placed in a sanitarium, and on August 11 Jim Denny called Hank to inform him that he had been fired from the Opry.

Chet told a story about Hank's label, MGM, wanting him to go into the studio and record, but Hank kept saying, "'My throat's sore. I can't record right now.' And they kept calling, wanting him to record something, and finally they said, 'What the hell's it gonna take to cure your sore throat?' And he said, 'I think about twenty-five thousand dollars would do it.' They sent the money and Hank recorded."[12]

Chet was in New York on July 29 and recorded—alone—"Stephen Foster Medley," comprising "Massa's in de Cold, Cold Ground," "Nellie Bly," and "Camptown Races." He also recorded a fiddle tune, "Black Mountain Rag," originally done by Curly Fox, "Hangover Blues," and a song he wrote alone, "Imagination." On "Hangover Blues," a song he wrote with Boudleaux Bryant, he "intentionally played sour notes in order to bring to mind the splitting headache feel of a terrible hangover."[13] All of these songs appeared on his *Galloping Guitar* album.

The next day Chet returned to the studio with Al Chernet on rhythm guitar, Marty Gold on organ, and Charles Grean on bass. He recorded "Meet Mr. Callahan," covering Les Paul's version of the theme song for a popular British TV show. The next song, "Chinatown," written in 1910, became a jazz standard. At the time there remained a concern with RCA Victor that instrumentals were a hard sell, so a number of guest vocalists appeared on Chet's recordings. RCA Victor artist Rosalie Allen, a New York–based yodeler and local TV star whom Chet had backed on her recordings, was featured as a guest vocalist. She sang "Guitar Polka" and "Dream Train." Being an instrumentalist was an advantage for Chet as a producer and record executive because singers on the label would not see him as competition for hit songs or for label attention and promotion.

On September 23, 1952—five days after his twenty-ninth birthday—Hank Williams recorded his last session. There were several canceled sessions before that one, indicating Hank's condition. He had flown into Nashville from Shreveport, where he was living, for the afternoon session at Castle Studio. Chet played his electric guitar with Hank and Eddie Hill on guitar, Don Helms on steel, Tommy Jackson on fiddle, Lightnin' Chance on bass, and Farris Coursey on drums. During that final session they recorded "Kaw-Liga" (written by Hank and Fred Rose), "I Could Never Be Ashamed of You," "Your Cheatin' Heart," and "Take These Chains From My Heart" (written by Fred Rose and Hy Heath). Hank Williams had only a little over three months left to live.

Homer and Jethro recorded an answer song to Hank's "Jambalaya" (a number-one hit on the *Billboard* country chart that year). "Jam-Bowl-Liar" had Chet playing guitar with Homer Haynes on rhythm guitar, Jethro Burns on mandolin, Charles Grean on bass, and Poppa John Gordy on piano. Three days later, Chet recorded "High Rockin' Swing" and "Fig Leaf Rag" (written by Chet and Boudleaux Bryant), accompanied by Jethro Burns on mandolin, Homer Haynes on guitar, Dale Potter on fiddle, and Charlie Grean on bass.

Chet, Homer, and Jethro, accompanied by various other studio musicians, recorded a number of songs as the Country All Stars. Those recordings were usually done after a session for a singer when there was time left. According to Jethro, "Somebody came up with the idea, let's do some instrumentals with the guys here. There wasn't any big thought behind them [they were] done primarily to fill studio time." During those two October sessions, the artist was listed as Homer and Jethro, although Chet usually played the melody. The song originally listed as "Untitled Number 1" was changed to "High Rockin' Swing." That was on the *Galloping Guitar* album, while two other songs were released as the Country All Stars. The numbers they recorded ranged from swing standards like "Stomping at the Savoy," "Sweet Georgia Brown," and "Marie" to twenties pop favorites like "Do Something" and "My Little Girl." Steel guitarist Jerry Byrd was often present.

Chet's recordings show that he loved a wide variety of music and often recorded songs from the early twentieth century and some from the nineteenth. He recorded many pop hits from his teenage years, with jazz and swing numbers prominent.

Chet's singles during 1952 included three with Rosalie Allen as vocalist: "It Wasn't God Who Made Honky Tonk Angels" / "It'll Surprise You," "I Laughed at Love" / "I Gotta Have You," and "Guitar Polka" / "Dream Train." There were two with the Country All Stars: "It Goes Like This" / "Midnight Train" and "Tennessee Rag" / "My Little Girl." Chet's solo releases in 1952 included "Meet Mister Callaghan" / "Chinatown, My Chinatown" and "Midnight" / "Rustic Dance."

CHAPTER 10

String Dustin' was the first album released under the Country All Stars name. The musicians included Chet, Homer, Jethro, steel guitarist Jerry Byrd, and fiddler Dale Potter. Byrd recalled, "Our imagination went beyond country music."

The All Stars recorded more tracks in 1953 during a session in New York, then, minus Chet, in Chicago with Homer and Jethro and two other musicians. A New York session in 1955 included Chet, Homer and Jethro, Charles Grean, and George Barnes.[1] Jerry Byrd later told John McClellan, "We did these in between sessions. It was another way to make $41. That was session scale back then," adding that, "We'd just pull a tune out of thin air and away we would whip it up! You take the intro, I'll fill the first eight bars, somebody else fills the second eight bars, you take the bridge, and here is our ending—roll tape! Let it rip! We would pull a tune out the air. That's the way we did it. We knew all those damn old tunes. It was something else!"

"Chet and I weren't the flashy jazz players," continued Byrd. "We stuck pretty close to the melody and we made it say something. It was a different religion, that's all. Jethro was a great improviser. We were too, but we never let it get in the way of the basic melody or the feel of the melody."

Chet and Jerry Byrd had a show on WSM radio, "Two Guitars," during the 1952–1955 period. "It was on the air for around two years," said Byrd. "We did the show to make a few extra bucks for our families. It was during the time we were playing the Opry. I came down from the north and he came in from the east. Somehow or another we just paired off. We gravitated towards each other, I guess. We did tons of recording sessions together and we worked out a lot of twin guitar stuff together. Back then, you had no electronic gadgets to help, no tracking, no overdubbing, none of that. The red light went on in the studio and you played your butt off until it went off. If you messed up, you started back at the beginning. No splicing!"

"Chet and I spoke the same musical language," said Byrd. The problem was that "Chet could never get with his dad. I think it hurt him until the day that he died. His dad didn't want to have much to do with him."

"Chet always looked like he smelled something," remarked Byrd. "Not strong, but he could faintly smell shit somewhere." Discussing some new guitar players, Chet told Byrd, "The guys these days are educated beyond their intelligence. They know all the chords but put them in the wrong song and in the wrong place."[2]

The Brown Brothers had closed their studio by 1953 and sold their equipment to engineer Cliff Thomas, who opened Thomas Productions Studio in a large metal building near Broadway. The building, which had been used as a storage location for RCA's recording equipment, became the label's main studio. In 1953 and 1954, Steve Sholes was Cliff Thomas's biggest customer among record labels. The label brought in a union engineer from New York to satisfy the requirement that all RCA Victor sessions have a staff engineer.

Si Siman became Porter Wagoner's manager after the singer joined KWTO in Springfield, Missouri. In spring 1952 Steve Sholes signed him to RCA and produced his first session at the KWTO studios. Their next session was in Nashville on Valentine's Day with Chet. Porter remembered that when recording at the Thomas Productions Studio "we had to stop when a big truck went by."[3]

In March, Sholes brought in Nashville musicians Chet, Jerry Byrd, and Grady Martin for sessions to back other artists. On March 17 and 18, Chet, with Byrd on steel guitar and Martin on guitar and fiddle, recorded five songs with Lone Pine and Betty. They were joined by Lone Pine's guitarist Raymond Couture and Charles Grean.

Harold "Lone Pine" Breau was born in Maine and during the 1930s was a member of the Lone Pine Mountaineers. Rita Cote was born in Quebec and grew up in Maine in a family of twelve children who spoke only French at home. In 1938, guitarist Ray Couture brought Harold to Rita's home because Harold and Couture needed a female singer. Although Cote could hardly speak English, she could sing in English and her and Breau's voices blended well. In June 1940 they married and began performing as Lone Pine and Betty Cody.

During their March 1953 recordings, produced by Steve Sholes, Betty remembered that Chet was "so interested. He was always working on doing a great introduction. He did some great guitar duet things—him and Ray Couture." Couture added, "Chet put those arrangements together right on the spot. He heard the songs once and he'd say 'I'll do this and you do this. Let's try it. 1-2-3-4' and we started to play."

Lone Pine and Betty's son, Lenny Breau, was around eleven when he asked Couture to show him how to play a song, "Messing Up the Frets," that Couture played each night during their show. Couture told him it was "pretty difficult" but played it for him. When Lone Pine and Betty returned from a tour "three or four weeks later he said, 'Hey Pan, see if I have it right.'" Couture "couldn't believe it. He was playing it better than I did. He had added things to it! He couldn't have been more than eleven. I used to tell Betty, 'That boy's a genius.'"[4]

On March 18 Chet, with Grady Martin on guitar, Jerry Byrd on steel guitar, Charlie Grean on bass, and Phil Kraus on drums, were in New York where they recorded a session at RCA Studio 1. "Oh By Jingo, By Gee! (You're the Only Girl for Me)" had been a hit for Frank Crumit, "Hello My Baby" was first a hit in 1899, and "The Bells of St. Mary's" was featured prominently in the 1945 Bing Crosby film of the same title. This was the first session where Chet used percussion on his recordings.[5]

Two days later in the same studio, with Homer Haynes on guitar, Jethro Burns on mandolin, and Charlie Grean on bass, Chet recorded "Country Gentleman," one of the most enduring instrumentals that he and Boudleaux Bryant wrote and which became his theme song. The song came about when Bryant went over to Chet's house while Chet was playing a tune. Bryant "added to it and showed me choruses to play and some good moves," said Chet. Boudleaux said, "Let's call it 'Country Gentleman,' which was the name of a farm magazine popular in the South."[6] Although the song never charted, Chet worked hard promoting it. Chet also recorded a W. C. Handy song, "Memphis Blues," "Alice Blue Gown," and "12th Street Rag," which was a hit for clarinetist Pee Wee Hunt in 1948.

Betty Jack (B. J.) Davis and Mary Frances "Skeeter" Penick met in high school and began singing together and soon landed a job singing on a WCPO-TV variety show in Cincinnati. They began singing at the Renfro Valley Barn Dance where the emcee was unable to remember

"Penick" one day and dubbed them the Davis Sisters. They moved to Detroit and were on the Big Barn Frolic on WJR radio for sixteen months. Early in 1953 they went to New York to audition for Steve Sholes without an appointment. They did not meet Sholes but did audition for Eddie Kissack with Decca. Kissack was hired by RCA Victor and alerted Sholes about the duo, and they auditioned in Nashville in May 1953. Sholes and Chet Atkins both listened and agreed to record them the next day. Sholes gave them two songs to learn: "I Forgot More Than You'll Ever Know" and "Rock-a-Bye Boogie" and told them they would record those with two other songs they had previously recorded as a demo in Detroit. They had not even signed a recording contract when they went into Thomas Productions to record with Chet on guitar and four other musicians. The first song was "I Forgot More Than You'll Ever Know" by Cecil Null.[7]

On August 1, the Davis Sisters performed on the Wheeling Jamboree then headed back to their home in northern Kentucky when a soldier fell asleep driving and hit them head-on, killing B. J. and injuring Skeeter. Two weeks later, "I Forgot More Than You'll Ever Know" entered the *Billboard* chart and became a number-one hit. Georgie Davis, B. J.'s older sister, joined Skeeter to continue the act as a duet.

Chet was in New York in November for a new Davis Sisters record. Though the Davis Sisters had one of the biggest hits of 1953, B. J.'s death meant the new duo could not capitalize on their success. Over two days the duo recorded four songs that were unreleased.

By September Sholes was relying heavily on Chet to be RCA's man in Nashville. Chet later told Chet Flippo in *Rolling Stone* magazine, "I would hire the musicians and we'd get into the studio—I've always been kind of domineering around musicians, so I'd tell everybody what to play." Atkins added that Sholes had another idea as well: "He kept saying how he'd love to build a studio in Nashville and have me run it."[8]

Chet once told Bill Ivey that the reason Sholes spent so much time in Nashville was because Sholes had caused an auto accident that left his wife "disfigured." Sholes's wife resented him after the accident and "made his life miserable."[9]

On September 17 Chet was in the Thomas Productions Studio to record a session accompanied by Louie Innis on guitar and Jerry Byrd on bass. The trio recorded "Peeping Tom," by Boudleaux Bryant and Chet, and "City Slicker," which Chet wrote by himself. They also recorded "Three O'Clock in the Morning" and "Georgia Camp Meeting."

Charline Arthur had lived in Paris, Texas, since she was four. As a teenager she met Ernest Tubb, who encouraged her to sing. By 1945 she was singing regularly on KPLT.

Charline married Jack Arthur and began singing in honky-tonks across Texas. Her first recording session was in late 1949 with Jim Beck at his studio in Dallas. In mid-1951 she recorded her next session at radio station KERB in Kermit, Texas. During her time at KERB she met Colonel Tom Parker, who was touring in Texas with Eddy Arnold. Parker told Julian and Jean Aberbach about Arthur, and the Aberbachs obtained a recording contract for her with RCA Victor. Her first RCA Victor session came in Dallas in February 1953.

Steve Sholes produced that session of four songs, three of which she wrote. The recording contract with RCA led to her being booked on tours with Big D Jamboree and Louisiana Hayride artists. At the end of 1955, she was runner-up in a poll conducted by *Country & Western Jamboree* magazine in the Best Female Singer category; Kitty Wells held the top spot. On September 21, 1952, Charline Arthur recorded four songs at Thomas Productions with Sholes producing. She was backed by Chet on electric guitar and five other musicians. One of the songs she wrote, the self-penned "I'm Having a Party All by Myself," was popular but did not chart.[10]

On Christmas Eve 1953 Chet finished the year at Thomas Productions accompanied by Louie Innis on guitar and Ernie Newton on bass. They recorded the Carter Family standard "Wildwood Flower," then "Kentucky Derby," which was written by Chet and Boudleaux Bryant. The song is "a perfect example of Chet's great interest in creating novelty records—an interest he would maintain throughout his entire career," noted Mark Reinhart. "Chet was very aware that vocal records were far more popular with the general public than instrumental records—and the few instrumental records that did become hits were often novelty numbers that used music to paint a funny, indelible picture in listener's minds." The song captured the sound and feel of an exciting horse race, with percussion providing the hoof beats. Within the song are snippets of "The Call to the Post," "The Old Grey Mare," and "The William Tell Overture" (popularly known as "The Lone Ranger Theme").[11] Chet wrote the instrumentals "Guitars on Parade" and "Simple Simon" that were on the session.

During 1953 Chet received a letter from Mattie Moss from Charleston, West Virginia, praising her son, fifteen-year-old Wayne Moss, and his guitar playing. The message was, "You've got to hear my kid!" Chet replied and told her to bring him to Nashville.

"So I came to Nashville at age 15 and played a bunch of Chet songs for Chet," remembered Moss. "My mother says, 'Isn't he amazing?' Chet says, 'No, he's average.' 'Well, what do you suggest he do?' she asked. 'Well,' said Chet, 'if I had it to do over again, I'd get in another line of work because there's too many headaches and heartaches in this business, but I don't know. He looks like he'd make a good plumber.'"

That scene with Chet made a deep impression on young Wayne Moss. "That could either crush you or make you determined," said Moss. "It made me determined. I went back to West Virginia to listen to a bunch of Les Paul and Johnny Smith, and Chuck Berry." Wayne Moss returned to Nashville during the 1960s and became one of the top session guitarists.[12]

The year 1953 was big for Chet. He had two singles with the Country All Stars, "Fiddle Patch" / "Fiddle Sticks" and "What's The Reason" / "Marie." Chet's solo single releases included "High Rockin' Swing" / "Fig Leaf Rag," "The Bells of St. Mary's" / "Country Gentleman," "Three O'Clock in the Morning" / "City Slicker," and "Barber Shop Rag" / "Centipede Boogie." Chet's ten-inch album, *Stringin' Along*, contained "Oh By Jingo!," "Indian Love Call," "Memphis Blues," "12th Street Rag," "Main Street Breakdown," "Hello Ma Baby," "Alice Blue Gown," and "Blue Gypsy."

CHAPTER 11

The year 1954 was pivotal for Chet. He and steel guitarist Jerry Byrd continued their fifteen-minute radio show, "Two Guitars," on WSM, appearing Monday through Friday, backed by Louie Innis on rhythm guitar and Bob Moore on bass.

The "Chet Atkins Guitar Method" folio was first self-published and then published by Acuff-Rose in 1954. The folio featured a picture of Chet with his D'Angelico guitar on the cover. Inside, the songs "When You and I Were Young Maggie," "I've Been Working on the Guitar," and "Country Gentleman" were shown in both notation and tablature with various exercises.

Artists connected with their fans through fan clubs, generally started by a fan who, with cooperation from the artist (and perhaps a manager), compiled a mailing list and sent out newsletters. Popular artists might have several fan clubs. The club organizers were amateurs, enthusiastic and effective in building a fan base.

Chet's first fan club was started by Margaret Fields, who was born in New Albany, Indiana. When she was around fourteen she began writing to movie stars and musicians and sent "about ten cards" to Chet, who finally responded with a typewritten note and postcard photo of himself. He was probably on KWTO at the time.

Margaret persisted through the mail and later found him in Knoxville with the Carter Family. She and her husband, Don, came to Knoxville to see him; she received a front-row seat to the Merry-Go-Round show. She handed June Carter a note for Chet, which led to them meeting and going out for soft drinks. Margaret remembered that Chet was skinny, was unfashionable, and "looked bad."

After Don and Margaret returned home, she received a letter from Chet: "I appreciate everything you all have done for me. I've been kicked around so much I just don't know how to take your kind of treatment. It will be fine if you start me a fan club. Maybe that's what I need."

Margaret sent letters to movie magazines, *Billboard*, and *Cashbox*, announcing the fan club, whose first members were Jimmy Johnson, Norva Baker, and Bill Johnson. "We also started corresponding with each other," said Margaret, "I think our fan club did what we were supposed to do. We wrote to every DJ and every place where we could get Chet featured." The fan club wanted Chet's records played in full rather than as "filler" while DJs talked over them.

The convention arose after Fields told members she was going to Nashville; members asked to meet up. About the third time that happened, Chet wrote to Margaret and told her and the fan club members to meet him at a restaurant on Sunday morning; he would pay for lunch and then take them to the State Capitol for a picture. That evolved into the group regularly going to Nashville.

The first year of the fan club they met in the WSM lobby for a show, but a politician's speech caused a cancellation. Chet came to talk and take pictures with members; Chet then came to their hotel with his guitar. In a member's room he "sat there for several hours playing his guitar." He let several of the members play his guitar as well. That first year of the fan club, Chet was voted an award by *Cashbox*. During a Grand Ole Opry show, Margaret presented the award to Chet on the stage.[1]

Margaret and Don Fields met Leona and Merle when, after his radio show, he invited the club to his home. Chet "sat in a recliner and set up his typewriter (he always typed his letters)" while Merle had breakfast and then Margaret read to her. Leona fixed lunch. Chet had to return to the studio and asked Leona for a shirt. She replied, "You only have two and one is in the wash." Later, when Margaret and Don got back to their hotel room, she lamented to her husband, "They're as poor as we are."

One evening after supper Leona and Margaret washed dishes and talked about the new sensation, "television." Margaret and her husband had one but the Atkins didn't. She and Margaret folded clothes in the family room while Chet filed his nails, applied clear polish, then picked "for an hour or two." The next morning Chet and Margaret visited several radio stations "as Chet and the Fan Club."[2]

Margaret compiled *Gallopin' Guitar News*, a mimeographed newsletter that featured news about Chet and other Nashville artists and had an "Ask Chet" section, where Chet answered questions from fan club members. It provided a boost to Chet's career, connecting him to his fans and others in the music industry. The Fields were on a tight budget; Margaret worked as a secretary and Don as a grocery clerk. Annual dues for the Chet Atkins Fan Club were a dollar a year and five 3-cent stamps.

In early 1954 Margaret Fields informed fan club members that Chet would turn thirty on June 20 and their annual Fan Club Convention would be in Nashville in July at a cost of sixty cents per ticket. She wrote that Chet "has really been keeping busy with radio and television shows." On radio he was featured Monday through Friday on the Martha White Flour and Coffee shows from 5:45 to 6:15 in the morning and their Friday night show from 8:30 to 9:30. There was also a Sunday morning program at 8:00 with the Carter Family. Chet was on the Noontime Neighbors show daily at 12:30. On Saturday nights, Chet was on the Cowboy Copas Show from 5:45 to 6:15 and on the Grand Ole Opry between 8:00 and 11:30. Besides all those radio programs, Chet was "featured on WSM-television several times each week."

One fan, Jimmy Johnson, went to WSM to meet Chet. Johnson reported that Chet walked in with "his guitar in one hand and his amplifier in the other." Johnson "rushed over" to Chet and said, "Boy, I've come 400 miles to see you!" They shook hands and Chet said, "Well, you must be Jimmy. Margaret told me all about you."

Johnson said that Chet was a guest on the Jimmy Dickens Show on WSM and "after the show we talked to Chet for a long time. Besides being a wonderful musician, he has a wonderful personality and is one of the friendliest persons I've ever met." Chet then invited everyone in the group with Jimmy over to his home where "Chet took us into his den where he played for us for over two hours. He was very nice about it and seemed to really enjoy it."

In early February, Chet injured several fingers on his left hand when he and another man were moving an amplifier, which slipped and smashed Chet's hand. One of his fingers became infected, so a doctor pierced a small hole in the nail to drain the wound. It took about ten days to heal, forcing Chet to miss two Opry appearances.[3]

On March 8 Chet went to the RCA studio in Chicago with Steve Sholes producing for a split session with Homer and Jethro. Chet performed "Get Up and Go" with a vocal by Red Kirk and an instrumental, "Pagan Love Song." The next day he recorded "Beautiful Ohio" (his second version), "Avalon," "Sunrise Serenade," and a song he wrote with Boudleaux Bryant, "Downhill Drag." "Avalon" was originally a hit for Al Jolson in 1920 and "Sunrise Serenade" was a hit for Glenn Miller. On the session were Homer Haynes on guitar, Jethro Burns on mandolin, and a Chicago musician, Holly Swanson, on bass. This was the last time that Chet, Homer, and Jethro appeared together on Chet's solo recordings, although they continued to record together as the Country All Stars.

On April 26, the "RCA Victor Country & Western Caravan," a package show of RCA acts including Hank Snow, Minnie Pearl, Hawkshaw Hawkins, the Davis Sisters, Hal "Lone Pine" and Betty Cody, Charline Arthur, Chet Atkins, and singer-emcee Eddie Hill, began a tour of the South and Midwest. The fourteen-location tour was promoted by Hank Snow's manager, Colonel Tom Parker. For their last show, in Little Rock, Arkansas, RCA brought in recording equipment and, under the supervision of Steve Sholes, taped the performance for an album; Chet performed two songs, "Downhill Drag" and "Yankee Doodle/Dixie." On the latter number, Chet played the two tunes simultaneously—"Yankee Doodle" on the bass strings and "Dixie" on the treble. "My father used to get this music magazine called *'Etude'* and there was a story in there about a pianist named Blind Tom," remembered Chet. "I think he was part of the P. T. Barnum museum. He could hear a tune one time and play it; (he) had a great ear. And he played 'Yankee Doodle' and 'Dixie' at the same time. So I thought, 'I wonder if I can do that on the guitar.' So I worked it out over a few weeks."

After the tour, Chet penned a letter for the *Gallopin' Guitar News*: "We have been making some transcriptions for International Harvester that features Marty Robbins" and "have had several inquiries about the guitar book Acuff-Rose is publishing for me. I can only tell you that it should be in the music stores very shortly."[4]

RCA Victor had recently released the album *Tennessee Jamboree*, which featured eight songs by artists Hank Snow, Johnnie and Jack, Minnie Pearl, Ken Marvin, Grandpa Jones, and Chet, who played "Georgia Camp Meeting."

An article in the *Nashville Tennessean* was headlined "Top Guitarist to Share Park Concert Spotlight with Duke of Paducah." The article announced a concert at Centennial Park on Sunday and noted that

Chet had recently been voted the Most Programmed Instrumentalist in the United States; he would perform "Country Gentleman," "Down Hill Drag," and "Kentucky Derby," accompanied by Jerry Byrd on steel guitar, Bob Moore on bass, and Louie Innis on rhythm.[5]

Around June 1952 the Atkins family moved into a house in the Belle Meade section of Nashville, where Chet built his first home studio and "workshop" in the garage. It was paneled in pine and had two single-track Ampex recorders, allowing him to practice and record at home. His daughter Merle remembered being constantly reminded by her mother to "be quiet" because daddy was recording.

Bass player Bob Moore remembered that he "spent weekends at Chet's house and we'd cut all weekend, just take our time and listen and go back and cut. We weren't following union three-hour [session length] rules at that time. He was a friend and I was 18–19. It was just mainly me and him."

Using the two Ampex machines, Chet dubbed multiple parts. They would each cut a track and then "play it back into another machine," where the two tracks were mixed down to one. "That leaves an open track on the second tape," said Moore. "So then he goes back in and he puts the [head]phones on and plays the tape back to himself through the earphones and he plays harmony with his guitar part that's on the first track, puts that on the second track. . . . He bounces back and forth like a golf ball in a tile bathroom. We'd work all weekend. It was slow going. We might get one song in one day."

Chet built his first home studio using two Magnecorders, then acquired a better version that used ten-inch reels. "Finally, I had an old RCA console built for a radio station," said Chet. "I was just mono in those days, like every one. Then I got an Ampex. Then I got a 3 track Ampex where I could have the band on the outer tracks and put myself in the center. "Les Paul was my inspiration, because I knew all about him," said Chet. Les Paul had built a studio at home.[6]

CHAPTER 12

In 1954, Ray Butts, a radio repair man from Cairo, Illinois, constructed an amplifier for a friend that allowed the guitar to be recorded and then played back a fraction of a second later, creating an echo effect. Butts knew that his creation was a major innovation, so he borrowed the amp from his friend and drove to Nashville, where he found Chet in the phone book.

"I told [Chet] I had an amp and he said 'I have several. What's yours got that's different?'" remembered Butts. "I told him I had one with an echo on it, and he got a little interested."

Chet and Butts arranged to meet at the WSM studios, and Chet was so impressed that he used the amp that evening on the Grand Ole Opry, then asked Butts to build him an "EchoSonic" amplifier, the second one ever constructed. After he received the amp he began using it on the "Two Guitars" show. In Memphis, Scotty Moore, who had just started working with Elvis, heard Chet's new sound and inquired about the amp. Moore received his EchoSonic amp from Butts in 1955 and used it on some of the last material Elvis recorded for Sun. That led Luther Perkins of Johnny Cash's Tennessee Two and Carl Perkins to order amps.[1]

During the 1930s Jimmy Webster worked as a musician and a piano tuner. Before World War II, Webster was only peripherally involved with Gretsch, but after the war he worked regularly, promoting their guitars. Webster originated many innovations, such as add-on gadgets and new models to set Gretsch apart from their competition.

Les Paul had been trying to develop a solid body guitar that would produce better sustain. Paul first developed the Log—a thick piece of wood wrapped in a guitar body, but the guitar was too heavy, and awkward, to play. After Fender developed their solid body, many guitar manufacturers took note but thought it might be a gimmick. The hollow body guitar was firmly established for both acoustic and electric guitars by this time, and Fender was a new upstart. However, in 1952 Gibson introduced the solid body Gibson Les Paul, but Fred Gretsch Jr. thought a solid body guitar was "nonsense."[2]

After Fender and Gibson showed there was demand, Gretsch introduced the Duo Jet, their first solid body, in 1953. The success of the Les Paul Gibson—over two thousand were sold in 1953—demonstrated the value of the endorsement of a well-known guitarist with a signature model. Advertisements for Gretsch highlighted established players, such as Al Ciailo (the Electro II), Mary Osborne (the Country Club), and Hank Garland (the Duo Jet). Yet those guitarists were studio musicians with limited recognition beyond other session players.

The search began for a well-known guitarist like Les Paul to endorse Gretsch; Jimmy Webster suggested Chet. Fred Gretsch was dismissive: "Why should I pay a hillbilly guitar player to use his name on our guitars?" Webster cited the advantages of having a well-known endorser, like Les Paul with Gibson, so Fred Gretsch finally agreed. Jimmy Webster contacted Chet, who declined. During his professional career, Chet had played a Gibson until he moved to Nashville and acquired his D'Angelico, which he was mostly pleased with. Chet was aware of Gretsch guitars—Louie Innis played an archtop acoustic—but they didn't appeal to him, primarily because there was no rod in the neck. The patent for the truss rod was held by Gibson until around 1954.

Chet was dismissive at first, but Jimmy Webster was persistent. He took Chet to a music store to try out some Gretsch models, which did not please Chet, but he was impressed that Les Paul had his name on a popular guitar.

Chet and Jimmy Webster spent a lot of time together during 1954 discussing guitars and Chet's potential endorsement. Finally, he decided to visit Gretsch headquarters in New York to discuss designing a guitar. Someone suggested he take an attorney with him, but "I didn't do that," said Chet. "I was afraid a lawyer would queer the deal by asking too much or something. When you're young like that, money doesn't matter." Chet agreed to terms with Gretsch on July 10, 1954. His royalties totaled 5 percent of actual sales prices, minus excise taxes. (The Musicians Hall of Fame has a copy of the original contract.)

The Gretsch group designed a Chet Atkins guitar. Fred Gretsch picked the orange color, and since Chet was known as a country guitarist and Gretsch wanted to break into that market, Gretsch designed a Western motif: a big "G" on the top of the guitar and a steer head on the top nut, with "Chet Atkins" written on the pickguard. Gretsch sent Chet a prototype Chet Atkins Hollow Body 6120. Chet wanted a Bigsby vibrato on it and didn't like the "f-holes" or "all this junk on it, the cattle and the cactus."

Although the designs did not appeal to Chet, he caved. "I was so anxious to get my name on a guitar, so I said 'Oh, that's fine,'" said Chet. "At the time I was full of ambition and I wanted to be known all over the world as a great guitarist, and that was one brick in the edifice that would help that happen." The 6120 had a sixteen-inch-wide body, and Gretsch offered another Chet Atkins guitar, a 6121 solid body, and introduced them in the December 1954 issue of *Music Trades*. The 6120 guitar became available for sale on January 1, 1955, priced at $360, with the case extra.

Chet never liked the solid body 6121 model because it was actually semisolid, but he could never convince the Gretsch brass of the need for a fully solid body. The 6121 was dropped from the Gretsch line a few years later.[3]

The first Gretsch that Chet regularly played was a modified 6120—it had uncut f-holes so it was actually much less of a true hollow body than the standard 6120. Chet's 6120 had two output jacks that allowed the guitar's treble and bass strings to be plugged into their own separate inputs. The pickups were wired in a manner that had the treble strings signal to one jack and the bass strings signal to the other. Chet had not liked the pickups and enlisted Ray Butts for assistance. "Gretsch was using pickups made by Row-DeArmond at the time," remembered Butts. "Chet didn't like the tone of those pickups. I was at his house one time and he said 'Why don't you make me a pickup?' so I started working on it. I had done some experimenting already on pickups, and had come up with the idea of humbucking."

"A guitar pickup, in purely electronic terms, is little more than a magnet and a coil of wire," stated Pat Kirtley. "To gain the required sensitivity, many turns of wire, sometimes in the hundreds or thousands, are needed. Besides sensing the vibrations of the strings, the coil also becomes sensitive to electrical fields . . . even at a distance. In a humbucking pickup, there is a second coil of wire wound in the opposite direction of the first coil. Electrical fields from a distance affect both coils equally, but since they are wound in opposite directions, the distant electrical fields are canceled out. The vibration from the guitar strings, being very close to the coils, is picked up at full strength."[4]

Butts had worked on humbucking when he "was building the [EchoSonic] amplifier. . . . I first built a homemade sample, installed it on a Gibson ES-125 and took it over to Chet and he liked that," said Butts. "Shortly after that, he told Gretsch he wanted to use it so I decided I should probably apply for a patent, and contacted a patent attorney in St. Louis. The basis of the patent was the humbucking design and use of adjustable pole-piece screws."[5]

On Chet's birthday, June 20, 1954, he went into the Owen Bradley Studio in Hillsboro Village with Louie Innis on rhythm guitar and vocals, Jerry Byrd on steel guitar, Ernie Newton on bass, and Buddy Harman on drums. The group performed an instrumental of the Bob Wills classic "San Antonio Rose" and "Set a Spell" (written by Chet and Innis), then Eddie "Red" Kirk, a former WNOX vocalist, sang "Mister Misery" (written by Chet and Louie Innis) and "Get Up and Go" (written by Mac McCarthy).

On September 26 Chet went to the Thomas Production Studio and recorded four songs. "South" was written in 1924 and introduced by Benny Molton's Kansas City Orchestra. "Alabama Jubilee" was first recorded in 1915, and in 1951 Red Foley turned it into a hit. "Corrine, Corrina" was recorded by Bo Carter and Charlie McCoy in 1928 and the Mississippi Sheiks in 1934. "Back Home in Indiana" was a popular Tin Pan Alley song published in January 1917 and introduced by the Original Dixieland Jazz Band. This session was the first for his album, *A Session with Chet Atkins*, which was his first twelve-inch LP and the first he developed as an album. His two previous albums, *Chet Atkins Gallopin' Guitar* and *Stringin' Along with Chet Atkins*, both collections of his singles, were on ten-inch discs.

The next afternoon the same musical lineup recorded five songs. "Red Wing" was recorded as a western swing number by Bob Wills during the 1940s. "Frankie and Johnnie," inspired by several murders, was published in 1904. "A Gay Ranchero" came from the Singing Cowboy films. "Ballin' the Jack" began as a dance before it was published as a song in 1913 and was introduced in the Ziegfeld Follies in 1913. "Honeysuckle Rose" is a classic Fats Waller song, introduced in the Off-Broadway Review *Load of Coal in 1929*. This collection represented Chet's wide ranging taste in music. These may have been the first sessions where Chet used a Gretsch, trying out one of the guitars that he and Gretsch were working on.

Hank Snow was an accomplished guitarist who played a Martin D-28 in a flatpicking style and played the lead guitar sections on his records. Steve Sholes suggested that Hank and Chet record instrumentals together, so in October, backed by Ernie Newton on bass and Buddy Harman on drums, they recorded four songs. "Darktown Strutters Ball" was first published in 1917 and popularized by Sophie Tucker. "The Old Spinning Wheel" was written by Billy Hill, who also wrote "The Last Round-Up" and "Empty Saddles." "Silver Bell" was written in 1911, while "Under the Double Eagle" was originally published in 1902. Hank played in his flatpicking style while Chet fingerpicked. Chet probably used a modified Gretsch 6120 with uncut f-holes, which allowed the guitar to sustain better. A single, "The Old Spinning Wheel" / "Silver Bell," was released under the name Chet Atkins and Hank Snow Guitar Duet.

In June 1954 the *Nashville Tennessean* reported that the United Methodist Television, Radio and Film Commission and RCA Victor would be tenants in a new building at 1525 McGavock Street being constructed by Cliff Thomas who, along with his wife Lillian, owned Thomas Productions, where RCA had been their biggest client, recording there for three years. Thomas Productions and the commission would each have their own studio. The Methodists would have a large studio in the rear of the building, while RCA would construct a small studio in the front. The article stated that the building would have two floors on the front and two on the left side, with offices for the Methodist staff, Thomas Productions, and "a representative of RCA Victor." Construction began in May and was expected to cost $100,000.[6]

At a small café next door to the new building musicians could grab a meal and play pinball, but the studio itself was subpar; there were complaints that bass notes "rolled around" due to ineffective acoustics. Sholes and Atkins soon had to field complaints from the Methodist executives because artists and musicians partied and left behind cans and bottles in the studio. The situation was far from ideal but represented an important step toward a permanent presence for

RCA Victor in Nashville. (The studio was known as TRAFCO, an acronym for Television, Radio, and Film Commission.)

Chet made his first recordings in the McGavock Studio on Tuesday, November 16, backed by Bud Isaacs on steel guitar, Bob Moore on bass, Buddy Harman on drums, Dale Potter on fiddle, and Poppa John Gordy on piano and celeste. The group recorded "The Birth of the Blues," from the 1926 Broadway Revue *White's Scandals*; "Have You Ever Been Lonely," which was published in 1943; "Caravan," a jazz standard written by trombonist Juan Tizol and Duke Ellington; and "Old Man River," from the musical *Showboat*. The next day Marvin Hughes replaced Gordy, but the rest of the lineup remained for a split session with Ruby Wells and Chet. After she recorded two songs, Chet recorded "Mister Sandman," a current hit by the Chordettes, and a Bob Wills song, "New Spanish Two-Step." Those songs completed the album *A Session with Chet Atkins*.

For "Mister Sandman," Chet probably played his modified Gretsch 6120 with the uncut f-holes through his EchoSonic amplifier that produced a "slap back" effect. "It was a lovely melody," said Chet, "and I just decided to see if I could play it. By that time, I was producing and could hear a tune, go home at night, and sit in front of the television and practice."[7]

On the morning of December 2, 1954, Chet Atkins read the front-page story in the *Nashville Tennessean* that Fred Rose had died at fifty-seven years old.

Fred Rose was a follower of Christian Science, which did not believe in medicine. Although Rose's doctor informed him he had a heart problem, he ignored medical advice. Chet did not ignore his doctor's report that he had a benign tumor on his jawbone and sought to have it removed. Soon after he left the hospital Chet went into the studio and found Fred "lying on the couch, very sick," remembered Chet. "We went in and tuned up and he came in for the session. . . . He had had a heart attack." On Saturday, December 4, a Christian Science memorial service was held, followed by burial in Mount Olivet Cemetery; pallbearers included Chet, Joe Lucas, Murray Nash, John R. Brown, Eddie Hill, and Boudleaux Bryant.

The deaths of Hank Williams in January 1953 and Fred Rose in December 1954 marked the end of an era for Nashville's music scene.

During 1954, Chet released the singles "Sweet Georgia Brown" / "Indiana March" and "In a Little Spanish Town" / "When It's Darkness on the Delta" as the Country All Stars. Chet, with Minnie Pearl, released "Georgia Camp Meeting" / "Jealous Hearted Me." Under his own name he released "Wildwood Flower" / "Simple Simon," "Kentucky Derby" / "Downhill Drag" and "San Antonio Rose" / "Mister Misery."

CHAPTER 13

On January 13, 1955, "Mister Sandman" entered the *Billboard* country chart; it lasted only two weeks, peaking at number 13, but was Chet Atkins's first hit single. The success of "Mister Sandman" changed his approach to songs—from that point forward he kept an eye on the charts for hit songs that he could cover. He was becoming increasingly well-known through his recordings as well as Gretsch advertisements. He was also influential as young guitarists attempted to master his fingerpicking style. His records were selling and the deal with Gretsch proved to be mutually beneficial. His dream of becoming a world-famous guitar player was coming to fruition. Chet was hungry for fame, worked hard and persevered, practiced constantly, and pushed the limits of his playing. Aided by the push given by Steve Sholes and RCA Victor, Chet's steady stream of singles and albums found increasing visibility and sales.

The first Gretsch 6120 hit the market in January 1955 with "Chet Atkins" emblazoned on the pickguard. In the coming years, Chet's Gretsch was a competitor to Les Paul's Gibson, as Paul's career faded while Chet's grew.

In late December 1954, thirty-four-year-old Al Gannaway produced a series of short films under the title *Stars of the Grand Ole Opry*. During the 1940s and 1950s Gannaway worked as a writer and producer in movies and television. In 1954 his Flaming Films company made an agreement with the Grand Old Opry to produce a series of black-and-white sixteen-millimeter films of Opry stars performing—but not during Opry performances. (Most of the initial filming was done in an auditorium on the Vanderbilt University campus.) Later, the Quonset Hut owned by the Bradleys and part of Bradley Studios was used. The thirty-minute shows were sponsored by the Pillsbury Flour Company and available for syndication.

The shows were first released in January 1955. On the first episode, Chet was introduced by Webb Pierce and played "Mister Sandman" and "Country Gentleman." He also engaged in a comedy routine with Minnie Pearl and Rod Brasfield. On the second show, Chet played "Frankie and Johnny" and "Tennessee Rag." He did not perform for the third segment, but for the fourth show he played "Sweet Talkin' Man" and "I'm All Right Now" with the Carter Family. Chet played "They Call Me the Lover of This Town" with fiddler Benny Martin on the fifth show and "Humoresque" and "Wildwood Flower" for the sixth. On the seventh show Chet played "Frankie and Johnny" and, with the Carter Family, "Parting of the Ways." For the eighth show Chet performed "Tennessee Polka" and "Country Gentleman," then "Arkansas Traveler" for the ninth and "Love, Love, Love," with the Carter Family, for the tenth.

For the eleventh and final show Chet played "Dark Eyes" and performed "Jilted" with June Carter. For his appearances Chet played a black 1956 Gretsch 6120, which the company had given him.[1]

The owners of KWTO radio had seen a decline in the demand for radio transcriptions prior to the introduction of television, so Si Siman, Ralph Foster, and John Mahaffey founded Crossroads TV Productions in an old movie theater in Springfield. Si Siman convinced Red Foley to leave the Grand Ole Opry and move to Springfield, where Foley signed a management contract with Siman and agreed to host the "Ozark Jubilee" TV show. It was a good time for Foley to leave Nashville; his wife Eva (who had recorded under the name Judy Martin) had committed suicide because of Foley's affair with Sally Sweet. Both Eva and Sweet's husbands had filed alienation of affection suits in court. Foley was drinking heavily, which caused conflicts with WSM and the Grand Ole Opry.

On January 22, 1955, the "Ozark Jubilee" premiered on the ABC network, and the first season ran until June, hosted by Red Foley. The regulars during the first year included Porter Wagoner, Jean Shepherd, Hawkshaw Hawkins, Tommy Sosebee, the Foggy River Boys, the Oklahoma Wranglers, and Bud Isaacs, while Webb Pierce made occasional appearances. The theme song was "Sugarfoot Rag" by Hank Garland. This was the first significant television show to feature country music.[2]

A letter from Chet appeared in the February *Gallopin' Guitar Newsletter* and stated, "Jerry Byrd and I are still doing the 'Two Guitars' shows from WSM. We lost our rhythm guitar player, tho, Louie Innis took a job with King Records in Cincinnati. Ray Edenton will replace him." Chet stated that he'd played a show on February 6 at the Mosque Auditorium in Richmond, but "Outside of that trip, I haven't been out of Nashville in a long time. If folks are as nice tho', as they were in Richmond, I'm gonna start playing more dates more often." He then added, "It's getting about time for me to make some more records. If any of you have any ideas on what I should record, I would appreciate your suggestions."[3]

On March 7 Chet, with Jack Shook on rhythm guitar, Bob Moore on bass, and Farris Coursey on drums, recorded four pop hits in the McGavock Studio. "Cherry Pink and Apple Blossom White" was a hit for Perez Prado in 1954, "Dance with Me Henry (The Wallflower)" was originally an R&B hit for Etta James that had been covered by Georgia Gibbs, "Darling, Je Vous Aime Beaucoup" was the current single for Nat "King" Cole, and "Tweedle Dee" was an R&B hit for LaVern Baker and a pop hit for Georgia Gibbs.

Although all the songs were current hits, "Darling, Je Vous Aime Beaucoup" was originally recorded in 1935 by Django Reinhardt. Those could be labeled "easy listening" recordings, a direction Chet was moving toward during the 1950s.

There was a split session with Nita, Rita and Ruby and Chet at the McGavock Studio in April. Anita Carter had recorded for Columbia during the early 1950s but returned to RCA, which formed a "supergroup" named Nita, Rita and Ruby, composed of Carter, Rita Robbins, the wife of guitarist Ray Edenton, and Ruby Wells, daughter of Johnnie Wright and Kitty Wells. (Ruby Wright used the name "Wells" because there was another recording artist named Rita Wright.) The group was a recording—not a touring—act. On Chet's session, the musicians included Ernie Newton, Buddy Harman, Jerry Byrd, Ray Edenton, Marvin Hughes, and Buddy Harman. His first song was "Hey, Mr. Guitar," a hit originally titled "Hey, Mr. Banjo" by the Sunnysiders in 1955. The lyrics were changed for Chet and the Anita Kerr Singers, with the addition of gospel singer Brock Speer, Millie Kirkham, and Don Footrell. That was the first time the Anita Kerr Singers appeared on one of Chet's records. This record never became a hit but offered Chet a moniker that stayed with him throughout his career: "Mr. Guitar."

The following day he recorded four songs during a five-hour session. "Unchained Melody" was written in 1936 but did not have a title. The song lay dormant for twenty years then became the theme song for the 1955 film *Unchained*. Orchestra leader Les Baxter released a version that reached number one on the *Billboard* Hot 100 in 1955. "Tennessee Polka" was a hit for Red Foley in 1949, while "Blues in the Night" appeared in the 1941 film *Blues in the Night*. For his version Chet borrowed a trick from Django Reinhardt, playing the same note on two strings an octave apart, then muting the strings. "Black Mountain Rag" was an old fiddle tune that was recorded by Curly Fox with Mose Rager in 1947 and became a showcase for fiddler Tommy Magness.

Kitty Wells blazed the trail for female singers with her hit "It Wasn't God Who Made Honky Tonk Angels," an "answer song" to Hank Thompson's hit "Wild Side of Life." Women who sang country music performed demurely; Charline Arthur wasn't like that.

The sessions with Chet were bumpy. "After Steve Sholes worked on my first couple of sessions, Chet Atkins came in and took over," she remembered. "He and I would get up in arms. He always had songs he wanted me to record that I didn't wanta record and I had ones I'd written that he wouldn't let me record. I'll give the Devil his due; I admire Chet Atkins's talents, but I didn't like his guitar style, even though he played it on my records. I just felt he didn't have the right substance for my vocal style, but he was the top dog and there was nothin' I could do. I remember the last time we recorded together, me and him had it out good and proper."

Part of the problem was that she wanted to record songs with a harder edge than the country music audience and RCA were accustomed to. She remembered that when she made guest appearances on the Grand Ole Opry "Grant Tuner had to screen my material. When I did 'Kiss the Baby Goodnight' he had to listen to it first and see how dirty it was. They made me leave out some of the real racy parts."[4]

In 1952 Jim Reeves signed with Abbott Records, owned by Fabor Robison, and enjoyed a hit with "Mexican Joe" in 1953, followed by "Bimbo." Both songs reached number one on *Billboard's* country chart.

Fabor Robison was a difficult man to get along with, dictatorial, possessive, and overbearing with artists. Robison expected artists to do as he said and was known for not paying royalties to artists. He had a nagging paranoia that led him to carry a small pistol. In 1955 Reeves's contract with Abbott Records had ended, but Fabor Robison had him tied up with management and publishing contracts, which did not end until June 1956. Reeves was determined to buy his way out of his contracts with Robison, but to do so he had to sign over all future royalties on his unreleased Abbott recordings. Robison had told Reeves that his records—seven of which had charted—were not selling so he couldn't pay him. Further, he insisted that Reeves record only songs from Robison's publishing company.

Despite having to surrender all royalties for his Abbott recordings, Reeves was so sick of Robison and Abbott that he signed with RCA. His first session for RCA occurred on May 31. Reeves drove to Nashville from Shreveport after stopping for the third annual Jimmie Rodgers Memorial Celebration in Meridian, Mississippi. During the drive to Nashville, he rewrote a song he had been working on, "Yonder Comes a Sucker," which reached the fourth spot on the country chart.

In June, Steve Sholes produced Homer and Jethro doing "The Ballad of Davy Crew-Cut." Chet played on the session. Davy Crockett was the rage of 1955. A five-part TV series, produced by Walt Disney, began in December 1955, and its theme song, "The Ballad of Davy Crockett," charted in 1955. The version by Bill Hayes reached number one, and there were additional chart versions by Fess Parker, who starred as Davy Crockett, Tennessee Ernie Ford, and Walter Schumann. Young boys were inspired to purchase coonskin hats and other merchandise.

The June issue of the *Gallopin' Guitar News* printed a letter from Chet that informed readers that "our 'Two Guitars' shows have been changed to 1:30 p.m. Tuesday, Wednesday and Thursday." Backing Chet and Jerry Byrd were Lightnin' Chance on bass and Billy Byrd on rhythm.

Atkins told his fans that there would be more TV appearances in the future because the Opry was scheduled to be broadcast on Saturday nights at six thirty on NBC. Chet noted, "My old friends Homer and Jethro were in last week and I recorded with them. I always enjoy that, they're pretty funny, I think. Also, Jethro's brother, Aytchie, visited me last weekend. He went up to the Opry and astounded all the boys by playing chords on the bass. He plays it like it was a little fiddle." After informing readers that Chet's latest single was "Hey, Mister Guitar" / "Unchained Melody," Margaret Fields reminded readers "to request a Chet Atkins record at least once a week on your local programs."

A special edition of *Country Song Roundup* featured RCA Victor. It featured several pictures of Chet as well as articles written by Chet and Steve Sholes. For the Q&A section, a reader asked if Chet preferred hollow or solid body guitars; he replied, "A solid one should have a longer sustaining tone and most players consider this an advantage. I think it's all according to the artist's taste. They both have their good features. I use both." "What record do you feel you do your best job on?," another fan asked, to which Chet replied, "I think they are all lousy and that I could have done a better job on all of them."

CHAPTER 14

At two in the afternoon of June 29, Chet was in the McGavock Studio, accompanied by Bob Moore on bass and local pop drummer Johnnie DeGeorge for the first session where Chet was listed as "producer" for his own recordings. On that session he rewired his pickups to be out of phase so the instrument sounded somewhat like a guitar, a mandolin, and tack piano. The idea came to him while tinkering with his EchoSonic amplifier. That new sound was heard on "Somebody Stole My Gal," a song from 1918 that was a million seller by Ted Weems and His Orchestra, and "Shine on Harvest Moon," from the 1944 musical film by the same name. The single was released on a 45 under the name "Chet Atkins and His Other Guitar."

The fifth annual Chet Atkins Fan Club Convention began on Thursday, August 11 and started "with a visit to WSM and the 'Noontime Neighbors' and 'Eddie Hill' shows," wrote Margaret Fields. "'Two Guitars' was on that afternoon, but Chet was at a recording session and missed the program." That evening they visited "Bill Morgan's Hayloft Hoedown" radio show on WKDA "and was thrilled when he played 30 minutes of Chet's recordings in honor of our convention." The group then went to the WSM studios and visited with Eddie Hill, who "had Chet tell his life story on the air and this I know everyone enjoyed," said Fields. "Chet very seldom talks over WSM, but this night he really gave out."

That night the group were special guests on the "Fan Fare" program on WSM. Chet was interviewed by Grant Turner, followed by a question-and-answer session. The Friday Night Frolic had Eddie Hill as emcee and featured Chet as a guest. "Chet picked two numbers on his guitar and played 'Draggin' the Bow' on the fiddle," wrote Fields. Chet was also a guest on the Mister DJ USA Show along with Ernest Tubb. On Saturday, the group visited WSM and had breakfast at the Opry. On the show were Chet, the Wilburn Brothers, Faron Young, and Eddie Hill.

On Saturday afternoon the fan club party was held at McGavock Studio. Fan club member Jo Davis remembered that she loved "the nice party Chet gave for us. . . . Chet spent the whole afternoon picking all his recorded tunes and anything else we requested. Watching Chet pick like he did left us simply spellbound; I just can't explain how it fascinated all of us. He told us he also enjoys playing classical music—which surprised some of us—and he played a few selections that were really impressive." After the party, the group went back to the studio shows at WSM and then to the Ryman for the Grand Ole Opry, where Chet appeared on the NBC portion. Margaret Fields presented Chet with a plaque that was awarded to the Country All Stars by *Jamboree Magazine* for the Best Instrumental Group of 1955. She noted that "Chet received two other citations from *Jamboree* as well as two awards from *Cashbox* this year."[1]

Gallopin' Guitar News reported that Chet's hobby was electronics, his favorite TV show was a boxing show, *Wednesday Night Fights*, he had a dog for a pet, his favorite color was blue, his favorite comedian was Bob Hope, and his favorite comic strip was "Lil Abner," but he did not have a favorite food or movie star. The newsletter reported that Chet had a series of articles in *Country and Western Jamboree* magazine on guitar playing.[2]

Paul Yandell was born in Graves County, Kentucky, and first heard "thumb style"—what fingerpicking is called in Kentucky—when he saw someone play "Shantytown, My Shantytown." His family listened to WCKY in Cincinnati and a DJ "played Chet's 'I've Been Working on the Guitar.' . . . That was my first introduction to Chet's music," said Yandell.

"When you begin to play guitar, especially finger style, or thumb style as we call it in Kentucky, you get to a point where you have to make a decision," said Yandell. "Are you going to play like Merle Travis or are you going to play like Chet Atkins? Some people go the Travis direction and some people go the Atkins direction. You have to commit yourself. I don't know of any guitar player that can play like Merle and also play like Chet because they are totally different styles, different chords, different time figures and a totally different outlook on a guitar."

"If you're going to play like Chet, first of all, you have to remember to alternate your thumb 90 percent of the time," said Yandell. "Like in the Key of 'C,' you play the fifth string and then the D string, sixth string and a 'D' string with hardly any exceptions. Now, Travis style, you don't alternate your thumb. You just sort of play the root note; you play two notes mostly. And that's the reason it sounds different. But you have to get your thumb down real steady and learn to play whole notes while your thumb is going. Then quarter notes and eighth notes. It's not easy. You have to practice, practice, practice. I went towards Chet," continued Yandell. "I was always fascinated by the vibrola he used and for years and years I didn't even know what he was doing. I thought he was bending the neck on his guitar!"[3]

Chet recorded a mixture of Christmas songs and pop tunes in October at McGavock Studio. He recorded "Jingle Bells," "Cecelia," "Arrivederci, Roma," and "Sleigh Bells, Reindeer and Snow," a song he wrote that was sung by his daughter, Merle. He recorded a medley of "Joy to the World," "It Came Upon a Midnight Clear," "Hark the Herald Angels Sing," and "Deck the Halls." He also recorded "Whispering," a 1920 hit for Paul Whiteman and his Ambassador Orchestra, and rerecorded "New Spanish Two-Step."

Studio logs show that Chet recorded his self-produced album *Chet Atkins in Three Dimensions* over three consecutive days in October, although he probably spent additional time recording in his home studio. Chet's "three dimensions" were folk, pop, and classical; he recorded four songs in each "dimension." That album was his first experience recording classical music and the first time he recorded with a classical guitar. Chet had first seen a classical guitar in New York when he visited his brother Jim in 1945 and met Jack Smith, guitarist for Fred Waring's group. In Nashville, WSM announcer David Cobb had a classical that Chet played before he purchased his own in New York.

According to session sheets, he recorded three songs on October 26. He played alone, although he occasionally added a bass and rhythm guitar. "Minute Waltz" was written in 1847 by Frederic Chopin as "The Waltz in D-flat major, Op. 64, No. 1" for solo piano. It was given the nickname "Minute Waltz" (as in "small waltz") by Chopin's music publisher. "Tenderly" was published in 1946 and the most famous recording was by Rosemary Clooney, who had a hit with it in 1952. Clooney used it as the theme song for her TV show. The evening after he made those recordings, Chet produced a session on Nita, Rita and Ruby.

The next day he recorded four songs. "Minuet—From French Harpsichord Suite, Prelude from Six Short Preludes" by Bach and "Schon Rossmarien" by Kreisler. "Tip-Toe through the Tulips" dated back to the 1929 Broadway musical *Gold Diggers of Broadway*. "Arkansas Traveler" was an old fiddle tune originally composed in the mid-1800s by fiddler/storyteller Sanford C. Faulker.

On October 28, his final day, he recorded four songs. "Ochi Chorrya" was a Russian romantic song from the nineteenth century; the phrase is translated into English as "Dark Eyes." Django Reinhardt had recorded the song, which became a standard number for jazz players. "Little Rock Getaway" was written and recorded by Joe Sullivan in 1935. "Londonderry Air" is best known as "Danny Boy," and "La Golondrina" (Spanish for "Little Swallow") was written by a Mexican physician in 1862.

Atkins dropped the "Galloping" from his billing on his *Three Dimensions* album; instead the LP was released as *Chet Atkins and His Guitar*.

Margaret Fields attended the 1955 Disc Jockey Convention in Nashville in November and noted that "Chet was a very popular choice for the top instrumentalist awards." That year Chet indeed was named Top Country Instrumentalist by *Billboard*, *Cashbox*, and *Jamboree*. He was named lead guitarist on the Jamboree All-Star Orchestra and the fourteenth most popular country artist by *Billboard*. Three of his five records were picked in the top five instrumentals of 1955 by *Jamboree*. Chet also increased his visibility by writing a "Guitar Pointers" column for *Country and Western Jamboree* magazine. After the awards, Fields attended the RCA Victor Luncheon at the Andrew Jackson Hotel. At the Friday night dance "Chet played for the entire dance with rhythm being furnished by Doug Kirkham [drums], Harry Floyd [bass], and Floyd Cramer [piano]."[4]

"La Goualante du Pauvre Jean" was written by Marguerite Monnot and recorded by Edith Piaf, the great French singer and Monnot's longtime collaborator. The song was released in the United States in 1950 with Piaf singing English lyrics (written by Jack Lawrence), accompanied by the Robert Chavigny Orchestra. The title was translated as "The Poor People of Paris." Chet recorded the song with Harold

Bradley on rhythm guitar, Bob Moore on bass, and Farris Coursey on drums. It was first released as "Jean's Song" in 1956, but a later version was released as "The Poor People of Paris (Jean's Song)," at a faster tempo. There is speculation that he recorded both the same day, although he may have recorded one in his home studio at a different time. On that same day Chet recorded two versions of "Honey," a hit for Rudy Vallee & His Connecticut Yankees. The "Two Guitars" show ran until the end of 1955.

During 1955, Chet had one single released with the Country All Stars, "Do Something" / "The Vacation Train," one single released with Hank Snow, "The Old Spinning Wheel" / "Silver Bell," and four singles released on his own: "Hey, Mr. Guitar" / "Unchained Melody," "Somebody Stole My Gal" / "Shine On Harvest Moon," "Jingle Bells" / "Christmas Carols," and "The Poor People of Paris (Jean's Song)" / "Honey." He also released four EPs: *Chet Atkins and His Guitar* ("Pagan Love Song," "Sunrise Serenade," "Beautiful Ohio," and "Avalon"); *Pickin' the Hits* ("Tweedle Dee," "Dance with Me Henry," "Cherry Pink and Apple Blossom White," and "Darling, Je Vous Aime Beaucoup"); *Chet Atkins in Three Dimensions*, volume 2 ("Blues in the Night," "Tenderly," "Little Rock Getaway," and "Tip-Toe through the Tulips"); and *Chet Atkins in Three Dimensions*, volume 3 ("Minuet and Prelude No. 2," "Intermezzo," "Schon Rosmarin," and "Minute Waltz"). Chet had three albums released in 1955: *Stringin' Along with Chet Atkins*, *Chet Atkins in Three Dimensions*, and *The Amazing Chet Atkins.*

CHAPTER 15

Elvis Presley's first release on Sun Records, "That's All Right, Mama" / "Blue Moon of Kentucky," had captured local and then regional attention for the Memphis-based label headed by Sam Phillips. Phillips pushed Jim Denny, manager of the Grand Ole Opry, to have Elvis appear on the show. Denny finally agreed, with Elvis making one appearance on Saturday night, October 2, 1954, at the Ryman Auditorium. He and his band, Scotty Moore and Bill Black, performed "Blue Moon of Kentucky." Later, Elvis told Gordon Stoker, one of the Jordanaires, in the studio when the mics were "open" so Chet could hear the conversation, "I really wanted to become a member of the Opry and that damn Mr. Denny said, 'We don't do that n***** music around here. Go back to Memphis.'"

"Out of his mouth he said it," said Chet. "I guess it must have been true. I never knew. I had heard it before, but I didn't know it was true."[1]

Colonel Tom Parker had arranged to represent Elvis with Hank Snow for Jamboree Productions and had booked him on a number of shows where the charismatic young singer encountered screaming girls. Parker had managed Eddy Arnold and Hank Snow, both RCA artists, and worked with Hill and Range Publishing through their representation of Arnold and Snow. Parker set his sights on RCA and traveled to New York to get Elvis signed. He called Phillips and asked how much it would take to buy Elvis's contract from Sun. Philips agreed to a price of $35,000, with an additional $5,000 for royalties owed to Elvis. Parker's offer was accepted.

Elvis had his first recording session for RCA in the McGavock Street studio on January 10, 1956, two days after his twenty-first birthday. Steve Sholes was in the producer's chair, and Elvis was backed by his band members, Scotty Moore with his guitar, Bill Black on upright bass, and D. J. Fontana on drums. Also on the session were Chet with his 1955 modified Gretsch guitar and Floyd Cramer, who had played piano behind Elvis on the Louisiana Hayride. Elvis had requested the Jordanaires for background vocals but Chet, who had been asked by Sholes to hire musicians and singers for the session, hired only one Jordanaire, Gordon Stoker, and two members of the Speer Family gospel group, Ben and Brock Speer. The Speer Family was signed to RCA.

Scotty Moore engaged in small talk with Chet about their EchoSonic amplifiers; Scotty had acquired his after hearing Chet's "Mister Sandman." Scotty asked Chet what they should do on the session, and Chet replied, "Just go on doing what you been doing."[2] The session began at two in the afternoon, and their first song, "I Got a Woman," which they had been performing on their live shows, had been a hit the previous year for Ray Charles.

Elvis had arrived at the session wearing pink pants with a blue stripe down each leg. After the first take, Chet called his wife, Leona, and told her to come down to the studio quickly. "I told her she'd never see anything like this again, it was just so damn exciting." Elvis was "dancing around and having a good time," remembered Chet, "and before you know it he split his pants so they sent out to the hotel and got him another pair and he threw the old pair out in the hallway." The receptionist asked, "What are we going to do with these old pants?" Chet replied, "You better keep them, he's going to be the biggest star in the business." The receptionist laughed at this remark "but a few months later she was trying to get on 'I've Got a Secret' (a television quiz show) because she had Elvis Presley's pants."[3]

The next song on the session was "Heartbreak Hotel," which the group had been performing on their shows. They spent the entire next evening recording "Money Honey," an R&B hit for the Drifters in 1953 that was part of their live shows. Just before Christmas, Sholes had sent Elvis acetate demos and lead sheets for ten songs and urged him to learn them. The next day they recorded two songs that Sholes sent Elvis, "I'm Counting on You" and "I Was the One," both published by Hill and Range. On those two songs Chet "took a far more active role . . . not only suggesting simple arrangements but offering a solid underpinning of his own guitar work."[4] Neither Sholes nor Chet was satisfied with the sound in the McGavock Studio, which was a bit muffled. "The studio itself was structurally bad for us," stated Chet. "It had a curved ceiling and we were always searching in the room, trying to find a dead spot for the bass (fiddle). In most places a bass note would roll around for a long time."

Chet later told Ralph Emery that "Elvis was a little scared when he came to RCA. We were all nervous that we might lose the magic that Sun Records had got on his records. It could have easily happened, we could have lost some small ingredient that was key to the sound. Luckily, we didn't."[5]

Elvis played the guitar on his appearances, which helped popularize the instrument. There was a mutual benefit: Elvis popularized the guitar, and the guitar popularized Chet Atkins.

Elvis's explosive success meant that Steve Sholes's daily activities centered around him, so Sholes gave Chet the responsibility for producing Hank Snow and Jim Reeves. "Steve Sholes had moved on to what the company considered more important things," remembered Chet. "So he turned Jim and Hank Snow over to me. That didn't go over too well, and they kinda resented the fact that Mr. Sholes was not making their records and they didn't know if I had any talent in the studio. Jim wasn't too warm at first, but he saw I had some talent."[6]

The success of Elvis led labels to look for artists—male and female—who could sing like him and capture the early rock and roll market. RCA found their "female Elvis" in Janis Martin, who "had a mother who was a show business/stage-type mother. . . . As a kid, I remember being a big fan of Eddy Arnold and, later, Hank Williams. I liked him because he had a little rock to his music." By the time she joined the Old Dominion Barn Dance in her teens "I got to where I was bored with the slow country songs and I didn't particularly care for bluegrass, either," she said. "It was the Black rhythm and blues that I really started to get comfortable with and then I started doing Ruth Brown and LaVern Baker songs. I just liked their music a whole lot more than the country music I was hearing then. Of course, that was also around the time that rockabilly music was starting to break loose down at Sun Records. So I ended up doing rock and roll music on a country show, which was kind of different then."

"People would tell me my stage delivery was almost identical to Elvis Presley's," she remembered, "even though I'd never even seen him perform, never even seen him on TV, at that point. It just wasn't natural for me to just stand up there and tap my foot. I'd get up there with a guitar and move all over the stage."

In late 1955 two staff announcers at WRVA, Carl Stutz and Carl Barefoot, wrote a rockabilly song, "Will You, Willyum," and asked Janis to sing it on the Old Dominion Barn Dance. The announcer taped the performance and sent it to Tannen, a music publishing firm in New York, who forwarded it to Steve Sholes. Janis Martin was fifteen when Sholes signed her to RCA. "It was RCA that came up with the publicity idea of the 'Female Elvis' bit," she said. "They kind of hung me with that, although I was proud of it at the time."

Chet produced an evening session on Janis Martin at McGavock Studio in March. "Drugstore Rock'n'Roll" was a song she wrote that was "about what we were all doing then; hanging out in a drugstore. Every drugstore [in the 1950s] had a soft drink fountain and a jukebox and an area for the kids to go and dance after school." "Drugstore Rock and Roll," her first RCA release, reportedly sold 750,000 copies and enjoyed international acclaim, but it never appeared on the *Billboard* chart.[7]

In early 1956 RCA formed a record club, patterned after the successful Book of the Month club. Their competitor, Columbia, had started a record club the year before. Members ordered records for a low introductory price and then agreed to buy others at the full retail price. At this time many music fans did not have access to a reliable and nearby record store. The record clubs also appealed to nonbuyers and those who rarely bought records. The ads for record clubs were prominently displayed in magazines. The middle-class audience became important for record club buyers and helped enhance sales of Chet Atkins records. An album featured in a record club could sell 50,000 units, with a hit perhaps achieving over 100,000 sales.[8]

Hank Snow had an Ampex recorder in his home where he practiced his songs. On March 20 he was well rehearsed for his next guitar duet session with Chet. First, Chet recorded "The Lady Loves Me," then he and Snow recorded "New Spanish Two-Step" and a song Hank wrote, "Reminiscin,'" accompanied by Ray Edenton, Ernie Newton, and Farris Coursey.[9]

"Heartbreak Hotel" entered the *Billboard* Hot 100 and country charts and reached number one on both. On April 13, Elvis returned to McGavock Studio for a session to record "I Want You, I Need You, I Love You" with Chet on guitar and Marvin Hughes on piano in addition to Elvis's band members Scotty, D. J., and Bill. Background vocals were again supplied by Gordon Stoker with Ben and Brock Speer.

The $35,000 risk in signing Elvis seemed like ancient history because Elvis's success not only supercharged RCA but also boosted Steve Sholes's prestige and responsibilities. Sholes was "RCA's Executive in Charge of Elvis" and moved into an expanded role that affected Chet when Sholes formally promoted him to manager of Nashville operations. Chet finally had some security with a regular paycheck amounting to $7,500 annually, a telephone credit card, and employee benefits with one of the biggest, most prestigious corporations in America. Chet had begun signing new acts during the time Sholes continued to produce Eddy Arnold and Hank Snow. This began a new phase as Chet became part of RCA's corporate culture, which expanded both his duties and his stress level. Chet no longer worried about finding jobs as a musician but those memories of his lean days remained. He cut back his recording for singers not on RCA although he continued to do outside sessions. The promotion also affected his personal appearances and severely limited his touring.

Chet had his work cut out for him. Tensions increased between RCA and their teetotaling studio landlords at the Methodist Television Radio and Film Commission. The Methodist staff, which included ordained ministers, bristled at the empty booze bottles littering the studio. RCA had only minimal office space, and Sholes and Chet were well aware of the studio's technical imperfections and acoustic problems.

Hank Locklin had signed with Four Star Records, owned by Bill McCall, in 1949. McCall entered into an agreement with Decca Records, where Decca would release Locklin's recordings but the songs had to come from McCall's publishing company and McCall reserved the right to pick the singles released. This is the same arrangement that McCall negotiated for Patsy Cline. McCall was notorious for not paying artists and songwriters their royalties. That was the background that caused Locklin to leave McCall and Four Star in 1955 and sign with RCA. In

May, Hank Locklin had his first recording session in Nashville at the McGavock Studio. Steve Sholes produced the session, and Chet arranged for the musicians and played guitar. They recorded four songs but none charted.

During another session, Locklin recorded two songs, both published by Hill and Range. Locklin had not known of the connection between Sholes and Hill and Range until that session when he discovered that "if you recorded anything by Hill & Range, they'd give you some money. So I made a little money on that. I called them and told them I'd recorded [their songs] and in a few days got a check." During a listening session, Sholes suggested Locklin record "Four Walls" but Locklin turned it down. "I didn't recognize how high-powered that thing was," remembered Locklin.[10]

Chet appeared on Tennessee Ernie Ford's television show in February and performed "Poor People of Paris." In May he went to New York to perform at a luncheon for television and radio executives. He made personal appearances in Denver, Miami, and several other cities and made a guest appearance with Minnie Pearl on Dave Garroway's *Today* program. In 1956 Eddy Arnold starred in a Wednesday night show on ABC-TV, filmed in Springfield, Missouri. Each week, Arnold and Chet flew to Springfield to do the show, which lasted about four months. Chet was also a regular feature on the Grand Ole Opry TV shows broadcast on ABC on Saturday nights as well as the Opry's radio show's "Prince Albert" section, broadcast over NBC.

In the Q&A section of *Gallopin' Guitar News*, Chet told readers he practiced thirty minutes each day and that when he doesn't play his Gretsch he plays a Gibson or his D'Angelico as a rhythm guitar and a Favilla classical guitar "that I spend a lot of time with." There was a letter from his brother Jimmy Atkins who was program director for KOA in Denver: "I had the pleasant experience of spending a few hours with Chet while he was in Denver on a show date and listening to him play several works. On several different occasions in the past I tried to get him to come to New York and swing over to the jazz and popular field of guitar. This he would not do. He used to tell me, 'Jimbo, country and western music is to me heart and soul. I like it [and] I like the people connected with the business and am determined to stay in the wagon yard.'"

The newsletter also printed a letter from Chet's father: "Chester was never robust and strong like some and for that reason I never put him to work like the other boys. This gave him more time to put in with his guitar. One expression of his which I heard so many times was 'If I can just get good enough to get on radio, I'll be satisfied.'" Finally, there was a letter from Steve Sholes, who wrote that Chet "is one of the hottest artists in Europe and also in the South American countries" and that Chet "has been my right hand man in helping me to record."[11]

CHAPTER 16

Chet celebrated his thirty-second birthday on June 20, 1956, by recording in the McGavock Studio. "Memphis Blues" is credited to W. C Handy, "father of the blues," and was published in 1912. "Oh! By Jingo! Oh! By Gee (You're the Only Girl for Me)" is a novelty song from the 1919 Broadway musical *Linger Longer Letty*. "Hello, Ma Baby" was written in 1899 at a time when the telephone was a novelty. The song became best known as the introduction to the Warner Brothers cartoon "One Froggy Evening" in 1955. "Indian Love Call" came from the 1924 operetta *Rose Marie*, the song "Alice Blue Gown" was inspired by Alice Roosevelt Longworth, President Teddy Roosevelt's daughter, whose favorite dress was a blue gown. It was first performed in the 1919 musical *Irene*. "The Third Man Theme" came from the film with that title. "Blue Gypsy" was written by Chet and Boudleaux Bryant. W. C. Handy first heard the tune of "St. Louis Blues" in 1892.

Chet had established a practice of working on his recordings alone at home, so there is no way of knowing whether the majority of a particular recording was done at RCA or at his home. The session was done because RCA decided to rerelease Chet's ten-inch album, *Stringin' Along With Chet*, as a twelve-inch LP, which meant increasing the number of songs on the album from eight to twelve. There are three versions of the *Stringin' Along* album; the first, released in 1953, was a ten-inch album with eight songs, then came a twelve-inch LP with twelve songs and then, dissatisfied with his playing, he recorded a new version of the songs on the original ten-inch album. That album, released in 1956, had three songs from the original album: "Gallopin' on the Guitar," "Main Street Breakdown," and "Twelfth Street Rag," all recorded with Homer and Jethro. For the twelve-inch album he rerecorded "Black Mountain Rag" and "Oh, By Jingo," which he had originally recorded in New York in March 1953.

Chet performed at a number of local events in Nashville. On Friday evening, August 17, he played a concert at the annual picnic, held at the Colemere Club, for the Nashville Advertising Federation. On Sunday, August 19, he played a concert at Centennial Park with the Louvin Brothers. On Friday evening, August 24, Chet Atkins and Faron Young entertained at the Miss Tennessee Ball at the Andrew Jackson Hotel.[1] On September 15, Chet performed "Alabama Jubilee" on the Grand Ole Opry's television show. On September 25, Chet appeared on Arlene Francis's show "Home" with Carl Smith, Martha Carson, Marty Robbins, June Carter, and the Jordanaires.[2]

Big news in Nashville's music world came on September 24 when Jim Denny was forced to leave WSM and the Grand Ole Opry. Denny had several businesses outside of WSM and the Grand Ole Opry that he would not dissolve after WSM president Jack DeWitt issued an ultimatum in August 1955 that WSM employees either work for WSM full-time or leave the station if they wanted to pursue their outside businesses. Denny had formed Cedarwood and Driftwood Publishing. The Grand Ole Opry artists and their managers were upset and concerned because Denny had been booking them. He met with the artists and promised them continued bookings, which constituted their livelihood. A number of artists thus left the Grand Ole Opry and joined Denny's booking agency. The Opry suffered from the loss of some of their greatest talent and from declining attendance. However, the break meant that the Opry no longer "controlled" country music like it had in the past, which allowed country music to grow as entrepreneurs opened new businesses in the years ahead.[3]

On Monday, October 22, Chet Atkins began recording his *Finger-Style Guitar* album. According to RCA session records, Chet recorded the entire album in one day, playing four songs that morning, then after taking a two-hour break, recording four more. Beginning at seven that evening, Chet recorded another four songs, with the thirteen-hour day resulting in twelve songs for the album. It is probable that Chet worked on some or all of those songs in his home studio and some of those hours were not charged to RCA Victor. Chet recorded all of those songs alone, playing his 1955 modified Gretsch 6120 through his EchoSonic amp, overdubbing rhythm and bass.[4]

"Dance of the Golden Rod" is a late nineteenth-century song; Chet used the arrangement by Merle Travis. He had recorded "Unchained

Melody" a year before but chose to rerecord it. The "Gavotte" is a French folk dance. "Malaguena" is a Spanish classic, written by Cuban composer Ernesto Lecuona in 1928 as part of a longer work, "Suite Andalucia." "Malaguena" is a Spanish dance named after Malaga, a port city in Spain.

During the afternoon session, Chet, with Buddy Harman on drums (using brushes), recorded four songs. "Glow Worm" is traced back to the operetta *Lysistrata* and was featured in the 1907 Broadway musical *The Girl Behind the Counter*. The first hit version was by the Mills Brothers in 1952. "In the Mood" was a huge hit for the Glenn Miller Band and featured in the film *Sun Valley Serenade*. "Heartaches" was published in 1931 but unknown until disc jockey Kurt Webster began playing it in 1947. "Swedish Rhapsody" was published in 1906 and is based on Swedish folk melodies. It appeared in the 1951 film *The Stranger Left No Card*. For the evening session, Chet recorded four songs. He transposed Brahms' "Waltz in A-Flat" to the key of A. "Adeita" is by Spanish composer Francisco Tarrega. "Petite Waltz" ("La Petite Valse") was a hit in 1950 for Guy Lombardo, while "Liza" was composed by George Gershwin, with lyrics by Ira Gershwin and Gus Kahn, for the Florenz Ziegfeld musical *Show Girl* (1929). Chet overdubbed rhythm and bass on "Liza."[5] Chet is pictured on the cover of the album with his orange Gretsch with pickups developed by Ray Butts.

On November 29, a little over a month after Chet recorded his *Finger-Style Guitar* album, he was back in the studio and recorded three songs with Bob Moore playing bass, Jimmy Riddle on harmonica, Floyd Cramer on piano, and Buddy Harman on drums.

"Peanut Vender" ("El Maniseor") was written by Cuban composer Moises Simons and created a craze for rhumba. It was recorded in 1931 by Louis Armstrong and was featured in the films *The Cuban Love Song* (1931), *Duck Soup* (1931), *Only Angels Have Wings* (1939; sung by Cary Grant), and *A Star Is Born* (1954; sung by Judy Garland). Django Reinhardt recorded the song in 1949. "Blue Echo" was written by Chet and Boudleaux Bryant. The title "Trambone," written by Chet and Bryant, alluded to the sound of a trombone, which Chet achieved by pushing down on his vibrato bar so the notes from the low strings slid into the melody. That session was the first of Chet's to feature Floyd Cramer on piano.

On the RCA sessions during 1955, Chet often played, although for sessions he produced he preferred not to play because he felt he could not concentrate fully on both jobs. The guitarists he used most as a producer were Hank Garland, Grady Martin, Harold Bradley, Ray Edenton, and Jack Shook. Other guitarists he booked included Eddie Hill, Billy Byrd, Jimmy Selph, Louie Innis, Ray Edenton, Spider Rich, and Velma Williams, who became a major studio rhythm guitarist during 1956.

Bass players were pretty evenly divided between Bob Moore and Ernie Newton, although Lightnin' Chance, Joe Zinkan, and Roy Huskey Jr. were also booked. When Steve Sholes came to Nashville he often brought along Charles Grean, who played bass.

For piano, Floyd Cramer was the most booked, followed closely by Owen Bradley, Poppa John Gordy, and Marvin Hughes. His major drummer was Buddy Harman, although he also used Farris Coursey, T. Tommy Cutrer, and Johnny DeGeorge. For steel guitar he used Jerry Byrd and Don Davis the most, followed by Bobby Garrett, Don Helms, Bud Isaacs, Jimmy Day, and Shot Jackson. The first-call fiddlers for sessions during the 1950s were Tommy Jackson, Dale Potter, Benny Martin, Howdy Forrester, and Tommy Vaden.

A "crisis" in country music began in 1956 because rock and roll singers, whose roots were in country, dominated both country and pop charts. During 1955 artists with number-one hits on the country chart included Carl Smith, Hank Snow, Webb Pierce, Porter Wagoner, Faron Young, and Eddy Arnold. In 1956, "I Forgot to Remember to Forget," "Heartbreak Hotel," "I Want You, I Need You, I Love You," "Don't Be Cruel," and "Hound Dog," by Elvis all reached number one on the country chart. Carl Perkins's "Blue Suede Shoes" was also a number-one country record. All of those records were also on the *Billboard* Hot 100 chart, which began in 1955 and represented the most popular recordings sold. Most of those records also appeared on the rhythm and blues chart.

The problem was that some country music from 1956 to 1958 no longer sounded like "real" country music, at least the country music represented by artists like Hank Snow, Webb Pierce, and Hank Williams. The demand for personal appearances by country music artists dropped and the demand for country records dropped as young people gravitated to rock and roll and saw country music as a relic of the past. Most barn dances left the air, and there was a decline in radio airtime for country music. Many wondered if country music as they knew it would survive. Labels, desperate to boost sales, sought to "modernize" and "update" country music during the late 1950s after the onslaught of rock and roll. Those in the country music business felt defensive and saw their battle as one for survival.

CHAPTER 17

Chet Atkins entered the RCA Victor Studio on McGavock with Grady Martin on bass, Buddy Harman on drums, and Floyd Cramer on piano on January 9. The group recorded a song written by Gus Jenkins, "Tricky," released as the Rhythm Rockers, Featuring Chet Atkins. That was the first Rhythm Rockers single, another attempt by RCA to capture some of Elvis's—and other rock and rollers'—audience. Chet played some bluesy licks on "Tricky." He was no stranger to the blues; back in Luttrell he'd listened to 78s of Blind Lemon Jefferson that his stepfather owned. During the 1940s he had heard and been impressed by T-Bone Walker, John Lee Hooker, and Lonnie Johnson, whom Chet considered "one of the greatest of all time."

The Chet Atkins Country Gentleman model guitar was introduced by Gretsch in 1957, named after Chet's song "Country Gentleman." "It was probably Gretsch's idea to put out another model," said Chet. "They were selling so many of the orange Gretsches they wanted to put out a little more expensive guitar. So the Country Gentleman had good tuning pegs, better wood selection, and the body was generally a little larger and thinner. I started to use the Country Gentleman on my records continually. I would use the 6120 once in a while—I know I've seen pictures of me with it in the studio—but I didn't use it as much as the Country Gentleman."

The Country Gentleman was the first Chet Atkins model to use the new Filter'Tron pickups. The Country Gentleman was also the first made by Gretsch with a "thinline" body, about two inches deep instead of the three inches of most archtops. The Country Gentleman was the first Chet Atkins model with a seventeen-inch body. It had "fake" f-holes, which were closed with plastic or wooden infits. Later, they were painted on the body of the guitar. The closed "f-holes" were created to solve the problem of feedback when guitarists played hollow-body electrics at a loud volume. When the amplifier's volume was turned up, the pickups picked up their own sound from the amp's speakers, then fed it back into the system. The loud soundwaves moved in and around the guitar's body, which agitated the strings and top and set up vibrations that created more feedback. Chet insisted that if the hollow body was more solid at certain points, which could be done by adding wooden reinforcement inside the body, it would cut feedback and allow the guitar to sustain. Atkins wanted a solid wooden section down the center of the body from neck to tailpiece, like Gibson had on their ES-335 model.

"I continually tried to get them to make the guitar more solid from the neck down to the end," Chet told author Tony Bacon. "I wanted more of a sturdy guitar that gave me more sustain. Originally the Country Gent did have two braces that went from the end of the guitar to the neck, but they didn't join it, so it still killed off the sustain. They finally made it semisolid back to the bridge and had a piece of wood going out to the back, which helped, but it didn't go all the way to the end of the guitar. They never could do that for me."[1] The early Country Gentleman was a single cutaway.

The development of the Filter'Tron pickups led to a conflict with Gibson. Ray Butts had created the Filter'Tron pickups that Chet used, which led Gretsch to adapt those pickups on their guitars. However, Seth Lover with Gibson had worked on the same type of pickup.

During the summer of 1957, Gretsch and Gibson displayed guitars equipped with humbucking pickups at the summer National Association of Music Merchandisers show in Chicago. Gibson claimed the rights to those pickups, but Butts had pictures of Chet playing a guitar with Butts's pickups in 1954. Finally, Gibson and Gretsch agreed not to challenge each other on the Filter'Tron pickup, and both companies were issued patents only weeks apart in 1959. Gretsch used Butts's humbucking design, which became standard for their top-end models, including those endorsed by Atkins in 1958. The term for those pickups became "Filter'Tron"; "humbucking" was never used. Since Butts served as a consultant to Gretsch—not a staff employee—he was never credited. "What counted most was that the tone of the pickups matched Chet's playing style very well," said Butts.[2]

Chet had an acetate of the song "Four Walls" that had been sent to him by Steve Sholes for Hank Locklin, but Locklin turned it down. During one of their song listening sessions to find material, Chet played it for Reeves; both thought the song fit a woman better. However, Chet and Reeves decided to give it a try.

They were not off the mark when they first heard it as a "woman's" song. The idea for the song came originally from Marvin Morris, who observed that his writing partner, George Campbell, was "a very busy pianist, writing by day and playing by night" supported by "the marvelous manner in which his wife took the rough edges of life with no complaint."[3] Reeves wanted to rehearse the song before they recorded it, so with Reeves and Atkins both working at WSM on radio shows, they managed to get together at the station to rehearse.

The idea for a different sound did not come from Atkins alone. He and Reeves had discussed songs and sounds and Reeves, aware of the records coming out of Nashville that crossed over to the pop chart, decided that he would for the first time record without a fiddle or steel guitar. Instead, on the session were Bob Moore on bass, Farris Coursey on drums, and Floyd Cramer on piano. Reeves wanted the Jordanaires on background vocals and waited until the group was available before he recorded the song. Reeves played rhythm acoustic guitar and Chet, who wore a lab coat during the session, played lead electric.

Reeves was a former disc jockey who knew how to handle a microphone to avoid popping "p's" and other problems. He wanted a warm, intimate sound but Jeff Miller, the former RCA engineer, would never have allowed someone to sing close to the mic. Engineer Selby Cofeen didn't mind. "Jim wanted an intimate sound and wanted to get real close and whisper the lyrics," said Chet. When Steve Sholes first heard the recording of "Four Walls," he was "amazed" and asked, "How did you get that beautiful vocal sound?"

On Thursday, February 7, the session began with "Four Walls." After it was recorded, Reeves said, "This is great, if they release it just like we're hearing it now. He didn't want more instruments added, he wanted the chorus up in the mix and that was how it was released." The "Four Walls" session proved to be groundbreaking and led to a permanent shift in Jim's studio recordings. On recordings after "Four Walls" he rarely strayed from his natural range. The session's only song with obvious country appeal was "I Know (and You Know)" written by Red Sovine.[4]

Jim Reeves had the image of an easygoing "Gentleman Jim," but he was quite difficult to work with. By the time he got to the studio, Reeves had rehearsed his vocals and was ready to record. The musicians, on the other hand, had most likely never heard a song before it was played in the studio, either on a demo or by someone singing it. During sessions Reeves would chastise, often harshly, musicians who did not play to perfection quickly. "He was an old maid," said Gordon Stoker of the Jordanaires. "He always complained he wasn't getting the best of this or that. I remember one late session we did, and the musicians had already done one, two, maybe even three sessions that day. Buddy Harman, the drummer, had gone into RCA Studio B to lie down and rest before Jim's session, and Jim came in and said, 'Well, that's what I always do—get a bunch of broken down musicians that are worn out before I get here.'"

Chet Atkins learned to tolerate Reeves's attitude and prickly personality because he recognized his perfectionism. It didn't make his job any easier, though. "Sometimes," Stoker said, "Jim would say something to one of the musicians and you'd feel a chill in the place."[55]

Reeves's vocal on "Four Walls" was a new sound in country music, sung by a "crooner" who appealed to the fans of singers like Bing Crosby. Many in the young country audience had left for rock and roll, so labels needed to capture an older market who did not care for rock. Most of that audience had come of age during the big band era led by singers like Frank Sinatra, Perry Como, Doris Day, Rosemary Clooney, and Dinah Shore. Although the "Nashville Sound" emerging in the late 1950s came to define an era in country music, it brought criticism from longtime fans of traditional country music, who wanted the steel guitar and fiddle to be prominent on country records.

A little over a week after recording "Four Walls," Reeves and his manager, Herb Shucher, announced a European tour beginning on April 1. Sholes worked with Teldec, the German distributor for RCA, and was prompted by strong sales of country records at military post exchange stores. The PXes accounted for half of RCA's country sales, and those records were often purchased by European civilians. In fact, country records far outsold pop in the military post exchanges throughout Europe.

On April 29, while Reeves was in Europe, "Four Walls" entered the *Billboard* country chart; it remained number one for eight straight weeks, stayed on the chart for twenty-six weeks, and reached number eleven on the pop chart. Jim Reeves and the Nashville Sound had caught the ears of the pop market. The city's impact on country music was enormous—the flag was planted for the Nashville Sound.

"All great things are an accident," said Atkins. "You don't just sit down and say, 'I'm going to develop this or that.' I wasn't trying to change the business, just sell records. I realized at that time you had to surprise the public and give them something a little different."[6]

CHAPTER 18

Ike Everly was a "thumbpicking" guitarist like Merle Travis. He and his brothers grew up in Muhlenburg County, Kentucky, and formed a band. They moved to Chicago, then Ike moved his family to Waterloo, Iowa, where he performed on KASL. After a year Ike moved his family again, to Shenandoah, Iowa, where he performed on KMA. Around 1950 Ike incorporated his two sons, Don and Phil, into his act. In 1952 Ike and his family moved to Evansville, Indiana, and then to WROL in Knoxville where, in 1953, the act dissolved.

The family moved to Nashville in 1955 after their son Don graduated from high school, and Chet Atkins played a role in that move. Ike had written to Chet, asking him to help his sons, who he believed were talented. Chet said he'd see what he could do. Chet had founded Athens Music as a publishing company; he signed Don as a writer and took a song he wrote, "Thou Shalt Not Steal," to Kitty Wells, who recorded it.

Chet introduced the Everlys to Troy Martin, who had numerous connections in the music industry—a "mover and shaker"—and found talent for record labels and publishing companies. Martin contacted Don Law, head of Columbia's Nashville division, about the Everlys. Law lived in New York but came to Nashville, Dallas, and Los Angeles to record country acts. The Everlys met Law in his hotel room to audition and he signed them on November 8. The next day they recorded four songs—one written by Don, two by Don and Phil, and one credited to Don and Jerry Organ, the real name of Troy Martin. The duo was backed by Carl Smith's backing band, the Tunesmiths. A single, "The Sun Keeps Shining" backed with "Keep a Loving Me," was released in February 1956 but failed to chart, so Columbia dropped the act. By this time Chet had a position at RCA and wanted to sign the Everlys but could not convince Steve Sholes, who gave final approval on all signings.

The Everlys visited publishing companies to audition their songs, and in Hal Smith's office at Pamper Music they told him they wanted a recording contract. Smith informed them that the only publisher powerful enough to obtain a record deal was Wesley Rose at Acuff-Rose publishing. That led to an appointment with Rose, who signed them. In 1957 Rose paid for a demo session for the Everlys and planned to record them on Hickory, a label owned by Acuff-Rose.[1]

Cadence Records was an independent label owned by Archie Bleyer, who started the label in December 1952. Cadence had a hit in 1954 with "Mr. Sandman" by the Chordettes and a number-one hit with "Ballad of Davy Crockett" by Bill Hayes in 1955. Bleyer wanted to get into country music—Elvis Presley, Carl Perkins, and the other rockabillies were considered country acts—so he contacted Wesley Rose, who brought Gordon Terry and the Everly Brothers to him. In exchange, Wesley wanted the acts to record only Acuff-Rose songs.

Boudleaux and Felice Bryant had written songs on a nonexclusive basis for Fred Rose. After Fred died in 1954, the Bryants agreed to write exclusively for Acuff-Rose, but after ten years their copyrights would revert back to them. The Bryants had a song, "Bye Bye Love," that they had pitched to Johnnie and Jack as well as several others, but everyone had declined. Bleyer liked the song and offered it to Gordon Terry, who turned it down. The Everlys liked it, so they scheduled it for their first Cadence session on March 1, 1957. Don Everly had run into Chet Atkins in the alley behind the Opry, told him they were going to record for Cadence, and asked him to come play some Bo Diddley guitar. Chet readily agreed.

The first song on the session, held at the McGavock Street studio, was "I Wonder if I Care as Much," and they recorded it twice. Nashville studio sessions are geared to record four songs in three hours but Bleyer, who came from pop music, was content to remain in the studio as long as it took to get a good take, even if only one song was recorded. The second song on the session was "Bye Bye Love," and Don Everly had tuned his guitar to an open G chord with a capo up the neck. Rhythm guitarist Ray Edenton was in standard tuning, but his G string was tuned an octave higher. Phil Everly's guitar was in standard tuning. Those acoustic guitars with Chet playing fills on his electric guitar created a driving sound.

During his career, Chet took credit for producing the Everly Brothers, but that is only partially true. On those first Everly sessions, Archie Bleyer did not play but "created an environment" in the studio and "had a good commercial ear," said Colin Escott in his

Classic Everly Brothers liner notes. Phil Everly told a reporter that "when somebody got stuck on some of the more obscure songs, Archie would come in and rearrange it a little bit. . . . [He] knew what he was doing."[2] Chet certainly played an important role as a guitarist and session leader. He brought session musicians together and was wise enough to let Don and Phil's acoustic guitars set the pace for their songs. Their harmonies came naturally.

It was less than a month after Chet produced "Four Walls" on Jim Reeves, which pointed country music toward the Nashville Sound, when he was in the studio with the Everly Brothers playing on a song that became a rock and roll classic. The Everlys saw themselves as country artists but Archie Bleyer was a pop producer who had hits on Cadence and lacked the inner connections of the country industry, so from the start Bleyer saw possibilities beyond country music, which Elvis and Carl Perkins had pioneered.

The success of "Bye Bye Love" sealed a connection between Chet and the Everlys that meant he remained an important part of their sound for years to come. Since Bleyer rented RCA's studios for Cadence sessions, it was easy for Chet to justify playing on Everly Brothers records.

On April 4, 1957, Chet Atkins was on the *Today Show* hosted by Dave Garroway on NBC, which was owned by RCA. On the way to New York, Chet's guitar was damaged (the neck came loose) but the Gretsch factory in Brooklyn repaired it. On his modified 1955 Gretsch 6120 he performed "Poor People of Paris." The show aired at seven o'clock in the morning, with Chet demonstrating his EchoSonic amp before playing a snippet of "Some Bach" and then "Blue Ocean Echo." During the eight o'clock hour he played "Caravan" and accompanied Helen O'Connell on a song.[3]

On April 17 Chet Atkins recorded "Martinique," "Dig These Blues," "Colonial Ballroom" (written by Chet with Chick Thompson), and a song he and Boudleaux Brant wrote, "Midnight." Those were issued on RCA as the Rhythm Rockers, Featuring Chet Atkins. Joining him in the studio were Bob Moore, Buddy Harman, Floyd Cramer, and Melvin Hughes.

A full-page RCA advertisement in *Music Reporter* announced a "Gallery of Hitmakers" and featured artists Eddy Arnold, Melvin

Endsley, Hank Snow, Shorty Long, Hawkshaw Hawkins, Pee Wee King, Porter Wagoner, Don Gibson, Hank Locklin, Nita, Rita and Ruby, Canadian singer Myrna Lorrie, and Don Windle. Most of those acts were produced by Chet Atkins.[4] Two weeks later a double-page spread in *Music Reporter* advertised releases by Dave Rich, the Browns, Elvis Presley, Jim Reeves, Jean Chapel, the Sons of the Pioneers, Stuart Hamblen, Ric Carty, and Chet Atkins and the Rhythm Rockers. Again, most of these recordings were produced by Atkins.[5]

Not every record that Chet and RCA Nashville released became a hit; of that list of singles in the advertisement, only the records by Eddy Arnold ("Gonna Find Me a Bluebird"), Elvis ("All Shook Up"), and Jim Reeves ("Four Walls") made the country chart. Chet was extremely busy producing records, but the fickle finger of fate was at work. The hits were big ones, and a big hit like "Four Walls" compensated for the many songs that failed.

On June 22 Chet was in the McGavock Studio to begin work on his next album, *Hi-Fi in Focus*. Backed by Bob Moore on bass, Buddy Harman on drums, and Floyd Cramer on piano, the guitarist recorded four songs. Like his *In Three Dimensions* album, Chet recorded a wide variety of material. "Anna" had been a hit for Italian singer Silvana Mangano and was featured in the film by the same name, while "Tiger Rag" was originally recorded in 1917 by the Original Dixie Land Jazz Band. Merle Travis had also recorded "Tiger Rag," a song he learned as a boy in Kentucky. "El Cumbanchero" was written by Puerto Rican composer Rafael Hernandez. Chet had originally recorded Fats Waller's tune "Jitterbug Waltz" in 1951.

Chet always claimed he was a "country" guitar player and a "country boy." He certainly had a country background, coming from the mountains of East Tennessee, but although he recorded a number of country songs as instrumentals, as a guitarist he was not limited to the boundaries of country music. When recording songs Chet drew from a very broad range of music that included jazz, pop, blues, classical, and opera.

Steve Sholes had signed Don Gibson to RCA in 1950, but none of his releases had significant sales, so Sholes dropped him. In April 1956 Chet played on a Faron Young session where the singer recorded "Sweet Dreams," written by Gibson. Faron's version entered the *Billboard* country chart in June and reached number two. Chet was impressed with the song and Gibson's songwriting.

"I just fell in love with the tune," said Atkins, who decided to sign Gibson, although Steve Shoes questioned his decision. Gibson's publisher, Wesley Rose, "was always insisting, 'Let's keep it country,'" said Chet, who set up a session for February at McGavock Studio. "On that first session we used steel and fiddles and did real country stuff and didn't sell two records," said Chet. "So I said, 'O.K. Wesley, we've done it your way, now let's do it my way.'"

Rose agreed that on the next session Gibson would record "Chet's way." During that evening session they recorded "Too Soon to Know," "Pretty Rainbow," "Blue Blue Day," and "Tell It Like It Is," three of them written by Gibson ("Pretty Rainbow" was by Vaughn Horton). Gibson was backed by Chet on guitar, Junior Huskey on bass, Floyd Cramer on piano, and Troy Hatcher, a friend of Don's from Knoxville, on drums, with the Jordanaires and Millie Kirkham providing background vocals. "It was right when rock'n'roll was starting," remembered Gibson, "and people like the Everlys were coming in. So we did 'Blue Blue Day' that way and it sounded pretty good."[6]

The day after the session with Don Gibson, Chet was in the studio with Hank Locklin, who needed a hit. He had recorded eight singles for RCA, but only one, "Why Baby Why," had charted. Chet was searching for different sounds that would help sell records during an era when rock and roll was eating country music's lunch. They first recorded "Livin' Alone," then "Send Me the Pillow That You Dream On," which Locklin had written and originally recorded during the summer of 1949 for Bill McCall's Four Star label. Locklin had been performing the song while in Texas; although it was a hit in the Texas market, Locklin was frustrated with McCall for not paying him royalties. Locklin reasoned that if it was released on RCA he would get paid.

The RCA version of "Send Me the Pillow That You Dream On" differed from the Four Star version, which featured a steel guitar and fiddle. The new version represented the Nashville Sound with a big chorus by the Jordanaires and Millie Kirkham. Grady Martin played lead guitar on this session, with Floyd Cramer's piano tinkling along.[7]

At the time of that session "Fraulein" was a huge hit for Bobby Helms on Decca; it entered the country chart at the end of March and reached number one. It was written by Lawton Williams, Locklin's Texas friend, who had written it for Ernest Tubb. Tubb and a number of other artists turned it down, but Helms "was so young and so new to the recording business that it never occurred to him that he could refuse to record the song." He recorded it at the end of 1956.

"Fraulein touched a nerve deep in the psyche of a society faced with dislocations of time and place, be they the difficulties of rural folk adjusting to life in the cities where there was work, or the problems of American servicemen adjusting to overseas posting," wrote Otto Kittsinger. There were a number of American servicemen stationed in Germany after World War II, so the song resonated with country listeners.[8] The success of "Fraulein" led Lawton Williams to write "Geisha Girl," which also struck a nerve because there were a number of American servicemen stationed in Japan. Lawton sent the song to Locklin, who played it for Chet, who agreed to record it.

That session resulted in two huge hits for Locklin. "Geisha Girl" was released first and entered the *Billboard* country chart on August 19, rising to number four and spawning (with "Fraulein") a number of "answer" songs: "I'll Always Be Your Fraulein" by Kitty Wells, "I Found My Girl in the U.S.A." by Jimmy Skinner, "I'm the Girl in the USA" by Connie Hall, "Lost to a Geisha Girl" by Skeeter Davis, and "Daddy's Geisha Girl" by the McCoys. Locklin's follow-up single, "Send Me the Pillow That You Dream On," reached number five on the country chart.

Hank Locklin did not become a major star with those two hit singles because, just before his session, he moved to a remote area in Florida with no telephone service. He paid to have a telephone installed in his daughter's home, twelve miles away, and each day drove to see if he had any calls for bookings.

SESAC, the Society of European Stage Authors and Composers, is a performing rights organization, like BMI and ASCAP, but is privately owned and for-profit. It was originally formed by Paul Heinecke to collect royalties for European composers who had recordings played on American radio. During the 1950s SESAC established an electrical transcription series where name artists recorded SESAC-licensed songs for radio airplay. The RCA brass must have given Chet permission to record those songs for the SESAC Repertory Library and release the songs on an RCA LP, *The Amazing Chet Atkins* (later reissued as *The Best of Chet Yet*).

The recordings are all quite mellow, with Chet playing straightforward melodies accompanied by backing singers. SESAC used Chet because he was a "name" act, but the playing was not energetic. In the studio with him was a singing group led by Anita Kerr, composed of Winifred Breast, Dottie Dillard, Kal Gavin, James Louis Holt, Millie Kirkham, Louis Nunley, and Gil Wright, who sang on the choruses. This was the first time Chet recorded with a large vocal group.

Three days after the SESAC session, Chet recorded six songs for his *Hi-Fi in Focus* album. "Portuguese Washerwoman" had been a hit for Lou Busch and His Orchestra, featuring ragtime piano player Joe "Fingers" Carr. "You Do Something to Me" was written by Cole Porter; "Shadow Waltz" appeared in the film musical *Gold Diggers of 1933*, and Bing Crosby, Rudy Vallee, and Guy Lombardo had all released it as a single. "Tara's Theme" was from the film *Gone With the Wind* and "Lullaby of the Leaves" was a number-one hit for George Olsen in 1931.

Chet was a friend and fan of Johnny Smith, a popular jazz guitarist who composed "Walk Don't Run." Like Atkins, Smith was influenced by Django Reinhardt. Roost Records was formed in 1949 and released "Walk Don't Run" from Smith's 1954 album, *Moods, Moods, Moods*. Chet wanted to record "Walk Don't Run" but first he met with Smith at Birdland in New York—owned by jazz saxophonist Charlie Parker—to play his version for Smith. Smith appreciated the "delightful" rendition and offered his blessing.

The song was a melodic reworking of the jazz standard "Softly, as in a Morning Sunrise," originally written as a vocal piece by Sigmund Romberg and Oscar Hammerstein II for the 1928 operetta *The New Moon*. It was recorded by Artie Show and the Modern Jazz Quartet. Johnny Smith took the chord structure and wrote his own minor-scale-based melody. Chet's version was substantially different as he completely cut out the riff played against a pattern of descending notes by backing musicians, focusing solely on the song's memorable A and B sections. Chet arranged his version as a fingerstyle piece and played its melody along with a simultaneous melodic counterpoint, primarily the lower string of the key. Originally Smith played it in D minor, with Chet doing it in A minor. The last third of Chet's version featured him moving to the key of D minor and playing the song's melody in a straightforward soloing style similar to Smith's.

"The founding members of the Washington state-based instrumental rock band The Ventures were big fans of the record and 'Walk Don't Run' was the song on the album that captivated them the most," stated Mark Reinhart in *Chet Atkins: The Greatest Songs of Mister Guitar*. "The band put together a simplified rocked-up version of the song, recorded it and released it as a single in 1959." The "rocked up" version of "Walk Don't Run" came because Ventures guitarist Don Wilson tried to learn Atkins's version but "found it too complicated" so the group "came up with their own way of playing it."[9]

About fifty RCA artists appeared in a *Music Reporter* advertisement on August 7. Major labels during that time had large rosters of performers, most of whom were signed for singles. It is interesting to note that there were a number of gospel acts on RCA, and although it was seldom publicized, Chet produced and/or played on most of those gospel recordings for the RCA Victor family.

On August 12 Chet was in McGavock Studio alone to record Fats Waller's 1939 classic "Ain't Misbehavin'," "Avorada," a traditional song whose title means "Little Music Box," and a song written by Johann Sebastian Bach, "Bourree." After a short break, he recorded "Johnson Rag" and "Yesterdays." Those songs completed Chet's *Hi-Fi in Focus* album.

CHAPTER 19

Archie Bleyer needed a strong follow-up to "Bye Bye Love" so he waited until he found the right song before the Everlys went back into the studio for two days of sessions on August 15 and 16. Chet appeared on those sessions. The first song they recorded was "Wake Up, Little Susie," written by Boudleaux and Felice Bryant. Once again the acoustic guitar played by Don in an open tuning was the defining riff. Archie Bleyer left for a convention on the second day, so Chet undoubtedly played a more prominent role as producer as the Everlys' guitars and harmonies and Boudleaux and Felice Bryant's songs came to define the Everly Brothers sound.[1]

In August RCA announced that they would open a new studio in Nashville "which will duplicate those in Chicago, Hollywood and New York." Chet would continue as the label's "Nashville man" in addition to being musical director and a recording artist.[2] Steve Sholes, who had headed RCA's country division for the previous twelve years, had been promoted to manager of RCA's single records for both country and pop, a new position that would take effect on September 1.[3] Sholes's promotion came as a direct result of the success of Elvis, who sold over ten million records in 1956. The change was both positive and negative for Chet, who would now have to spend more time with administrative work and place his role as executive ahead of his role as artist, although Sholes continued to be a shield between Chet and the New York office.

During the late summer of 1957, RCA recording manager Bill Mittlenberg drew up plans for a new studio facility on a napkin. RCA broke ground for a full-blown studio and office complex on the corner of Hawkins Street (now Roy Acuff Place) and Seventeenth Avenue South (now Music Square West). The one-story building, sitting on a quarter of an acre, spanned 65 by 150 feet and cost $39,515 to build. Dan Maddox owned the building and land and leased it to RCA Victor.

Inside the building were offices for Chet and Ed Hines, manager of RCA's custom services, in addition to a studio.

In October RCA engineer Les Chase came down from New York to work with Selby Coffeen and local RCA staff engineers to set up the tape machines, a mixing board, and other equipment. The first recording session took place at the end of October, with an official opening in November. A picture of Chet Atkins in *Music Reporter* described him as "guitarist extraordinaire" and "A&R director in Nashville for RCA-Victor." It showed him receiving a gold plaque commemorating his tenth anniversary with the company. Jack Burgess, manager of RCA's single records department, presented the plaque and stated the new studio was "the house that Chet built."[4]

On August 27 Chet, Bob Moore, Farris Coursey, and Marvin Hughes were in the studio to record "Hidden Charm," written by Spider Rich. Coursey not only played drums but also slapped his thighs with his hands, much like he did on Red Foley's hit "Chattanoogie Shoeshine Boy." "Hidden Charm" was the last song Chet recorded in McGavock Studio.

Jimmie Driftwood and his wife Cleda were schoolteachers from Timbo, Arkansas. Driftwood was born James Morris, but his grandfather played a trick on his grandmother by bringing her a batch of sticks wrapped in a blanket to show her their new grandson. "Why, it ain't nothing but driftwood," she said as she took the bundle. The Driftwood name stuck. Driftwood had written songs to help students learn history, recording eight songs for Cardinal Records that were released in 1952. One of them, "Howdy, Neighbor, Howdy," later became Porter Wagoner's theme song.

Wagoner and his steel guitarist, Don Warden, had started a publishing company and were looking for songs. Red Gale, guitarist and fiddler in Porter's band, recommended Driftwood to Warden, who invited Jimmie and Cleda to Nashville. The couple drove over to Nashville in their pickup truck during the spring of 1957 and checked into the Clarkston Hotel. They first met with Buddy Killen with Tree Publishing, but Killen turned them down. The next day they met Don Warden and Porter Wagoner. Jimmie, Cleda, and Warden went to Driftwood's room, where he "sang more than a hundred songs, playing the homemade guitar his grandfather, John Morris, had made." That guitar, known as "the Contraption," featured a neck made from a piece of fence rail and the sides from an old ox yoke with the body from his grandmother's headboard.[5]

After singing those songs Jimmie began, "In 1814 we took a little trip"—the first line to "The Battle of New Orleans"—but he stopped abruptly, his confidence in the song shaken. Warden urged Driftwood to continue. "I told him to sing it all. It was the best thing I had heard so far." Driftwood had written the song in 1936 to the melody of an old fiddle tune, "The Eighth of January," which is the date that General Jackson defeated the British in New Orleans.

Warden took Jimmie and Cleda to the Friday night Opry, where they played songs for the singers and musicians there. The next morning they drove back to Timbo. Not long after Don Warden visited them with publishing contracts. Don introduced Driftwood and his songs to Chet, who set up an appointment in his office at RCA. Chet offered Driftwood a recording contract, stipulating that he would use the name of Jimmie Driftwood—not Jimmy Morris—that he would spell his name "Jimmie" because "it looked more southern and 'folksier' than 'Jimmy'" and that Jimmie "would play the guitar that his grandpa Morris had made for him."[6] For someone obsessed with the guitar, Chet found it appealing to record with a unique handmade guitar.

On Sunday, October 27, 1957, Jimmie was in the RCA studio with Chet and bassist Bob Moore and they recorded eleven songs, including "Battle of New Orleans." After the session, Jimmie and Cleda drove back to Arkansas, where she continued teaching third grade and he continued as a school principal.[7]

The Driftwood album that Chet recorded "sounded old-fashioned and that was kind of the way Chet wanted to do it," said engineer Bill Porter. "Old fashioned technically. More consistent with the bluegrass sound of years ago."[8]

Before Chet produced a session for Don Gibson in June when the singer recorded "Blue Blue Day," Gibson had sent him a demo tape with two songs, "I Can't Stop Loving You" and "Oh Lonesome Me." Gibson had written both songs the same afternoon in Knoxville "sitting in the trailer feeling low" as his television set and vacuum cleaner had both been repossessed. "I Can't Stop Loving You" came when he "sat down to write a lost love ballad." He wrote "Ol' Lonesome Me," but when someone at Acuff-Rose transcribed it they thought he sang "Oh Lonesome Me." For the demo Gibson recruited drummer Troy

Hatcher, who used a beat he learned from an East Tennessee Black band. Chet remembered that "there was a drummer on the demo playing 'boom-ba-boom, boom-ba-boom.' I said, 'bring him with you'" for the session, set for the morning of December 3 in the new studio.

For the session Chet played his guitar through his EchoSonic amp. "I just wanted to make 'Oh Lonesome Me' like Don's demo," said Chet. "His demo was great. In order to get the bass drum on there real prominent, we miked the bass drum. Up until that time, people just picked up the drums with one mic. Whoever happened to be playing loudest, that's what was loudest on the record. So we miked the drum. As far as I know, that's the first time a drum had been miked." Playing rhythm guitar was Velma Williams and Chet had her "play a special beat, and we were all doing something special." Playing bass was Joe Zinkin, and Floyd Cramer was on piano with the Jordanaires on background vocals.

The second song they recorded was "I Can't Stop Loving You," which Don insisted on recording "but Wesley and Chet said it was just a simple old ballad. I said, 'Well, if it ain't that good, just put it on the backside of "Oh Lonesome Me."'" The third and fourth songs were "Tell It Like It Is" and "It Has to Be Me." All of the songs were written by Gibson.

On December 4, the day after the Don Gibson session in the new RCA studio, Chet recorded his last solo session for 1957. Accompanied by Bob Moore, Buddy Harman, and Floyd Cramer, he recorded four songs. "You're Just in Love" was sung in the Broadway musical *Call Me Madam* by Ethel Merman. During the early fifties it was popular as a duet. "Don't Blame Me" was introduced in the 1932 musical *Clowns in Clover*; in 1948 Nat King Cole had a number-one record with it. "Jungle Drums" was by the Cuban composer Ernesto Lecuno, and "Czardes" (sometimes spelled "Csardes") was written by Italian Vittorio Monti in 1904. These were the first songs recorded for what became his *Chet Atkins at Home* album.

That same day Chet produced a session on Johnnie and Jack in the new studio. The session marked the duo's first with a saxophone. Sax player Andy Goodrich, a local African American musician who had studied music at Tennessee State University, arrived at the session late, just in time to record "Camel Walk Stroll" with Johnnie and Jack. Harold Morrison and Joe Zinkan wrote the song. "Rock and roll was tearing us up pretty bad," remembered Morrison. "Everybody was trying to do something different just to sell some records. It was tough!"[9]

CHAPTER 20

On January 9, 1958, Chet recorded five songs for his *Chet Atkins at Home* album. The first song was "Sophisticated Lady," a Duke Ellington standard written in 1933. Next up was "Muskrat Ramble," credited to Kid Ory, who composed it in 1921. That was followed by "April in Portugal," also known as "The Whisp'ring Serenade," which was a hit for Les Baxter and his orchestra in 1953. "Martha" came from a popular opera that premiered in Vienna in 1847. Chet knew "Nagasaki" from Django Reinhardt's version, which was originally a Tin Pan Alley novelty hit written in 1928.

Chet continued work on his *At Home* album on January 30. On that session was his old friend from his Knoxville days on WNOX, bassist Aytchie Burns. The session began with "Say Si Si," written by Cuban composer Ernesto Lecuona in 1935 and was first a hit in 1936 by Xavier Cugat's band with singer Desi Arnaz. In 1940 it was a hit by the Andrew Sisters. "Ay-Ay-Ay" was a public domain song that Chet arranged. Chet recorded a number of PD songs, as the label could avoid songwriter royalties, making the albums more profitable. By listing songs as "traditional" or "arranged by," Chet received reduced songwriting royalties.

The song "Yankee Doodle" dates back to the mid-eighteenth century. "Dixie" has been traced back to the mid-nineteenth century, just before the Civil War, and is credited to Daniel Decatur Emmett. Chet had been working on combining the two songs for several years; he had done a short version on a live recording in 1954 that was on the *Country and Western Caravan* album. On his version on the *Chet Atkins at Home* album, he played his Gretsch in the key of A in standard tuning, offering the melody of "Yankee Doodle" on the lower strings and "Dixie" on the higher strings.[1] The last song on the session was "In the Chapel in the Moonlight," first performed by Shep Fields and a hit in 1953 for Kitty Kallen with the Jack Pleis Orchestra.

On February 6 Chet finished recording the songs for his *At Home* album with "Villa," another version of "Yankee Doodle Dixie," "Siesta" (written by Chet and James Rich), and "Bopra," a Chet original that has "disappeared." He was accompanied by Bob Moore on bass and Buddy Harman on drums.

Teenagers accounted for half of the $400 million spent on record sales, according to a 1958 article, which added that "a big chunk of that will be for recordings made in RCA—Victor's Nashville studio." The article quoted Atkins, who stated his philosophy about finding talent to record: "First, I try to sign the best artist possible, then try to find a song that exactly suits his style," he said. "Next there is a search for a gimmick or an arrangement different enough for the public to go for it. Then we hire a band with five or six members and a singing group."

"You've just got to have them," said Chet about background vocalists. "The public almost demands a group singing in the background."[2]

On March 6, almost exactly a year from the day they had recorded "Bye Bye Love," the Everly Brothers were in RCA's new studio to record again. The Bryants had been writing songs aimed specifically for the Everlys and when the Everlys and Archie Bleyer heard "All I Have to Do Is Dream" they knew it was a hit. Chet opened the song with a tremolo chord through his EchoSonic amplifier and is prominent with his fills.

In April it was announced that Owen Bradley had been named C&W A&R director for Decca Records in Nashville. Owen had been in the music industry since 1939 and joined WSM in 1940, then was made musical director in 1946. Bradley led a big band that performed regularly and had been associated with Decca since 1947.[3] Chet and Owen Bradley are considered two of the architects of the Nashville Sound.

On May 3 Chet was in the RCA studio and, with Bob Moore on bass, Floyd Cramer on piano, and Buddy Harman on drums, recorded an old Texas fiddle tune, "Jessie Polka" (renamed "Jessie"), and a song he wrote, "Slinkey." This was Chet's final session in mono. Chet had adapted an electronic tremolo device from an old Fender amplifier for "Jessie" and used guitarist James Burton's iconic riff on Dale Hawkins's "Susie Q" at the beginning of "Slinkey." Chet played his electric guitar through a Fender amplifier with lots of tremelo on "Slinkey."[4]

Chet always liked novelty records, and the Slinky, coiled wire that could "walk" down stairs, was a novelty toy. Chet changed the spelling slightly, adding an "e" to make it "Slinkey," either because he wanted to avoid copyright problems with the toy manufacturer or he misspelled it; the former is more likely.

Elvis, RCA's biggest moneymaker, was drafted into the army in March and spent six weeks in basic training. He had a short respite before training with the tank corps, and RCA wanted to record songs that could be released as singles during his tour of duty in Germany. RCA's new studio in Nashville had proven to be a place where hit songs were cut after Don Gibson's success with "Oh Lonesome Me," "I Can't Stop Loving You," and "Blue Blue Day."

Gibson's "Blue Blue Day" had not been a hit when first released in 1957, but after "Oh Lonesome Me" was number one for eight straight weeks and "I Can't Stop Lovin' You" reached number seven on the country chart, the DJs decided to give the record a second listen. "Blue Blue Day" then reached number one on the *Billboard* country chart just as Elvis came to Nashville on June 10.

Elvis lacked fond memories of recording in Nashville because Chet did not hire the Jordanaires as he requested. Elvis had not recorded in Nashville for two years before driving his nine-passenger black Cadillac limousine, with the Jordanaires, Colonel Tom Parker, and some of Elvis's Memphis buddies—but no girlfriend—in tow, from Memphis to the studio.

Under the supervision of Steve Sholes and Chet, Elvis recorded five songs, "I Need Your Love Tonight," "A Big Hunk O'Love," "Ain't That Loving You Baby," "A Fool Such as I," and "I Got Stung" during the all-night session. Chet was in the studio playing guitar, with Hank Garland and Elvis also on guitar, Bob Moore on bass, Floyd Cramer on piano, and both Buddy Harman and Elvis's drummer D. J. Fontana on drums. The Jordanaires offered backing vocals; it was the first time bass singer Ray Walker joined the group for a session.

Elvis first recorded "I Need Your Love Tonight" and "A Big Hunk O'Love," then moved on to "Ain't That Loving Your Baby," but it didn't seem to have the energy of the first two. After several tries, Chet came out of the control booth, picked up a guitar—as Elvis said "Boogie, Chet!"—and played a walking bass line on guitar that helped the rhythm. After eleven takes and two different versions, they moved on to "(Now and Then There's) A Fool Such as I," a 1953 hit for Hank Snow. Chet played rhythm guitar.

Around six o'clock in the morning, Elvis walked out of his first session in Nashville's new RCA studio and headed back to Memphis.[5]

The July 7, 1958, issue of *Music Reporter* announced the formation of the Country Music Association at the Country and Western Disc Jockey Association's convention held in Miami. During that convention, the Disc Jockey organization was dissolved and the Country Music Association was formed "to include all members of the recording industry associated with C&W." Planning representatives for the new organization were Wesley Rose, Hubert Long (manager of Ferlin Husky and Faron Young), Dee Kilpatrick (WSM's Grand Ole Opry manager), Bobby Lord of "Country Music Jubilee," and Don Law, C&W head of Columbia Records. During the summer a "caretaker committee" oversaw the development. The purpose of the CMA "will be the widening of country music programming, the opening of doors now barred to it, and assuring greater prosperity for its artists, producers, promoters, and writers," in short, an effort to save country music from the rock and roll invasion. A board of directors, comprising representatives from different aspects of the recording industry was elected, with Wesley Rose as chairman.

In December it was announced that Connie B. Gay, chairman of the board of the Town and Country Network, had been voted president of the Country Music Association. Officers elected included Eddy Arnold and Harold Moon as vice presidents, Mac Wiseman as secretary, and Hubert M. Long as treasurer. The board and officers agreed to meet three times a year, beginning January 10–11, 1959, in Nashville. Applications were sought for an executive director who would guide the day-to-day activities.[6]

Gretsch introduced the red Tennessean 6119 in 1958, which cost less than the Country Gentleman and was basically a one-humbucker version of the 6120, introduced in 1958. There were now three Chet Atkins models in the Gretsch line: the Tennessean ($295), the 6120 ($400), and the Country Gentleman ($525).

Janis Martin toured with Hank Snow, Porter Wagoner, and Faron Young and appeared on Jim Reeves's shows during 1957. She had formed her own band, the Marteens, toured heavily and took a screen test for MGM, but her records did not chart well. RCA did not know that when she was fifteen Martin had secretly married her childhood sweetheart, who was in the army and stationed overseas. During her European tour of American military bases, she visited her husband: "I got pregnant and it kind of busted the little teen idol image." Record labels liked to present their artists as young, attractive, and single for mass appeal. She performed only one more session for RCA. Chet produced that session in RCA's studio on July 7. They recorded four songs but none charted, and Martin was subsequently dropped.[7]

Three days after the Janis Martin session, the Everly Brothers were in RCA's studio to record two songs, "Devoted to You" and "Bird Dog," both written by Boudleaux Bryant. "Devoted to You" opens and closes with Chet playing a tremolo guitar through his EchoSonic amp. It appeared as the B side of the single and reached number ten on the pop chart. "Bird Dog," which the Everlys hated and thought was too corny, was a number-one record.[8]

During a session on July 24, Chet had several goals: to record with his brother and to try out the new stereo equipment installed at RCA, which included an Ampex three-track recorder and a new RCA custom-designed recording console. That session would be the first stereo recording for Chet.

Jim Atkins's career as a singer and performer was effectively over by 1958; it had peaked in the late thirties to early forties when the Les Paul Trio disbanded. Jim then joined the Pinetoppers on Coral Records and recorded with them; Chet sat in on some of those sessions. By 1958, at age forty-seven, Jim had worked for years as a manager and executive in broadcasting; his current job was as program director at KOA-AM in Denver. Ironically, Chet had worked at that station with Shorty Thompson before his first recording sessions with RCA. Jim was a hero to Chet, opening doors for him in radio, and had been a source of songs for Chet, who recorded a number of songs he first heard when Jim performed them with the Les Paul Trio.

For most of the session Chet used his new Gretsch Country Gentleman, which had existed for less than a year but was quickly becoming his favorite; it featured a mahogany finish with uncut f-holes. Jim Atkins played rhythm guitar, with Bob Moore on bass, Floyd Cramer on piano, and Buddy Harman on drums. Beginning at ten in the morning they recorded "Asleep in the Deep," used in the 1943 Merrie Melodies cartoon "Wackiki Wabbitt." Chet heard "Out of Nowhere," first recorded by Bing Crosby in 1931, on the 1939 recording by Django Reinhardt and Stephane Grappelli. "Even Tho" was a number-one hit on the country chart for Webb Pierce in 1959. "When Day Is Done" charted for Paul Whiteman, Nat Shilkret, Harry Archer, and Art Kahn, all in 1927. They finished the first session, took a two-hour break, and resumed with "I'll Be with You in Apple Blossom Time," a hit for the Andrews Sisters in 1941. The final song Jim recorded was "Swanee River," a number-one hit for Al Jolson in 1920. It was a jazzy pop session with Chet playing melodic solos and jazzy fills.

After Jim's vocals, Chet, Bob Moore, Buddy Harman, and Floyd Cramer recorded five instrumentals. They began with "My Funny Valentine," written by the Broadway team of Richard Rodgers and Lorenz Hart, followed by "I Know That You Know." Next came "Zing Went the Strings of My Heart," originally in *Thumbs Up* in 1934, with the most famous version by Judy Garland in the 1938 film *Listen Darling*. The fourth song that evening was "I'm Forever Blowing Bubbles," a vocal number for the Broadway musical *The Passing Show of 1918*. The final song, "Country Style," was written by pop songwriters Johnnie Burke and Jimmy Van Heusen.

Before Jim left Nashville to return to Denver, he and Chet went to the Belle Meade Mansion and posed on the front porch of the original log cabin for an album cover photo. A cover for *My Brother Sings* was drawn up and the project was given a catalogue number—but the album was not released. The fact that Jim was not signed as an artist to RCA is a possible reason that the label canceled the project.[9]

CHAPTER 21

Printers Alley is located between Third and Fourth Avenues North and between Union and Commerce Streets in downtown Nashville. The name dates from the 1940s when it was the site of printing companies. During the mid-1950s it became known for having clubs where liquor was sold illegally. Liquor by the drink was not legalized in Nashville until 1968, but bars stretched the rules by charging for a "service." The clubs in Printer's Alley stretched along a two-block area that featured strip joints and seedy clubs in addition to a few more "sophisticated joints."

Nashville Tennessean reporter David Halberstam observed that "everything was closed on Sunday (except churches, of course), and restaurants couldn't serve alcohol, so there were few good restaurants. However, there was an underground nightlife of private clubs, illicit gambling, drinking and sex in smoky jazz and blues dives and country honky-tonks with cops and politicians on the take." This was where Chet and other session musicians could play blues and jazz.[1] By the end of 1958, Chet, Hank Garland, Floyd Cramer, Bob Moore, Buddy Harman, and Boots Randolph were jamming regularly in Printer's Alley.

One day W. O. Smith, an African American faculty member at Tennessee State University and jazz bassist, received a phone call from Buddy Harman "that would change my life." Harman and pianist Bill Pursell were in a quartet led by Hank Garland that performed regularly at the Carousel, a club owned by Jimmy Hyde that featured jazz. The regular bass player, Chuck Sanders, had been drafted, so Harman asked Smith to join them.[2]

Smith had joined the Tennessee State faculty in 1952 and became part of a string quartet with Brenton Banks on first violin, Maureen Stovall on second violin, Dave Kimbrell on bass, and Smith on viola. They were a "novelty," a Black string quartet that played classical music. Later, Smith became bassist in a jazz group with Andy Goodrich, a TSU graduate, on alto saxophone, Brenton Banks on piano (and sometimes violin), and drummer Morris Palmer.

"Nashville was a hotbed of Black jazz," recalled W. O. Smith. "The rub was that nobody knew about it except for the Black community, some white jazz performers and the cognoscenti. This was a town deeply mired in country music, the product that gave it national recognition. However, the jazz practitioners knew or knew of each other, Black and white, and some of the country music cats crossed over to the Black clubs and looked for a jam session. That didn't work the other way, of course."[3]

The group Smith was asked to join was white and he didn't know any of the members. "They turned out to be a fantastic group," said Smith. "Buddy could swing with the best of the jazz drummers" while Hank Garland was "a major-league jazz guitarist" and pianist Bill Pursell "was up to it all the way. He had the technique of a classical pianist, brought from the Eastman School of Music and Peabody Conservatory."[4] Buddy Harman was the staff drummer at the Grand Ole Opry, and Hank Garland played on the Opry—just a few blocks away—so the group could not start until Harman and Garland finished their Opry gigs. When Garland arrived he first had dinner, so the group generally started later than scheduled.

W. O. Smith "noticed that every Saturday night near midnight, we were visited by a representative of Nashville's finest. Always it was a ranking officer and the rank was geared to the prestige of the club. The Carousel never got less than a Captain."[5] A number of other clubs in and around Nashville were centers for gambling and bookmaking. There was an after-hours club on Music Row in a house that is still standing.

Smith's tenure with Hank Garland's quartet ended when Garland's regular bassist, Chuck Sanders, returned from the service. Morris Palmer, drummer in Smith's TSU group, sometimes subbed for Harman, but Smith's departure ended integrated musicians playing before a paying crowd. Printer's Alley was "rigidly segregated," remembered Smith. The police "had conspired with the club owners not to have any more mixed bands."[6]

A jazz quartet comprising Andy Goodrich on alto sax, Brenton Banks on piano, drummer Morris Palmer, and W. O. Smith on bass became a quintet with the addition of trumpeter Louis Smith. They decided to visit various clubs and offer a "free audition"; the Ebony Club hired them before they moved to the Black Poodle. "We rarely mingled with the customers unless we received a specific invitation," said Smith, but "we were visited nightly by the town's leading white jazz musicians," including Hank Garland, Buddy Harman, Bill Pursell, Tupper Saussy, and Chet Atkins.[7] Musical jams occurred after the club closed and the paying white customers had left. After a time, Chet had his own Sunday night shows at the Carousel.

The Printer's Alley evenings were soaked in jazz. Chet and his buddies' jam sessions at the Carousel Club allowed them freedom to delve into musical areas that their more rigid studio work didn't permit. Chet insisted he wasn't as strong an improviser as Hank Garland, Jethro Burns, or even Floyd Cramer, but he certainly was among the elite jazz players on those club stages.

A true musician plays not for money but because they must, because the music must be released from their soul, flowing from a deep well that spills out like a cascading waterfall. Without doubt Chet Atkins was a true musician.

Boots Randolph had been playing in a Decatur, Illinois, club when Homer and Jethro came in and joined him for a jam. "Both of them were great players," said Randolph. "We sat up all night and played all the old standards. Jethro could play his butt off on the mandolin. Nobody challenged him because he was great. He was the king of jazz mandolin."

Boots had sent a tape to Spider Rich, who subsequently invited Boots to play on some of his demos, which Rich then took to Chet. Chet listened to a demo and told Rich he wanted to meet Randolph. Around this same time Jethro was in Chet's office where Chet played the demo for him. "That's Boots Randolph!" Jethro called out. "How do you know him?" asked Chet. Jethro recalled jamming with Randolph in Illinois.

Chet "was playing down at the Carousel Club every Sunday night," said Randolph. "He asked me to come over and jam a bit," which led to Chet hiring Randolph for session work. "When I came to town, you know, I was kind of a hot rod type player," said Randolph. "They wanted to bring some of this country stuff into a pop/rock type sound. Brenda Lee was one of the first to use this type of sound through Owen Bradley." Chet told Randolph, "I need you to move down here because we want you on these records" or "someone else is going to grab that spot."

Randolph had a wife and two young daughters and had just bought a house in Decatur. He was playing six nights a week at a local club but reasoned that if Nashville failed to pan out, he could always return to that club. In Nashville Randolph joined Chet at the Carousel Club on Sunday nights. They "packed the place! We would play standards and maybe a few country tunes," said Randolph.[8]

On August 9 Elvis Presley completed tank training at Fort Hood, Texas; that same day his mother Gladys was taken to Methodist Hospital in Memphis. Elvis obtained a seven-day emergency leave from the army and arrived back home in Memphis on August 12. On August 14 Gladys Presley passed. Chet Atkins drove from Nashville to attend the funeral service.

On August 16 TV viewers could see Chet on "Jubilee U.S.A.," the new name for the "Ozark Jubilee" TV show. Host Red Foley introduced Chet as "the master himself, the one and only." Chet performed two songs from his recently released *At Home* LP, "Vilia" and "Say Si Si."[9]

Red Foley had run into IRS issues related to back taxes. Though the charges were disputed, the negative publicity scared off sponsors for the TV show and made executives nervous. That led to a change—Jim Reeves "subbed" for Foley for eight weeks.

It was standard fare for country artists to record gospel albums during their career. On September 4 Chet was in the control room while Jim Reeves recorded eight songs for a gospel album, backed by session musicians and the Anita Kerr Singers. This three-hour session was the first where Velma Williams backed Reeves; knowing how demanding and difficult he could be, she arrived early and introduced herself to Reeves while they were alone. "Mr. Reeves, I'm Velma Smith," she said, "and I will be your rhythm guitarist today." He looked at her and mumbled something under his breath that sounded like, "What has Atkins gotten me into?" She continued, "I'll tell you, Mr. Reeves, I'm going to try my best to please you, and if there's anything that I do that is not up to par with what you would like, I only ask that you come and tell me." After the session he went to Smith, kissed the back of her neck, and told her, "Velma, I think we're going to get along just fine." From that day forward they collaborated beautifully.[10]

On October 23, 1958, Chet was in the Radio Recorders Annex Studios in Hollywood for a session with a full orchestra (eighteen string players) produced by Dick Peirce. He was also accompanied by jazz guitarist Howard Roberts, Clifford Hills on bass, Larry Bunker on drums, and Geoffrey Clarkson on piano. Dennis Farnon, a well-known Canadian musician, arranged and conducted the orchestra. Chet had never before recorded with an instrumental ensemble that large.

The *Chet Atkins in Hollywood* album was the brainchild of Ed Welker, the A&R head of pop in New York, who thought it would be interesting to have Chet's version of film songs past and present. He contacted Chet and arranger Dennis Farnon, who was also a West Coast executive with RCA, and both agreed.

Ironically, two of the songs he recorded later became major hits for other artists. When Don Everly heard "Let It Be Me," he decided the Everly Brothers should record the song as a vocal. The Browns did not hear Chet's version of "The Three Bells" but later recorded it as a vocal.

Chet had recorded the former Les Paul hit "Meet Mister Callaghan" in 1952. "Theme from Picnic" had been a hit for Morris Stoloff in 1956, and "Theme from Limelight" (also known as "Eternally") was the theme for the 1953 Charlie Chaplin film. "The Three Bells," originally known as "Les Trois Cloches," was a hit for French singer Edith Piaf in 1948 and the group Les Compagnons de la Chanson in 1952. The Hollywood session was the third time Chet recorded Fats Waller's "Jitterbug Waltz."

While these were his first solo recordings with a full orchestra, they weren't his first with arranged strings. Four years earlier he'd played on Anita Carter's first Columbia solo session, with a string quartet accompanying.

Chet Atkins in Hollywood reflected his growing stature at RCA because the label spared no expense. In later years Chet teamed with Arthur Fiedler and the Boston Pops Orchestra for joint recordings and live performances, which led to appearances with other symphony orchestras. After the session the original recording was shelved in Hollywood, then sent to New York. Chet took the basic tracks home and rerecorded his parts in his home studio, then sent the revised version to New York, where it was stored. This led to confusion when the album was rereleased in 1961 but lacked Chet's rerecorded parts.

In 1958 Chet built a new home in the Forest Hills section of Nashville where he would live for the rest of his life. In the basement of the house was a studio measuring twenty-five by fifteen feet and a twelve-by-eighteen control room. In one corner of the studio was Chet's work bench, where he tinkered with his guitars and electronics. The studio contained up-to-date equipment. Later he added three-track stereo gear that was identical to the gear RCA installed in their studio. The equipment was expensive—eight thousand dollars—but allowed Chet to record at home and take his time. Chet told reporter David Halberstam, "I can take my time here. Can't take my time at the studio. We're making money there and when you're making money you really can't take your time. Here I can work at my own pace, when I feel like it, and do it right. This way, I have even more flexibility. It enables me to do what I try to do every time I make a record: keep searching for a better sound."

Chet continued to use the RCA studio for basic tracks and arrangements, then worked on his solos at home. Ever the perfectionist, Chet did not feel rushed in his home studio. It is difficult to ascertain which work he completed at RCA versus at home, or even how much time he spent working in his home studio. He was always conservative when he submitted a bill to RCA and undoubtedly spent more time than he billed.

The move-in date for the new Atkins home was October 23—the same day Chet was in Los Angeles recording his Hollywood album—so the entire move was left up to Leona.

The seventh annual Disc Jockey Convention was held in Nashville on November 21; Chet and other RCA executives attended. Simon Crum, the alter ego of Ferlin Huskey, had released a single, "Country Music Is Here to Stay." *Music Reporter* borrowed that title for its article, which stated that "country music is $50 million of the record industry's annual sales," adding that "up to 2500" will attend the convention. Through the efforts of the Country Music Association, "radio stations started programming more hours of C&W than before" as the CMA "carried out a public relations campaign for the country music industry." The same article singled out Steve Sholes, "who has done more toward breaking down the barriers . . . which he calls artificial . . . between country music and the wider markets" and cited his success from signing Elvis, Eddy Arnold, and Jim Reeves.[11]

There were pictures of Chet Atkins and Owen Bradley over a feature titled "Nashville Booms as Music Mecca." In the section on Atkins the magazine stated, "Football has its triple threat half back. The music industry has Chester Atkins. One of the finest artists in the nation with his self-styled guitar playing, Chet Atkins is rising to the fore as one of the best C&W A&R men in the trade" and noted that in his first year in charge of country A&R for RCA Chet produced a number of hits and released several albums of his own. "Chet's long association with country music, his own ability as a talent picker plus his good taste and way of handling people, has made him one of their most valuable employees," according to the article.[12]

A double page ad listed twenty-six RCAs artists, most of whom Chet produced.

Rock and roll has deep roots in country music; Elvis Presley, the Everly Brothers, Jerry Lee Lewis, Carl Perkins, and other rockabillies had records on the country charts. That led Jim Denny with Cedarwood Publishing, W. D. Kilpatrick, head of WSM's artist service bureau, Wesley Rose with Acuff-Rose, Jack Stapp with Tree, and Don Pierce with Mercury-Starday to meet with the trade magazines in an effort to stop putting rock and rollers on the country music charts. On the *Music Reporter*'s chart at that time, over half of the discs in the top ten on the country chart were by rock and roll singers.

During the 1956 to 1958 period, artists such as Elvis Presley, Carl Perkins, Jerry Lee Lewis, and the Everly Brothers enjoyed number-one songs on the country charts. Other artists, including Marty Robbins, Sonny James, Ferlin Husky, and Johnny Cash, appealed to the pop/rock audience and released music that did not seem to fit the definition of country.

In the October 20, 1958, issue of *Billboard*, the two country charts, "Most Played C&W by Jockeys" and "C&W Best Sellers in Stores," were combined into one chart, "Hot C&W Sides." From that point forward rock and roll seldom entered the country chart during the 1950s, although its influence could be heard in country recordings.

Ironically, many of the young country-based artists playing rock and roll during that period were later welcomed into the country fold. Some, like Johnny Cash, Marty Robbins, Sonny James, and Ferlin Huskey, elected to remain identified as country artists throughout their career. Others took a while longer. When Elvis died in 1977 his records were played more on country than on rock stations; in 1998 he was elected to the Country Music Hall of Fame.

CHAPTER 22

In July 1958, Mitch Miller's album *Sing Along with Mitch* entered the *Billboard* pop chart. It was number one in the nation for eight consecutive weeks and remained on the chart for almost four years. The album was a rebuke directed to rock and roll; the songs were old, familiar tunes. In November his second album, *More Sing Along with Mitch*, entered the *Billboard* chart and was also a huge hit. Then in December *Christmas Sing-Along with Mitch* was released and reached the number-one position.

Billed as Mitch Miller & His Orchestra and Chorus, he had a hit single in 1955 with "The Yellow Rose of Texas" in the same year that "Rock Around the Clock" by Bill Haley and the Comets hit. In 1956 he had a hit with "Theme Song from '*Song for a Summer Night*,'" and in 1958 another hit with the "March from the River Kwai and Colonel Bogey" from *The Bridge on the River Kwai*. Miller's debut included familiar songs that adults could sing from memory. In later years he would be better known for his intense hatred of rock and roll rather than for his hit albums and TV show.

Miller's success with his sing-alongs led Chet Atkins, on January 2, 1959, to be in RCA's studio with session musicians and eight backing vocalists to record "Peek a Boo Moon," "Backwoods," and a Merle Travis song, "Walkin' the Strings." The album was *Hum & Strum Along with Chet Atkins* and Chet, like Mitch Miller, led a listener participation album for those at home singing and playing. However, Chet did not enjoy a network TV show.

On the next "Hum and Strum" session, Anita Kerr had her group with the Jordanaires sing "Beautiful Brown Eyes," the classic "Tennessee Waltz," and the traditional "Birmingham Jail" while Chet played his guitar. Two days later, on February 3, Chet was in the studio for two more sessions recording songs for his *Hum & Strum Along with Chet Atkins* album. On the first session he recorded "The Prisoner's Song," "In the Good Ole Summertime," "Titanic," and the Hank Williams classic "Cold Cold Heart." On the second session he recorded "John Henry," "Goodnight Irene," a big hit for the Weavers in 1950, and "Music! Music! Music!," a number-one pop hit for Teresa Brewer in 1950. On February 5 Chet recorded two more songs, "Bill Bailey" and "Sweet Bunch of Daisies," which he had originally recorded in 1951 with the Beasley Singers.

On the first day of February Chet was in the RCA studio with Velma Williams Smith on guitar, Hank Garland on guitar, Bob Moore on bass, Buddy Harman on drums, and Floyd Cramer on piano. They recorded five songs. "Hello Bluebird" was written by Cliff Friends, who wrote Hank Williams's first hit, "Lovesock Blues"; "Rainbow" was written by Percy Wenrich and Alfred Bryan; Chet and Boudleaux Bryant wrote "Country Gentleman"; a classical piece, "Piano Concerto in B-Flat Minor," was by Tchaikovsky; and "Show Me the Way to Go Home" was by Irving King, a pseudonym for British songwriters Jimmy Campbell and Reg Connelly. Anita Kerr produced this session.

On March 31, 1959, Bill Porter began working as an engineer at the RCA studio in Nashville. Porter would be a key element in the success of Chet Atkins as producer. The engineering job came open because Bob Ferris, who "would probably make you mad in about five seconds," had "caused problems with Chet" too many times. According to Bill Porter, "Bob made some smart remark to Chet and that was it, he was transferred to another studio."

Bob Ferris cleared the calendar on his last day in order to teach Porter the system. On Monday morning Porter panicked, wondering what he had done and why. Chet entered the control room: "You look kind of troubled." "I told him I was having trouble figuring how everything works," replied Porter.

"Chet was good to me," said Porter. "He said, 'Don't worry about it. I'll help you.' He took the time and helped me get a handle on things. Because I was the new guy on board, nobody in the custom labels would use me. I was unknown. RCA had no choice but to use me because they employed me." The session began at seven o'clock in the evening and Chet told Porter after the first song, "Here, sit down and mix this first tune."

"I just wasn't ready for the pressure," remembered Porter. When the song was finished, Porter told Chet, "I can't do this anymore." Chet looked at Porter and said, "What? We got another two hours to go.

What's wrong with you? Sit down, Bill, and finish this session." Porter "got through it and from then on I kind of calmed down."[1]

In the studio was a stand with a red bulb on top and a switch for the engineer to turn on the light, indicating to musicians they were recording. There were no monitors, headphones, or windscreens on the mics, which hung on booms. The musicians did not have charts, although some made notes. Musicians heard the song, ran through it once or twice, and then recorded the master by memory. The acoustics at RCA's studio were not good when Porter arrived so he took sixty dollars from the petty cash fund and bought some fiberglass acoustic ceiling panels that he and assistant engineer Tommy Strong cut into triangles and hung at various heights. The studio sound improved dramatically. Those who saw the triangles called them "Porter's Pyramids."

As a producer "all Chet wanted to hear going into a session was the raw song, with minimum accompaniment, either with piano or guitar," said Porter. "He didn't hear the tune re-arranged but on the spot he would have a concept about the arrangement. He would usually have Anita Kerr help with the arrangements, if needed. Anita was a fantastic musician, certainly a crucial component to the sound on those sessions. Chet called the shots. He picked the songs. He always had good material because the publishers and songwriters trusted him." Porter noted that "if somebody was having problems during the session, Chet was very respectful. He never embarrassed anyone. He limited the interaction with the artist and musicians unless they were really having trouble. He might make a suggestion to the artist if a word or two needed some vocal inflection to improve the take."

"Chet was more in tune to the band because he was an instrumentalist," continued Porter. "If somebody played out of tune it would drive him crazy. He would sit there and say, 'Oh no! I am going to push the talk back button and say something and I don't want to embarrass the guy.' So sometimes he would just say, 'Bill, we got a little tuning problem.' He would press the button and say, 'Everybody check and see what's going on.' Usually this did the trick. When this didn't work Chet would ask me to turn down the level on the out of-tune musician. Chet just didn't want to hurt anyone."[2]

During the mid-1950s albums were issued only by the hottest country artists. It was principally a singles market and 78s constituted a larger percentage of the country market than for most other kinds of music. At first the industry looked at the album market as separate from the singles market, and many albums were recorded and released with no hit single. For the most part such albums consisted of covers of hits by other artists or the culls that had not earlier been deemed fit for release as a single. Eventually it occurred to the label businessmen that they could increase album sales by including a hit single, and for a time country albums generally consisted of one single and filler. The idea of an album with several hit singles emerged later.

The first *Billboard* charts for country appeared in 1944 and were labeled "folk." However, Senator Joseph McCarthy's communist witch hunts outed folk singers Pete Seeger, Sis Cunningham, and Woody Guthrie as potential communists. The industry sought to distance itself from the "folk" label, so in 1949 "folk" was replaced by "country and western," which seemed appropriate at the time since the singing cowboys were still popular.

Country artists had often recorded old or "folk" songs, but the commercial success of Harry Belafonte, whose songs "The Banana Boat Song (Day-O)" and "Jamaica Farwell" were labeled "Caribbean folk," led the way to "Tom Dooley" by the Kingston Trio, which became a number-one hit on *Billboard's* pop chart after its release in September 1958. Folk music seemed compatible with country, which also had story songs and traced its roots to the British Isles and Appalachia. As country music evolved, the term "country and western" or C&W on *Billboard's* charts was changed to "country" in 1962. Although the term "country and western" persists, the misnomer is indicative of a lack of awareness of contemporary country music.

In 1958 John D. Loudermilk moved to Nashville from North Carolina. Loudermilk, a talented musician, had written "A Rose and a Baby Ruth," a hit for George Hamilton IV in 1956, and "Sittin' in the Balcony," a rock hit for Eddie Cochran in 1957. "Chet had heard about me," said Loudermilk. "He sent out word that he wanted to meet me. I came over to meet him and that started a lifelong friendship." Loudermilk gave Chet a copy of "Recuerdos de la Alhambra" when they met.

Loudermilk had given himself a year to make it in the business and time was running out. On what was to be his last day Chet invited him to lunch and offered him a job at RCA. When Loudermilk went to work for Chet he "learned how to listen to songs. The first thing I learned was that you always play or present your best thing first. Steve Sholes taught Chet how to listen. Steve told Chet, 'I listened to songs when I started out for two years and didn't find one thing that was worthwhile. The worthwhile things come through disc jockeys and personal friends. They come in with notes from people. They come in the back door of your office. They don't come in through the front door.' Chet told me that and I said, 'I will listen with that in mind.' He said, 'Just listen to the first song and if there is nothing in the first song, there won't be anything after that. People generally play their best first.' I never found one thing in the year I worked for him."[3]

CHAPTER 23

A session for Eddy Arnold was set for April 24 and Chet and Eddy "used to talk about the session before it started," said Bill Porter. "Sometimes it was a week before. They'd come in and talk about the songs and pick out either three or four, whatever they wanted to do. If they were doing an album it was more than that. If it was just a singles session he always had one more than they figured they could do, just to see what would actually happen. That was primarily Chet's idea. Trying to get the maximum. And then if the thing was really grooving along, if there was ten minutes left or something like that they'd get in one more and sometimes that was a hit. Eddy just came in and sang. . . . He didn't get into analyzing things or directing the show at all."[1]

Three days later Arnold was back in the studio to record Jimmie Driftwood's "Tennessee Stud." Arnold had a difficult time recording the song, remembered Bill Porter. "For some reason he couldn't figure out where to come in and we did 72 takes on that song. Not all the way through, but 72 starts. It was about eight bars in. Even Chet was starting to get upset with him."[2]

On June 22, 1959, "Tennessee Stud" by Eddy Arnold entered the country chart in *Billboard* and was his first hit in almost two years. A month earlier "The Battle of New Orleans" by Johnny Horton had entered the country chart and become a ten-week number-one record and number one on *Billboard's* Hot 100. Both songs were written by Jimmie Driftwood, whose first album, *Jimmie Driftwood Sings Newly Discovered Early American Folk Songs*, was released in 1958. Tillman Franks, Johnny Horton's manager, heard "The Battle of New Orleans" on Ralph Emery's all-night show on WSM. Although most stations refused to play the song, which contained "damn" and "hell" in the lyrics, Emery could get away with it on his late-night show. Tillman Franks was convinced "Battle of New Orleans" would be a hit for Horton, so they arranged to get together with Driftwood for a rewrite. The new version featured cleaned-up lyrics.[3]

On the first day of July 1959, Chet, along with Hank Garland on guitar, James "Spider" Rich on rhythm guitar, Bob Moore on bass, Buddy Harman on drums, Floyd Cramer on piano, and Boots Randolph on saxophone, worked a split session; first Boots recorded "Sweet Talk" and then Chet recorded a Django Reinhardt song, "Django's Castle (Manoir de Mes Reves)," which became known to American musicians after "I did it first," said Chet. "It was called 'Manoir de Mes Reves.' I got somebody who spoke French to tell me what it meant and they said 'Castle of My Dreams.' So I called it 'Django's Castle' and recorded it and after that a lot of jazz people did it and the publisher, Gene Goodman, Benny's brother, called up and got all of Django's publishing rights, which I could have gotten if I'd been smart enough." The song had first been recorded by Reinhardt in 1942 and became so popular that he rerecorded it several times before his death in 1953. On Chet's recording he used a modified DeArmond foot-operated pedal that he adapted, changing the volume control with a "tone pot that moved from extreme bass to extreme treble." Author Mark Reinhart noted that "when the pedal was moved, it gave Chet's guitar a crying sound similar to that of a trumpet note being muted and then unmuted," adding that this "modified pedal was the first of its kind ever used with an electric guitar."[4]

During 1959 Gretsch provided Chet with a new Country Gentleman with a slightly wider neck than the standard; this single cutaway became his favorite Gretsch for the next nineteen years.

The Browns, Jim Ed, Maxine, and Bonnie, grew up in Arkansas and signed with Fabor Records, the same label that had Jim Reeves. The Browns recorded "Looking Back to See" in 1954 and joined the Louisiana Hayride. In the fall of 1954 they toured with Elvis Presley, who was also on the Hayride. They toured the Southwest for about a year as Elvis caused an uproar with his performances. In 1954 the Browns consisted only of Jim Ed and Maxine, adding sister Bonnie for their next chart record, "Here Today and Gone Tomorrow." The Browns were dissatisfied with Fabor Robison, who had a habit of not paying royalties. Reeves asked the Browns if they would join him when he contacted Steve Sholes about joining RCA Victor; they agreed. In 1956 Steve Sholes signed the Browns to RCA after they bought their way out of their Fabor contract.

The Browns first met Chet Atkins at a McGavock Studio session. As the musicians ran down the songs, "One particular gentleman stood out from the rest," wrote Maxine Brown in her book, *Looking Back to See*. "He had a nice, down-home smile that seemed to put everyone at ease. He strolled over to us and said, 'Hi, kids, my name is Chet Atkins. I want to welcome you to the RCA Victor family. Jim Reeves has told me all about you—so I've been looking forward to this for a long time. I'm going to be producing your session and also pick guitar.'" From that time forward said Maxine, "Chet would play the biggest, most important role in our career and lives."[5]

The Browns had songs that reached the charts between 1957 and 1959, but Maxine had a small child and a troubled marriage; she then became pregnant again, which severely limited the Browns' touring and finances. This forced the group's hand to quit the music business, so they called Chet to alert him. "I understand, kids," he reportedly replied. "I don't blame you at all," but then reminded them there were several months left on their RCA contract. "Why don't the three of you come on back to Nashville and do one last session?," asked Chet. "We'll call it the Browns' farewell. Pick out any song you've always wanted to record and I promise we'll do it."[6]

In Arkansas Bonnie had heard "The Three Bells" by the Andrews Sisters with the Gordon Jenkins Orchestra and Chorus. The Browns rehearsed it at home and on their way to Nashville. They met with Chet and sang the songs they wanted to record. Chet told them he loved their choice of "The Three Bells" but never shared that he had recorded it as an instrumental for *Chet Atkins in Hollywood*.

They went into the RCA studio and recorded "The Three Bells" and "Wake Up Jonah." Chet brought in Anita Kerr to help with the arrangement and the Anita Kerr Singers added background vocals. The songs came off well; Chet shared, "This is the big one. You've got the biggest hit ever . . . I've just recorded you a million-seller. There's no way you'll be quitting the business."

Chet so intensely believed "The Three Bells" could be a huge hit that he flew to New York to meet with RCA's top executives. According to Maxine Brown, "Chet said to the executives, 'I've produced a lot of hits but you have never promoted any of my artists. This time, I want you to listen to what could be the biggest record RCA ever had,'" and added, "If you don't get behind the Browns and this record, then you'll have to hire a replacement for me as A&R in your Nashville office."

"You would have to have known Chet," said Maxine, "who was normally low-key, to realize how out of character this was for him, especially when it came to standing up against the giants at RCA. Chet seemed to feel that there was something special in that recording and it rubbed off on us. His confidence in this one was exactly the encouragement we needed."[7]

Engineer Bill Porter had been working at RCA for only a few months and had to edit the tape before shipping it to New York. Preparing the tape, Porter "stretched the introduction" and thought he had "messed up," but he found "an alternate tape with a good intro and spliced it," without telling anyone. "That was a need to know situation," remembered Porter, "and I figured nobody needed to know."[8]

On July 4 RCA released "The Three Bells"; it remained number one on the *Billboard* country chart for ten consecutive weeks, was number one on the *Billboard* Hot 100 for four weeks, and stayed on that chart for almost five months.

Bill Porter was not involved in the earliest Everly Brothers hits like "Bye Bye Love" or "Wake Up Little Susie," but on July 7 he engineered a session where they recorded two songs written by Don Everly, "('Til) I Kissed You" and "Oh, What a Feeling."

"The biggest problem I had with them was they sang pretty loud," said Porter. "It was always a problem with them because sometimes they sang so hard and so loud but they also wanted the band up around them, too. They challenged you."[9]

On recording sessions, "Chet had an idea but not a preconceived idea. More of a concept for an arrangement of a song," said Porter. "It wasn't a rigid idea. Archie Bleyer was rigid. If it didn't fit what he thought it should fit, he'd fight with the arranger and fight with the engineers and fight with the artist."[10]

Buddy Harman and John D. Loudermilk came up with the idea of writing a semi–rock and roll song using a novelty instrument, and since Chet had an affinity for novelty records and unique sounds, the idea that he would record a song with a "boo boo stick," a section of heavy cardboard tubing cut to different lengths to give different tones, was appealing. The first version of "Boo Boo Stick Beat" did not quite come off, so they did a second version four days later where Chet played his new 1959 Country Gentleman. Although Buddy Harman is credited with playing the "boo boo stick" on this recording, he was joined by John D. Loudermilk and Floyd Cramer. The new version was a bit different after Chet and Buddy Harman came up with new ideas for the remake. The recording is in the key of B, with Chet only vamping on some B-based chords while Bob Moore slapped some riffs on his bass built around the B note. Chet used his modified DeArmond pedal for a wah-wah effect.

During the recording of "Boo Boo Stick Beat" the Chet Atkins Fan Club Convention was held so the studio was filled with club members. That caused dissension among members because three members from South Carolina "circulated a petition asking for my removal as president, saying the recording session took time away from the party, that I should not have brought my three-year-old daughter and that a new male president should be appointed," said fan club president Margaret Fields.

"I didn't need any more," remembered Fields. "My doctor had given me orders to 'straighten up' or he would send me to Our Lady of Peace Hospital in Louisville, which meant 'shock treatments.'" Margaret told Chet about the petition, but "he just laughed and said to forget about it. But it was clear to me that this was the end of the fan club." The Chet Atkins Fan Club formally ended in 1960. Back home, the Fields continued to visit and exchange letters with Chet.[11]

Chet and others had high hopes for "Boo Boo Stick Beat." "They thought that it was gonna come out and make a big rage like the hula hoop, but it didn't happen," Bob Moore recalled. The next day Chet joined Homer and Jethro in the studio to record "The Battle of Kookamonga," a comedic "answer song" to "The Battle of New Orleans."

In August, still flying high from their success on "The Three Bells," the Browns returned to the studio needing a strong follow-up. At the end of the second day Chet invited the group to have dinner with him at a restaurant in Printer's Alley. According to Maxine Brown, a "slightly inebriated" man insisted on singing at dinner. Finally the bartender relented and the man stood and sang "Scarlet Ribbons" a cappella. As soon as the man finished singing the group knew they had their follow-up song.

The "slightly inebriated" man who sang that song, probably directed by Chet, was Archie Campbell, an old friend of Chet's from their Knoxville days. The next day, September 24, they recorded "Scarlett Ribbons."[12]

CHAPTER 24

In October, Chet's *Mister Guitar* album was released with liner notes by *Nashville Tennessean* writer David Halberstam, who stated, "At present, Atkins's records sell better at Nashville's two major record-and-book stores, which cater to local eggheads, than they do at the country-oriented Ernest Tubb record store. Atkins's albums, like those of Floyd Cramer, transcend the country music field and appeal to suburban adult audiences."

During an afternoon session on October 7 for his next album, Chet was joined by Velma Williams Smith on guitar, Bob Moore on bass, Buddy Harman on drums, Floyd Cramer on piano, Boots Randolph on saxophone, and Anita Kerr, Dottie Dillard, Louis Nunley, and Gil Wright on vocals. The group recorded "Blue Rhapsody" (the title was later changed to "Teensville"); "Til There Was You," from the Broadway musical *The Music Man*; "Theme from *High Noon* (Do Not Forsake Me, Oh, My Darling)," a hit by Tex Ritter featured in the 1952 film *High Noon*, and the Boudleaux and Felice Bryant song "Take a Message to Mary," which had been a pop hit for the Everly Brothers that year. Those songs were intended for Chet's *Teensville* album.

The next day Chet returned to the studio with Boots Randolph and, with the Anita Kerr Singers providing background vocals, recorded "Sleep Walk," a number-one pop hit for Santo and Johnny in 1959, "One Mint Julep," an R&B hit for the Clovers in 1952 (and later a hit for Ray Charles), "Come Softly to Me," a number-one pop hit for the Fleetwoods in 1959, and "White Silver Sands," a pop hit for Don Rondo in 1957 (it had also been a hit for the Owen Bradley Quintet that year). "Night Train" had been a hit for Jimmy Forrest in 1952. "Hot Toddy" had been a pop hit for Red Foley in 1953. Chet used his adapted foot pedal to provide "wah wah" effects on those songs, many of them rooted in rhythm and blues, and Boots Randolph showed off his R&B chops.

The song "Teensville" was written by Wayne Cogswell, a guitarist who played on Sun's rockabilly releases by Ray Harris. Cogswell had recorded the song as Wayne Powers and sent it to Chet. "Teensville" comes pretty close to a rock number, but without the wild abandon that rock and roll is known for.[1]

On this album Chet attempted to compete with Duane Eddy and other rock guitarists. There were a number of rock and roll guitar hits during the 1956 to 1959 period. In addition to Duane Eddy and his hits "Rebel Rouser," "Forty Miles of Bad Road," and "Ramrod," there was "Rumble" by Link Wray and the Ray Men, "Raunchy" by Bill Justis, and "Honky Tonk" by Bill Doggett. However, Chet was never a rock and roll guitarist.

After his orchestral experience and success with the album *Chet Atkins in Hollywood*, Chet wanted more than ever to create a string section in Nashville, an ambition Owen Bradley shared. Anita Kerr became the key to success.

By 1959 Anita Kerr was working with Chet and RCA on a regular basis. She and her group of singers appeared on Chet's LPs *Mister Guitar* and *Teensville*. The Anita Kerr Singers stayed busy in studio but also made numerous appearances with various artists such as Eddy Arnold, Jim Reeves, and Patsy Cline—as well as their own appearances—on radio shows, at the Opry, and on national television. They were as much a part of the Nashville "A Team" as Buddy Harman, Bob Moore, and Floyd Cramer. In addition to leading her background vocal group, Anita increasingly worked as an arranger and producer.

Chet and Owen had used members of the Nashville Symphony, but they just played notes on the page and lacked the ability to "swing," so there was a sterile feeling to their recordings. At a club in Printer's Alley—probably the Black Poodle—Anita Kerr heard a group of African American musicians, including pianist Brenton Banks, who regularly performed with W. O. Smith, Andy Goodrich, Morris Palmer, and Louis Smith. The members of Smith's group were all on the faculty at Tennessee State University.

W. O. Smith described Brenton Banks as a "superb musician" and remembered "a gig where the piano was a minor third low. Instead of having everybody else play in a key a minor third lower, Brenton transposed his own playing a minor third higher. It meant that while we were playing in B-flat, Brenton played in D-flat, a key with more flats. I knew of very few musicians who could pull that off."[2]

Banks was a graduate of the Cleveland Institute of Music, a jazz and classical composer, an excellent pianist, and a top-flight violinist. That gave Anita Kerr the idea that Banks could be a key string musician for studio work because he could get classical violinists to "swing." "The string players were in the Nashville symphony orchestra so they were not used to working on pop songs and with a rhythm section," remembered Kerr. "That's why after a few months I suggested to Chet and Owen that I thought that Brenton Banks, whom I had heard play jazz piano, would be a good addition. I had heard that he also played good violin so what could be better for the string section than having a man as concert master who could help them to keep with the beat more closely?"[3]

In Los Angeles an idea had evolved about an "academy" for music awards; the movies had the Academy of Motion Pictures Arts and Sciences, which had presented Oscars since 1929, and the National Academy of Television Arts and Sciences had presented Emmys since 1949. That idea led to the formation of the National Academy of Recording Arts and Sciences, which held its first regular meeting on June 26, 1957, at the Beverly Hilton Hotel. Only creative music industry employees could become members, which eliminated executives, publishers, disc jockeys, and others strictly on the business side of the industry. The awards were named Grammys.

The first ceremony was held in the Grand Ballroom of the Beverly Hilton. The organization grew out of a reaction against rock and roll, which upset an industry rooted in big band and pop. The song of the year was "Nel Blu Dipinto Di Blu (Volare)," and *The Music from Peter Gunn* by Henry Mancini won Album of the Year. Vocalist honors went to Perry Como and Ella Fitzgerald. Elvis Presley, who had been responsible for about half of RCA's sales in 1958, was not nominated because there was no category for rock and roll or rhythm and blues. There was a category for "country and western," and that Grammy went to the Kingston Trio for "Tom Dooley." Although Chet was not a nominee, he was the producer for three nominations in the country and western category. The Everly Brothers were nominated twice, for "All I Have to Do Is Dream" and "Bird Dog," and Don Gibson was nominated for "Oh Lonesome Me."

In 1957 in *Western World* Frank Sinatra called rock and roll "the most brutal, ugly, degenerate, vicious form of expression it has been my displeasure to hear" and described Elvis's music as "deplorable, a rancid-smelling aphrodisiac."[4]

That summed up the view of the pop music establishment in 1959.

During 1959, the NARAS group in California reached out to their New York counterparts to establish a chapter, so the second awards ceremony was held simultaneously in Los Angeles and New York. The Song of the Year was won by a country and pop hit, "The Battle of New Orleans" by Johnny Horton, and Album of the Year was *Come Dance with Me* by Frank Sinatra. Sinatra and Ella Fitzgerald earned vocalist awards. The Mormon Tabernacle Choir won Best Performance by a Vocal Group, but "The Three Bells" by the Browns was nominated. In the Best Performance by a Top 40 Artist category Nat King Cole won, but Elvis's "A Fool Such as I" by was nominated. Elvis was also nominated in the Best Rhythm and Blues category for "A Big Hunk O'Love." Those recordings were done in Nashville at the new RCA studio (later known as RCA Studio B) while he was in the army.

Johnny Horton and "Battle of New Orleans" took honors in the Best Country & Western Performance category. The other four nominations were all produced by Chet: "Tennessee Stud" by Eddy Arnold, "Set Him Free" by Skeeter Davis, "Don't Tell Me Your Troubles" by Don Gibson, and "Home" by Jim Reeves. In the Folk category the Kingston Trio won their second Grammy, but "Tennessee Stud" by Eddy Arnold and the album *The Wilderness Road* by Jimmie Driftwood—both produced by Chet—were nominated.[5]

Chet recorded four songs on December 8. "Delicado" was a number-one hit in 1952 for Percy Faith and his Orchestra. "Sabrosa" was written by Cuban band leader Rene Touset, who had joined Desi Arnaz in California. "Maria Elena" was first recorded by Western Swing band leader Adolph Hofner with his Texans in 1940. In 1941 it was recorded by Lawrence Welk, and the Los Indio's Tabajaras recorded it in 1958. Chet recorded his "super lick" for the first time on "Maria Elena." On a Spanish (nylon string) guitar he played the lightning fast riff of thirteen notes in blinding speed through the use of hammer-ons, pull-offs, and sweep picking. He had previously recorded "The Peanut Vendor" in November 1956. On his first version Chet played his electric guitar, but on this version he played a classical guitar.[6]

Chet was in the studio on December 12 and recorded "Begin the Beguine," from the musical *Jubilee* and written by Cole Porter. "Macheta" was written by violin prodigy V. Scherzinger. "Poinciana (Song of the Tree)" was first recorded by Glenn Miller's band in 1943, before Bing Crosby recorded it for the 1952 film *Dreamboat*. "Yours" was a 1941 Jimmy Dorsey hit, a feat repeated in 1952 by British singer Vera Lynn.

During the period 1957 to 1959 Chet preferred to record and produce with guitarists Hank Garland, Grady Martin, Ray Edenton, and Velma Smith, drummer Buddy Harman, pianist Floyd Cramer, and bassist Bob Moore, yet he hired other musicians on occasion. Farris Coursey was hired on a few sessions, and Jim Reeves and Dave Rich played guitar on sessions for other artists. Jerry Shook, James "Spider" Rich, Jimmy Selph, Eddie Hill, and Louie Innis also played guitar on RCA sessions. Jerry Byrd, Lighnin' Chance, Junior Huskey, Joe Zinkan, and Ernie Newton were booked to play bass on occasion, and Marvin Hughes to play piano. Chet's favored musicians were sometimes unavailable, as they also played for Owen Bradley with Decca, Don Law with Columbia, and Ken Nelson with Capitol Records. They would often play three or four sessions a day.

Most of the major labels had organized a system of monthly release schedules for LPs. From the end of 1958 and into the first quarter of the year the revenue from LP sales exceeded that from singles. In radio the big news was "top 40 programming," which featured a smaller number of records being played regularly. Broadway cast recordings and movie soundtracks dominated album sales.

During 1959 Nashville and country music enjoyed a banner year with successful crossover hits from country artists such as Jim Reeves, Don Gibson, Johnny Horton, Johnny Cash, and Marty Robbins. Chet Atkins released three albums, *Chet Atkins in Hollywood*, *Hum & Strum Along with Chet Atkins*, and *Mister Guitar*, and two singles, "One Mint Julep" and "Teensville."

CHAPTER 25

On January 4 Chet and Hank Locklin met in Chet's office to hear a demo of "Please Help Me I'm Falling," written by Don Robertson and Hal Blair. Chet had first played the song for Jim Reeves, but he turned it down. Ironically, Hank Locklin had passed on "Four Walls."

Robertson played piano on the demo, and his "bent" or "slipped" note style inspired Chet to give a copy of the demo to Floyd Cramer so he could learn the style. Don Robertson was developing a style to record as an instrumental artist. Chet "thought Don had played that style piano because it fit the song so well."[1]

The next day it took only one take for the studio musicians and Hank Locklin to nail "Please Help Me I'm Falling" during an afternoon session.[2] The song was released in March and spent fourteen weeks in the number-one position on *Billboard's* country chart. It reached number eight on *Billboard's* Hot 100 chart and inspired an "answer song" from Skeeter Davis, who recorded "(I Can't Help You) I'm Falling Too," with Chet producing.

After the Hank Locklin session Chet alone recorded "Siboney," written by Ernesto Lecuona, one of Chet's favorite composers, and "El Relicario." "Tzena, Tzena, Tzena" had been a hit in 1950 for Gordon Jenkins and the Weavers, featuring Pete Seeger. "The Streets of Laredo," also known as "Cowboy's Lament," is an old western song, first published in 1910 in John Lomax's book *Cowboy Songs and Other Frontier Ballads.*

On February 23 Chet recorded four songs. "Lambeth Walk" came from 1937 British musical comedy *Me and My Girl* and was recorded by Django Reinhardt in 1939. "In a Little Spanish Town" was a hit for big bands led by Paul Whiteman, Ben Selvin, and Sam Lanin in 1927. Chet had recorded the tune with Homer and Jethro, released as the Country All Stars. "Lullabye of Birdland" became a jazz standard after a 1952 recording by the George Shearing Quintet. Chet acquired the arrangement for "Hot Mocking Bird," a nineteenth-century ballad, from steel guitarist Bud Isaacs. "Tammy," from the film *Tammy and the Bachelor*, was a number-one hit in 1957 for Debbie Reynolds.

The next day Chet recorded four more songs. "Goofus" was a 1931 chart hit for Wayne King, and in 1950 Les Paul recorded it. "Whispering" was a number-one hit for Paul Whiteman in 1920. "Theme from a Summer Place" was a number-one hit in 1960 by Percy Faith and His Orchestra; it was on the radio—and on the pop chart—when Chet recorded it. "Marie" was written by Irving Berlin and was a hit for Rudy Valley in 1929 and then for the Four Tunes in 1953. Chet had originally recorded the song with the Country All Stars. Those eight songs formed the core of his *Chet Atkins Workshop* album.

In March Elvis was discharged from the army and came to Nashville for a recording session. RCA was anxious to have a new single and album to release after the almost two-year hiatus. On the session Elvis and his band member Scotty Moore played guitar, joined by Hank Garland. Elvis's drummer, D. J. Fontana, was on the session along with Buddy Harman. Bob Moore was on bass, Floyd Cramer was on piano, and the Jordanaires provided background vocals. In the control room were Chet and Steve Sholes with engineer Bill Porter and a studio staffer, Jackie Nisely. The Jordanaires—Gordon Stoker, Hoyt Hawkins, Neal Matthews, and Ray Walker—provided background vocals.

"The usual tone of a recording session is one of controlled urgency, as running into overtime for the musicians can become very expensive for the record company," said Chet. "But with Elvis, we had long before decided that things just had to be allowed to take their natural course if we were to get the best results." That meant that Elvis started by singing some gospel songs with the Jordanaires, then played on the drums as the group "just let him move around the studio as the fancy took him. Whenever he stopped singing or doing anything, nobody said a word."

During the all-night eleven-hour session, Elvis recorded "Make Me Know It," "Soldier Boy," "Stuck on You," "Fame and Fortune," "A Mess of Blues," and "It Feels So Right." As soon as the session was finished, a tape of "Stuck on You" and "Fame and Fortune" was rushed to the pressing plant, where 1.4 million copies were pressed. Within forty-eight hours after Elvis walked out of the studio, copies of the single were shipped to radio stations. On April 4 "Stuck on You" entered the

Billboard Hot 100 chart and hit number one. "Fame and Fortune" reached number 17.[3]

On the last day of March Chet was in the studio to record "Boo Boo Rhapsody," a recording that has been lost, but on April 28 he recorded "Rainbow's End" with Buddy Killen and Doug Kirkham on "boo boo" sticks. That is most likely a remake of "Boo Boo Rhapsody.

That evening, Chet produced the first songs Jim Reeves did with a string section. The rhythm section consisted of Reeves and Hank Garland on guitar, Bob Moore on bass, Buddy Harman on drums, Marvin Hughes on keyboard, and the Anita Kerr Singers on backing vocals. The string session comprised Brenton Banks, Howard Carpenter, Solie Fott, Lillian Vann Hunt, Vernale Richardson, and Wilda Tinsley. On that session they recorded "I'm Getting Better" and five other songs. "I'm Getting Better" hit number three on the country chart and number thirty-seven on the pop chart.

"The way the strings worked," said Chet, "was I called Anita Kerr, but she wouldn't write string arrangements before the date. I'd hire a few violin players. I'd say, 'Write something for the violins, Anita' and she'd grab a pencil and write something, but it didn't give her time to get fancy and cute. I found I got the best results out of her when I did that. It was only when a large orchestra was used that Anita Kerr wrote out arrangements ahead of time."[4]

"He'll Have to Go" by Jim Reeves started showing up on *Billboard's* country chart at the end of 1959 and during the first week of February 1960, it knocked Marty Robbins's "El Paso" from the number-one spot. It stayed number one in the country charts for fourteen weeks. The song, written by DJ Joe Allison and his wife Audrey, was originally recorded by Atlanta-based artist Billy Brown on Columbia. Chet heard the record earlier that year and played it for Jim Reeves. "The boy who recorded it didn't have much of a voice because he couldn't hit those low notes," said Chet. After waiting to see if Brown's version was a hit, Chet and Jim decided to record it. The opening line in the song, "Put your sweet lips a little closer to the phone," was inspired by Audrey Allison's soft voice; her husband often told her those words when he called her.

"I heard it played on the radio," said Reeves. "I heard the original recording by Billy Brown. It sounded good to me. I went to Johnny Talley at WENO and asked him to lend me the record. I took it home and played it almost every day for three weeks. I sent it to Chet Atkins and he liked it too."

"It was Jim's idea to bring in Bob Moore to play electric bass," said Anita Kerr, "because Chet didn't normally think that way."[5] Bill Porter noted that Jim Reeves "was a guy that was totally in charge of his recording career and he picked the songs, in most cases, and he did the arrangements." Porter did not view Jim Reeves as a country artist. "The arrangements may have been that way but the type of singing he did wasn't country," stated Porter. "I think he was leaning towards the pop field because he knew that's where most of the money was. A lot of his songs, I think, may have had some country messages but they were not country arrangements. So he was trying to get the best of both worlds."

"Reeves looked down on hard country artists," continued Porter. "Sometimes at a session he'd make a comment. Somebody would have alluded to some hard-core country something and he'd say, 'I ain't gonna put that on my record.'"[6]

A tipping point for the Nashville Sound occurred in 1960 when Chet and Owen Bradley began using string sections regularly. Prior to that time they had only used background vocalists to enhance recordings. On March 27 Owen Bradley used a string section consisting of Brenton Banks, Howard Carpenter, Lillian Vann Hunt, and Vernal Richardson, all on violins, for a Brenda Lee session. Reeves did not like Brenton Banks being on his records. He "always fussed and griped about Banks," said Leo Jackson, lead guitarist in Reeves's band.[7]

On April 3 Elvis was back in the studio to finish *Elvis Is Back*, with Sholes and Chet producing. The musical lineup was the same as the previous session; in a productive night Elvis recorded twelve songs, including "Are You Lonesome Tonight?"

On April 14 Chet recorded three songs for his next album. Accompanied by bassist Bob Moore he recorded "Bonita" (written by James "Spider" Rich), "Whatever Will Be, Will Be," a hit single by Doris Day from *The Man Who Knew Too Much*, and "Sleep," which had been a number-one hit for Fred Waring's Pennsylvanians in 1924 and became his theme song. It had also been a chart record for Les Paul in 1953.

Nashville musicians Chet Atkins, Hank Garland, Boots Randolph, Brenton Banks, Floyd Cramer, Bob Moore, Buddy Harman, and eighteen-year-old vibe player Gary Burton went to Newport, Rhode Island, during the July Fourth weekend in 1960 to perform at the Newport Jazz Festival. RCA had planned to record the live set, but a large number of teenagers and college students arrived and discovered that all the seats had been sold and no hotel rooms were available. On Saturday night, July 2, fueled by alcohol, a riot broke out and the performance was canceled. However, the group began jamming on the front porch of the mansion RCA had rented for them; what started as a jam became an album.[8]

After the Riot in Newport by the Nashville All Stars was issued later in 1960 and showed Nashville musicians in a jazz setting. The group recorded a Chet Atkins original, "Nashville to Newport," Gershwin's "'S Wonderful," and "All the Things You Are" by Oscar Hammerstein and Jerome Kern. They also recorded "Riot Chorus," written by Hank Garland and Boots Randolph, as well as "Relaxin'" by Jimmy Guinn, both of which appeared on Hank Garland's *Jazz Winds from a New Direction.*

The Other Chet Atkins was released in September; the cover was an original oil painting of Chet in a gaucho outfit.

Chet and Eddy Arnold wanted to create a country music festival patterned after the Newport Jazz Festival and went to Knoxville in August to discuss the project with Jack Comer, a promoter, and Fred McCallum, manager of the under-construction city coliseum. Plans were made for the first festival to be held in July 1961 at the University of Tennessee. When a reporter asked Eddy Arnold why the festival was not going to be held in Nashville, Arnold replied, "In Nashville they take us for granted. I haven't been with the Opry for 12 years but I've always said Nashville should put up signs on the highways welcoming people to the Opry. The Chamber of Commerce should do this to give the Opry fair recognition.[9]

Chet was in Hollywood at RCA Victor Studio 1 on September 6 to record the theme song for the film *The Dark at the Top of the Stairs*, composed by Max Steiner. Backed by a large orchestra, Chet played his Gretsch electric; Al Hendrickson and Alfred Viola also played guitar. Later, Chet had the tape shipped to Nashville and worked on his guitar part until he was satisfied. Chet was back in RCA's Nashville studio two days later and recorded "Hocus Pocus," written by Spider Rich, who also played guitar on the session.

What to label "country" music was an ongoing issue. *Billboard's* first country chart in 1944 was labeled "Jukebox Folk Records." In 1949 the chart became "Country and Western," then in 1962 "Hot Country Singles," as the term "Country" began to replace "Country and Western." However, professionals thought the term "country" inhibited the music's appeal.

The *Music Reporter* noted that "for some years now there has been an underlying discontent in some places that 'country' is not expressive enough for this universally loved and widely played music. 'Country music' is not necessarily 'country' in the sense that it derives from the farmhouse or those remote places having primarily an agricultural economy. It's not strictly 'blue grass' because it's generally broader, richer and of more musical stature," adding that "for the record novice . . . the name may cause country music to be subconsciously downgraded. To be a devotee of country music today, most people know, implies no lack of sophistication."

In his column in the *Music Reporter*, Charlie Lamb, writing about the popularity of country music, stated that "despite its contribution to the arts and proven commercial value [country music] still does not command unanimous acceptance." It was his opinion that "many are prejudiced by connotation of the words 'country music.' Mebbe it needs a new name."[10]

During 1960 Chet Atkins was pictured with forty-seven other artists in an advertisement showing the stars of the Grand Ole Opry. Shortly after the Opry announced that a number of artists, including Chet, had been fired for failing to make the required number of appearances. However, Chet was never a member and always appeared as a "guest artist." "I never worked for the Opry," said Chet. "I never signed any papers or nothing. In 1960 I got so busy producing records that I stopped playing the Opry and the paper said a whole bunch of us was fired because we hadn't appeared enough . . . I thought it was kinda funny."[11]

Chet's suggestion to Floyd Cramer that he write a song in the slipped note style paid off. By November "Last Date," produced by Chet, was number two on the pop chart and number eleven on the country chart. The song stayed at number two for a month, unable to dethrone "Are You Lonesome Tonight" by Elvis. Floyd had played on Elvis's record, and Chet had produced both.

Floyd explained his "slipped note" style of piano playing: "You hit a note and slide almost simultaneously to another. It's sort of a near-miss on the keyboard. You don't hit the note you intend to hit right away, but you 'recover' instantly and then hit it. It is an intentional error and actually involves two notes."[12]

Don Robertson was shocked when he heard "Last Date" on the radio and went to see Chet, who explained what had happened to create the Floyd Cramer hit and that he had no idea that Robertson was developing that style for his own career as an instrumentalist. That "slipped note" style made a hit for Hank Locklin's "Please Help Me I'm Falling" and for Floyd Cramer's "Last Date" and became the defining sound for Cramer as an instrumentalist—but it stopped Robertson from having any chance to claim that style as his own and derailed his instrumentalist career.

Chet's last 1960 recording session occurred on November 8 when he covered three former Elvis hits, "Blue Moon of Kentucky," "Heartbreak Hotel," and "It's Now Or Never." The former was never released, but the other two appeared on *Guitar Genius*, released on Camden and containing five Jim Atkins vocals from the aborted *My Brother Sings* album.

Chet Atkins released three albums in 1960—*Teensville*, *The Other Chet Atkins*, and *Chet Atkins' Workshop*—and was featured on *After the Riot at Newport*. He also released the *Chet Atkins Favorites* EP, which included "Malaguena," "Trambone," "Cecilia," and "El Cumbanchero."

It had been fifteen years since the end of World War II. Although in 1945 Nashville did not have a single recording studio or label, by the end of 1960 it was the third largest U.S. recording center, behind New York and Los Angeles, and was known universally as "Music City U.S.A."

CHAPTER 26

In 1961 Anita Kerr joined RCA as Chet's assistant. She had worked with him in the past as an arranger, and the Anita Kerr Singers had sung on recordings that Chet had produced, but she was unable to join RCA until she was no longer under contract with Decca. Her role included working as a vocal group leader, arranger, and occasional producer for Eddy Arnold, Hank Snow, Willie Nelson, Jim Reeves, and Floyd Cramer. She was also a recording artist, recording as Anita & th' So-And-So's. Although she served as a producer at RCA, she never received production credit.

Anita's first venture with Chet was as string arranger and producer of his album *Most Popular Guitar*. The sessions began in February when Chet recorded "My Dear Little Sweetheart," composed by Johnny Smith. The song was in the film *Lili* in 1952 and became a hit for Dinah Shore. He also recorded "Rock-a-Bye-Baby," written by Mann Curtis and Guy Wood. On those songs were strings and backing vocals by the Anita Kerr Singers.

In March Chet recorded four songs: "Stay as Sweet as You Are" from the 1934 film *College Rhythm*; "When Day Is Done," first recorded by Harry Pollack's Club Maurice Diamonds in 1926; "East of the Sun (West of the Moon)," first recorded by Hal Kemp in 1934; and "It Ain't Necessarily So," written by George and Ira Gershwin for *Porgy and Bess*. That same month Chet recorded an additional three songs: "Vanessa," first recorded by Hugo Winterhalter in 1952; "My Prayer," recorded by Glenn Miller and by the Ink Spots, and a 1956 number-one record for the Platters; and "Intermezzo," from the 1936 Swedish film *Intermezzo: A Love Story*.

George Hamilton IV had a hit with "A Rose and a Baby Ruth" when he was a student at the University of North Carolina. The song peaked in 1957 on the ABC-Paramount label, for which Hamilton continued to record, releasing pop chart singles. However, Hamilton wanted to be a country artist.

His manager, Connie B. Gay, put him in touch with Jim Denny, who signed Hamilton. His old friend John D. Loudermilk, produced sessions of country songs over a six-month period, so Hamilton received country airplay on several songs. Hamilton's contract with ABC-Paramount was set to expire in mid-1961, so he asked Chet to produce him. Chet agreed to give it a try.

Atkins produced Hamilton's first RCA session which resulted in a top-ten hit, "To You and Yours (From Me and Mine)," written by Bill Anderson. His next session yielded another chart record, "Three Steps to the Phone," written by Harlan Howard. "If ever there was a true role model/mentor in my life it would be Chet," remembered Hamilton later. "He's always been my hero because he's so Lincolnesque—just a very gentle, intelligent, quiet but witty, sensitive, poetic man."[1]

Chet had a skeleton in his closet when it came to George Hamilton IV. In 1956, when Hamilton's "A Rose and a Baby Ruth" was hitting, Chet recorded "A Rose and a Baby Ruth" with a group composed of Jerry and Jan Crutchfield, two brothers from Kentucky, and himself. The group was named the Country Gentlemen, the same name Hamilton's band used on their original recording.

On February 15, 1961, Chet produced a session with Eddy Arnold, backed by guitarist Velma Smith, pianist Bill Purcell, and a new bass player in town, Henry Strzelecki. Strzelecki first came to Nashville with Baker Knight for a session in January 1957. Knight had written hits for Ricky Nelson and several others. Baker Knight and the Knightmares were signed to Decca, and Owen Bradley produced the session, part of an ongoing effort by Music Row to capture the rock and roll audience. During the session Bob Moore was waiting in the wings in case Strzelecki couldn't cut it. "We played for four hours and when we finished the only person that said anything to me at all was Hank Garland," said Strzelecki.

In November 1960 Strzelecki visited Nashville and reconnected with Hank Garland and sat in with Garland's band at the Carousel Club in Printer's Alley. His first session came when Garland hired him to play on an Eddy Arnold album. Chet Atkins was the producer on those sessions and that's how Strzelecki met Chet, who began to use him regularly on recording sessions.

As a producer, "Chet was meticulous in the fact that he never did quite let us know exactly why he would want us to do it again or not," said Strzelecki. "He'd just say, 'Let's try one more time' if he wanted us to record the song again. But usually it was a nice way of telling us that we hadn't got it cut yet. He was very nice about doing that."

During a typical session for Chet, the musicians came into the studio and "the first thing we would do is get a cup of coffee and then we'd get set and we'd be ready to listen to the first song and they'd either bring a tape in and play it for us or somebody would pick for us on the guitar. The writer would come in sometimes if the artist didn't know it well enough at the time, and then teach it to all of us. Most of the time it was the artist because they did know the songs and they had gotten together with Chet the day before and they would figure out what they were going to do with the song."

"Chet always had a lot of ideas for the songs he produced," said Strzelecki. "He would have licks, basically, to go in his songs. In other words, guitar licks, piano licks. If the bass was playing too much or the drums was playing too much, which was usually the case, he'd tell us, 'Now simplify that and you've got it.'"[2]

Chet was widely respected as a record producer. Eddy Arnold stated that "Chet was a great producer. He would talk very slowly and understated, 'Do you think you can sing it better, Eddy?' I'd say, 'I might be able to Chet.' That was how he was, low key. Chet had a great ear."

"He treated everybody honestly," said Arnold. "Chet's whole life his attitude was just honesty. He was just Chet. There were no airs about him at all."[3]

"Chet was a great producer," said Ray Edenton. "He was a great fellow as far as I'm concerned. Chet was so far above others, especially the rhythm players as far as what he knew. He would never ask you to play something he knew you couldn't play. He knew what you could play and what you couldn't play. I had been on several sessions back in those days with him when he was producing somebody. I said, 'Chet, it'll take me two hours for me to learn that song.' He'd say, 'Don't worry about it. I'll play it.' He would just walk into the studio and play it. He never put pressure on you to do it."

"Chet could be very stern," continued Edenton. "Chet didn't have much to say, but he heard everything. He might be sitting in the control room playing his guitar but he still heard it. If you hit a bad note into that microphone he would come up and say, 'Play it this way.' There was this artist in the control room with him one time and this person said to Chet, 'Why don't you go out into the studio and produce this thing?' He said, 'They've got six producers out there now. They don't need any more.'"[4]

"Chet was a really great producer but he never really asserted himself much," said Buddy Harman. "He let us, the band, do it our way. If he had an idea, he would tell us about it but he mainly left it up to the musicians. Of course, he always had a good group of players who could handle it."[5]

Sometimes during a session Chet's humor would kick in. During one session, steel guitarist Jimmy Day was laying out and Chet pushed the talk-back button on the console and said, "Jimmy, there's a wonderful opportunity here for a steel guitar." He once corrected Carl Story, who was singing "Once-t." Chet reminded him, "There's no 't' in 'Once.'"[6]

Chet was quiet in the studio with an occasional smile or a "I like that" if he thought the song might be a hit, but he didn't lavish praise on an artist who had just recorded a song. "I knew there were so many ingredients that went into making a hit that it scared me to get someone's hopes up," said Chet. "There were so many times that I made what I thought was a great record, and then it was lost because of sales and promotion."

Chet had only once pronounced a song a hit as soon as it was recorded—Floyd Cramer's "Last Date. "I was sure about it," he told Ralph Emery. I "knew it was a hit sound and that it would change the whole industry as far as piano playing went."[7]

During the 1960s there were four major record producers in Nashville—Owen Bradley with Decca, Don Law with Columbia, Ken Nelson with Capitol, and Chet with RCA. Each of them handled producing a little differently. "Every session was different, whether it was because of the producer or the artist," said Buddy Harman. "Owen was probably the most involved from a production standpoint. He'd usually worked out an arrangement well ahead of time, but still left the musicians room to improvise. Ken Nelson and Don Law were more prone to have the musicians work things out. Don was the only one who wasn't a musician, so he gave us a lot of leeway. Chet varied. Sometime he was very involved, and of course, he'd play guitar a lot of the time. But there were other times that he stayed in the control room."[8]

There were other producers in Nashville, some on staff with the major labels and some with small, independent labels. Part of a producer's job in Nashville was to listen to songs from songwriters and publishers and find something that fit the artist. Sometimes a song was almost "there" but needed some touching up before it could be recorded and a producer might make—or suggest—those changes. Songwriters expected feedback that let them know whether a song that was put on hold would actually be recorded. Some of the less ethical producers demanded cowriting credit or a piece of the royalties before they would cut a song.

As a producer, Chet "touched up a lot of songs he didn't take credit for," said Billy Ed Wheeler. "He also created some great introductions to songs as the producer. In other words, he made those songs work because of his ingenious way of writing the intros and getting you into the song." When it came to taking credit for a song that he didn't write, "Chet never did that," said Wheeler.[9]

"Chet could have taken advantage of the songwriters when he was producing, by owning a percentage of the music," said Wayne Carson. "This is a common practice. He never did this, never one time." Other producers might "figure out a way of putting it through their production company so they can get a piece of the action. Chet never did this. He could have made so much money by abusing the songwriters that way. Chet thought too much of the songwriters and their talent to exploit them. Chet thought, 'I have my money, you have your money. This is your talent and this is my talent. We will all get our fair share.'"[10]

Although Chet could have been a musician on every record he produced, he felt he had better success when he didn't play on records he produced because "I found . . . that if I was out in the studio all the time I'd miss something and be unhappy with the session when I got through. Once in a while I'd play on a tune but most of the time I stayed in the control room and listened."

Chet had started out making $7,500 a year and the budgets "topped out at around $3,000, but "when I started out making a lot of hits, I got them to raise my salary to $30,000."[11]

Artists and songwriters are often needy people with insecurities because they need constant support and encouragement. They also need others—the producer, executives, studio musicians—to make them successful. Those artists looked to Chet because they needed him to come up with hit songs, make hit records, and then have the record company get behind them. It was a lot of responsibility. In his later years Chet said, "If I had to do it over, I think I could have been a much better producer. I look back and think I should have smiled more, or danced around the room like Paul Cohen did if he liked a record. Paul would jump up and down and say 'This is a hit!' That is one of the best attributes a producer can have—the ability to enjoy the music and make the artist enjoy the experience."[12]

As he began working regularly on sessions Henry Strzelecki soon learned the rules of being an effective studio musician. "Number one is you had to be there on time. You were not late," stated Strzelecki. "On a recording session, it was strictly business. You were not late and you were there. If you were booked for the normal three-hour session, unless it was on a break or a playback and they were trying to do something else, you didn't leave your post. You did not leave where you were sitting and you didn't go and use the telephone. We had to sit there and learn the songs. Back then, we remembered the songs, we didn't write out numbers. We remembered everything and the musicians were so good they could memorize a song after listening to it once."

"Back then they didn't allow the bass to be very loud nor the drums because they really were just introducing drums into country music," said Strzelecki. "They didn't use drums on the Opry. Drums were just more to be seen than heard at that time, and not much bass either. When we went to electric bass, they started putting a lot more bass on the records and they tried to get it on but what would happen is the grooves (on a record) are only so big and they only take so much. You lost a lot of bottom because the grooves were only so wide."[13]

"Chet always asked Buddy to play percussion a little lighter on his sessions," said Bill Porter. "He was concerned the drums would cover the guitar. Chet was always working with the idea that less is more. There are times when things get too busy and the textures cancel each other out."[14]

In 1961, Gretsch changed the Country Gentleman from a single cut-away to a double cut-away. The company copied Gibson, which had sold double cut-aways since 1958. The fake "f-holes" of the Country Gentleman were not stenciled on. Chet's 1959 single cutaway continued to be his favorite guitar and the one he used on most of his sessions when he used an electric guitar.

Jimmy Webster introduced the mechanical damper, also known as a mute, so the strings on a guitar could be deadened with the flip of a switch instead of pressing the palm of the hand on the strings. He also introduced a padded back to the guitar to make it more comfortable.

Chet never liked the new "gimmicks" developed by Webster. "He was always coming up with ideas, like the Gretsch 'tuning fork' and the pad on the back, the mute and all that bullshit. I never liked it! He said, 'You got to give them something different all the time. It's like a car, you've got to come up with something new: they want new features.' And I guess he was right. He was a hell of a salesman."[15]

CHAPTER 27

John D. Loudermilk said that Chet "came to me one day and said, 'John, I'm getting too deep into jazz. I need a song to bring me back to my roots. I picked up this guitar and 'Windy and Warm' just fell out," said Loudermilk. "I had never played those licks before in my life. I did a lot of things in open tuning. There was nobody in town that could write that stuff down. The stuff he recorded of mine was in open tuning but he changed them to standard tuning. He lost the musical flavor by doing it that way. There is just too much going on. You can't keep everything going on in standard tuning. Anyhow, that is where 'Windy and Warm' came from."

"Every time I saw Chet's hands, I would touch his hands," said Loudermilk. "They were just muscles. He had the most beautiful hands. Many times I would sit and marvel at them. I'd laugh and say, 'Sir, may I look at your hands?' His fingernails were always immaculate. I looked at his hands as the perfect work of art."[1]

On April 5 Chet recorded "Windy and Warm" in the RCA studio for a 45 single release. Chet played the song on a nylon-string classical guitar at a relatively slow tempo. The record did not chart.

There was a conflict in the NARAS group of music industry professionals between those who wanted to award "serious" music (i.e., jazz and classical) and those who leaned toward awarding popular music. That was reflected in the nominees for the Grammy Awards presented in April 1961 in Los Angeles and New York. Nominees for Album of the Year included Harry Belafonte, Frank Sinatra, and Nat King Cole as well as *Brahms: Concerto No. 2 in B Flat* by Sviatoslave Richter and a comedy album by Bob Newhart, *The Button Down Mind*, which won the award.

Chet did not receive a nomination, but his influence as a producer was felt. In the Record of the Year category, Elvis was nominated for "Are You Lonesome Tonight." Nominated for Song of the Year was

"He'll Have to Go," written by Charles Grean and Joe and Audrey Allison. In the Male Vocalist category Elvis was nominated for "Are You Lonesome Tonight" and Jim Reeves for "He'll Have to Go." In the "Folk" category the album *Songs of Billy Yank and Johnny Reb* by Jimmie Driftwood, which was produced by Chet, was nominated. The Best Country & Western Grammy was won by Marty Robbins for "El Paso," but nominees "Please Help Me, I'm Falling" by Hank Locklin and "He'll Have to Go" by Jim Reeves were produced by Chet.

On May 1 and 2, Chet supervised three sessions where Don Gibson recorded his *Girls, Guitars and Gibson* album. Gibson had been beset with problems from drinking and drugs, but a detox facility in Ashville, North Carolina, helped him come clean.

"That was one of the best times of my life in recording," remembered Gibson. This was the first Nashville recording session for Colorado jazz guitarist Johnny Smith, who was invited by Chet. The two were friends, and Chet invited him because Smith could sight read music and "just to make it possible that we could get together and visit."[2]

Chet had an incredibly busy week; on Sunday, May 6, he was in Miami at a music business convention, then on Tuesday, May 8, he was in the studio with pop star Rosemary Clooney. Chet, with Richard Peirce helping in production, oversaw a session where Clooney recorded three songs, then four more the next day.[3]

"One of the reasons I came here," said Clooney, "was because of the Nashville musicians. It's the only group in the world that works together day after day, session after session. . . . Of course," gesturing with her eyes and hands, "another reason was Chet Atkins. He has an ear for a hit—and I need a hit."[4]

That same week Chet produced a session on Ann-Margret, a young Swedish dancer and actress. She told a *Nashville Tennessean* reporter that she "got her big break by wearing black tights and an orange sweater when she auditioned for comedian George Burns, who was at the Sahara Club in Las Vegas."[5]

Jim Denny with Cedarwood Publishing sent Chet a song, "I Just Don't Understand," for Ann-Margret. It had been written by Kent Westberry and Mary John Wilkin, and on that demo Charlie McCoy played harmonica. Chet told Denny before the session that he wanted to record the song on Ann-Margret and wanted the harmonica player to play exactly what he played on the demo. On the day of the session, Denny took Charlie McCoy over to the studio to introduce him to Chet, whom McCoy had auditioned for in 1959 playing guitar and singing “Johnny B. Goode.” “You played a black Gibson Les Paul Custom, right?,” said Chet when he was introduced to McCoy, who was surprised that Chet remembered him.

When McCoy arrived at the studio, “I was overwhelmed,” he said. “First, Ann-Margret was a beautiful blond bombshell, just eighteen years old, and my twenty-year-old self was entranced. And then I looked around the room, saw the band I was going to be working with, and had to pinch myself.” That band included Floyd Cramer, Bob Moore, Buddy Harman, and three guitarists—Hank Garland on lead, Ray Edenton on rhythm, and Harold Bradley on tic-tac bass.

“Chet was a very soft-spoken man,” remembered McCoy. “He seemed to enjoy giving young musicians a chance to make it in the business, often hiring people who showed great potential and using them for sessions until they were in great demand. Then he would let them spread their wings and give a new crop of musicians an opportunity to prove themselves.” At the end of the session Chet said to McCoy about the early audition, “You should have played that harmonica for me. We might have done something.”[6]

After the session Bob Moore asked McCoy if he was available for an upcoming Roy Orbison session. McCoy was; in fact, his appointments book was empty. During the Orbison session, McCoy played harmonica on the intro to “Candy Man,” and from that point forward his appointments book began filling up.

Chet’s philosophy of producing “seemed to be to hire some of the best musicians he could find—especially the younger ones who needed an opportunity to prove themselves—and give them the room to create,” said McCoy, who noted that “Chet also had a knack for pushing people to play things that were out of their comfort zone.” Chet once asked McCoy to play some notes on a vibraphone for a tune “that didn’t need harmonica.” That led McCoy to buy a set of mallets and practice to learn the vibraphone. Along the way McCoy learned a valuable lesson about being a session musician. He had grown a bit cocky and, during a session, “I started feeling my oats, playing nearly every lick I knew.” Grady Martin pulled him aside: “You’re playing too much. Listen to the words. If you can’t hear and understand every word, you’re playing too much.”

“This was the best advice that anyone ever gave me about studio playing," said McCoy. "For the rest of my career, I let this be my guide: Less is more."[7]

On Tuesday, May 23, Chet began recording his Christmas album, so engineer Bill Porter decorated the studio so everyone would get into the Christmas spirit. It was not easy; the weather was warm and beautiful. On the second session of the day, Velma Williams Smith replaced Ray Edenton on rhythm guitar and Morris Palmer replaced Buddy Harman on drums. Palmer was an African American jazz drummer who was known as "the singing drummer." According to W. O. Smith he was perhaps "the finest jazz drummer east of the Mississippi and south of the Mason-Dixon line," a "driving metronome who inspired top play and interaction. He only tolerated the best and was uncompromising in his relationships with others who dared to play with him. Everything had to be just right."[8] The next day there were back-to-back sessions again, and Chet recorded six songs and a medley.

Chet used both his electric and classical guitars on this album, which was released with all of the electric guitar numbers on side one of the LP and those on classical guitar on side two. Although most of the songs were traditional numbers, Chet recorded "Jingle Bell Rock," a hit for Bobby Helms in 1957.[9] Anita Kerr produced the *Most Popular Guitar* and Christmas albums but was uncredited.

Elvis was in Nashville to record on June 25. The producer for the session was Steve Sholes; although Chet isn't listed on that session, if Sholes was in town and Elvis was recording, Chet was there. Chet did not like the all-night sessions that Elvis preferred. "When Elvis first signed with RCA he recorded in the afternoons, but when he got so big he started coming in during the night so fans wouldn't congregate outside the studio," said Chet. "I finally started going in around ten o'clock p.m. just to say hello, then leave."[10]

On September 6, Chet and Eddy Arnold were in the studio, and the singer recorded some of his old hits with background vocals by the Anita Kerr Singers. Looking for a "smoother" sound, Arnold recorded with a musical lineup of Floyd Cramer, Henry Strzelecki, and Buddy Harman, with Velma Williams and Hank Garland on guitars. Two days later Hank Garland was in a near-fatal car accident near Springfield, Tennessee, which left him severely brain damaged and ended his career as a musician.

Shortly before the accident, Garland "was having trouble with his wife, marital problems," said Henry Strzelecki. "He said to me, 'If anything ever happens to me, go see Chet. He will take care of you.'" Garland had been booking Strzelecki on sessions because the producer often called the session leader and told him to book the musicians. Garland often served as session leader. "It wasn't two weeks later when he had his wreck," said Strzelecki. "I don't know what happened there; he either had a premonition or something. He injured his brain and could never play again. We thought maybe some of his ability would come back. They put him on a lot of sessions, but turned the mic off and just let him sit there."[11] Garland was thirty-one when his music career came to an end. Chet always claimed that he was the best guitarist in Nashville.

There was a session for Porter Wagoner where the singer recorded "Misery Loves Company," written by Jerry Reed. That session marked the arrival of Reed as a hit songwriter.

Jerry Reed moved to Nashville in 1961 and made an immediate impact on Chet Atkins. Reed was part of the Atlanta group that included Ray Stevens and Joe South, all signed to Bill Lowery's organization. Reed began playing at an early age and cut his first record, "If the Good Lord's Willing and the Creek Don't Rise." Lowery signed Reed to his National Recording Corporation (NRC) label in 1958. His song, "Crazy Legs" was covered by Gene Vincent.

Reed was drafted and spent two years in the army. At the beginning of 1962 his song "Misery Loves Company" became a number-one hit for Porter Wagoner. He soon became a session guitar player. Chet noted that he had begun losing interest in the guitar—had thought he had done all he could do—until he heard Jerry Reed play. Inspired by Reed, Chet's playing was rejuvenated.

On October 3 Chet recorded songs on back-to-back sessions for his *Down Home* album. His previous releases had been in the "easy listening" or "cosmopolitan" (often referred to as "countrypolitan") vein, and he wanted to get back to a more "country" sound. Backing him on the first session was Henry Strzelecki on bass, Floyd Cramer on piano, Charlie McCoy on harmonica, Boot Randolph on saxophone, and Morris Palmer on drums. The overall feel of the album is "relaxed." The songs came from a wide variety of sources. "I Am a Pilgrim" has been traced back to the early nineteenth century. “Give the World a Smile” was the theme song of the gospel group the Stamps Quartet. “Steel Guitar Rag” is credited to Leon McAuliff, who recorded it with the Bob Wills Texas Playboys in 1936. “Little Feet” is a children’s song with the lyrics “Put your little foot right down.” “Never On Sunday” came from a film by the same name in 1960. “Girl Friend of the Whirling Dervish” is a novelty song that was in the film *Garden of the Moon* in 1938. “Salty Dog Rag” is traced back to the early 1900s and was first recorded by Papa Charlie Jackson. “Trambone” was written by Chet, who played the bass string like a trombone slide, hence its name. That was the second time he recorded the song. “Yellow Bird” is a Haitian song originally titled “Choucoune.” Arthur Lyman had a hit with it in 1961. “Yellow Bird” and “Wild Orchids” were held for his *Caribbean Guitar* album, released the next year.

During 1961 a revised *In Hollywood* album was released with a new cover: a photograph of a voluptuous blonde in tight gold slacks. The changes were more than just packaging. According to Pat Kirtley, who has extensively researched the *Hollywood* album, during the original recording Chet’s guitar was plugged directly into the board to avoid “bleed” of his guitar with the orchestra. That recording was submitted to RCA in a box marked “Master-Chet Atkins in Hollywood.” Chet had a copy of those orchestral tracks shipped to him in Nashville, where he rerecorded his parts and submitted that version to New York, which was stored in a box with the same label. The two boxes sat side by side; when the album was rereleased the first tape was pulled and used instead of the second one, which had Chet’s overdubs.[12]

Chet also released two studio albums, *The Most Popular Guitar* and *Christmas with Chet Atkins*, and a compilation album, *Chet Atkins Plays Great Movie Themes*, in 1961.

CHAPTER 28

"Everybody says Chet was great at picking songs, but he was great at picking musicians," said Henry Strzelecki. "He was the ultimate at knowing who was good and who was not. . . . When you got someone like Chet, who was willing to go to bat for you, people would never question what he said or recommended. Chet should be credited for using Velma at a time in a business with so many biases against women."[1]

During 1962 Chet's go-to musicians were Grady Martin, Ray Edenton, Velma Smith, Sam Pruett, and Harold Bradley on guitars; Henry Strzelecki, Bob Moore, Junior Husky, and Joe Zinkan on bass; Floyd Cramer and Bill Purcell on piano; and Buddy Harman on drums. Chet did not like a loud or active drummer.

During a recording session Chet would first "get a sound check on each instrument," said Strzelecki, then "convey certain licks he wanted played. Then he would piece it together. He knew what the final outcome would be because he had it in his head."

There was some new talent in town, so Chet booked Jerry Kennedy, who had moved from Shreveport where he was on the Louisiana Hayride, and Jerry Reed on guitars, Pete Drake on steel (rare for the Nashville Sound), and Charlie McCoy on harmonica and as "utility" who could play almost any instrument. Harold "Pig" Robbins was getting more session work on piano. For horns, either Dutch McMillin or Boots Randolph was called when a sax was needed, while Bill Justis and Cam Mullins were first-call trumpet players and arrangers. There were two groups of background singers. Chet booked the Anita Kerr Singers, although Anita wasn't always with them. Instead, Millie Kirkham or Winnie Breast joined Dottie Dillard, Louis Nunley, and Gil Wright. The Jordanaires, Hoyt Hawkins, Neal Matthews, Gordon Stoker, and Ray Walker, were the male group on first call. The string section almost always had Brenton Banks on violin.

According to studio logs, on three consecutive days in February Chet recorded most of the songs for his *Caribbean Guitar* album. On the first day he recorded "The Enchanted Sea," a hit single for the Islanders in 1959. "Moon Over Miami" came from the 1941 film by that name. "Jungle Dream" was a current release when Chet recorded it. He finished that day by recording "Bandit," which has a western feel. The next day Chet recorded "Theme from Come September," from the 1961 film. "Temptation" was first heard in the film *Going Hollywood* by Bing Crosby. "Come to the Mardi Gras" was first recorded by Patricio Texeira in 1937. "The Banana Boat Song," also known as "Day-O!" was a Harry Belafonte hit in 1957. On February 21 he recorded "Mayan Dance" to finish the album. On that same session he recorded a song written by Jerry Reed, "Scare Crow," which was the first instrumental by Reed that Chet recorded.

On March 8, Chet recorded "Montego Bay," "Down Home," which was written by Jerry Reed, and "Melissa" by Tupper Saussy, a talented musician and unique character who taught English at Montgomery Bell, an exclusive boys prep school in Nashville. Those last two songs were on Chet's *Our Man in Nashville* album.

Chet signed Bobby Bare to RCA in 1962. Bare had recorded "All-American Boy" in 1958 before he entered the army. It was released as "Bill Parsons" on Federal Records (Parsons had been on the session) and reached number two on the pop chart in 1959. Bare said he was "cocky" when he met with Chet. He told Chet "to get me as many new musicians as he could get. Then I played him this horn sound and he said, 'Well, Okay—we'll use horns.'" Bare "knew what everyone else was doing, with fiddle and steel guitar, and I didn't want to do any of that—I wanted to do the opposite." Chet played for Bare "Shame on Me," by Bill Ennis and Lawton Williams, and the singer loved it. The session's second song was "Above and Beyond," a hit for Buck Owens in 1960.[2] "Shame on Me" was released in May 1962 and enjoyed crossover success.

In 1962 Wayne Carson, the son of Shorty Thompson from Chet's days in Denver, came to Nashville with Si Siman to see Chet. "He was walking out of his office and Si says 'I brought Wayne over to see you,'" remembered Carson. "I had my Guild guitar with me and this was my shot. I was damn nervous. . . . Chet, being the consummate professional, understood how I felt. . . . He never cracked a smile or a frown. . . . No telling what he was thinking. I know now Si was probably thinking 'Damn! Where did I find this guy?' I finished and Chet said, 'interesting.' I never knew exactly what he meant. He asked me if I had anything else and I said I did. . . . He just said, 'Play whatever you want to.'" After Carson finished, Chet thanked him. Chet and Si left Carson and walked into another room. A few moments later Si returned and told Carson that Chet "didn't think you were ready yet but he liked your songwriting." Chet hated telling songwriters that he didn't like their songs.[3]

On May 23 Chet recorded well-known traditional songs, "Amazing Grace," "Farther Along," "Lonesome Valley," "In the Garden," "When They Ring the Golden Bells," and "Just a Closer Walk with Thee," for a gospel album, *Chet Atkins Plays Back Home Hymns*. In June he filled out the album with "The Old Rugged Cross," "Take My Hand Precious Lord," "Just as I Am," and "Were You There."

RCA did a series of releases of "Our Man In . . ." that featured Al Hirt in New Orleans, Arthur Fiedler in New York, and Chet in Nashville. In 1962 Chet recorded three songs for his turn in the series. "A House in New Orleans," also titled "House of the Rising Sun," is a traditional song traced back to the British Isles about a life gone wrong in New Orleans. The Animals found success with it in 1964. "Alexander's Ragtime Band" is a classic song written by Irving Berlin in 1911. "Goodnight Irene" was written by Lead Belly and folk song collector Alan Lomax and was a number-one record in 1950 for the Weavers.

In August Chet recorded "Drown in My Own Tears," written by African American songwriter, producer, and music executive Henry Glover, who worked with country and R&B artists for King Records in Cincinnati. "Drown in My Own Tears" was a number-one R&B hit for Ray Charles in 1956. "Lonesome Road" sounds like an African American folksong but was written in 1927 by Nathaniel Shillkret, an early Victor executive. Chet was in the studio again in August to record four songs. "Spanish Harlem" was a hit for Ben E. King in 1960. "A Little Bitty Tear" was written by Nashville songwriter Hank Cochran and was a current hit for Burl Ives. "Streamlined Cannon Ball" was written by Roy Acuff and "The Old Double E Shuffle" by John D. Loudermilk.

When RCA Victor opened their recording studio in Rome, Bob Yorke, head of A&R in New York, met Gerald McGrath with Teal Records, which manufactured and released RCA product in South Africa. McGrath informed Yorke that Jim Reeves sold more records than Elvis in South Africa and asked if Reeves, along with Chet Atkins and Floyd Cramer—who were also popular in South Africa—would tour that country. Yorke contacted Dick Broderick, head of RCA's International Division, who arranged a three-week tour of civilian venues, bypassing military bases, where country entertainers usually performed overseas.[4]

Before the tour RCA released *In Suid Afrika*, which had four songs by Reeves in Afrikaans, the language of whites in South Africa, including "Ek Verlang Na Jou," a hit for other South African artists. Reeves learned the song from composer Gilbert Gibson, who wrote out the lyrics phonetically and sent them to Reeves. Chet recorded Afrikaan songs, "Weste Windje," "A Young Man with a Dream (Outa In Die Langpad)," "Mossie Se Moses," and "Marie." Floyd Cramer recorded the other four songs on the album.[5]

On August 16 Jim Reeves, Chet, Floyd Cramer, and Reeves's band the Blue Boys, with comedian Dick O'Shaunessy (a veteran of the 1957 European tour), left Nashville and flew to New York, then to Rome, and finally to Johannesburg, where the group was amazed to find a screaming crowd, estimated at three thousand, greeting them as if they were Elvis. Their names were announced over a loudspeaker and the group attended a press conference in the terminal. The group found their path blocked to the cars that would take them to their hotel. Reeves's Italian suit was torn to pieces; the other members also had their clothes torn. A police escort finally arrived and pushed the crowd back.

"We made it to the cars," said Leo Jackson, one of the Blue Boys, and "all the way—it was about four or five miles—to the hotel, people were lined up." The motorcade was escorted by three policemen on motorcycles. At a busy intersection, the motorcade was stopped by cars whose passengers demanded autographs. Reeves, Chet, and Cramer had never encountered a frenzied crowd like this. Finally, they arrived at their hotel, where another crowd awaited. "When we got to the hotel," said Jackson, "they were grabbing at us, at our clothes, and they tore some of our clothes." The troupe was trapped again.

"We did make it inside," said Jackson, "and Floyd, he was really shook up. . . . You could tell that the [hotel management] people had talked to the help in the hotel and told them not to bother us because it looked like they were scared to death when we walked into the lobby. But when Floyd threw his sunglasses onto the floor and they broke, this girl couldn't contain herself. She ran out from behind the counter and picked up the pieces: 'Oh please! I've got to have this. I've got to have this.' So, Floyd let her keep them, but he was that shook up that it scared the hell out of him."

The troupe was scared. Reeves's hand was bleeding because someone had tried to strip a ring off his finger. The crowd was yelling "Jim Reeves! Jim Reeves!" so he went to his room's window and blew kisses and waved until the crowed was dispersed. "It was the only time a crowd really scared me with its size," remembered Chet.[6]

The group traveled in a small plane and were met by screaming crowds when they landed. They performed in Pretoria, Durban, Port Elizabeth, Cape Town, Bloemfontein, Kimberley, Nelspruit, and Salisbury. Jim Reeves was the main attraction, but Chet and Floyd had fans there as well. The group was accustomed to setting up their own equipment but were surprised to find "big [trucks] carrying all this stuff," remembered Jackson. "We had private planes to fly us everywhere. I saw the guitar when I went onstage. I would tune it, and when we got through, I'd set the guitar down and that's the last time I'd see it until the next show. . . . We'd go offstage and have beer, girls and food." Reeves loved flying and had been taking flying lessons, so he occasionally took over the controls.

At Port Elizabeth one reviewer wrote that he thought Chet "got more applause and louder applause than the number-one billing, Mr. Reeves. There is no doubt that this moon-faced Texan knows how to sing, but he lacked showmanship sparkle that a person expects from a top entertainer. After the gigantic build-up, it was an anti-climax when he walked on to the stage." Reeves sang two Afrikaans songs, "Ou Kalahari" and "Ek Verlang na Jou," during the shows.

Tour organizers arranged for the group to see some of the country and attend native events when they had free time. They watched a rugby match in Johannesburg, but when it came time to return to Cape Town a storm arose as they prepared to take off. Although the airport was closed, the pilot received special clearance for their flight to leave. The pilot was aware that a canceled concert would cost the promoter money and disappoint the rabid fans. "I got suspicious," said a terrified Cramer, "when all air traffic out of Johannesburg was grounded." The plane they flew on had a fuselage made of wood and canvas. They took off in clear weather but soon encountered a storm, shaking the plane. Ice built up on the wings, so the pilot climbed to seventeen thousand feet in the unpressurized plane—a potentially dangerous situation. The pilot told his passengers to remain calm, then flew over the storm and made a sharp decent into Cape Town airport. Reeves and Cramer were shaken but made the concert.

In early September, when the troupe left South Africa, Reeves promised the fans and promoters that he would return. Back in Nashville Reeves received an offer to star in a film based in South Africa.[7]

On December 10, Chet had an all-day session for his *Travelin'* album. The first song he recorded that day was "Wheels," written by Norman Petty, most famous for producing Buddy Holly. Then came "Exodus," usually titled "Theme from Exodus," from the Otto Preminger film. He rerecorded "Muskrat Ramble," then "Volare," originally titled "Nel blu dipinto di blu," a number-one hit in 1958 that won two Grammys in 1959. Chet then recorded "Baubles, Bangles and Beads," from the 1953 musical *Kismet*. The final three songs were "Winter Walkin,'" written by Jerry Reed, "Sweetness," composed by Jethro Burns, and "La Dolce Vita," from the 1960 Fellini film by that name. Accompanying Chet were Floyd Cramer, Bill Pursell, and Henry Strzelecki, with Willie Ackerman on drums. Hank Garland was credited as a musician.

On the last day of 1962 Chet was in the studio and started the session with his second version of "Baubles, Bangles and "Beads." The next song was "Calcutta," a 1961 hit for Lawrence Welk. "The World Is Waiting for the Sunrise" was a million seller for Les Paul and Mary Ford in 1951. It was first published in 1919 and was recorded by jazz musicians, including Django Reinhardt and Benny Goodman. "Mossie Se Moses" was written by South African musician and songwriter Nino Carstens.

CHAPTER 29

Chet was overwhelmed handling RCA administrative duties, producing artists, and recording his own albums to the point that he had developed an ulcer, so in early 1963 he hired Bob Ferguson, who had managed Ferlin Huskey, to assist. In 1960 Ferlin had a huge country/pop hit with a song Ferguson wrote, "Wings of a Dove." Ferguson had two publishing companies and occasionally sent Chet demos. Chet's secretary told Ferguson that Chet was looking for someone to fill an A&R position. Out of the twenty applicants, Chet chose Ferguson. Part of that job entailed listening to demos; one day Chet told Ferguson, "I just listened to a tape recorded audition by the greatest girl singer I've heard in years. Her name is Connie Smith." "When Chet says something like that, then asks you if you want to produce her, the only answer is 'yes,'" said Ferguson.

RCA already had three female singers, Skeeter Davis, Norma Jean, and Dottie West, and it was difficult finding good songs for them. Bill Anderson, who had written a string of hits, offered to write songs for Connie if Chet signed her, which he did. Her first release was "Once a Day," a number-one hit. "Chet had an ulcer when I went there and a year later he was out playing golf and I had the ulcer," joked Ferguson.

Chet continued to pursue an audience of "young people," as he referred to the youth market. In 1960 he released his *Teensville* album and decided to record a new album, *Teen Scene*. During two straight days of sessions in February he recorded "Sweetie Baby," written by Roye Lee and Chet, and "I Will," a minor hit for Vic Dana in 1962. "Walk Right In" was a number-one hit by the Rooftop Singers in 1963 and featured group members Erick Darling and Bill Vanoe playing twelve-string guitars, quite rare at that time. The final song, "A Little Evil," was written by guitarist Jerry Shook. The next day Chet began the session with "Susie-Q," a hit for Dale Hawkins in 1957. "I Got a Woman" had been Ray Charles's first hit. "Rumpus" was recorded by Floyd Cramer in 1960 and then by Al Hirt in 1962. The last song on that session was "Indiana," also known as "Back Home Again in Indiana," which was introduced by the Original Dixieland Jazz Band.

After a brief break the third session began with "Alley Cat," a worldwide hit for Danish pianist Bent Fabric under the name Frank Bjorn, which had won a Grammy for Best Rock Recording. Next up was "I Love How You Love Me," written by Brill Building songwriters Barry Mann and Larry Kolber that was a hit for the Paris Sisters in 1961. The song "Bye Bye Birdie" came from the Broadway musical by the same name. "Teen Scene" was written by Chet and Jerry Reed. The final song recorded was "Guitar Country."

George Hamilton IV was scheduled for a session, and the first song recorded was "Abilene," which Hamilton and John D. Loudermilk had heard on the radio sung by Bob Gibson. "John and I understood 'Abilene' to be an old cowboy song, a public domain number," stated Hamilton. Loudermilk "rehashed it a little bit, arranged it, and helped get the song together."

"The folk revival was happening and we were doing an album with some folky kind of tunes. I took the song into Chet, he kind of liked it, and we recorded it," recalled Hamilton. "There was another song on the session called 'Mine' written by a guitar player, Jerry Shook, that I was all excited about. I remember calling Chet up a week or so after the session and he said, 'George I think we're going to release that "Abilene" as your next single.' I said 'No! What on earth for, Chet?'" Chet told Hamilton that some RCA Victor executives from New York had been in town and wanted to hear what Hamilton had recorded, so he played that song for them. "They seemed to like it," said Chet, "so I thought I'd quit while I was ahead."

"That's exactly how 'Abilene' was chosen as the single," remembered Hamilton.[1] The song entered the *Billboard* country chart on June 15 and reached number one, then one week later it entered the *Billboard* Hot 100 and rose to number fifteen.

The Kingston Trio, Peter, Paul and Mary, the Lettermen, and other folkies were popular on the pop charts in 1963. Hits included Peter, Paul and Mary's "Puff, the Magic Dragon," "Blowin' in the Wind," and "Don't Think Twice, It's All Right" (the last two written by Bob Dylan), "Hello Mudduh, Hello Fadduh!" by Allan Sherman, and Trini Lopez's "If I Had a Hammer." Folk music was selling albums. In Nashville,

Bobby Bare ("500 Miles"), Johnny Cash ("Ring of Fire" and "Busted"), and George Hamilton IV ("Abilene") were all classified as folk.

On April 18 Chet was in the studio with Bobby Bare, and they first recorded "Detroit City." Working on the intro, Charlie McCoy and Boots Randolph came up with the novel idea of McCoy playing the bass guitar while Randolph turned the tuning peg for the low E string up from a low E to F then F sharp, then back down to F while alternating with the B note to end on the full E chord.[2] "Detroit City" was a hot single during the summer of 1963; it reached number six on the country chart and number sixteen on *Billboard's* pop chart.

In 1962 Chet and Anita Kerr collaborated as producers on a recording that they felt represented the pinnacle of success for the production techniques they had developed when "End of the World" became a hit for Skeeter Davis.

Chet found "End of the World" from songwriters Arthur Kent and Sylvia Dee. Kent had written "You Never Miss the Water (Till the Well Runs Dry)," recorded by the Mills Brothers, "Don't Go to Strangers," by Etta Jones, and "Take Good Care of Her," an R&B hit by Adam Wade. Lyricist Sylvia Dee set the mood for the song while thinking about her father's funeral. When Chet and Skeeter went over songs before a session, Chet would sit and sing with her to see if her voice "fit" a song. They recorded the song in B flat, then modulated to B for the talking section—Chet's idea.

"End of the World" became a huge hit in 1963, reaching number two on both the country and Hot 100 charts and appearing on the R&B chart. Chet Atkins always felt that the song was his greatest success as a producer because Skeeter was a harmony singer—not a lead vocalist. The fact that he managed to find a song that fit her voice and create a production that enhanced her delivery to produce a hit was always a source of pride for Chet.

An article in *Music Reporter* at the end of June, headlined "Chet Atkins Music City's Mr. RCA Victor," stated that Chet was "the busiest executive on the Nashville scene, a status he doesn't discount with any degree of vehemence." That busyness involved finding songs for RCA's roster of artists, meeting with publishers and artists to discuss songs, and keeping a lookout for new artists to sign. There were phone calls with executives in New York and then hours and days in the studio, supervising recordings. He also had to find songs and rehearse them for his own albums.

In addition to his activities as a major record company executive, Chet stated, "You must remember that I have two careers going: I am Victor's A&R man and I am a guitar player. I practice every day. . . . It is necessary to keep something fresh or new coming all the time, or the public moves to somebody else. . . . I must observe a rigid work schedule to keep the pace."[3]

Chet loved to play golf, and in 1959 his wife Leona took up the game. Leona was a natural and in July won the ladies tournament at Hillwood Country Club, where they were members. Chet had tried to get into the Belle Meade club, which was closer to his home, but Nashville's "aristocracy" didn't want a country guitar picker rubbing elbows with them.

"Chester and I play together on Saturdays and he always beats me," said Leona, who told a newspaper reporter that she had grown up as one of sixteen children on a farm outside of Williamsburg, Ohio. In 1946 she and her twin sister Lois sang as a duo on WLW in Cincinnati. That same year they both met their husbands and were married.

"I seldom travel with my husband," said Leona, before adding, "He hasn't done much traveling lately. His day at the office begins around 8:30 in the morning and ends around 4:30 in the afternoon." According to the article, after work he returned to their home. "Chester did all the wiring for the stereo outlets himself," said Leona. "He's electronics-minded." In the kitchen was a ham radio and "he talks on that thing while I'm cooking supper." The couple did not have a maid, and Leona revealed that "I do most of my own work. I like it. As to entertaining, we usually do that here at home too, mostly for visiting recording artists. Just about the only time I attend a recording session at the studio is when Rosemary Clooney is in town. I knew her when we lived in Cincinnati." Chet's studio in the basement of their home had a wall filled with his awards.[4]

In October, session logs show that Chet recorded for three straight days. On October 1 he did a four-song session for his *Guitar Country* album. The session began with "Freight Train" by folksinger/guitarist Elizabeth Cotton, who was left-handed but played her guitar "upside down," which gave her fingerpicking version of the song a unique sound. "Freight Train" became a regular part of Chet's repertoire. Chet then recorded "Yes Ma'Am," written by Jerry Reed, and "Dobro," by Chet and Cy Coben, but that version was unreleased. That day Chet also recorded "A Little Bit of Blues," by Jerry Reed. The next day Chet began with "Kentucky," written by Karl Davis. Chet knew Merle Travis's version of "Nine Pound Hammer," released in 1946, but the origins of the song date back to the story of John Henry. "Vaya Con Dios," which means "Go with God," was a number-one hit for Les Paul and Mary Ford in 1952.

The session on October 3 began with "Gone," which had been a number-one country record for Ferlin Huskey in 1957. The next song was "Copper Kettle" (also known as "Get You a Copper Kettle"), which was popularized by Joan Baez in 1962. Next was "Sugarfoot Rag," an instrumental composed by Hank Garland and released in 1949. Chet then rerecorded "Dobro" and "Rose Ann," written by Jerry Reed. In December Chet recorded three songs: "George's Theme," written by Tommy Burk and George Gillis, "Summer Sunday," by Johnny Duncan, and "Sidewalks of Nashville," by Lou Gottlieb.

During 1963 RCA released three albums by Chet Atkins, *Teen Scene*, *The Guitar Genius* (on the Camden label), and *Travelin'*. *The Guitar Genius* album featured tracks from the *My Brother Sings* album. Five of the ten songs on the album featured Jim Atkins singing.

CHAPTER 30

The year 1964 began for Chet with an appearance on *The Jimmy Dean Show* on January 9. The TV show featured a segment saluting the "Nashville Sound" and featured Chet accompanying Dean on Jim Reeves's hit "He'll Have to Go," Homer and Jethro on "How Much Is That Hound Dog in the Window," and Molly Bee on "The End of the World." At the end the entire cast sang "Does Anybody Here Play the Piano."[1]

The Beatles made their American TV debut on the *Ed Sullivan Show* on February 9, and Chet was at home watching as guitarist George Harrison played a Chet Atkins Country Gentleman Gretsch while 73 million people watched. The next day Gretsch guitars were flying out of instrument stores, which meant a lot of royalties for Chet.

George Harrison had first heard of Chet when he attended a concert in Liverpool by Duane Eddy, who mentioned Chet during his introduction to "Trambone." Eddy played a Gretsch during his live performances, which led Harrison to buy Chet's albums. Harrison fell in love with the Gretsch brand and in July 1961 purchased his first Gretsch, a Duo-Jet.

The Beatles had barely left the United States when Chet produced an afternoon session on Homer and Jethro where the two did parodies of Beatles songs, "I Want to Hold Your Hand" (the Beatles' first number-one hit in the United States) and "She Loves You." Chet accompanied Homer and Jethro on guitar, aided by Grady Martin, Henry Strzelecki, and Buddy Harman.

On Tuesday, February 11, Chet recorded "Around the World in 80 Days," from the 1956 film by that title. The next day he recorded three songs: "So Rare," a hit for Jimmy Dorsey in 1957, "Satan's Doll" by guitarist Johnny Smith, and "Love Letters," from the 1945 film. On Monday, February 17, Chet recorded four songs: "I Remember You," sung by Dorothy Lamour in the film *The Fleet's In*; "Bluesette," a hit for Toots Thielemans in 1961; "Early Times," a Jerry Reed song; and

"Jordu," first recorded by the Duke Jordan Trio in 1954. A day later Chet recorded "Gravy Waltz," the theme song for *The Steve Allen Show* on TV. "Kicky" was a Jerry Reed tune, and "Summertime" was the classic song composed by George Gershwin with lyrics by DuBose Heyward for the musical *Porgy and Bess.*

RCA arranged a three-week European tour for Jim Reeves, Bobby Bare, the Anita Kerr Singers (Anita, Dottie Dillard, Gil Wright, and Louis Nunley), and Chet; the group was billed as Nashville Stars on Tour. The artists were accompanied by two of Reeves's band members, guitarist Leo Jackson and pianist Dean Manuel. Studio musicians Kenny Buttrey and Henry Strzelecki joined as well. Jim Reeves did not like for his band members to back other artists but had to allow it on this tour.[2] RCA wanted their artists to play primarily before European audiences, although a few American military bases were included. The money was minimal but the exposure was beneficial.

The group left New York on April 2 for Hamburg, West Germany, where they were greeted with a reception by the European organizers, who boarded the plane and passed out cowboy hats. "To the Germans, we were supposed to be cowboys," remembered Strzelecki. "They gave us all hats, and we had to wear them when we got off the plane."[3] Prior to the trip the German office of RCA had released "I Love You Because" by Jim Reeves, which did well in Germany.

The troupe performed in Hamburg on April 4 and 5, then performed throughout Germany and Austria, before Copenhagen, Stockholm, and Oslo on successive days. On April 16 they were back in Germany and performed in Frankfurt, then traveled to Amsterdam, Carlsruhe, Brussels, and Munich. During the two-week tour the Anita Kerr Singers opened the shows with a short set, followed by Bobby Bare, whose hit "Detroit City," with its chorus "I wanna go home," connected with the rowdy servicemen far away from their homes. Bare's song "500 Miles Away from Home" also lit a fire in the GIs.

Chet followed Bare and had to tolerate the GIs yelling for Bare to return. During a performance at the Capri Enlisted Men's Club in Friedberg, Germany, Chet told the rowdy audience, "We came here to play for you. You won't even let us play. You act like a bunch of animals. Act like Americans." Chet generally played "Levee Walking," "Wildwood Flower," "Yes Ma'am," "Malaguena," a medley of "Greensleeves" and "Streets of Laredo," "Peanut Vendor," and "Tiger Rag."

During the show in Friedberg Reeves thought the cheering audience created too much noise. He tried to silence the rowdy servicemen, but they continued to yell "We want Bobby Bare," accompanied by breaking glass and stomping feet. A newspaper reported that "Reeves turned abruptly and walked off the stage in a huff followed by hoots of derision." A few nights later Jim "refused to appear before a military audience in Munich—forcing cancellation of the show—and then he did the same in Gelnhausen."[4] Reeves faced criticism from the press for calling the audience "animals," although Chet was the one who used that term. "It was Chet Atkins, and that surprised me because Chet is so easy going," said Leo Jackson. During a show in Germany, the performance was taped for the album *Nashville Stars on Tour*, released in Germany

"Bobby Bare would get drunk and go out and sing 'I Want to Go Home,' 'Detroit City,' 'Five Hundred Miles Away From Home' and the servicemen would cheer and shout 'Yeah, I wanna go home, too,'" remembered Chet. "And then Jim would come out and try to sing his quiet songs and he couldn't get the audience quiet. I think Jim resented that. He said he'd never play in an enlisted men's club again. In Munich, Jim refused to play at a NCO club, which created a storm of controversy. He'd cuss these people out," continued Chet. "He'd say, 'You built a $300,000 building and you put a $50 PA system in it.' They were threatening to report all this to *Stars and Stripes* but Jim didn't care." Along the way, Reeves lost his toupee. "He couldn't go onstage without that toupee," remembered Chet, so "we rushed around and got another one from somewhere."[5]

During the tour the performers had to get up at five in the morning to catch a plane at seven or eight for the next city. They did the show, then held a press conference, and did not leave the venue until one or two in the morning. Reeves, Chet, the Kerr Singers, and Bare were exhausted by the end of the tour. During most of his interviews, Reeves complained about the tour's logistics. "We have been getting an average of three hours sleep during this tour," he told the *Billboard* correspondent in Oslo. "This tires the members of the troupe, and we are not at top form when we perform. I'd rather not repeat a promotion tour like this."[6]

During the tour Anita Kerr met Alex Grob of Switzerland, who was RCA Victor's promotional director for Europe, and they soon married. By 1965 Anita had decided to leave Nashville for Los Angeles, where she and her husband spent the next five years. In 1970 they moved their family to Switzerland.

Chet's daughter Merle and wife Leona flew to Europe during the RCA tour. They never saw a show, instead spending their time shopping and visiting tourist attractions. After the tour the Atkins family went to Rome before returning to Nashville.

The May 1964 Grammy Awards had Chet Atkins's fingerprints all over them. Chet received his first Grammy nomination, interestingly in the Best Rock & Roll Recording category for *Teen Scene*. In the Country & Western category, "Detroit City" by Bobby Bare won. In the Best Performance by an Orchestra or Instrumental, "Java" by Al Hirt won. The large Hirt, known as the Monster, had a million-selling album, *Honey in the Horn*, produced by Chet. Chet also produced Hirt's follow-up album. The Grammys event was held in three different locations: Los Angeles, New York, and Chicago, which now had a NARAS chapter. Nashville did not have one.

On May 18 Chet was in the studio for an evening session with Jim Reeves, backed by studio musicians, a string section, and the Anita Kerr Singers. "The relationship between Jim Reeves and Chet Atkins was, for the most part, anathema to the Reeves-Fabor Robison antagonism at Abbott Records," stated author Michael Streissguth in his biography of Reeves. "Chet would approve [a song Jim wanted to record], but more than likely if Jim liked it, Chet liked it. Or if Chet liked it, Jim liked it. There was a mutual respect." Chet came to learn that Jim had definite ideas about the songs he should record and how and let Jim have his way. And Jim acknowledged that Chet had a knack for producing hit records. Chet called the shots in Nashville for the suits back in New York, so Jim avoided clashing directly with Chet or even Chet's right-hand woman, Anita Kerr. However, RCA engineer Bill Porter told historian John Rumble that Chet feared a time would come when "that infamous Reeves temper would flare in his direction."

"To a certain extent, Jim Reeves dictated more to Chet than most people," said Bill Porter. "[Chet] seemed to be sort of apprehensive when [Jim] was around—pins and needles a little bit. Not that [Chet] would be intimidated by him, but he didn't seem to want to get into a controversial argument, so he kept things even as much as he could because Reeves was doing the right thing."[7]

Chet had come to learn the ways of stars, whose egos can explode. Chet allowed the creativity to flow and interceded—gently—only when a course correction was needed.

On the first day of June, Chet recorded three songs. "Wimoweh" was originally titled "Mbube" (the Lion) and was composed by South African composer Solomon Linda in 1939. "Levee Walking" was written by Jerry Reed and Henry Strzelecki, and "Drina" was written by Bosnian composer Stanislav Binicki in 1914.

In July 1965 Jim Reeves came to the RCA studio, changed out of his golf outfit, and, with Chet in the producer's chair and backed by studio musicians including a contingent of horns and strings, recorded five songs. The next session started at ten o'clock that night. During the second session Bob Ferguson came into the studio, maybe because Chet did not like late-night sessions or perhaps he thought that Ferguson could bring in some new ideas. At any rate, partway into that session, remembered Ferguson, "Chet closed up his briefcase and said, 'I believe I'll head home.' I was dumbfounded. He said, 'It's going to be all yours. . . . Jim's got the songs and you know what to do.' So, he just walked out the door."

"Actually, Chet and Jim had planned out the recording . . . so I wasn't producer in the sense that I worked out the songs with the musicians," continued Ferguson. "They had done that. We went through a rehearsal . . . and he turned around and stepped to the microphone and sang it without a hitch. He was great at that." Chet had left to see if the notoriously difficult Reeves could get along with Ferguson. They did work well together, but that was the last studio session that Reeves would ever do.[8]

Chet and Hank Snow recorded an album, *Reminiscin'*, that was an extension of the acoustic instrumental duets the two had recorded in the 1950s, but on this album they were backed by Nashville studio musicians as well as a string section of five violins. On July 13 they recorded two songs. The next evening they recorded "Unchained Melody," "Beautiful Dreamer," "My Isle of Golden Dreams," and "Brahms' Lullaby."

Chet recorded five songs on July 29: "I Love Paris," written by Cole Porter, from the musical *Can-Can*; "Al-Di-La," composed by Carlo Donida with English lyrics by Ervin Drake; "Why Don't They

Understand," which had been recorded by George Hamilton IV in 1958 and the Anita Kerr Singers in 1963, both produced by Chet; "Stranger on the Shore," the theme song for the BBC TV drama; and "Danke Shoen" (German for "thank you very much"), a hit for Wayne Newton in 1963.

It was announced that RCA planned to construct a new building and studio, and on July 30 a sketch of the $750,000 project was presented during a press conference. Groundbreaking for the new building was the next day. Chet had asked Jim Reeves to attend, but Reeves told him he would be out of town on business.

On that morning Bill Walker arrived in New York from South Africa. Reeves had met Walker when he worked with the arranger on the film *Kimberly Jim* and invited Walker to move to Nashville and score his shows. After his arrival, Walker called Reeves and told him he wanted to see the Broadway production of *Oliver!* that evening before he came to Nashville. Reeves told Walker to call Steve Sholes, who got him tickets. After speaking with Walker, Reeves and his piano player, Dean Manuel, flew to Arkansas to look at some property that Reeves was interested in buying. They planned to spend the night in Arkansas and fly back the next day.

That evening Chet was in the studio recording with Bob Ferguson supervising. Chet had booked Bill Pursell on the session, but after Pursell arrived he discovered that Chet had changed his mind and did not want a piano on the session. Chet recorded "English Leather," an instrumental written by Jerry Reed, and "Soul Journey," written by Chet and Tim Spencer of the Sons of the Pioneers. Sometime around eight that evening the phone in the studio rang. Someone from the airport was asking if they knew where Jim Reeves was. Ferguson told them that they had not seen Reeves at the studio and that Chet was unable to come to the phone because he was recording. Ferguson and Pursell began making calls and discovered that Reeves's plane was overdue at the airport.

Chet began recording again, but Ferguson did not inform him of the calls because there was no confirmation that Reeves's plane, with pianist Dean Manuel as a passenger, had actually crashed.[9] There were storms and heavy rains in the Nashville area, but Reeves decided to fly through them, even though air traffic control told him landing would be extremely difficult.

Chet finished his session before Bob Ferguson told him about the emergency. "Oh, no—not Jim." That evening, rescue workers formed search parties while helicopters flew low over the area. The search continued the next day in Brentwood, just south of Nashville. A number of Nashville singers and musicians, including Chet, Eddy Arnold, and Bill Pursell, joined the search. On Sunday, August 2, the searchers found the wreckage and Eddy Arnold identified Jim Reeves.

The memorial service for Reeves was held on Tuesday, August 4. Chet Atkins, Eddy Arnold, Red Foley, Skeeter Davis, Floyd Cramer, Ferlin Husky, Webb Pierce, Dottie West, the Jordanaires, and other music luminaries were present. Memorial services for performers generally feature a lot of music, but at Reeves's service not one song was sung, although some recorded music was played. Reeves's body was sent first to Shreveport and then on to Carthage, Texas, where he was buried on Wednesday.[10]

"Welcome to My World" was a defining song in the Nashville Sound era. Backed by studio musicians Thumbs Carllile, Velma Smith, Bob Moore, Floyd Cramer, and Farris Coursey, with a string section and the Anita Kerr Singers, the song had reached number one earlier that year and was still on the chart at the time of Reeves's death. That initiated a string of eight consecutive hits beginning after his death. On August 8, the album *The Best of Jim Reeves* entered the country chart and remained in the number-one position for eight weeks. The last album Reeves released during his lifetime, *Moonlight and Roses*, reached number one on *Billboard's* Country Album chart in July 1964. In England "I Love You Because" was closing in on a million in sales.

Two days after Reeves's funeral, Chet was in the studio with the Browns, who recorded three songs during an evening session.

Chet recorded four songs on August 26 with Bob Ferguson producing. "Mack the Knife" was composed by Kurt Weill with lyrics by Bertolt Brecht and was introduced in 1928 in *The Three Penny Opera*. In 1959 Bobby Darin had a number-one hit with it. "Song from the Moulin Rouge" came from the 1952 film *Moulin Rouge*; the biggest hit was by Percy Faith's Orchestra in 1953. "As Long as He Needs Me" was written for the musical *Oliver!* Back in the studio on September 9, Chet, with producer Bob Ferguson, recorded "It Don't Mean a Thing (If It Ain't Got That Swing)," a jazz classic by Duke Ellington. "Josephine" was recorded by Les Paul and Mary Ford in 1951 and "Travelin'" was by James Arnold Miller.

Chet resumed work on his *My Favorite Guitars* album, which he had begun on June 1. On November 11 he recorded six songs. The session began with "Say It With Soul," written by Nashville session guitarist Wayne Moss. "Sukiyaki" was a huge international hit by Kyu Sakamoto. "One Note Samba" was first recorded by Jao Gilberto in 1960. "Cloudy and Cool" was written by John D. Loudermilk as an answer to his song "Windy and Warm." "El Vaquero" was written by Chet and Nashville session guitarist Wayne Moss. The session finished with "Chopin Waltz No. 10 in B Minor." Chet recorded the song on his Juan Estruch classical guitar and changed the key to A minor in standard tuning.

Problems emerged at the RCA studio that caused Bill Porter to leave in November. Porter and Anita Kerr started a publishing company, which the New York executives declared was a "conflict of interest" and ordered him to cease. Porter argued that Chet had a publishing company, but the executives were adamant. Steve Sholes came to his defense and wanted Porter to remain, but he bolted to Columbia Records. Chet openly admitted that he got his "sound" from Porter's engineering; after Porter left Chet's sound was never the same and he recorded fewer hit records than he had with Porter.

During 1964 RCA released four Chet Atkins albums: *Guitar Country*, *Progressive Pickin',* *My Favorite Guitars*, and a duet album with Hank Snow, *Reminiscing*. They also released *The Best of Chet Atkins* and, on the Camden label, *The Early Years of Chet Atkins & His Guitar*. Chet also appeared on *Nashville Stars on Tour*, recorded in Germany but unreleased in the United States. RCA also did not release *Guitar Over Europe*, with a picture of Chet at the Roman Colosseum on the cover, because there were so many Chet albums in 1964.

CHAPTER 31

In January 1965 engineer Jim Malloy began work at Nashville's RCA studios. Malloy and Chet had met the previous year when Chet was in Los Angeles to produce an album for the Anita Kerr Singers; Chet and Malloy developed a rapport and became friends. According to Malloy, "The more Chet and I talked, the better I liked the idea of moving." Steve Sholes arranged for Malloy's transfer to Nashville.

Jim Malloy was an important addition to Chet's staff in Nashville, and by the time he left LA was considered one of the top engineers in that city. He had won a Grammy for *Charade*, been nominated for *The Pink Panther*, and was booked six months to a year in advance. Malloy had done extensive work with Henry Mancini and also worked with Benny Goodman, Bing Crosby, Frank Sinatra, Sammy Davis Jr., and Ike and Tina Turner. "Chet was a unique record producer," remembered Malloy. "He was a great studio musician himself. He could go out in the studio, tell the guitar players, bass, drums . . . what to play and it would work. But that wasn't Chet's way. Chet would sit very calm and relaxed in the control room and let the musicians figure out what they wanted to play."

"Chet let everybody do their job," continued Malloy. "He said to me one day, 'If you hire great musicians, have a great engineer and hit songs, then let them all do their jobs, they'll cut hit records for you.'" Malloy added that Chet "was not locked into a particular sound. Chet wanted to cut great records and when he brought me here, we started using horns, strings, harps or whatever instruments made the records sound like hits."[1]

Bob Beckham was working for a publishing company, pitching songs. The first time he went to see Chet his office door "was opened about this much [Beckham held his thumb and finger about an inch or two apart]. There was a songplugger in there from New York. He was really giving Chet hype on this song. . . . Finally Chet raised up and gets the acetate." Chet put the acetate on the record player, took the lead sheet, “leaned back, put his feet up on his desk and put that lead sheet over his face. As the acetate was playing, he’s blowing this lead sheet up in the air, letting it flutter up and down on his face. The song finished playing. Chet took the acetate and put the lead sheet around it with a rubber band and says, ‘That’s a good song.’ The guy just stood there for a minute and said ‘Well, thanks!’ The guy didn’t get his cut and I had to follow him in there.”[2]

On Tuesday, February 9, Chet produced a session on pop star Perry Como, who had arrived the day before with a cold and spent the day rehearsing. The cold “doesn’t bother his singing,” said Chet, so they decided to go ahead with the three sessions scheduled.[3]

Como had a long history with RCA, joining Victor in 1943. His first number one, “Till the End of Time,” came in 1945. During the late forties and fifties Como had a string of number-one hits. Steve Sholes had convinced Como to record “Don’t Let the Stars Get in Your Eyes,” originally a country song by Slim Willet. Como hated the song: “The meter’s wrong. I don’t understand it.” But Sholes insisted on one take. Como did and the song entered the *Billboard* pop chart in December 1952, reaching number one and selling over two million records. So Sholes’s suggestion that Como record in Nashville with Chet Atkins encountered much less resistance.

By early 1965 the fifty-one-year-old Como did television specials but had not had any major hits since 1958. Sholes believed that sessions in Nashville under Atkins might give Como a chance for another hit. Como was used to recording in New York with a studio full of musicians, but when he walked into the Nashville studio he discovered a handful of musicians ready to provide the Nashville Sound. Como was surprised to find the musicians had only the Nashville number system on their music stands.

“I looked over to see the arrangements and all I see is ‘I-IV-V-II,’” said Como. “I say, ‘what’s this?’ and they say ‘that’s the arrangement.’ It was just a chord sequence, and they’d change the key and make up the arrangement as they went along.” For musicians, that was the definition of the Nashville Sound. Arrangements for Como’s songs in Nashville were done by Anita Kerr. The Ray Charles Singers had backed Como on previous sessions but instead of eight to twelve singers Kerr’s group included just four. The biggest difference was in the approach used by Kerr, who sang from a lyric sheet, working up the harmonies during the recording session. "We couldn't have done that in New York," stated Como.

Chet and Kerr were both well aware of Como's style, and only wanted to give it the Nashville touch. Como was soon comfortable with the backing and arrangements, although there was little social interaction between him and the musicians.

Como recorded some new songs, like "Stand Beside Me" and Willie Nelson's "My Own Peculiar Way," along with country hits such as Nelson's "Funny How Time Slips Away" and the Eddy Arnold hit "I Really Don't Want to Know." A new song on the session, "Dream On (Little Dreamer)," was released in April and reached number 25 on *Billboard's* pop chart. The album was titled *The Scene Changes*, with the subtitle *Perry Goes to Nashville*.[4] In 1965 the pop charts were dominated by the Beatles and the British Invasion, so Como was competing with acts a generation younger.

Several people claimed to be the reason Chet signed Waylon Jennings to RCA, but the fact is that one day Chet called Waylon, who remembered that Chet offered him a recording contract: "To be on RCA and have Chet Atkins produce me. To have him call me and tell me he would like to sign me, having never even seen me. I'll never forget that day. I was sitting at home, and I could hear this real gentle, kind voice on the other end of the phone, saying 'We'd sure like for you to record for RCA. Would you be interested?' . . . It was impossible to say no. . . . Chet was a legend."[5]

Waylon was living in Phoenix, performing at J.D.'s, a popular local club, when he first recorded with Chet. On the first session they recorded three songs, then two days later recorded five more, including "I'm a Man of Constant Sorrow," the Roy Orbison hit "Dream Baby (How Long Must I Dream)," written by Cindy Walker, and "Stop the World (And Let Me Off)." The next evening they recorded four songs.

"Chet let me bring my band in the studio," remembered Waylon, who brought guitarist Jerry Gropp, bassist Paul Foster, and drummer Richie Albright. "We'd been playing 'Stop the World (and Let Me Off)' in the clubs, and had it all worked out." On one song, "I started playing the break. I looked over in the control room and realized 'I'm playing guitar in front of Chet Atkins!' So I just grabbed me a string and held on for dear life."[6]

In addition to Waylon, Gropp, Foster, and Albright, Chet added guitarist Fred Carter Jr., bassist Henry Strzelecki, and Floyd Cramer on piano with backing vocals by the Anita Kerr Singers. Waylon's album was titled *Folk-Country* and was an attempt to capture the young urban folk audience.

On March 29, 1965, RCA held a grand opening for their new studio and office building. The local newspaper reported that "musicians, songwriters, disc jockeys, music publishers, managers and executives of Nashville's most vocal industry flocked en masse" to the opening to see the new studio. The three-story stone and brick building had offices for RCA's A&R staff and commercial sales offices on the first floor. Trumpeter Al Hirt played while about five hundred guests mixed and mingled. Elvis was not there but sent his "gold-plated, crushed-diamond coated Cadillac with gold vanity case, telephone, bar, refrigerator and electric shoe buffer."[7]

The building was owned by Chet, Owen Bradley, and Harold Bradley. Steve Sholes had arranged for Chet to have ownership of the building and lease it to RCA because the label refused to give him producer's royalties. As an executive, Chet was on a straight salary, although he did receive artist royalties. Chet had intended to be the sole owner, but his wife cautioned him about tying up so much cash. His accountant, Joe Kraft, offered to bring Owen Bradley into the ownership. Owen agreed but said his brother Harold also wanted in. Owen offered to let Chet have half with Owen and Harold splitting the other half, but Chet wanted each to own a third. Chet later lamented that was the biggest mistake he ever made. He should have been the sole owner.

The first Grammys were dominated by chapters in Los Angeles and New York. In 1960 NARAS attempted to create a "hillbilly chapter" in Nashville, but it folded after six months. However, by 1964 Nashville could no longer be ignored. NARAS executives came to Nashville in March 1964 and negotiated with Wesley Rose to establish a Nashville chapter. By the time they left, Rose had bargained for six categories for country music: Album, Single, Song, New Artist, and Male and Female Vocalists. This meant that country music had more Grammy awards than rock and roll, R&B, and jazz combined. At that point there were fewer than fifty members of NARAS in the Nashville community.

On Tuesday evening, April 13, 1965, NARAS held their first annual Grammy awards dinner in Nashville at the Carousel Club in Printer's Alley. The event was held simultaneously with awards dinners in New York, Los Angeles, and Chicago. The awards show honored top recordings from 1964, and Roger Miller, whose hit "Dang Me" swept the awards, won five Grammys.

Chet was nominated in the Best Country Album category for *Guitar Country*; *The Best of Jim Reeves* was also nominated in that category. RCA acts made a good showing. *Grand Ole Opry Favorites* by the Browns was nominated in the Best Vocal Group category (the Beatles won for "A Hard Day's Night"). In the Best Country Single category, "Four Strong Winds" by Bobby Bare, "Here Comes My Baby," by Dottie West and "Once a Day" by Connie Smith were nominated. In the Country Male category, Bare's "Four Strong Winds," "Fort Worth, Dallas or Houston" by George Hamilton IV, and *Hank Locklin Sings Hank Williams* were all nominated. In the Country Female category, "He Says the Same Thing to Me" by Skeeter Davis and "Once a Day" by Connie Smith were nominated. The song "Sugar Lips," written by Buddy Killen and Billy Sherrill for the Al Hirt album *Sugar Lips*, produced by Chet, was nominated for Best Instrumental. "Sunrise and Sunset" by George Beverly Shea was nominated in the Gospel category. Entertainment for the evening was provided by Chet, Boots Randolph, Bill Purcell, and singer Kaye Golden.

Eight days after the Grammys, Chet recorded four songs: "The Last Letter," by Rex Griffin; "The Letter Edged in Black," first recorded by Mary Hyers in 1898; "Understand Your Man," a number-one hit for Johnny Cash in 1964; and "Catch the Wind," the first hit for Scottish singer-songwriter Donovan in 1965.

Two days later Chet recorded four more songs, including "Alone and Forsaken," a Hank Williams song, written in a minor key. He also recorded "Yakety Axe," whose roots go back to a performance by James "Spider" Rich at the Armory in Hopkinsville, Kentucky, where he took several fiddle tunes and melded them tougher. Boots Randolph heard the song and, inspired by the saxophone break in "Yakety Yak," the Coasters song from 1958 written by Jerry Leiber and Mike Stoller, recorded his version, "Yakety Sax," in 1958. It was released on RCA but was not a hit. Boots then signed with Monument Records and rerecorded the song; it entered the *Billboard* Hot 100 in 1963 and reached number 35. Chet had been given a guitar version of the song by Jerry Reed, who had worked up a version that Chet copied. Charlie McCoy played the harmonica solo.[8]

Soldiers in World War I popularized the song "Old Joe Clark," which was based on a Kentucky mountaineer who was murdered in 1885. "Back Up and Push" was recorded in 1929 by two groups, the Augusta Trio and the fiddle band the Georgia Organ Grinders. Three days later, Chet recorded three more songs. First up was the Bob Dylan classic "Blowin' in the Wind," then "How's the World Treating You," which Chet wrote with Boudleaux Bryant. He finished with a song he wrote, "My Town." He was backed by Ray Edenton on guitar, Jerry Smith on piano, Charlie McCoy on harmonica, Buddy Harman on drums, and Henry Strzelecki on bass. The Anita Kerr Singers provided vocals on several songs.

On June 26 "Yakety Axe" entered the country chart and rose to number four and remained on the chart for nineteen weeks. It was a popular instrumental on country radio and crossed over to the pop chart.

Chet did his first album with the Boston Pops, led by conductor Arthur Fiedler, on June 10 and 11 at Symphony Hall in Boston. The album was titled *Pops Goes the Country* and featured the hundred-piece symphony with Henry Strzelecki on bass and John Greubel on drums for support. Chet recorded twelve instrumentals for the album—six each day. He recorded two "standards" in his repertoire that he had previously recorded, "Country Gentleman" and "Windy and Warm." Chet had previously recorded a version of "Alabama Jubilee," a song written in 1915, on *A Session with Chet Atkins*, released in 1954, but he slowed the song down a bit for his second recording. Other songs recorded with the symphony were "Tennessee Waltz," "Cold Cold Heart," "My Hometown," "Love Offering" (written by Jerry Reed), and "Prancin' Filly," which was written by Chet's Dad.

Chet recorded "Yours" with his Del Vecchio resonator guitar, an acoustic guitar with metal cones built into the soundboard, creating a louder sound than a regular acoustic. Chet related in his book *Me and My Guitars* that he was intrigued when he heard the Los Indios Tabajaras record of "Maria Elena," a hit in 1963. "I just couldn't get over the guitar sound Nato was getting," stated Chet. "The tone and sustain were astounding for an acoustic guitar." Chet was impressed so he "investigated and discovered the existence of the Brazilian-made Del Vecchio resonator guitar."

"The Del Vecchio is a strange looking thing," continued Chet. "The round resonator ports on the top have grille covers that make them look like built-in speakers. Combining the nylon string, classic sound with a resonating sound box produces the most impressive acoustic sound I've ever heard out of a guitar." Chet got in touch with Nato Lima and requested him to find one for Chet to buy. "It took some time, but Nato finally agreed to sell one of his to me." The price was $375 "but I would have paid more," said Chet.

As Chet investigated the Del Vecchio, he "learned that they aren't made that well. You can buy them out of Brazil pretty cheap, but you never know what you're going to get." The one he received from Lima "was a good one, but the bridge on them is usually off, sometimes by as much as a quarter inch, and they aren't fretted accurately, so they won't play in tune. You can go through a hundred of them and maybe find one you want to keep." Instead of endlessly searching for a quality Del Vecchio, Chet bought one and sent it to a professional luthier and had him overhaul it. He also had one custom built.[9]

During an interview with Mark Pritcher, Nato Lima said that he was introduced to Chet by RCA producer Herman Diaz. "We got together and played and tried guitars," said Lima, who needed documentation for his immigration into the United States. Los Indios Tabajaras was signed to RCA, so Nato went to Herman Diaz because he thought that RCA had lawyers who could help. Diaz told him that "the lawyer has no power in that situation" but a letter from Chet Atkins, "the greatest guitarist in the country," would help. Chet's letter was all Nato would need: "Chet Atkins, that is important. That is the only letter you need. You don't need anything more. You can stay and work."[10]

In 1965 Chet, Boots Randolph, and Floyd Cramer began performing "Festival of Music" concerts. X. Cosse, husband of singer Martha Carson and Chet's manager, booked them in various cities where they were backed by various Nashville musicians. They played about two concerts a month during a weekend. On a Tuesday evening in September the Master's Festival of Music did a concert at Municipal Auditorium in Nashville to a near capacity audience. Boots Randolph opened the show with a medley of "Yellow Rose of Texas" and "Dixie."

Randolph then played "The Shadow of Your Smile," before Floyd Cramer performed "By the Time I Get to Phoenix" and a sprightly rendition of "Gentle on My Mind" before a Hank Williams medley of "Your Cheatin' Heart," "Why Don't You Love Me," and "Jambalaya." Chet Atkins then closed the show.

Chet wanted to play and perform; he *had* to play his guitar and the Festival of Music shows were a way for him to get out of town and perform. The shows were a relaxed presentation of middle-of-the-road music, and Chet clearly enjoyed performing. However, there was another side to the concerts: "The whole deal with them, they made X. Cosse book these shows around golf tournaments," said David Conrad. "They would come and play . . . Pro-Celebrity. At night, they would have a concert and pick up a few thousand bucks before going home."[11]

In October RCA sent Chet for a tour of Japan with the Browns, Skeeter Davis, and Hank Locklin to promote the Nashville Sound. Chet brought along Jerry Reed, Henry Strzelecki, Hank Wallis, and Kenny Buttrey. Before the tour Chet recorded an album for the Japanese market. The Tokyo Grand Ole Opry had just started, so the group played that show. The group was based in Tokyo and took the train to various other cities to perform sold-out concerts. They also did some TV shows and held interviews to explain and promote the Nashville Sound. Maxine Brown noted that "Chet was a master at this."[12]

In Japan Chet met with Isamu Asanuma, whom he had first met in 1961. Asanuma remembered one of Chet's Japan concerts: "The hall was filled with people, and outside there were a lot of fans who couldn't enter; however, Chet took a small guitar amp outside on the balcony and played a few tunes for the outside fans. Oh what a splendid guitarist he is!" Later that night Asanuma took Chet to a yakitori (grilled meat on a stick) shop and "Chet really satisfied the entire shop. Yakitori shops are common places in Japan, so I thought Chet could really discover Japan by exploring there."[13]

A group of RCA artists—Bobby Bare, Skeeter Davis, Connie Smith, Nat Stuckey, and George Hamilton IV—did a twenty-one-day tour of Europe, but Chet appeared with them only during the final two nights in London at the Royal Albert Hall. During the tour Bare received a gold record for "Detroit City," then had his necktie torn off by autograph seekers. When they returned to Nashville a reporter met them at the airport and noted that "Atkins was his usual diffident self, walking through the rain to the doorway of the ramp with his cased guitar on one arm and Mrs. Atkins on the other. He said the others were the ones to talk to about the tour, since he had only performed with them the last two days of it." The group had performed in Finland, Norway, Holland, Germany, Denmark, and Sweden before London.[14]

On December 6 and 7 Chet and Hank Snow were in the studio to record an album of instrumentals, *The Guitar Stylings of Hank Snow*. On the first session the duo recorded "Waltz You Saved for Me," "Lay My Head Beneath the Rose," "Among My Souvenirs," "Whispering Hope," "King's Serenade," and "The Whispering Tradewinds." During the next evening they recorded "Wabash Blues," "Sentimental Journey," "Am I Losing You," "I Get the Blues When It Rains," "Sweet Marie," and "Birth of the Blues." Accompanying Chet and Snow were Velma Smith on guitar, Pig Robbins on piano, E. R. McMillin on clarinet, and a string section.

Four days after Christmas Chet was in the studio to record "From Nashville with Love," written by John D. Loudermilk, with Chet on his classical guitar.[15] Chet released one studio album during 1965, *More of That Guitar Country*, which was also released in England.

CHAPTER 32

In January 1966 Chet was in the studio with Don Gibson for two sessions with Brazilian guitarists Los Indios Tabajaras. Gibson, Chet, and Floyd Cramer had met Los Indios while doing a series of TV shows for Jimmy Dean in New York in late 1965. Chet suggested to Gibson the idea of doing an album with the duo, and after an evening of jamming in a hotel room Gibson agreed.

Los Indios was made up of Natalicio (Nato) and Antenor Lima, two sons of a Tabajaras chief from an isolated province in northeastern Brazil who claimed to have learned to play guitar on an old instrument that had been discarded by a white explorer before World War II. They were discovered in Rio de Janeiro and signed to RCA in 1943. In 1963 Los Indios had a pop hit with "Maria Elena."

Chet and Gibson initially planned to record an album with Los Indios, accompanied by Junior Huskey on bass and Buddy Harman on drums. On the morning of January 19 the group recorded three songs, "Address Unknown," "My Adobe Hacienda," and "Lonely Street," but it was a struggle. During the afternoon they recorded "Cryin' Heart Blues," "Too Soon to Know," and "I Can't Tell My Heart That." The afternoon session also did not turn out well. The Lima brothers spoke little English, so an interpreter was needed. "I thought they were improvisational musicians but they were really more like classical musicians," said Chet. Gibson recalled that "When the one who played the lead wanted to sing on 'Lonely Street,' I said, 'Chet, I can't take it no more.' Chet replied 'I can't either,'" so they quit after six songs "and just sat down and listened to them play."[1]

Jim Reeves left behind a number of tapes, many of them demos for his publishing companies, and told his wife Mary that if anything happened to him "these tapes would be her insurance policy." On one of those tapes was "Distant Drums," written by Cindy Walker. Walker had sung it to Jim, but according to Walker, Chet nixed it. However, before she left town Jim recorded a version for her. "I don't believe you'll have any trouble getting a record on it now," he told her. Roy Orbison was the first to record it.

Reeves had recorded many songs on a tape recorder in his small home studio, checking to see if they fit him. Mary Reeves met with Chet in his office with the tape of "Distant Drums"; Chet called in Jim Malloy to listen and determine if it could be made into a record. As they listened, Malloy noticed that Reeves "had played wrong chords on the tape and his steel guitar player had played some answers that should have been played by trumpets. The steel player's amplifier had not been mic'd so it had leaked into Jim's mic but there was no presence to the sound of the steel." That actually helped.

The original recording was made on tape at 7 ½ ips (inches per second), not studio quality, which is 15 or 30 ips. They wondered if "Distant Drums" could be converted to studio quality. Malloy transferred the demo to a 15 ips tape and equalized Reeves's voice, adding a filter to eliminate the rumble from Reeves's voice and the steel guitar. After editing, a listener "would hear Jim singing the words and then the tape would go blank until he sang again." When Reeves sang, "you would hear, occasionally, a little of the steel guitar."

Chet and Malloy played the edited version of the tape for arranger Bill Walker. Malloy told Walker that two things needed to be done in his arrangement: hide Jim's guitar and hide the leakage from the steel guitar. On February 9 musicians Leo Jackson, James Kirkland, Bob Moore, Jerry Carrigan, Mel Rogers, and Floyd Cramer overdubbed their parts on "Distant Drums" and two others Reeves had recorded.[2] "Distant Drums" entered the *Billboard* country chart in April 2, 1966, and rose to number one. It was released in England and became Reeves's first number one there.

The tapes that Reeves made extended his career as a recording artist by almost twenty years. After his death he had six records reach number one on the country chart—"I Guess I'm Crazy," "This Is It," "Is It Really Over," "Distant Drums," "Blue Side of Lonesome," and "I Won't Come In While He's There"—and chart records that extended into 1984. In all, Reeves had thirty-four chart records after he died.

"If Jim had lived he would either have been very big, or the most unhappy guy in this world," observed Chet. "I often think that what made Jim so mean and so hard to get along with was that he wanted to be perfect, and he knew he wasn't. . . . He wanted the best songs, the best arrangements and perfect records. When they weren't perfect, it tore him up."[3]

The year 1966 began with a release from Charley Pride, a brand-new singer on RCA. Pride had come to Nashville in February 1963 after a frustrating tryout with the New York Mets when manager Casey Stengel refused to watch him during their Spring Training camp. Pride was living in Montana, working at a smelter and singing in clubs. He met Red Sovine when he came there to do a show. Sovine encouraged Pride to try his luck in Nashville and gave him the address of Cedarwood Publishing Company. There Pride happened to run into Jack D. Johnson, a manager who was looking for a Black country singer. Pride and Johnson talked and then Johnson put him on a bus back to Montana, where a management contract was waiting. Pride signed and waited. Finally, in the summer of 1965, having had no success while waiting, Pride decided to meet Johnson in Nashville.

Johnson gave Pride seven songs to learn and arranged for a studio session at RCA Studio B with Jack Clement producing. Clement had produced Johnny Cash at Sun and had written "Guess Things Happen That Way" and "Ballad of a Teenage Queen." Pride recorded three songs on August 16, "Snakes Crawl at Night," "Atlantic Coastal Line," both written by Mel Tillis, and "Just Between You and Me," written by Clement. When Clement brought the recordings to Chet, he was impressed but said, "Let me check with Harry Jenkins, something he had never said before," according to Clement.[4] Jenkins was Chet's immediate boss at RCA.

Chet decided to sign Pride and at a company meeting in California played his tape for the RCA executives, who were excited. Then Chet said, "I need to tell you that's he's colored." That caused questions and concerns but "Chet lobbied hard for RCA to take a chance on me," said Pride. By the end of the meeting it was agreed that RCA would sign Pride but take a cautious approach in marketing him, sending out his records without broadcasting that he was Black.[5]

That first record did not chart, but the second single, "Just Between You and Me," with "Detroit City" on the B side, entered the *Billboard* country chart in December. It was a top-ten record and launched Pride's career.

Nashville was a center for civil rights activities, which most of the white population loathed. From February 13 to May 10, 1960, Nashville students from Tennessee State, Fisk University, and Baptist Theological Seminary staged a series of sit-ins. John Lewis, James Lawson, and Diane Nash were student civil rights leaders in the city. In 1961 Nash led a group of marchers to the steps of Mayor Ben West's courthouse and asked, point blank, if he felt it was fair to discriminate against someone because of the color of their skin. The mayor agreed it was not right, which led to Nashville's lunch counters and restaurants being integrated.

Chet was more progressive than many southerners when it came to race relations. He jammed with Black musicians and hired them for sessions. He did not make derogatory comments about African Americans or throw around the N-word; he appreciated musicians of all colors. Chet had worked with Nashville Symphony conductor Willis Page, who insisted that musicians be hired without regard to race, ethnicity, sex, or religion. Nashville Symphony therefore became the first multiethnic symphony in the nation, and its first African American musicians were Booker T. Rowe and W. O. Smith.

Ray Charles's album *Modern Sounds of Country and Western Music* was released in April 1962, and the follow-up was released six months later and had an immediate impact on country music. Chet loved that album—he had produced a number of those songs on RCA acts. Chet was a longtime fan of Ray Charles—when Charles performed in Nashville in November 1961, Chet and Leona Atkins were in the audience.[6]

Many Nashville citizens did not like long hair on men, counterculture clothing like jeans or tie-dyed T-shirts and their connection to liberal politics, "free love," and drugs. Those clothes and long hair were political statements, antithetical to the conservative political view most Nashville whites embraced. Country music was a counter to the counterculture during the sixties and is partly why it thrived. While young people marched against the Vietnam War, demonstrated on campuses, were sexually liberated, and had an affinity for drugs, especially marijuana and LSD, the country audience was conservative and espoused traditional family values.

The rock and rollers in New York and Los Angeles looked down on Nashville, considered country music backward, prejudiced, racist, and the antithesis of cool. But some changed their views on Nashville when Bob Dylan recorded his 1966 *Blonde on Blonde* in the city. Dylan opened the doors for rock musicians to record in Nashville.

The Dylan sessions ran smoothly, although Al Kooper, a former member of Dylan's band who was on the sessions, ran into some trouble when he visited Buckley's Record Shop. Kooper "got accosted by . . . juvenile delinquents, about five of them, and they wanted to start some trouble." After a phone call the group's bodyguard drove in and picked him up.[7] Bob Dylan would eventually record all or part of five albums in Nashville.

Waylon Jennings came to Nashville to record for the third time in February 1966. Backed by studio musicians and the Anita Kerr Singers, with Priscilla Hubbard replacing Anita Kerr, Jennings recorded three songs on the evening of the 16th. The next day there were a few changes in the musical lineup and the session began with a Gordon Lightfoot song, "(That's What You Get) For Lovin' Me," then three more songs. For the afternoon session, "Chet came up with the left-field idea of doing a version of the Beatles' 'Norwegian Wood,'" remembered Waylon. "It was this kind of unpredictability that endeared Chet to me."[8]

CHAPTER 33

On Tuesday evening, March 15, 1966, the Grammy Awards were held in Los Angeles, New York, Chicago, and Nashville, at the Hillwood Country Club, where "a tuxedo and mink-clad crowd" of over four hundred attended. The Nashville event was hosted by Eddy Arnold.

There were forty-seven categories for the Grammys, a result of the NARAS board trying to correct the problem from the previous year of an overabundance of country categories at the expense of rock and rollers. The new categories created for rock and roll were not supposed to be open to country artists, who had six categories—but they were. Out of those forty-seven categories, Roger Miller was nominated in ten and came away with five Grammys that evening.

Chet received three nominations. *More of That Guitar Country* was nominated in the Best Country & Western Album category that was won by Roger Miller's *King of the Road* album. Also nominated in that category was Eddy Arnold for his *My World* album. "Yakety Axe" was nominated in the Best Country & Western Single category, which was won by Miller's "King of the Road." Also nominated in that category were "Is It Really Over" by Jim Reeves and "Make the World Go Away" by Eddy Arnold. In the Best Instrumental Performance, Non Jazz category, Chet was nominated for "Yakety Axe" but lost to "A Taste of Honey" by Herb Alpert & the Tijuana Brass.

Album of the Year went to Frank Sinatra for *September of My Years*. Other nominees in that category were *Help* by the Beatles and *My World* by Eddy Arnold. Record of the Year went to "A Taste of Honey" by Herb Alpert & the Tijuana Brass. Also nominated were "King of the Road" by Miller and "Yesterday" by Paul McCartney. Song of the Year, a songwriting award, was captured by "The Shadow of Your Smile." Other nominees included "King of the Road" and "Yesterday." Best Vocal Male was captured by Frank Sinatra for "It Was a Very Good Year." Other nominees included Paul McCartney for "Yesterday" and Roger Miller for "King of the Road." In the Best Performance by a Vocal Group, the Anita Kerr Quartet's *We Dig Mancini* triumphed over the Beatles *Help* and albums by Herman's Hermits, the Statler Brothers, and the We Five. In both the Best Contemporary Rock and Roll Single and Best Contemporary Rock and Roll Male Vocal categories, Roger Miller won for "King of the Road" over "Yesterday" by Paul McCartney. In Best Contemporary Rock and Roll Performance by a Group, the Statler Brothers won for "Flowers on the Wall" over the Beatles' "Help," Herman Hermits' "Mrs. Brown You've Got a Lovely Daughter," and the Supremes' "Stop! In the Name of Love." Performers who received no nominations that evening included Bob Dylan, the Beach Boys, and the Rolling Stones.

Reporters and critics of the Grammys labeled it "a Confederate Coup" and "a Confederate forage into pop territory." NARAS was embarrassed.[1]

It was a big night for Chet. In addition to his three Grammy nominations, RCA acts Jim Reeves, Eddy Arnold, Norma Jean, Bobby Bare, Anita Kerr, Carl Belew, Skeeter Davis, Dottie West, George Beverly Shea, the Statesmen Quartet with Hovie Lister, and the Blackwood Brothers were all nominated. During the evening, a big band under the direction of Owen Bradley played an overture while Chet, with Boots Randolph, Don Bowman, Don Gibson, and the Statler Brothers, provided entertainment.

In March Chet recorded four songs. He started the session with "What'd I Say," a Ray Charles song from 1959. "Prancin' Filly" was written by his father, Arlie Atkins; "Solo Soul" was by Cindy Walker. "Ain't We Got Fun" was introduced in a revue, *Satires of 1920*. On March 23 Chet was in the studio to record "A Taste of Honey" for his *It's a Guitar World* album. The song was originally a waltz in the Broadway musical *A Taste of Honey*. It was recorded by pop singer Lenny Wright in 1962, but Herb Alpert & the Tijuana Brass had a top-ten hit when they recorded it in 1965 as an up-tempo "swing" number. Chet copied Alpert's version of the song, which had triumphed over Chet's "Yakety Axe" at the Grammys a week before. Backing Chet were Ray Edenton (guitar), Henry Strzelecki (bass), and John Greubel (drums).

There was an altercation between Chet and fiddle player Tommy Jackson on Friday night, April 1. Jackson was arrested at the Grand Ole Opry for "threatening to harm Chet Atkins." Chet swore out a peace warrant alleging that Jackson "threatened me and I feared for my life." Jackson had waited in RCA's parking lot the previous night, and when Chet stepped out of his car Jackson beat him and threatened his life. He reportedly landed a number of punches before he was pulled away.

The trial was set for Monday at one o'clock in General Sessions Court. "Jackson said he threatened Atkins, whom he described as an old friend, after they argued about a personal matter involving Jackson's family," according to a newspaper article. "The judge quoted Jackson as saying he got drunk Friday night and invited Atkins to 'go outside' with him, but the famed guitarist declined."[2]

In September 1964 Chet had decided to record an album of Beatles songs. He was unsatisfied with the recordings he had made earlier of "Things We Said Today" and "I Feel Fine," so they were unissued. In October 1965 Chet and Bob Ferguson returned to the studio for the Beatles project. On the first day they recorded "Yesterday," "Can't Buy Me Love," "I'll Follow the Sun," and "I'll Cry Instead." The next day brought "She's a Woman," "From Me to You" (unissued), "She Loves You," and "And I Love Her." On November 1, the final day of recording, Chet did "If I Fell," "A Hard Day's Night," "Things We Said Today," "I Feel Fine," and "Michelle."

On April 9, 1966, Chet's *Picks on the Beatles* album entered both the Country and Pop album charts in *Billboard.* On the cover was a twelve-string Gretsch guitar with long-hair wigs on four mannequin heads. The back of the album had two pictures of Chet: one in a long-haired Beatles wig and another of him with short hair, playing his Gretsch. The album reached number six on the country chart but only number 112 for pop.

In the liner notes Beatle George Harrison wrote, "I have appreciated Chet Atkins as a musician since long before the tracks on this album were written; in fact, since I was the ripe young age of seventeen. Since then I have lost count of the number of Chet's albums I have acquired but I have not been disappointed with any of them. . . . Whilst listening [to this album] I got the feeling that these songs had been written specifically with Chet in mind." "Chet's own style of picking," continued Harrison, "has inspired so many guitarists throughout the world (myself included, but I didn't have enough fingers at the time)." "One thing remains very clear to me at the end of this LP," concluded

Harrison, "and that is why this sleeve note must end here. Chet Atkins did not get to be a great guitarist by writing sleeve notes, but by years of devoted practice on the instrument he so obviously loves."[3]

Elvis was booked into the RCA studio for three days, May 25, 26, and 27, to record a gospel album. A few days before the sessions Chet went into Felton Jarvis's office and told him that he thought Felton would make a good producer for Elvis. "I'm going to carry you over," said Chet, "and maybe you all will hit it off." Chet disliked producing Elvis because of the all-night sessions.

Elvis and his entourage traveled by chartered Greyhound bus from Memphis and arrived around eight in the evening. Chet introduced Felton to Elvis, and the two began to talk. They talked about Elvis's records, how the voice seemed to be too far out front with the musicians buried in the track. Elvis wanted a hotter sound, like the Beatles. It was clear that the pair clicked, so Chet excused himself and left before the session began.[4]

Chet recorded four songs during a session on May 31: "Something Tender," by George Barnes; "La Fiesta," by Byron Williams; and "After the Tears," by Chet with Shirley Nagel. He also recorded "Romance."

Chet was in the studio on July 22 with Jerry Reed and Ray Edenton on guitar, Jerry Smith on piano, Boots Randolph on saxophone, Roy Huskey on bass, Wayne Moss on bass, and drummer Jerry Carrigan to record a song written by Priscilla Hubbard, Jerry Reed's wife, who recorded under the name Priscilla Mitchell. Priscilla had replaced Anita Kerr in the Anita Kerr Singers. "Prissy" became a single but never appeared on an album. He also recorded "Colonel Bogey," sometimes known as the "Colonel Bogey March," the theme for the 1957 film *Bridge on the River Kwai*. This was Chet's first recording of that number, which became popular during his appearances, but this version was unissued. The last song on the session was "Sempre," written by Sonny Osborne of the Osborne Brothers.

Chet signed Jimmy Dean, who had a major pop and country hit in 1961 with "Big Bad John" and an important television show on ABC, to RCA. "Jimmy Dean was a big kid," remembered Jim Malloy. "He loved to have a good time" and "whenever he came into the studio to record, he would jokingly give everybody a bad time. He was always fooling around." Malloy said that "One night, he brought a smoke bomb into the control room and set it off on the producer's console right in front of Chet Atkins. It started making a hissing sound and smoke was everywhere. It scared Chet Atkins and me both. . . . When the smoke cleared and we came back in the control room, the smoke bomb had burned a big hole in the producer's console. Jimmy was standing in the control room laughing until he saw the hole in the console." When the smoke had cleared Chet was "mad and told Jimmy if anything like that ever happened again, he wouldn't be on RCA."[5]

Chet became wealthy through his real estate investments, including a 141-unit project in a four-story building on the east side of Hillsboro Road. Chet owned the property; his partner was W. B. Cambron, with the Gaines Construction Company. By the time the project was approved the Zoning Board had scaled it back to 128 one-bedroom units in a "garden-type building."[6]

Chet's album *Pops Goes the Country* with the Boston Pops conducted by Arthur Fiedler entered the *Billboard* pop album chart on June 18 and reached number 62. Almost two months later—on August 13—the album entered *Billboard's* country album chart and reached number 36.

Most American music fans first heard the sitar when George Harrison played it on the Beatles' "Norwegian Wood." He delved into Indian music and was taught by Ravi Shankar, the most prominent Indian sitarist for classical Indian music. Always exploring new musical avenues, Chet delved into Indian music on September 6 with sitarist Harihar Rao.

Rao was born in Mangalore, India, in 1927 and moved to the United States in 1964. He studied ethnomusicology and wrote several books on the sitar. A close friend of Ravi Shankar, Rao sought to bring the sitar to jazz. The songs that Rao and Chet recorded that day were "Et Maintenant (What Now My Love)," "Ranjana," "Na Voce, 'Na Chitarra e'o," and "E Luna."

Chet did that session on the same day he produced one on Hank Snow. Chet then spent two days in the studio with Waylon Jennings. On September 22 he did an afternoon session with Eddy Arnold where the singer recorded five songs. On October 10 and 11 there were sessions with Hank Snow for a Hawaiian-themed album where the singer recorded thirteen songs.

On November 3 Chet recorded four songs. "Lara's Theme," also known as "Somewhere My Love," was the theme for *Dr. Zhivago*. "Cast Your

Fate to the Wind" was released in 1962 by jazz artist Vince Guaraldi. Then he recorded "Here Come the Cossacks" before "Star-Time," written by blind Texas songwriter Leon Payne.

Also in November, Chet and Harihar Rao recorded "A Taste of Honey," the Beatles song "For No One," "Pickin' Nashville," written by Joe Layne and Jimmy Wilkerson, and "January in Bombay," written by Chet.

The year 1966 marked a profound transition in Chet's career. He was one of America's best-known guitarists with an international audience and fans who extended from country to pop. At the same time Chet was a successful and influential producer who had created major hits and a consistent series of chart records with many renowned artists. Chet's own albums were consistent sellers, but he both dreaded and enjoyed his success as an executive and producer. Artists depended on Chet to find hit songs, which entailed listening to countless demos. He also had administrative duties with RCA. On the outside he seemed placid and undisturbed, but inside Chet was a tight bundle of nerves. He considered himself an artist and craved time to work on his own recordings, but at the same time he was responsible for a large roster of RCA artists. He felt constant pressure from the New York office and from himself.

Chet loved being with RCA, a top U.S. corporation, reaching heights that a poor farm boy from East Tennessee could hardly have imagined. Chet was an introvert but needed to be surrounded by label personnel, songwriters, artists, and Nashville music community members. At RCA he was fortunate to be a magnet for artists and songwriters, who mostly came to him. As an artist he was free to choose what songs he wanted to record and the RCA promotion staff toiled to get his records on the radio and into record stores. He was secure in his position as an executive, but while he loved the position he hated the job. Since he had a studio in his home he could work on his records for endless hours and to perfection. His early work had an energy that his late sixties and seventies recordings seemed to lack. Chet's artistry did not really fit with the youth of the sixties, who embraced rock and roll. His audience—and Chet himself—wanted a smoother, middle-class adult lifestyle kind of music.

Nashville and the country audience were conservative politically as well as socially. While Chet was more progressive in terms of race relations, he still fit comfortably in a society with conservative political and social inclinations.

Steve Sholes remained close but was distant; he had been transferred to Los Angeles handling pop releases. Sholes protected Chet but could not shield him from onerous duties like having to drop artists from the RCA roster, especially when they were friends. Chet had to deal with executives in RCA's corporate headquarters in New York. "I didn't get a hell of a lot of help on a lot of the stuff I sent up there," remembered Chet. "I'd go up [to New York] for meetings all the time and I'd dread it so much because they'd always want me to drop a bunch of good people like Boots and Roger Miller." The New York executives' interest in the Nashville office and country music could be summed up as "New York doesn't care," as long as the country acts made money.

In 1966, Dolton Records issued *Play Guitar with Chet Atkins* as part of their instructional "Guitar Phonics" series. The twelve-page instructional booklet with Chet featured "Nine Pound Hammer," "Red Wing," "Windy and Warm," and "Hello My Baby." Chet released three studio albums that year—*Chet Atkins Picks on the Beatles*, *From Nashville with Love*, and *Music from Nashville, My Home Town*—and an album with the Boston Pops, *Pops Goes the Country*.

Chet with Homer and Jethro in the 1950s. Chet Atkins Family Archives.

Chet, Leona, and Merle Atkins. Chet Atkins Family Archives.

Chet rehearsing with Arthur Fiedler, conductor of the Boston Pop Orchestra. Frank Empson, *The Tennesseean*.

Chet and Leona Atkins.

Chet in the studio, producing a session on Jim Reeves.
Country Music Foundation.

Chet in a school picture in Georgia, 1937. Chet is in the second row, second from the right. The author's collection.

Chet's school in Mountain Hill, Georgia. Photo by author

Chet with Buddy Harman on drums and Bob Moore on bass. Country Music Foundation.

Chet's family. From left, Lowell, Chet, and Jim Atkins. Billie Rose is in front. Chet Atkins Family Archives.

The Carter Family: Mother Maybelle, Helen, Anita, and June.
Chet Atkins Family Archives.

Chet in Knoxville, 1943. Chet Atkins Family Archives.

Chet in the hat he wore when performing. This is in 1988.
Chet Atkins Family Archives.

Chet at KNOX in Knoxville, December 1944.
Chet Atkins Family Archives.

Chet in 1997, the elder statesman of guitarists.
Chet Atkins Family Archives.

Chet performing on stage. Hope Powell, courtesy of the Hope Powell Collection by Singleton/Curb.

Chet at KNOX in Nashville with the Old Fashioned Gospel group. Chet started as a fiddler on WNOX. Chet Atkins Family Archives.

The Best of Chet album. Chet Atkins Family Archives.

Chet in the studio. Chet Atkins Family Archives

Fern and LaVerne. Chet Atkins Family Archives

Paul McCartney at Chet's home in 1974. Chet Atkins Family Archives

CHAPTER 34

Chet's day-to-day life as head of RCA's Nashville office involved listening to songs, either on reel-to-reel tape or on acetates. Sometimes he met with artists or songwriters who played their songs for him—either live or on tape—but more often the tapes and acetates were simply dropped off. As he listened, he usually held his guitar and practiced the fingering for a song over and over so it would be automatic when it came time to record or perform the song. Many accomplished musicians no longer practice, but Chet practiced his entire life; he was always looking for new sounds and new songs. Sometimes he took his guitar to a session but did not play on the session. Instead he played quietly in the control room as the musicians learned a song. His guitar was also there in case it was needed. Chet never wanted to undermine another guitarist, but he stood ready to provide his input.

When Chet found a song he liked and would be good for one of his artists, he either sent the acetate or called the artists to his office. Before a session Chet generally met with the performers and went over the songs. Sometimes the artists brought in songs they had found and played them for Chet for his input.

His RCA duties included administrative paperwork. Chet had to write letters, ensure forms were completed, and sign off on contracts with the Musicians Union. His assistant handled much of this paperwork, but he still had to stay on top of things.

The search for songs was ongoing and constant. He might hear a song on the radio and would obtain a copy. In addition to songwriter demos and the radio, Chet listened to albums because he might find a song buried in the tracks. People he knew might recommend an album or song. His ears were always open, always listening for songs.

Chet developed close, personal ties with his artists; he listened to their troubles, problems, and joys. When Skeeter Davis was married to Ralph Emery, Chet spent a good deal of time listening to her talk about their marital problems. He knew about the private and public lives of his artists and often found himself in the role of counsellor, giving advice.

Although Chet always appeared calm, he was a worrier. He constantly felt the stress of having to create hit records and turn profits. He wanted to please Steve Sholes. Chet was reserved and admittedly shy, but he could be talkative with friends and those he knew. He knew how to meet strangers who idolized him and put them at ease, although he was aware that he made those people nervous. He had come a long way from that poor mountain boy who was unsure of himself and painfully shy. He did not want to sound like a "hillbilly," so he practiced pronouncing words to remove the thick, mountain accent. He had grown comfortable with his responsibilities and as a leader in the Nashville music community. Still, his memories of poverty never left him, and although he had become wealthy, he was not comfortable thinking of himself that way.

Chet Atkins loved being Chet Atkins. He had always wanted to be famous and had attained fame—but in a more limited way than artists with big hits. He attended music industry gatherings, and although he was quiet and reserved, he was inquisitive and conversational. He had a curious mind and loved to read and learn. In his home were books on World War II and other history topics. Chet was always embarrassed about his lack of formal education, but he had acquired a self-education through experience. In that sense Chet was more "educated" than many of those with degrees.

Don Gibson was scheduled to record during an evening session but had been drinking heavily and was in no shape to record. Chet "kept trying to get Don to let the band lay down the music tracks so Don could come back and do his vocals when he was in better shape," said Maxine Brown. "But Don wouldn't hear of it. He acted like he'd been insulted. Before we knew it, Don shoved himself right up against Chet and slapped the fire out of him right in front of everybody. Don had his girlfriend with him and she was throwing a few punches herself."

Waylon remembered a slightly different version when Gibson was "having trouble singing." Chet came out of the control room and suggested they postpone the session and "get together another time." On the way back to the control room, Chet said to Gibson's girlfriend, "Don's not straight tonight and we can't record," and the girl "slapped him in the face, right across the mouth. Upholding her honor, Don threw his guitar on the floor and took up a karate pose. 'I'll kill you,' he said."

Chet just stood there motionless, not knowing what to do. Finally, Gibson relaxed and decided not to hit him. Meanwhile, Maxine and Bonnie Brown chased the girl down the hall yelling, "You bitch, you can't hit Chet Atkins!" Chet "had a gash on his lip and blood coming from his nose," remembered Maxine. Chet then told the Browns, "There's no use wasting three hours of session time" and told them to find some songs to record. The Jordanaires had been on the afternoon session and helped them find songs.[1]

"It was that kind of manic pressure that started driving Chet crazy," stated Waylon. "He was a musician; he didn't like being an executive—the paperwork, the bottom-line pressure. He found it very difficult to go out and tell a singer 'You're flat on this note,' or that he would have to drop them from the label because they weren't selling. It tore his insides out. He was an artist himself, and he empathized with their fears, hopes, and desires. He took it all too much to heart."[2]

On Friday night, January 20, TV viewers could watch Chet on the *Porter Wagoner Show* as Porter introduced him as "the greatest guitar player who has ever picked one up." After he played "Colonel Bogey," Porter came back on camera and told Chet how much he enjoyed his new album with the Boston Pops. Chet replied that there were ninety musicians on the session or "half an acre of fiddlers." For his second selection, Chet played "Kentucky," accompanied by Porter on rhythm. When comedian Don Bowman walked into the picture near the end of the song, Chet quipped, "You should be at home working on your material."[3]

Chet was in the studio on February 6 and recorded four songs. "You'll Never Walk Alone" was from the Rodgers and Hammerstein 1945 musical *Carousel* and had been a hit for Gerry and the Pacemakers in 1965. "Battle Hymn of the Republic" is known as the Civil War anthem for the North. Chet rerecorded "Colonel Bogey" and then recorded "El Paso," the Marty Robbins hit from 1959 and 1960 that won a Grammy.

On February 27 Chet was in the studio to record "Tears," a song by Django Reinhardt and Stephane Grappelli. This would be for his album *Chet Atkins Picks the Best*. "Tears" was written in 1937, and Chet's version was arranged similar to Django's, but he slowed down the tempo. Also on that session, produced by Bob Ferguson, Chet recorded "How Insensitive," the English title for the Brazilian song "Insensatez." "Nuages" is one of Django Reinhardt's best-known songs; the title means "clouds." Reinhardt's first of thirteen recordings of the song came in 1940. The film *Anna*, released in the United States in 1953, had the song "El Negro Zumbon," often known as "Anna." Chet also recorded "Lovely Weather."

Photographer Jimmy Moore shot the cover for *Picks the Best*. Moore met Chet when John D. Loudermilk took him to Chet's office and shared, "You're a damn fool if you don't use him because he's the best." Chet paused a few moment, raised his head, and said, "Well, I won't be a damn fool." *Picks the Best* was the first album cover Moore shot for Chet, who often recommended him to other artists.[4]

Jerry Reed and his wife Prissy (Priscilla Mitchell) struggled when they moved to Nashville in 1962. "When we moved to Nashville, sometimes I just hung on by my teeth," said Reed. "Came close to quitting, but I went in there whimpering when I was feeling sorry for myself. . . . Chet didn't have to say 'come over here and let me record you,' did he? But Chet sees a lot of things that other people don't see."

Reed was signed as an artist to Capitol and then to CBS and recorded several singles at Columbia. He became a busy session guitarist but was not succeeding as an artist. Every time Reed was ready to throw in the towel, Chet urged him to persevere. "One day Chet said, 'There ain't nothin' happening with your records because you're recording wrong,'" said Reed. "You ought to play that guitar like you do over at the house. Why don't you come over here and let me record you." The first album on Reed produced by Chet was *The Unbelievable Guitar and Voice of Jerry Reed*, released in February and containing the instrumentals "The Claw," "Reedology," "Jerry's Breakdown," and "Lightning Rod." There were two songs, "Guitar Man" and "U.S. Male," that Elvis later had hits with. Reed's first single was "Guitar Man" and it was his first chart single.

Chet "was a great coach," said Reed. "Chet can get you on top of the world. He can look and say 'Hey that's great, let's record that.' . . . He got whatever I was out of me. Chet Atkins is the difference in my life."[5]

At the Grammy Awards, held in March 1967, Chet's album *Picks on the Beatles* was nominated in the Best Instrumental Performance (Other Than Jazz) category but lost to "What Now, My Love" by Herb Alpert & the Tijuana Brass. Additionally, a song Chet had recorded, "Prissy," was nominated for Best Instrumental Theme category, a composer's award. It was a good night for Chet the producer. Nominated in the pop category was Jim Reeves for Best Vocal Performance Male for "Distant Drums." Three albums he produced, *Funny Way to Make an Album* by Don Bowman, *Have a Laugh on Me* by Archie Campbell, and *Wanted for Murder* by Homer and Jethro, were nominated in the Best Comedy Performance category. Comedy albums were major sellers during the 1960s, and Chet, who always enjoyed a good joke, saw the success of Bob Newhart, Alan Sherman, and the Smothers Brothers prove there was a large market. Comedy was an important part of country shows.

The Best Sacred Recording Grammy went to *Grand Ole Gospel: Porter Wagoner and the Blackwood Brothers*; others nominated in that category were *Connie Smith Sings Great Sacred Songs* and *Southland Songs That Lift the Heart* by George Beverly Shea.

Cortelia Clark was a blind Nashville blues singer who sang on the streets. Peabody University student Mike Weesen made a studio demo of Clark, and it came to the attention of Chet and Bob Ferguson. Felton Jarvis was assigned to record him, and he and Weesen persuaded Chet and RCA to allow them to record Clark on the street. After the recording of Clark's songs (which included the Everly Brothers' "Bye Bye Love") street noises were overdubbed. The album was released on RCA, and although it sold fewer than a thousand copies, it won a Grammy in the Best Folk Recording category, triumphing over offerings by Pete Seeger, Peter, Paul and Mary, Leadbelly, and Ravi Shankar.

Chet hired Red O'Donnell, a local reporter for the *Nashville Banner*, to write his life story. O'Donnell held interviews with Chet, Steve Sholes, Leona Atkins, and others and wrote the book over four days.

The book, published by Athens Music, Chet's publishing company, featured forty-six pages of text, around eighty pictures, and a foreword by Bob Jennings and retailed for $2.50. The book's format is horizontal and measures six inches tall by nine inches wide. It opens with a quote from Chet, "It beats working," and goes on to say, "As far back as I can remember, I had a horror of having to make a living at hard labor. In the very beginning, the guitar, or maybe music itself, was a means whereby I could avoid the necessity of earning bread by the sweat of my brow."[6]

The book lists Atkins accomplishments, goes into his early days, and then tells the story about when he and his wife were on a Caribbean cruise in 1966 and he picked up a guitar and played it while another passenger listened. When Chet put the guitar down, the other passenger told him, "You play pretty good, but you're no Chet Atkins." Chet always loved that story.[7]

Talking about his early life Chet stated, "The people around Luttrell were poor and disillusioned. They sang a lot, though, mainly because there wasn't much to do. We had no modern conveniences. I never knew what electric power was until I was almost a teenager. Most of the families used coal oil lamps. If you were really fancy, you got an Aladdin lamp. Proper diets were unheard of. About 1930 I had some sores on my body. I didn't know what caused them. I know now it was from malnutrition. Nevertheless we were fond of music. I guess you would have called us a musical family."

Chet's wife Leona proclaimed that he was "the best friend I've ever had." She continued, "I get awfully mad at him sometimes. I don't understand his moods, which sometimes last for almost two days," before adding, "But if you don't get mad—a man and a wife—you miss the pleasure of making up. Chester isn't the boss around the house," continued Leona. "But he makes the decisions. Something will come up and we'll discuss it but, in the end, he'll decide what is to be done—after telling me 'you're the boss.'"

"He's genuinely sentimental," said Leona, "but like other males, frequently doesn't remember birthdays and anniversaries. He can't cook a lick. He'd starve to death if he had to prepare his own meals. He is never too busy to practice on his guitar. He even practices before breakfast. He'll come home tired and worn out from the studio and pick up the guitar after we've eaten. I'll be in another part of the house sewing or reading and hear his music slowing down. I'll check and discover he has fallen asleep playing the guitar."

"Chester has a marvelously comforting philosophy about life," concluded Leona. "'There is nothing you can't do if you really want to,' he contends. And I agree. It's happened for us many times."[8]

In the book O'Donnell tells the story of a testimonial dinner given by RCA for Steve Sholes in 1961. During that dinner, George Market, then RCA's vice president in charge of recording, asked Sholes what single contribution that he had made to the label's record division did he consider the most important. Sholes replied "Chet Atkins," then added, "Everybody expected me to say Elvis Presley, I am sure. I had negotiated for Elvis to join the company and Elvis has done—and still does—exceedingly well. But my vote for Chet is without reservation," adding that Chet "is one of the largest record sellers. He has produced more than anybody else in the business and signed and helped develop many artists. He not only is the best I've had anything to do with but, in my opinion, the best anybody else has had anything to do with."[9]

"I had no fear of his capability as a producer," said Sholes. "I had watched him work around other musicians in sessions and I was aware that the musicians and artists respected him. I knew his ability better than he did. I frankly didn't know how he would do in an administrative post, but he gave me a pleasant surprise. He developed quickly and in depth; he is a man with a golden ear."[10] "If I had never done anything for RCA Victor except to sign Chet Atkins," concluded Sholes, "the company should be content with paying me the salary it has over the past three decades."[11]

Chet told Red O'Donnell, "I have never done anything in personal appearances or on record that satisfied me totally. I keep my eyes and ears open for ideas all the time. I'll cut an album and I'll think: What am I going to do next? Then I keep on thinking and waiting and hoping and sooner or later another idea will come. The late Fred Rose had it right. He once told me, 'There are plenty of ideas all around. You just have to think of them.'"

"I never force an artist to do something, a specific tune," continued Chet. "I do try to reason with them if I really believe in a particular song. I usually go on my first inclination because I think it's the best. Bobby Bare convinced me of this. He contends—and I subscribe to his theory—if you change your mind after your original reaction, you're just second-guessing and you really don't know."[12]

"I'm frequently asked what makes a hit record," said Chet. "Work like heck and develop your talents is my answer. A good voice or ability with a musical instrument isn't enough. You've got to get the right writers and the right A&R man and the right engineer and the right product promotion. As for entertainers, use your basic intelligence and never kid yourself into thinking you're something you aren't. Be yourself. Most of all, realize your limitations and then develop your talent to the highest degree. The route to stardom isn't the same for everybody. There is no standard 'open sesame' to success. I think if you set your goals and try conscientiously, you'll succeed. Then, when you think you've got all the ingredients to be a star, go where it's happening. Let the right people hear you play or sing. By and by, somebody who can help will listen. If you are honest and sincere with yourself and your work and let the right person hear you, I think it will happen for you."

He admitted he was a high school dropout, and "I've always had a complex about that," said Chet. "I never had much formal education or went to college and that always bugged me. I've tried to educate myself. I bought books on mathematics and English. I worked algebra problems just to prove to myself I could. I also bought books on English composition."

"I'd give anything to be able to write," stated Chet, but noted that writing is "a full-time job. You've got to get your mind attuned to it and have songwriting on the brain all the time. You've got to listen to people and keep a pad to jot down ideas so you can rush home and write the song. I just don't have the time."

Chet stated that in order to succeed "you've got to have drive. And it really isn't something you have much to do with," adding that "I don't know where I got my zeal and aggressiveness. I hardly inherited it. I'm sure my Dad had ambition—but in another direction."

"I've had a wonderful life. I've done everything I've wanted to do and I don't know why I've been so fortunate," said Chet. "There are so many joys and pleasures about my music. Like when a record I've produced for somebody becomes popular. I get a special kind of thrill out of that."[13]

Fred Harvey Jr. asked Chet and O'Donnell to appear at an autograph party for the book in his Harvey's department store and suggested a Saturday at three o'clock in mid-July. The party didn't lack for promotion—there was a window display and ads in newspapers. Red O'Donnell "readily agreed" to appear, but Chet "was reluctant. He preferred to play golf—but finally promised he would be there. Five minutes before the autograph party began, a king-size rainstorm hit downtown Nashville. It poured most of the afternoon. About 90 minutes later, when only about a dozen books had been sold, Chet turned to me and said, 'You don't know many book buyers, do you?' He then thanked Fred Harvey Jr. for the party and left."

Chet paid O'Donnell a flat fee of a thousand dollars to write the book, and with the money O'Donnell and his wife took a trip to Nassau in the Bahamas.[14]

"Chet's Tune" was written by Cy Coben and recorded by "Some of Chet's Friends" to commemorate Chet's twenty years on RCA. "Some of Chet's Friends" included Jerry Reed, Floyd Cramer, Eddy Arnold, Willie Nelson, Dottie West, Archie Campbell, Bobby Bare, Norma Jean, George Hamilton IV, Skeeter Davis, Jimmy Dean, Hank Locklin, Jim Ed Brown, Hank Snow, John D. Loudermilk, Connie Smith, Homer and Jethro, Waylon Jennings, Porter Wagoner, and Don Bowman. All of those artists had been produced by Chet. Musicians backing the singers were Jerry Reed, Wayne Moss, Chip Young, Weldon Myrick, Charlie McCoy, Norbert Putman, Jerry Carrigan, and Floyd Cramer. There was a section of strings and backing vocals by Dottie Dillard, Priscilla Hubbard, Louis Nunley, and Gil Wright. The recording was produced by Bob Ferguson and Felton Jarvis and was done without Chet's knowledge. The 45 was released with a picture sleeve and made the top 40 on *Billboard's* country chart that summer.

CHAPTER 35

On Sunday, May 28, 1967, over eight thousand gathered at Municipal Auditorium in Nashville to honor Chet Atkins for his twentieth year as an RCA artist. The event was sponsored by RCA to benefit "Furbelows and Fanfare," a project of the Junior Board of the Florence Crittenton Home, a home for unwed mothers that provided social welfare for infants.

Two days before the tribute show the Carter Family—Maybelle and her daughters, Helen, Anita, and June—sat with Chet for an interview with a reporter from a local newspaper. The Carters recalled that when Chet joined he was reluctant to talk "but we forced him to. We even made him smile." Chet was signed to an exclusive six-month contract with the Carters in Springfield before they moved to Nashville. "We had never had an outsider in the family before, but we needed him," remembered June Carter.

"We played an awful lot of schools, courtrooms and theaters back then," remembered Chet. The Carters "changed my luck. They came along at a time when I needed them. I was broke. When I started playing with the Carter sisters, I started making money." The five agreed that there were never any arguments or disagreements. "I respected Maybelle too much," said Chet. "She would have slapped me down."

"These people gave me my chance to come to Nashville," said Chet. "I'll always be grateful for that. This is where things were happening and I was glad to be back again." Helen remembered "his constant rehearsing and practicing on the guitar," adding, "I think he was disturbed that we disturbed him as much as we did." Maybelle concluded, "He was like one of the family. He was more like a son to me than anything else. He was always there, ready to work."[1] It had been twelve years since Chet and the Carters had worked together. They saw each other only occasionally but remained close.

The show at the Municipal Auditorium was hosted by Jimmy Dean: "Chet's done as much for me, if not more, than anybody around in the record business."[2] Arthur Fiedler flew in the day of the show and spent two hours rehearsing the eighty-piece orchestra of Nashville musicians.[3] The event began with a patron's reception and dinner that featured an exhibit of two hundred paintings, one hundred of those by Mimi Bickley, local artist and teacher, whose pupils included Charles "Red" Grooms." "Patrons" of the tribute were presented with a recording of "Chet's Tune" and the biography of Chet written by Red O'Donnell.[4]

During the show Arthur Fiedler and the orchestra performed "Amparite Roca," "Oberen Overture," "Mame," and "Winchester Cathedral," in addition to a medley of TV western themes: *Bonanza*, *Maverick*, *Gunsmoke*, *Wyatt Earp*, and *Rawhide*. Chet performed "Country Gentleman," "Alabama Jubilee," and a couple of songs with the Carter Family. Other performers on the program included Boots Randolph, Floyd Cramer, Dottie West, Archie Campbell, John D. Loudermilk, the Jordanaires, and Homer and Jethro.[5]

RCA general manager Norman Rascusin presented Atkins with a plaque honoring him for his twentieth year as an artist with the label and tenth year as head of RCA's Nashville division. Lowell Blanchard, who hired Chet back in the forties for WNOX in Knoxville, presented him with an award pointing out his "exceptional guitar virtuosity and a continuing inspiration to guitar players and the entire music world." Chet took the stage and proclaimed it "the Greatest dad-burned day I've ever had," stating, "I'll go on picking this dad-burned guitar as long as I'm able."

Chet named people who were important to his career, beginning with his family and including Merle Travis, Tandy Rice, John D. Loudermilk, and Elmer Alley (who produced the tribute), his manager X. Cosse, Fred Rose, and Eddy Arnold. For the final number of the concert, Boots Randolph and Floyd Cramer brought Atkins a black, jewel-studded stool with "Mr. Guitar" on it and, with Chet and the symphony led by Fiedler, played "Tennessee Waltz."[6]

On July 14 studio logs show Chet with producer Bob Ferguson recording "Scherzino Mexicano" by Manuel Maria Ponce and "Morenita Do Brazil" by Farranto. The songs had a distinctly Latin feel. "Yellow Bird," "Malaguena" by Ernesto Lecunona, "Lagrima" by Tarrega, and "Cancion Triest" all had Latin origins. He also recorded "Ave Maria" by Franz Shubert, a song he wrote, "Acutely Cute," and one he wrote with Jerry Reed, "To Be in Love." "Manha De Carnaval" came from the

1959 film *Black Orpheus*. "I Feel Pretty" was from the musical *West Side Story*. Chet had recorded "Yellow Bird" for his second classical guitar album, *Class Guitar*. Chet probably used his Juan Estruch classical for this recording.[7]

On August 31 Chet recorded five songs for an instrumental album titled *Chet* that was released on Camden, the budget label for RCA. That album was aimed directly at the country audience. He recorded "Foggy Mountain Top," a Carter family song credited to A. P. Carter. Chet let Sonny Osborne and Charlie McCoy play breaks on the banjo and harmonica, respectively. Chet finished the song by playing his "superlick" several times. "Just Out of Reach (Of My Two Empty Arms)" was recorded by Faron Young and Patsy Cline, but Solomon Burke had the most success with it in 1961. "Goin' Down the Road (Feelin' Bad)" is a traditional song, originally named "Lonesome Road Blues" and first recorded by Henry Whitter in 1923. Woody Guthrie was among many others who recorded the song. "Wabash Cannon Ball" is credited to A. P. Carter but dates back to 1882 as "The Great Rock Island Route." The Carter Family released it in 1932, and Chet played it throughout his time with the family. "Bandera" is an instrumental written by Chet.

The sessions for *Chet* on September 14 were produced by Ethel Gabriel, the first female A&R producer for a major label. Gabriel was named head of Camden Records when that label was near failure. Gabriel's leadership transformed the label's fortunes. Subsequently she came to Nashville in 1967 to produce a session on Chet Atkins for Camden.

"Truck Driver's Blues" is considered the first truck driving song. It was written by Ted Daffan, who also wrote "Born to Lose" and "I'm a Fool to Care." "Release Me" was a country hit in 1954 for Ray Price and Kitty Wells, but the biggest hit came from Englebert Humperdinck in 1967. "Oklahoma Hills" was written by Woody Guthrie, but his cousin Jack Guthrie made some changes and recorded it as a western swing number, which is the most popular version. "Oh, Baby Mine" was an R&B hit in 1953 for the Four Knights. It was a country hit for Johnnie and Jack in 1954, produced by Chet. "Make the World Go Away," written by Hank Cochran, was a worldwide hit in 1965 for Eddy Arnold and produced by Chet.

Paul Yandell met Lenny Breau in Canada. "I was with Kitty Wells and we traveled up there all the time," said Yandell. "Every time we were up there, we'd call Lenny and have him come over to the room to play for us after our show. He had a thirty-minute show on the Canadian Broadcast Company. We were up there one time and he came by the room with a seven and half inch tape, the audio from the show. He asked me to take it to Nashville to see if he could get a record deal."

Yandell took the tape to Jerry Kennedy at Mercury Records, but Kennedy's roster was full. Yandell then went to RCA and left it with Chet's secretary. "That afternoon around 4 o'clock, Chet called me," said Yandell. "Hey Paul! This is Chet. Who is this Lenny Breau?' I said, 'It's Lone Pine's boy.' 'How is he doing those chimes, those harmonics?' I said, 'I don't know, Chet.' Chet said, 'Boy, that is really something!'"

Lenny began playing the guitar when he was eight and joined his parents as lead guitarist, billed as Lone Pine Junior. From his earliest days he played the fingerpicking style of Chet Atkins and Merle Travis. At fifteen he made his first recordings and worked as a studio musician. Lenny's interest in jazz led him to incorporate jazz improvisations with his family's group, which led to a slap on the face from his father. He left the group after that and began performing with jazz musicians. He moved to Toronto in 1962 and formed a jazz group, Three, that recorded a live album in New York and appeared on the TV shows of Jackie Gleason and Joey Bishop. Breau then moved back to Winnipeg and began working as a session guitarist. He had his own show on CBC (Canadian Broadcasting Corporation) Television. Breau performed jazz on a seven-string guitar. Yandell told Chet that Breau wanted to get a record deal and Chet asked, "How can I get in touch with him?"" Two or three weeks later Chet had Lenny in Studio B.[8]

Country music awards had been given by the trade magazines *Billboard* and *Cashbox* since the second Disc Jockey Convention in 1953. The board of directors of the Country Music Association was against giving out awards, afraid that there would be hurt feelings because only one artist could receive each award. The board finally relented—possibly because the trade magazines wanted additional advertising revenue—so the first CMA Awards were held on Friday, October 20, 1967, at the Municipal Auditorium.

The show was hosted by Sonny James and Bobbie Gentry and broadcast live over WSM radio but was not televised. The big winner that evening was the song "There's Goes My Everything." It won Song of the Year for songwriter Dallas Frazier and Male Vocalist for

Jack Greene, who released the song; and the album it appeared on won Album of the Year. Eddy Arnold won Entertainer of the Year, Loretta Lynn won Female Vocalist of the Year, and the Stonemans won Group of the Year. Chet Atkins won Instrumentalist of the Year, over Roy Clark, Floyd Cramer, Pete Drake, and Boots Randolph. The Buckaroos won in the Instrumental Group category.

Inducted into the Country Music Hall of Fame that year were Steve Sholes, Jim Reeves, J. L. Frank, and Red Foley.

Chet continued to work with Gretsch, designing and developing ideas for future models. One of his ideas was a guitar with the low E and A strings replaced with the E and A strings from a bass guitar, which meant the strings were an octave lower than a regular guitar's. It was called an octabass guitar. On November 28 Chet recorded three songs on the octabass guitar for his *Solo Flights* album. "Drive-In" was written by James "Spider" Rich, and Chet tuned his guitar a half step higher than standard (F-B flat-E flat-A flat-C-F) but played in E fingering so it sounded like the song was in the key of F. Chet played the octabass on all songs on the first side of the album, while the second side featured Chet playing an acoustic guitar. That album was the only time Chet recorded with an octabass.[9]

The album *Solo Flights* is a bit of a misnomer because Chet did use other musicians (Henry Strzelecki on bass and Jerry Carrigan on drums) for some numbers. "Mercy, Mercy, Mercy" was first recorded by Cannonball Adderley's band. At the time Chet recorded it, it was a pop hit for the Buckinghams, who added lyrics to the song. "Autumn Leaves" was number one for four weeks in 1955 by Roger Williams.

Chet released three studio albums in 1967: *It's a Guitar World*, *Picks the Best*, and *Class Guitar*. A compilation album, *Chet*, was released on the Camden label.

CHAPTER 36

Chet and producer Bob Ferguson were in the studio on the second day of 1968 to record eight songs, although the basic tracks were probably the only things recorded in the studio before Chet's parts were recorded in his basement studio. "Three Little Words" was recorded in 1930 by the Rhythm Boys, featuring Bing Crosby, backed by Duke Ellington's Orchestra. "Cheek to Check" appeared in the film *Top Hat*, starring Fred Astaire and Ginger Rogers. "Gonna Get Along Without You Now" was recorded by Skeeter Davis, who had a top-ten hit on the country chart with the song in 1964; it was produced by Chet.

"When You Wish Upon a Star" came from the 1940 film *Pinocchio* and won the Academy Award for Best Original Song. The song opened every Walt Disney TV show. "Georgy Girl" was composed for the film by the same name and was a hit for the Australian group the Seekers and nominated for an Academy Award. The melody for "Cindy Oh, Cindy" was originally recorded by Vince Martin and the Tarriers in 1956. "Choro Da Saudade" was composed by Agustin Barrios, a Paraguayan classical guitarist and prolific composer. "Music to Watch Girls Go By" was originally recorded by the Bob Crewe Generation as an instrumental. In 1967 Andy Williams recorded it as a vocal.

The Nashville office of RCA added a new member to their A&R staff when Danny Davis joined in January 1968. Davis, a trumpet player, had worked as a producer for MGM, where he produced crossover hits by Johnny Tillotson and Connie Francis. He was then hired by RCA in New York to work with Jose Feliciano and Nina Simone, before he was assigned to Nashville. He joined the Nashville office with the title executive A&R producer and soon formed the Nashville Brass ensemble, which made him one of RCA's best-selling album artists.

Chet was exhausted and needed help. His workload was overwhelming, and he was never satisfied with his performances. He was frustrated because he really wanted to spend more time as a guitarist, but other demands constantly pulled him away.

The Grammys were held on a Thursday evening in February. The presentations in Nashville were held at the National Guard Armory. Chet was a presenter that evening, and "Chet's Tune" was nominated for a Grammy but did not win. However, his album *Chet Atkins Picks on the Best* won a Grammy, Chet's first.

On Monday, March 11 it was announced that Chet had been promoted to vice president in charge of production for RCA's Nashville office. He had held the title of general manager in Nashville since 1957 and had been with the company for twenty years.[1] That same day his father, James "Arlie" Atkins, died in Maynardville, less than twenty miles from Knoxville. The seventy-nine-year-old Atkins was married to his fifth wife, Jewell, who was his childhood sweetheart. According to Chet, his father could never court Jewell when they were young "because her old man would get a shotgun after him. So when the old man finally died, he left his fourth wife and went back to East Tennessee and married her."

Arlie suffered a heart attack on a Sunday evening. He went over to his next-door neighbors and told them, "I'm dying. Jewel will be back in a few days. Take care of the chickens and feed the cow."[2] On Tuesday evening Chet and family members received mourners at a funeral home in Maynardville.

When asked about his father, Chet shared, "He played the first music I ever heard. He sang me to sleep when I was a baby and played the violin when I was in the cradle. He instilled a desire in me to be somebody musically." Chet added that his dad "gave me all my talent, of course. I used to travel around with him when he would teach and I learned a lot by listening to him. He was a very thorough musician. He studied from a lot of different instructors and knew their compositions and all that. He was a tremendous influence on all of us kids."[3]

Chet had a complex relationship with his father. He loved him and wanted to please him but always felt that he fell short. He still remembered that, when he was a young boy, his father had promised him a fiddle but never delivered.

After the funeral Chet returned to Nashville and spoke to a reporter about his RCA promotion. "The difference will be that I'll get to play the guitar more," said Chet, adding that "I'm really a guitar player. I just stumbled into the office job years ago, but I've got to practice and I haven't had time for it." By this time Chet was performing about thirty concerts and recording several albums each year. He had a staff of eight or ten engineers, with forty artists signed to the label. The marketing and publicity campaigns were primarily done from New York. "I looked around for material for everyone, so I sort of neglected myself," said Chet, who stated that he had told RCA executives of his desire to spend more time as a guitarist, so they had approved an expansion of staff to help. The reporter noted that "Mr. Atkins said that he liked producing records but that he was pleased to be more free of administration."

Chet was replaced as manager of the label by Danny Davis.[4] Steve Sholes stated that Chet had done well as an executive: "Most musicians are mostly poor in that area." Years later Chet said of his promotion to vice president, "I really didn't want that title. I was ashamed of it." The reason, he explained, was in part because he didn't like to be thought of as an executive. "I wanted to be known as a guitar player and it also embarrassed me because I didn't even have a high school diploma."[5]

Chet was torn. He felt pride in being an executive with RCA and loved being in the music business in Nashville. If Chet had been just another artist on the RCA label, he would not have had the freedom to record as much as he did. He recorded a lot of his songs in his home studio, then listed them as originating in the RCA studio. Chet had the opportunity to pick the material he wanted with no one questioning his choices, and he had freedom to hire whomever he wished.

The administrative work, paperwork, meetings, and trips to New York were a drain and interfered with his guitar playing but also allowed him to help run RCA, to understand the label's New York executives and what it took to prepare records for release. He could sign artists he wanted to sign and had direct access to the corporate hierarchy. When Chet received his promotion to vice president, he hoped that he could leave behind the administrative job and concentrate more on playing and producing. He had cut back on producing, but there were still artists he wanted produce: Eddy Arnold, Hank Snow, Waylon Jennings, and Willie Nelson. Those artists were top talent, and Chet was a man who appreciated talent in others. There was a lot of prestige attached to being a vice president, but he still had to battle corporate accountants and other red tape. Chet was still shy, complex, and at times tormented, and his stress grew. A key problem was that for most people both inside and outside the music industry,

Chet Atkins *was* RCA, so everything that concerned RCA in Nashville came to him.

On Monday, April 22, Steve Sholes flew into Nashville to attend a meeting of the Country Music Foundation. He rented a car at the airport, and as he drove across the Cumberland River Bridge, he suffered a heart attack and died. This loss dramatically impacted Chet, especially coming a little over a month after the death of his father. Sholes had signed Chet to RCA, hired him as a session leader, and then named him manager of RCA's Nashville office and was instrumental in promoting him to vice president. Sholes always had Chet's back—the buffer between the "suits" in New York and Chet in Nashville. When there were problems with the label, Chet could always call on Sholes—and often did.

Two days after Sholes's death, Chet was in the studio and recorded six songs. "Sweet Georgia Brown" was first recorded by Ben Bernie in 1925 and had been the theme song for the Harlem Globetrotters. "Blue Angel" was written by Nato Lima of Los Indios Tabajaras, and "I always thought [he] wrote it about the [Blue Angels] airplanes that fly in formation," said Chet, "but one night when I played Carnegie Hall and he was in the audience, I asked him and he said he wrote it about the club called the 'Blue Angel' where [Los Indios] played when they first came to New York years ago."

"It's a great tune," continued Chet, "but I had a lotta trouble learning it because Nato recorded it on a guitar that was tuned up a minor third [in pitch]. I think I put a capo on my guitar and imitated what he did; I don't play it exactly like he wrote it but it's pretty close. I learned it [from a Los Indios record] and years later I listened to their record again and I had changed it so much; I rearranged it completely and unconsciously. I didn't intend to do it but I play it entirely different than when I first learned it."

Chet recorded the song on his Juan Estruch classical guitar with a Baldwin Prismatone pickup, backed by Jerry Reed and Earl Porter on guitars, Boyce Hawkins on organ, Bobby Dyson on bass, and Buddy Harman on drums. "Blue Angel" was released as a single when the *Hometown Guitar* album was released, but it did not chart.[6] Chet also recorded "Blue Guitar," "Huntin' Boots," "Get On with It," and "Reed's Ramble."

One week after Sholes's death Chet was in the studio with Hank

Snow for a session. In many ways, the death of Sholes marked the end of an era for Chet, for Snow, for RCA, and for the music industry in general. During the sixties Snow had seen his own music change. He had started the era still putting most of his efforts into singles and chart hits and ended it putting his best efforts into concept albums. Throughout all the radical changes in the music during during this period Snow stayed his course, stubbornly clinging to the classic styles and songs that brought him his initial fame. By the decade's end Hank was being sent material he could not possibly record—even with the promise that it would propel him back into the top ten. "I can't record a song unless I believe in it," said Snow. When the new songs didn't measure up, Hank returned to classics or found new songs modeled on the classics. Hank never turned his back on the past or the great country sound of his early years.[7]

Chet's investments in real estate led him to purchase land on Nolensville Road where a Minnie Pearl's Fried Chicken shop would be built.[8] Chet and Ray Stevens eventually co-owned a lot of property. Stevens would find properties and alert Chet, who supplied the finances. "He never questioned me," said Stevens.[9]

On May 10 Chet recorded twelve songs with Bob Ferguson producing. Chet rerecorded some of the songs from his 1961 album *Chet Atkins at Home*: "Sophisticated Lady," "Say Si Si," "Vilia," "Martha," "In the Chapel in the Moonlight," "Czardas," "Nagasaki," and "April in Portugal." In addition he recorded "Cattle Call," written by Tex Owen and Eddy Arnold's theme song. "The Last Thing on My Mind" was written by Tom Paxton, who recorded it in 1964. It was also the debut single for Porter Wagoner and Dolly Parton on RCA. "Blues for Dr. Joe" was written by Chet, and "Yesterdays" appeared in the 1933 musical *Roberta*.

David Conrad was visiting a friend in Nashville who loved Chet Atkins's playing. *The Boyce Hawkins Show* was a local television production on WSM, and in June 1968 Chet was scheduled to perform on the early morning show on Thursday, but not wanting to get up earlier than usual, insisted the show be taped on Wednesday evening.

Conrad and his friend went to the taping and were sitting in the bleachers while Chet was sitting on a stool, by himself, as the show started. Conrad's friend urged him to meet Chet, but Conrad was reluctant, wanting to wait until the show was over. His friend told him that everyone else would want to meet him then, so Conrad walked over with the book Red O'Donnell had written on Chet and introduced himself: "I am David Conrad from North Carolina." Chet asked, "What are you doing up here?" Conrad replied that he was visiting friends. Chet had to hand his guitar to Conrad in order to autograph the book. "Hold this," said Chet as he took the book. Conrad remembered that "he was looking for a suitable page to sign. He never did anything in a hurry." As Chet did this he told Conrad, "Play me a little something." Conrad put his foot on a rung of the stool and played "Quiet Nights." After he signed the book, Chet handed it to Conrad and took back the guitar. "You've got a nice touch there," said Chet. "You want to play on this show with me tonight?" David said, "I don't have anything prepared. I better not." As the announcer said, "Here he is—Chet Atkins!" Chet turned and said, "You'll be fine. Sit there until I call you."

David was in a bind. "I got a choice," remembered Conrad. "Stay there like he told me to do, because he is going to call me and if I'm not there, then that embarrasses him." Chet played a song, and then Hawkins asked him to play another, but Chet replied, "Well, Boyce, I found a kid out there in the studio. His name is David Conrad and he is from North Carolina." Conrad was amazed. "He remembered everything I said to him in those few seconds back stage, just tossed it off!" Then Chet said, "Let's get him out here. He'll pick a tune for us!"

Conrad walked over, shook hands, and sat down between them. Hawkins said, "Chet says you're a pretty good guitar player but I need you to play for the folks. You've got to prove it!" and with that he handed Conrad a cheap classical guitar. Conrad was trying to tune it while Hawkins asked him what he was going to play. Conrad said, "I would like to play 'One Note Samba' by Jobim. I like Bossa Nova a lot." Conrad continued trying to tune the guitar in an awkward situation. Then Chet got up, took the guitar from Conrad, and handed David his Juan Estruch classical guitar. "I think he would rather play this one," said Chet. Conrad yelled "A-flat," and the band and Conrad began playing. Chet was sitting, noodling, and tuning the other guitar, then when it came time for the bridge, Conrad knew only the chord progression so he yelled, "Take the bridge!" and Chet "just ripped on through it and played the heck out of it."

After they finished that song they played "Satin Doll" and "Girl From Ipanema." When the show concluded, the crowd surged around

Conrad as well as Chet. At that point Conrad was thinking, "I'm not going home. I'm not going to college. Momma can just send all my stuff over here!" Finally, David and Chet made their way back to each other and Conrad told him, "This was one of the most wonderful things of my life. I'm committed to this! What can I say? Where do we go from here?" Chet looked at him and said, "Well, you're going back home to North Carolina and go to college and I'm going to go get a haircut" and laughed.

Chet could see Conrad was disappointed but told him, "Nah, you go back home. I'm going to be here anytime you want or need me. Stay in touch. I'm not going anywhere. Go to school and come back and I'll be here and we'll pick another one."[10]

On June 14 it was announced that RCA had promoted Chet again; this time he was responsible for the entire Nashville operation of the Record Division of RCA, which meant he would handle all the policy responsibilities for RCA's Nashville operation that had formerly been handled by Steve Sholes. It was the best of times and the worst of times; he received a promotion that he could not turn down for duties he did not want to carry out but had to do it because his mentor, Sholes, who formerly handled those duties, was gone. Sholes was like a father figure to Chet as well as the entire Nashville operation for RCA; now Chet would have to take on that role, even though he yearned for less day-to-day involvement in the administration of RCA's Nashville office.

Reflecting back on that time, Chet told author Alanna Nash that if Sholes hadn't died "I'm sure that I would have. But when he died I made up my mind that I was going to slow down, so I started hiring people, and gradually I turned all the artists over to other A&R men, with the exception of Hank Snow and Jerry Reed."[11]

On August 14 Chet recorded "Slick," "Prayer Meetin'," "Lady Madonna," and "Grazing in the Grass." On August 23, with Felton Jarvis and Bob Ferguson producing, he recorded a session of current and near-current hits by pop artists. He recorded Simon & Garfunkel's hit "Mrs. Robinson," featured in *The Graduate*, "Sleep Safe and Warm (Lullaby from Rosemary's Baby)" from *Rosemary's Baby*, and "Sealed With a Kiss," which had been a hit for Bryan Hyland in 1962 and was a current hit by Gary Lewis & the Playboys. "Stoned Soul Picnic" was written by Laura Nyro and a hit by the Fifth Dimension, and "The Sound of Silence" was a hit by Simon & Garfunkel 1965–1966. "Slick" was written by Herb Alpert and followed his hit, "This Guy's in Love with You." Atkins probably bet on "Slick" being a hit, but it wasn't. "Lady Madonna" was a Beatles song, and "Grazing in the Grass" was a hit in 1968 for South Africa performer Hugh Masekela and was featured in *The Graduate*.

CHAPTER 37

On a Tuesday evening in September the Master's Festival of Music performed a concert at Nashville's Municipal Auditorium to a near capacity audience. Boots Randolph opened the show with a medley of "Yellow Rose of Texas" and "Dixie." Randolph then played "The Shadow of Your Smile," before Floyd Cramer performed "By the Time I Get to Phoenix" and a sprightly rendition of "Gentle on My Mind." He then did a Hank Williams medley of "Your Cheatin' Heart," "Why Don't You Love Me," and "Jambalaya." The special guest was clarinetist Pete Fountain, who performed "Way Down Yonder in New Orleans," "High Society," and "Skater's Waltz" with his quintet, before he performed solo on "Just a Closer Walk with Thee." The quintet did "When the Saints Go Marching In" before performing "Going Out of My Head."

Homer and Jethro performed parodies of "King of the Road" and "Something Stupid" for the audience, before Chet took the stage and played "Zorba the Greek," "Lara's Song (Theme from *Doctor Zhivago*)," and "How Insensitive." Jerry Reed joined Chet, and they played "Memories of the Alhambra," which Chet said was the "only classical work" the audience would hear that night. The show finished with all the musicians on the stage belting out "Hello Dolly," which was a number-one hit for Louis Armstrong in 1964.[1]

Guitarist John Johns first met Chet in May 1960 and around 1968 was a student at the Peabody Conservatory of Music in Baltimore. Aaron Shearer, a prominent classical guitar teacher at the Peabody Conservatory, needed money to fund a guitar scholarship and knew that John had a relationship with Chet and asked him how to make contact so Shearer could meet Elvis and ask for scholarship money. Shearer flew to Nashville and met Chet, who told him that he couldn't even get to Elvis. Shearer was disappointed, but he and Chet talked about Johns and Chet remembered him.

About a year later "Mr. Shearer had promised me that scholarship for my senior year of study," but the funding had been cut in half "and the next thing I know I was called into the Dean's office at Peabody," said Johns. In his office the dean put an envelope on his desk and said, "Here is what came for you." Johns opened a check from Chet Atkins payable to the Peabody Conservatory for the other half of his scholarship.[2]

On September 6 Chet was back in the studio with Felton Jarvis and Bob Ferguson producing to record more recent hits. He did "Light My Fire," a hit for the Doors in 1967, "Harper Valley P.T.A.," a crossover hit for Jeannie C. Riley, and "It Never Hurts to Ask," by Tupper Saussey. In October came an announcement from the president of Aurora Publishers that they would publish a book and record by Chet Atkins with guitar lessons. *Play Guitar with Chet Atkins* featured Chet playing and instructing "Nine Pound Hammer," "Red Wing," "Side," "Windy and Warm," and "Hello My Baby."[3]

During 1968 the Country Music Association's board of directors knew that the best way to promote country music was to have their awards show telecast on network TV, but no company approached them offering to sponsor. Irving Waugh, the head of WSM, and Jack Stapp, chief of Tree Publishing, both had connections with major advertising agencies. They traveled to New York to visit J. Walter Thompson, which handled advertising for Kraft, about sponsoring a telecast of the CMA Awards on their "Kraft Music Hall" program. The agency was set to sponsor a show hosted by Roy Rogers and Dale Evans from Texas but during the visit decided to let the husband-and-wife team host the CMA Awards Show from the Ryman Auditorium. There were no big-name stars outside the world of country music, and the awards show was not televised live because the advertising executives were not convinced that it would draw an audience.

The show was taped on October 18 and saw Glen Campbell win Male Vocalist and Entertainer of the Year honors, Tammy Wynette won the Female Vocalist award, and Porter Wagoner and Dolly Parton won Group of the Year honors. The album of the year was *At Folsom Prison* by Johnny Cash, the Single of the Year was "Harper Valley P.T.A.," recorded by Jeannie C. Riley, and Song of the Year was "Honey," written by Bobby Russell and recorded by Bobby Goldsboro. Chet Atkins won Instrumentalist of the Year for the second time.

On the evening of November 20 TV viewers could watch Chet present Porter and Dolly the CMA Award for Vocal Group of the Year after deadpanning, "This is kinda easy, but I'd rather be playing the guitar." Later, when Chet received the CMA Award for Instrumentalist of the Year from Dick Clark, he thanked Django Reinhardt, Les Paul, Merle Travis, and "the fella that invented the guitar years ago."[4]

Chet was in the studio for three successive days in November to record twelve songs. In the studio with Chet were Jerry Reed, Richard Morris (vibes/bells), William Sanders (bass), and a string section that included seven violins, two violas, and two cellos. (Brenton Banks was on this session.) Chet wanted to do an album of instrumental versions of current hits on the radio. He also began recording *Relaxin' with Chet*, which contained eight songs from his *Chet Atkins at Home* album from 1958. Chet was also working on *Lover's Guitar*, with him playing his classical and Del Vecchio guitars. On November 20 he recorded four songs, including three by Francisco Tarrega, the Spanish composer who is often considered the father of the classical guitar: "Cajita de Musica," "Recuerdos de la Alhambra," and "Estudio Brillante." Chet also recorded "Cancion del Viento (Song of the Wind)," by Mexican composer Alfonso Esarza Oteo.

"The Look of Love" was written by the hit songwriting team of Burt Bacharach and Hal David and was first recorded by Dusty Springfield for the James Bond film *Casino Royale*. "Hawaiian Wedding Song" is traced back to a song written in Hawaiian that, translated to English, meant "Waiting There for Thee." It was renamed for Elvis's 1961 rendition in *Blue Hawaii*. "Theme from *Zorba the Greek*" was written for the 1964 film starring Anthony Quinn. "Those Were the Days" was a hit for Mary Hopkins in 1968. "Until It's Time for You to Go" was written by Canadian singer-songwriter Buffy Sainte-Marie and appeared on her 1965 album *Many a Mile*. "If I Should Lose You" was composed for the 1936 film *Rose of the Rancho*. Chet's friends Jerry Reed and John D. Loudermilk each supplied a song. "La Madrugada" was by Reed and "The Odd Folks of Okracoke" was written by John D. Loudermilk.

On December 12 Chet was on the *Joey Bishop Show* on ABC with guests Mel Torme, Kaye Stevens, and comedian John Byner. Four days later Chet was on the *Mike Douglas Show* and brought along Jerry Reed, who accompanied him on "Zorba the Greek" and "What'd I Say."[5]

During 1968 RCA released three studio albums by Chet, *Hometown Guitar*, *Solid Gold 68*, and *Solo Flights* and a compilation album, *Chet All the Way*. Photographer Jimmy Moore shot the cover for

Hometown Guitar in Chet's hometown of Luttrell. Chet and Moore "left Nashville early one morning in a rent-a-car with cameras, film, guitars and a truck load of clothes and several boxes of those little cigars Chet liked to chew on," said Moore. "As we drove into Luttrell, Chet began to talk: 'There is the place where I heard a jukebox play for the first time and over there is where I saw my first guitar and over there is where I started to learn to play.' As we pulled up in the yard of his childhood home I noticed a little gray-haired lady sitting at the top of the steps on the porch," said Moore. "It was his mother, Ida Sharp Atkins. Chet reached out and hugged her and said 'Mom this is Jimmy Moore, a friend of mind from Nashville.'"

For the album cover shoot, "Chet and I went down to the old railroad station to see if we might use it for the album cover picture," said Moore. "We both thought it was a good idea, because the old wooden sign hanging on both ends of the depot identified the stop as Luttrell." After taking pictures, Chet and Jimmy went back to Mrs. Atkins's home, where "his mother made sure I was stuffed with dinner, which was fried chicken, mashed potatoes, vegetables and apple pie."[6]

By 1970, the failures of Chet's early career were behind him, and he was comfortable in his role as head of RCA's Nashville division and secure in his role as a pillar in the Nashville musical community. He enjoyed wealth and fame, although not like the superstars who sang. He was confident as a guitar player—widely considered to be the best guitarist in Nashville—but he still practiced.

Paul Hemphill wrote *The Nashville Sound*, released in 1970, the first book-length look at the country music industry in Nashville. Hemphill interviewed Chet and devoted a chapter to him. He noted that at ten o'clock sharp Chet drove into the parking lot of the RCA Building in his Cadillac, got out, locked his car, then walked into the back door, nodding to people who were in the hallway. Hemphill described Chet as "a stringy, unobtrusive East Tennessean" wearing "a soft royal-blue blazer and a polka-dot tie." As soon as Chet was in his office he took a phone call from a friend in Paterson, New Jersey, who wanted his advice about selling guitar lessons through the mail. Then a songwriter came to play a song as Chet lit a cigar stub.

Hemphill traced Chet's background and early years and then discussed the challenges country music faced from rock and roll. He gave Chet credit for the success of the Nashville Sound and country music in general. "It was time for experimentation and change, and few people were more prepared to guide Nashville through its most trying period than Chet Atkins, who had the back-country roots of all the great country musicians but had gone a giant step further by developing interests in such diverse areas as poetry, classical music, philosophy and electronics," wrote Hemphill, who said Chet was "not simply a 'picker,' but a master musician who was at home on the stage of the Opry as he was guesting with the Nashville Symphony or playing at the White House."

He noted that Atkins "quietly pulled country music out of a rut and kept pace with the new technology and changing tastes, and in the mid-Sixties when the phrase, 'the Nashville Sound,' was coined, it amounted to a tribute to him," continuing that "the Nashville Sound is the loose, relaxed improvised feeling found on almost anything recorded out of Nashville today, and if any one man could be credited with creating it, the man would be Chet Atkins." Hemphill called Atkins "the most respected musician on Music Row," adding that Chet produces "three or four recording sessions each week."[7]

The writer noted that Chet is "one of the wealthiest men on Music Row" due to his real estate and stock investments, "yet his wife cuts his hair." His office "is highlighted by a boomerang-shaped velvet sofa and a nude statue carved from rare Philippine wood and an ashtray engraved TO CHET—THANKS—TRINI. It was given to Chet by Trini Lopez, who came to Nashville to record his album, *Welcome to Trini Country*."[8]

Chet met with singer Stu Phillips and arranger Bill Walker to discuss an upcoming session. As they went over songs Chet put a tape of "Rings of Grass," written by Shel Silverstein, on the reel-to-reel recorder. Silverstein was a friend of *Playboy* publisher Hugh Hefner, who had published illustrated articles in *Playboy* featuring Silverstein's time in a nudist camp. "Ol' Shel's probably got the worst voice of anybody alive, but I'm not knocking anybody with a deal like he's got," said Chet. "Can you imagine him and Hefner and thirty Bunnies in that house?"

Phillips picked up the lyric sheet as they listened to the tape and began singing while Chet grabbed a guitar leaning against the wall and began playing along. After listening to the demo a second time, Chet suggested using his "tree cymbal" on the recording. "It's shaped kinda like a Christmas tree about two feet high," said Atkins. "Got those doughnut-looking cymbals that get bigger from the top to the bottom of the pole they're on. You rake a drumstick up or down, and it makes a pretty good sound."

"Where'd you find that?" asked Phillips.

"Pakistan," replied Chet. "You can import one for about a hundred dollars. Makes a nice decorative piece."

"A hundred dollars for a decorative piece?"

"I've got mine at the house," said Chet.

"You're rich, all right."

After discussing other songs as possibilities for the upcoming session, Phillips sang a song he had written while Chet "strummed his guitar with the cover to a book of safety matches"[9]

"In a way, the session that morning had said all there is to say about what has been happening in Nashville lately," wrote Hemphill. "Here, in a town that once belonged to Roy Acuff and Ernest Tubb and Uncle Dave Macon and The Solemn Ole Judge, you have a suave Canadian singer and an Australian arranger and a guitar picker from the Clinch Mountains kicking around a song written by the bald and bearded philosopher-in-residence of the Playboy Mansion."[10]

Waylon Jennings was frustrated because he wanted to record with his own band, but there was an invisible barrier between studio musicians and road musicians. Time was valuable when recording in a studio, so Nashville producers booked session musicians because they were certain to get three or four songs—and sometimes five or six—in a three-hour session. Producers and session musicians regularly worked together; producers knew that session musicians were talented and very fast. The same could not be said for road musicians, who might not learn a song as quickly or provide a memorable lick quickly under pressure. Nashville producers knew session musicians but did not know road musicians. Under the gun to keep costs down, producers were concerned that the costs would be higher if they hired road musicians. According to Jennings, Chet treated road musicians as "aliens."

"That was part of the problem," said Waylon. "It was his framework, part of a Nashville sound that had been engraved in stone. They had a system. It was like an assembly line, and they rolled off records like clockwork, working more for efficiency than emotion, a song per hour and maybe a fourth if there was ten minutes till the three-hour session was scheduled to end. Chet wanted me to be myself," said Waylon, "but he wanted me to be myself with musicians he knew were great."

Chet used some of Waylon's band on the early sessions, but after those first sessions he " got nervous and called in the studio pickers. In his view, he probably had a point. Bands that work in clubs with the artist aren't very fast about learning new arrangements, or changing things on the spot," said Waylon. "Chet would get together with me and discuss who to hire in the studio, and we would wait to get to the session to work out the arrangement," continued Waylon. "At first I was a little hesitant about suggesting things, but Chet appreciated ideas. He believed that, in the record business, you sell an awful lot of records by not following trends; instead, the idea was to start a trend of your own. We both had the same idea, but we were coming at it from different directions."

"He listened to everybody," said Waylon, "which is probably why he was a great producer. He was making so damn many records, though, juggling twenty or thirty acts, that he could hardly concentrate on each one. Still, despite his many artists, as well as his executive duties at RCA, he would always look to get something different in each record, trying to spot something in the rhythm section he could feature, to make the record sound distinctive."

RCA had a contract with the engineers union that required an RCA engineer in all sessions. "Chet thought there was nothing wrong with that. 'Studios are all alike,'" he told Waylon. "Same equipment, everything." However, at RCA in Nashville, Studio B was older and smaller, so there was a "warmth" between the musicians and the singer. Studio A was newer and bigger, with high ceilings and room for an entire orchestra.

Artists using drugs made Chet nervous. "About the third time I visited with Chet, he asked me if I did drugs," said Waylon. "I thought, well, I'm not going to start this out wrong. I said 'yeah.' Godomighty, he was mad. From then on, he was watching me. He didn't know how to deal with that, and he couldn't stand to see somebody throw their life away. He did not understand drugs, and he didn't understand people on them," continued Waylon. "Chet didn't want to understand them. He'd been through Don Gibson, and then Roger [Miller], and then here I come. Chet was from East Tennessee, where they drink moonshine all the time. When he thought high, he thought whiskey. He never took a pill in his life. 'I think you got so many beats in your heart,' he'd say. 'Why shorten them?'"

"If anything, Chet was too nice," said Waylon. "He would internalize so much that he grew a tumor, and suffered cancer of the intestines.

The business literally made him sick. The stress was too much," adding that "Chet was at a point where he was just tired, and he was wanting out of it. He needed to go back and play his guitar."[11]

"Waylon wanted to make his own records," said Chet, "and, at the time, we had Bob Ferguson, Ray Pennington, Felton Jarvis and Danny Davis as staff producers. I knew that if all the artists started producing for themselves, then all these guys would be out of a job. I was trying to protect them when I voiced my sentiments that I didn't think it was good for the artists to produce themselves." Chet later admitted that "I was wrong, but I felt real close to Ferguson and some of those guys."[12]

Chet was a musician who had to fulfill the roll of a "company man." Steve Sholes, who was the ultimate "company man," had protected Chet when he had to deal with the New York executives. After Sholes's death Chet had to call New York to get approvals for marketing and promotion "and they held him, and us hillbillies, at arm's length. They still ran everything from both coasts, and we were caught in the middle," said Jennings.[13]

On March 16 Chet and the Masters Festival of Music with Boots Randolph and Floyd Cramer made their first appearance on the *Ed Sullivan Show* on CBS. Chet played a solo of "Autumn Leaves" and then joined Boots and Floyd on "Yakety Sax," "On the Rebound," and "Rock a Bye Your Baby with a Dixie Melody."[14]

During 1969 there were dramatic changes in country music: Glen Campbell and Johnny Cash had network TV shows, and Bob Dylan was recording in Nashville. It was the year when men landed on the moon, when demonstrations against the Vietnam War on college campuses were considered a major threat to the nation, and when Richard Nixon was inaugurated. RCA artists did two or three albums a year and released a steady stream of singles. Many of those albums contained hits by other artists because they were proven hits and the sales department in New York pushed for albums that sold; Chet did his best to stack the odds in his favor.

The executives and studio musicians were not part of the Baby Boom generation, and the music coming out of Nashville was becoming outdated. Studio musicians and record executives were all part of the Great Depression and World War II. The men of that Greatest Generation shielded their emotions and were not introspective.

The session musicians were technically proficient and prided themselves on their flawless playing, but the Baby Boomers sought a deeper sense of meaning and emotion in music. In country music the stories and emotions are important, but music is the business of entertainment, which the Baby Boomers felt was shallow. Mainly, it was a shift in generations and the longtime A Team players were gradually being replaced by younger A Team players. The session players knew each other and played together on countless recordings, developing a camaraderie, knowing what each could play. They also banded together to keep new musicians outside their circle. Loyalty was a key factor in this generation, but when the winds of change blow hard that loyalty can be detrimental. Major labels, which were part of major corporations, were loyal only to the bottom line; those who were not showing a profit were dropped. Accountants can be heartless in the music business.

CHAPTER 38

Muscle Shoals, Alabama, was a hot R&B recording center during the sixties and seventies, with two studios, FAME and Muscle Shoals Sound, hosting a number of R&B artists and turning out great R&B hits like "You Better Move On" by Arthur Alexander, "When a Man Loves a Woman" by Percy Sledge, "Mustang Sally" by Wilson Pickett, and "Sweet Soul Music" by Arthur Conley. Musicians who were an important part of the Muscle Shoals sound included Norbert Putnam on bass, David Briggs on keyboard, and Jerry Carrigan on drums. All three were in-demand musicians for the Muscle Shoals sessions, but local studios avoided the Musicians Union, so Putnam and Briggs were underpaid. That's a major reason that all of them moved to Nashville, where they had to adapt to country music. Chet Atkins and Owen Bradley were two major producers in Nashville, so the Muscle Shoals boys were going to have to fit in with Chet and Owen after they moved two hours up the road.

The first session that bassist Norbert Putnam did with Chet Atkins came when he played on a session for Skeeter Davis, who was recording *Skeeter Davis Sings Standards* in RCA's big Studio A. When he entered the studio Putnam saw eight violins, four violas, two cellos, a harp, a French horn, and a rhythm section consisting of David Briggs on piano, Farrell Morris on vibes and percussion, Harold Bradley on tic-tac bass, Jerry Carrigan on drums, and three guitars—two electric and one acoustic. The Nashville Edition, four singers led by Hershel Wiggington, were also there. Standing in front of the musicians was Ray Stevens, who had arranged the orchestration and was conducting.

When the clock struck ten, everyone was tuned and ready. Ray Stevens counted "a one, two, three" and the musicians began playing "Dear Heart," a Henry Mancini standard. Jim Malloy was in the control room at the board—but Norbert couldn't see Chet Atkins. Then, as the song was ending, Chet came "sneaking into the control room for the first time." When the song ended Chet pressed the talkback button: "Skeeter, honey, where in the world are you?"

"Oh, hi, Chet, they've got me over here in the corner, all baffled off. I'm afraid I can't see you or the control room, but I'm sure glad you're here."

Skeeter was surrounded by large baffles to control the sound, and she could see Ray Stevens only through a small window in one of the baffles.

"Well, honey, your voice sure sounds mighty fine this morning. Would you like to try and make one?" Skeeter agreed and the red light went on as Ray Stevens counted off the start. When the music began Chet snuck out of the control room into the hallway and practiced his putting until, as the song ended, he came back in.

"Skeeter, how did that feel to you?" asked Chet. "Well," she said, "it felt pretty good to me." "Well, honey," said Chet, "if it felt good to you, let's give the boys a ten-minute break and then move on to the next song."[1]

Millie Kirkham, who sang background on a number of records, said about Chet's producing, "Chet didn't do anything—the musicians and singers did it all."[2] There's a bit of truth to that—Chet was often hands-off until or unless help was needed.

Chet's *Solid Gold '69* was released that same year, and Norbert Putnam played on that album and provided insight into Chet as an artist. The album was produced by Bob Ferguson and Putman was "a little surprised" when Ferguson called him and said, "Putt, Chester's going to do a new record album and he was wonderin' if you could arrange the *strangs and thangs*." (That was Putnam's imitation of Ferguson's pronunciation.) Ferguson explained that "Chet had heard an arrangement Putnam wrote for a Burt Bacharach tune and really liked it." The album would be "Broadway and Hollywood tunes," and it made Putnam nervous to be faced with arranging an entire album. When Putnam expressed his concern, Ferguson replied, "I'm sure you'll do just fine" and told Putnam he'd set up the sessions "as soon as Chet picks out the tunes."

Putnam thought the sessions would be weeks away, then discovered they were only a week out. Putnam called Ferguson to tell him he didn't think he'd have enough time but was assured, "Ah, Putt, don't worry. You won't need to write anything for the tracking date. Chet will just play the tunes like a normal session and everybody can write their own charts. Then you can take your time with the string parts, which we'll overdub later. Don't worry, it'll be easy!" There were three sessions—nine hours—scheduled to get twelve songs.

When Putnam arrived at Studio B before the ten o'clock morning session, A Team players were waiting: Hargus "Pig" Robbins on piano, Jerry Carrigan on drums, Ray Edenton on rhythm guitar, and Jerry Reed and Wayne Moss on electric guitar. Chet's famous Gretsch was missing. "Suddenly, there was a loud commotion as Bob and Chet entered the studio," said Putnam. "They were shaking hands and laughing, sharing stories with the guys and, within minutes, Jerry Reed had Chet bent over his guitar, intently watching as Jerry played some amazingly difficult riff he'd just invented." Putnam noticed that Ferguson placed a large stack of records by the RCA console phonograph, then raised his hand and asked for quiet.

"Fellers, we're goin' to do some of this Hollywood Broadway stuff," said Ferguson, "and since we've just finished pickin' out the songs, poor Chester hasn't had a chance to learn any of it. Soooo, we'll just go ahead and cut the backing tracks—I've got a list of the keys—and Chet's got a golf game to get to and, oh yeah, I've brought along most of the records so we'll just take the changes off that. We'll do the tracks and Chet can overdub his part at his home studio." Ferguson paused, then said, "*Oh . . . and then Putt's gonna write the strangs and thangs.*" After he walked around the room, Ferguson said, "Okay then, it's ten o'clock and if there are no questions, let's go ahead and get started." Chet waved good-bye as Ferguson walked with him to his car. "Well, this wasn't exactly what I'd hoped for," remembered Putnam. "I really wanted to see the great man play the guitar, show us the tunes, talk about the arrangements."

The first song on the session was "The Age of Aquarius" (listed on the album as "Aquarius"), from the Broadway musical *Hair*. This wasn't an everyday three-chord country song, and the musicians struggled to write their charts, but pianist Pig Robbins had the chords and harmonies figured out quickly. The musicians recorded the Beatles song "Blackbird," Joni Mitchell's "Both Sides Now," which was a hit for Judy Collins in 1968, and "Son of a Preacher Man," written by Nashville songwriters John Hurley and Ronnie Wilkins and a hit for Dusty Springfield. "I'll Never Fall in Love Again," written by Hal David and Burt Bacharach, was a hit for Dionne Warwick, "Folsom Prison Blues" was a Johnny Cash song, and "Jean" by Oliver came from the film *The Prime of Miss Jean Brodie* and was written by Rod McKuen. "Love Theme from Romeo and Juliet," also known as "A Time for Us," was a number-one pop hit for Henry Mancini. "Lady Madonna" was another Beatles song.

On each of the songs an arrangement was worked out by the rhythm section and they began playing it. "Wow," thought Putnam, "some bunch of country musicians, I thought, as they played the complicated changes perfectly. I would not be quick to underestimate this group of 'country boys.'" A few adjustments, then the red light came on and the song was recorded. Putnam wished that Chet was sitting in the same room, playing his Gretsch and smiling, but as he listened to the playback of each song he "began to understand the tremendous amount of trust and respect that Mr. Atkins had for this group of men. He had literally entrusted us *totally* with his new album, without a second thought."

The musicians completed the album in the allotted time. A few weeks later Ferguson called Putnam and told him that Chet had finished his guitar parts. Putt drove over to RCA and picked up the tape. As he listened to the songs, Putnam "couldn't help but admire the impeccable taste and flawless technique displayed by the great master. I imagined him sitting there, alone in his private studio, punching in the various eight-bar phrases, one at a time." Because multitracking was now part of recording "Chet could stay home and slowly, at his leisure, complete his solos."

Putnam observed during other sessions with Chet that he "would never pick up a guitar in the studio and play a part in front of Grady Martin or Wayne Moss or Jerry Reed" and realized the reason was "he didn't want to stress out the lesser gods."[3]

Chet was an investor in a hotel chain, Tudor Inns of America, and was named to their board of directors at the end of May. In addition to being on the board for the motel chain, Chet was also on the board for the State Mental Health Association and the Music City Golf Tournament and was past director of the Tennessee Heart Fund Association and served on the board for the Country Music Association.[4]

During the summer an article in *Billboard* announced a $600,000 "renovation plan" of the RCA building and studio owned by Chet, Owen, and Harold Bradley. The plan called for the installation of additional sixteen-track equipment and "expanded office space." The tenants on the second floor were removed, and construction was set to begin on

August 1 for a "complex of suites" for Chet and the four producers on staff headed by Danny Davis and including Bob Ferguson, Felton Jarvis, and the just-hired Ronnie Light. There would be an office for Dot Boyd, administrator, and an audition and conference room. The second floor would house the main reception area.

The first floor, where Chet's office was located, would house a new overdub studio with sixteen-track equipment and the office of Ed Hines, who headed RCA's custom sales. On the second floor Chet would have a large office. Also, a large office area for Wally Cochran, director of public relations and country promotion, would be built. The engineering area would be on the first floor, and there would be new equipment for the original RCA studio, now known as "Studio B."[5]

On June 6 Chet recorded a second album with Arthur Fiedler and the Boston Pops at Symphony Hall in Boston. On the album, titled *Chet Atkins Picks on the Pops*, were "Delilah," "Ode to Billy Joe," "Scarborough Fair/Canticle," "Wimoweh," "By the Time I Get to Phoenix," "This Guy's in Love with You," "Spanish Harlem," "Galveston," "The Last Waltz," and a medley of "The Battle of New Orleans" and "Sugarfoot Rag." This was the last album he recorded with the Boston Pops, although he appeared with them several times on *Evenings at Pops* broadcasts on Public Television.

Chet remembered that Fiedler, who was seventy-four at the time of the concert, "spent intermissions from recitals drinking a boiler-maker, then returned to his podium before one of the world's finest pop orchestras." Members of the orchestra "could talk to Fiedler," said Chet, "but only after making an appointment."[6]

On the evening of July 23 Chet was in the studio with Hank Snow for a duet guitar album and they recorded "Limbo Rock," "Hold Me Tight," "Tammy," and "Jamaica Farewell." The next day they recorded "Everybody Does It in Hawaii," "I Saw the Light," "The Green Leaves of Summer," and "Difficult," which was written by Chet and James "Spider" Rich. On July 29 Snow recorded "Wheels," "Tiptoeing" (written by Snow and Chet), and "Poison Love." Chet and Hank wanted to sing "Poison Love" and added vocals on October 27. At the end of the song they ribbed each other, with Snow telling Chet to stick to the guitar and Chet telling Snow to stick to singing.[7]

Chet played in the Music City Pro-Celebrity golf tournament, which the Aurora Publishing team won. The following week it was announced that Chet was on the board of directors for Aurora, which had been formed in April and was the first commercial publishing house in the South without political or religious affiliation. The company was formed to "publish books and other materials in the graphic arts and produce recordings in several specified areas of interest." The first book was a cookbook by Minnie Pearl, and there were over forty others in various stages of production. The announcement stated that "Atkins will take an active part in the operation of Aurora Publishers, Inc. and provide additional variety to its board." Chet "has been working on a three-man committee to select figures for a country music wax museum to be established here by Aurora," stated the announcement.[8]

The *Kraft Music Hall Presents the Third Annual Country Music Awards* TV show in 1969 was the first CMA Awards Show that was broadcast live. The evening belonged to Johnny Cash, who won Entertainer of the Year and Top Male Vocalist; his *At San Quentin* won Album of the Year and "A Boy Named Sue" won Single of the Year. Chet presented Johnny and June Cash their award for Vocal Group of the Year, while Song of the Year was "Carroll County Accident," written by Bob Ferguson and recorded by Porter Wagoner. Gene Autry was elected to the Country Music Hall of Fame; "I'm back in the saddle again" he exclaimed. Chet repeated as Instrumentalist of the Year.

The year 1969 was big for Merle Haggard, whose "Okie from Muskogee" gave a voice to the "silent majority" of country fans who did not like the liberal counterculture.

In October Chet recorded "Country Champagne," and on December 2 he was in the studio with producer Bob Ferguson and recorded "Yestergroovin'," "Liberty," and "Rocky Top." Although Chet was cutting back on his producing duties, he continued to produce Hank Snow. In December he was in the studio with Snow for an album of Jimmie Rodgers songs titled *Hank Snow Sings (In Memory of Jimmie Rodgers)*. Chet also continued to produce Eddy Arnold and in December recorded "Mary in the Morning" and a song written by Bobby Goldsboro, "With Pen in Hand." Four days after Christmas

Arnold was back in the studio for three straight days of recording. On the morning of New Year's Eve he recorded three songs, including "Soul Deep," a song written by Wayne Carson Thompson that had been a pop hit for the Box Tops.

The albums of the late 1960s followed the successful pattern set by RCA during the early part of the decade. There were collections of cover versions of others' hits or albums with a certain theme, like girls' names or places. During 1969 Chet released three studio albums, *Lover's Guitar*, and *Solid Gold 69*, and *Chet Atkins Picks on the Pops*, and a compilation album, *Relaxin' with Chet*, was released on Camden. Chet, with Homer and Jethro, released *The Nashville String Band* album.

CHAPTER 39

Chet was interested in promoting music education, especially for guitarists, and called a press conference on the afternoon of January 14 to announce the creation of a scholarship fund "to make higher education possible for people who have an outstanding talent as a guitarist or songwriter." There would be a national search for winners, with final competitions in Nashville in August after a series of regional competitions. The scholarships would be presented during the Chet Atkins Guitar and Song Festival. Thirty-seven people would sit on a board of directors, "representing a wide cross-section of the local and national music industry, as well as large financial interests." The board would sponsor $11,000 in scholarships for deserving musicians of promise.[1]

Chet continued work on his *Yestergroovin'* album in January when he recorded three songs. "Cherokee" was written by British dance band leader Ray Noble, while "How High the Moon" was recorded by the Les Paul Trio in 1945 and reached the number-one position on the *Billboard* chart in 1951. "Inka Dinka Doo" was written by Jimmy Durante and Ben Ryan and was introduced in the 1934 film *Palooka*. It became Durante's theme song during his career. The next afternoon the group recorded "Makin' Up," "Steeplechase Lane," which was written by Jerry Reed, and the Billy Grammar hit "Gotta Travel On." On the third day of recording the group started with "Tennessee Pride," then did "Bring Me Sunshine," which was first recorded by the Mills Brothers in 1968. The session ended with "Love Beads," which was released as a single.

On February 8 Chet, Boots Randolph, and Floyd Cramer appeared on the *Ed Sullivan Show* on CBS. Chet performed "Blue Angel," while the trio played "San Antonio Rose" and a Hank Williams medley of "I Can't Help It (If I'm Still in Love with You)," "Jambalaya," and "I Saw the Light."[2]

On March 11 the Grammy awards were again hosted in Los Angeles, New York, Chicago, and Nashville. Chet received a nomination for his *Solid Gold '69* album in the Best Country Instrumental category, but Danny Davis & the Nashville Brass won.

Chet's work with Jerry Reed as his producer led them to record a duet album, *Me and Jerry*. Chet usually laid down basic tracks for his records in the RCA studio then took the tapes home to tinker with his parts, but on the *Me and Jerry* album Chet and Reed recorded their guitar tracks first in Chet's home studio, then took the tracks to the RCA studio to add backing. Producing the sessions was Bob Ferguson.

On May 7 Chet and Jerry did two sessions backed by musicians Jerry Carrigan, Larrie Londin, Henry Strezlecki, and Farrell Morris. During the morning they recorded "MacArthur Park," "Old Man River," and "Tennessee Stud." "MacArthur Park" was written by Jimmy Webb and was a hit for Richard Harris in 1968. On "Tennessee Stud," the song's writer, Jimmie Driftwood, along with Eddy Arnold, Doc Watson, Chet, and Reed, all sang a line or two. Chet played his Del Vecchio Dinamico resonator guitar, Reed a classical guitar.[3] The second session that evening they recorded "The January–February March," "Wreck of the John B.," and "Bridge over Troubled Waters," written by Paul Simon and a hit for Simon & Garfunkel in 1970. The group then did "Stump Water" and "Nut Sundae," both written by Reed, and a Beatles song, "Something." Accompanying Chet and Reed were Farrell Morris on congos/drums/percussion, Larrie Londin and Jerry Carrigan on drums, and Henry Strzelecki on bass.

In 1962 Owen and Harold Bradley sold their Quonset Hut studio to Columbia Records. In the sale was a "noncompete" clause that said the Bradleys could not open another studio within thirty miles of the Quonset Hut. Owen looked at a map, measured thirty miles from Music Row, and landed on Mount Juliet, a rural suburb east of town. That's where he built Bradley's Barn Studio, where his son Jerry often engineered sessions.

Jerry had gone to college with Harry Warner, who worked at Roesch-Patton Funeral Home. Funeral hearses doubled as ambulances and Jerry often accompanied Warner on emergency calls. Warner had met Chet but was not close to him until one day they were both in the parking lot at Arnold's, a popular meat-and-three restaurant in Nashville. Chet hosted a party in his office each weekday at five o'clock, providing drinks for a group of guests and regulars who included Ray Stevens and publisher Bob Beckham. That day Harry was in Chet's office to "party" and continued going over each day at five to join the group. These parties became a fixture for Chet and his friends.

Jerry Bradley ran Forrest Hills, his father's publishing company, and had an office on Music Row, across the back parking lot from RCA. Bradley was leaving his office when Chet and Harry came out of the RCA building to get in Chet's car to go to dinner. "Why don't you come with us?" asked Chet. "Ahh, nah. I don't have a coat on," said Jerry. "Ah, c'mon, go with us" said Chet, so Jerry got in the car and the group went to the Carousel in Printers Alley for dinner. On their way down to the Carousel, Jerry said to Chet, "Hey, if you ever have a job open, keep me in mind." Jerry remembered that Chet "took a drag off his cigar, didn't say anything." After dinner, when Chet and Harry dropped Jerry off, Bradley said, "Hey, Chet, don't forget what I said—if you ever have anything, give me a holler." Chet took a drag off his cigar and said, "Well, you might make a pretty good executive." "Aw, shit, I don't want to be an executive," replied Jerry. "I'd have to get a coat and tie." Jerry then laughed and got out of the car.

Two weeks later, Jerry's secretary, Cecile, told him "Chet Atkins called you." "Well, anybody that knew anything knew that Chet didn't call you much about songs," said Jerry. "If he wanted to put a song on hold he had somebody else call you." Jerry hadn't pitched Chet any songs and wondered what he wanted. Jerry called his father, Owen, and told him about the message from Chet. Jerry told Owen that he had a feeling that Chet was going to offer him a job. Owen replied, "What do you want a job for? Hell, you got a job. Tell him you're looking for an *opportunity*." When Jerry met with Chet he was offered a job, but Bradley told him, "I got a job. I really don't need a job. Now if you've got an opportunity over here I might. . . ."

"Well, I'll have Harry Jenkins (Chet's direct boss at RCA) give you a call."

Jenkins flew in to Nashville and they talked; Jenkins offered him $20,000 a year to start. Jerry replied, "I'll take it, but in two years I want to be makin' twenty-five." "I'll tell you what," said Jenkins. "I'll give you $25,000 right now." Danny Davis was leaving RCA to devote full attention to the Nashville Brass. Bradley knew that Felton Jarvis was also going to leave—but the RCA brass did not know that yet.

Jarvis was going to work full-time for Elvis with an independent production deal. Finally, it all came together and Jerry moved into Danny Davis's former office.[4]

On Tuesday, June 9, there was an article in the local newspaper that stated, effective Monday, June 15, thirty-year-old Jerry Bradley had been hired by RCA as Chet's assistant and a producer for the label. In the announcement Chet said that Bradley would be "in charge of the operation when I'm not here." Bradley would also direct recording sessions for some of the label's artists, yet to be designated. "Jerry has all the qualifications for the job," stated Atkins. "He has been well trained for the past nine years in all facets of recording."[5]

On the evening of June 29 there was a press party at the BMI offices hosted by Frances Preston and Richard Parker, general manager of the local PBS station, WDCN-TV, for a preview of the show *Evening at Pops* that featured Chet with Arthur Fiedler and the Pops Orchestra. Watching the hour-long show were thirty members of the press while Chet sat on the floor in the board room with his elbows on his knees.

The program began with Fiedler and the Pops Orchestra performing the "Washington Post March" and "An Outdoor Overture" before Chet walked onstage with his guitar. A reporter wrote that when Chet walked onstage he "was the understatement of both man and instrument, excitement with the blasé look of a man on a stroll through his living room" as he began to retune his guitar. "I'd been playin' the guitar about 20 years before I found out I couldn't tune a guitar too well," said Chet. "By that time, I was too rich to quit." Chet kept his eyes on his left or chording hand and gently tapped his foot as he performed "Alabama Jubilee," "In the Pines," "Wildwood Flower," and "On Top of Old Smokey." "Classical pieces," Chet wryly stated as he watched the broadcast.

The first annual Chet Atkins Guitar and Song Festival was held on Friday and Saturday evenings, August 7 and 8, at the Municipal Auditorium in Nashville. President of the Song Festival was Chet's manager, X. Cosse. Chet was honorary chairman of the board, while Chet's brother Jim Atkins, Joe Kraft, Red O'Donnell, and a "who's who in Nashville business" served as board members. "The Guitar and Song Festival events have been in Chester Atkins' mind for some time," stated Cosse. "All he requests is that we develop a plan that will be permanent and offer a system under which the moneys (to support it) will grow each year. In brief, he said, 'make it non-profit, but make it successful!'"[6]

There was a full house at the Municipal Auditorium for the festival on the first day to listen to the four finalists in the acoustic category. The first prize check of $1,500 was presented by Chet to Douglas Niedt, with the second prize check of $750 going to Angel Nico Anastos. In the "electric guitar category" the winners were Fred Hamilton, John Pell, and Joe Schuler. In all, eight winners received $6,000 in prize money, while the charity event sent proceeds to the Florence Crittenton Home.[7]

On October 10 *Me and Jerry* entered the *Billboard* country album chart and reached number 13.

The CMA Awards Show was broadcast from the Ryman Auditorium and hosted by Tennessee Ernie Ford. The big winner was Merle Haggard, who won for Single and Album of the Year for "Okie from Muskogee" and Male Vocalist. Song of the Year honors went to Kris Kristofferson for his hit "For the Good Times," recorded by Ray Price. Tammy Wynette won Female Vocalist, while Porter and Dolly carried home the Duo award. Jerry Reed won the Instrumentalist Award, and Entertainer of the Year was Charley Pride. The Carter Family and Bill Monroe were inducted into the Country Music Hall of Fame.

At the end of October Chet was elected to the board of governors for the Nashville Area Chamber of Commerce.

On November 23 Chet and Jerry Reed began recording their follow-up album, *Me and Chet*, accompanied by Johnny Gimble (mandolin), Junior Huskey, Larrie Londin, Jerry Smith (piano), and Farrell Morris (vibes, marimba shaker). They recorded "El Condor Pasa," written by Peruvian composer Daniel Alomia Robels. Simon & Garfunkel recorded it on their *Bridge over Troubled Waters* album, released in 1970. "Just One Time" was written by Don Gibson and was a hit for him in 1960 and "Chaplin in New Shoes" had previously been recorded by Chet.

On the afternoon of December 9 Chet and Reed recorded four songs. "Walk Right Back" was a hit for the Everly Brothers in 1961. "Vesti La Giubba" came from the opera *Pagliacci* and was a hit for Victor recording artist Enrico Caruso in 1904. They also recorded

"Tuck Me to Sleep in My Old Kentucky Home" and "Together Alone." On the eleventh, Chet recorded "For the Good Times," written by Kris Kristofferson, and "Snowbird," a current hit by Anne Murray. The 45 single never charted but won Chet his third Grammy for Best Country Instrumental Performance. "Theme from Love Story," also known as "Where Do I Begin," was a hit for both Andy Williams and Henry Mancini in 1971. A week later a string session was overdubbed on "Just One Time," "Chaplin in New Shoes," "Snowbird," and "Theme from Love Story."

CHAPTER 40

In early January it was announced that Chet and Leona's daughter Merle was engaged to be married to Will Russell in County Tipperary, Ireland. It was a large affair; Merle married a doctor whose father was the only doctor in the Irish village, so the whole town turned out. Chet was not known for being overly friendly to the young men who came courting his daughter, according to Merle. However, "he loved Will."[1]

Merle remembered that when she was young her parents would drive from their home in Nashville to Luttrell to visit her grandmother. It was an unpleasant trip for young Merle, who easily became carsick and rolled around in the backseat of their Oldsmobile. There were no interstates back then, just winding two-lane roads.

Growing up Merle had memories of "daddy practicing. I remember him sleeping. I remember him having really bad asthma when I was little. My earliest memories were of that little recording studio at our old house on Lincoln Court and having to be quiet." Her dad was "very aware of everything." He was a proud man but she "knew the way to get to Daddy was to be funny. To make a joke out of things. That was how we discussed things we really didn't want to talk about." Her mom "devoted her whole life to Daddy," said Merle. "Everything revolved around him in her world, and in mine too!"

Merle was in high school when the Beatles hit and remembered that "it was a terrific thing for me to say, 'George Harrison plays one of my Daddy's guitars!' It was a big deal." She remembers one of his favorite sayings, "That's my opinion and it oughta be yours too!"[2]

Merle's wedding was the biggest social event in County Tipperary. A number of her husband's friends from high school and fellow students in medical school attended. "The reception was at Cashel Palace in Tipperary. So we go and we have this big reception," said Merle. "X. Cosse, Daddy's manager, came from the States. Anita Kerr was living in Switzerland at the time and so she came—a few people like that."

"You didn't ever ask Daddy just to play, you know? He wasn't gonna be anybody's dancing bear. He was just very—it wasn't a snobby thing;

I don't know what it was. It was just something if he felt like he could do it, he would do it. There was a little band playing and all that. The next thing I knew, Daddy was sitting on a stool playing and Anita Kerr was singing 'Danny Boy' with Daddy. . . . Anyway, it was just beautiful. Just absolutely beautiful."[3]

The first live broadcast of the Grammy Awards came on March 16, 1971, from the Hollywood Palladium on ABC. Chet won the Country Instrumentalist award for his album *Me & Jerry*. He was also nominated for *Yestergroovin'* in that same category.

Chet was in the studio on June 1 and 2 to record six songs for his *Pickin' My Way* album. On the first morning Chet recorded "One Side of Love," "Floatin' Down to Cotton Town," and "I Never Knew." On the second morning he recorded "Pickin' My Way," "Wouldn't It Be Loverly" (from the musical *My Fair Lady*), and "Lover Come Back to Me."

In June an article, "At Home with the Chet Atkins," appeared in the local newspaper. A reporter visited Chet and Leona's home in Chickering Hills and noted that the home is "not like the homes of other people in the entertainment world—at least not like those who need to be noticed and dress, talk or act in a way to assure it." The home was described as "traditional," a white brick house with "black shutters, with a nice roomy entry hall with a slate floor, dining and kitchen wing to the left, bedrooms to the right, and a big square living room in white with a baby grand piano, mahogany furniture and a marble fireplace. Opening off the living room was a paneled den with a wall of mostly non-fiction books and scores of records to the left, a cozy brick fireplace in the corner and a few of the most prized trophies on a desk at the back. There's a patio off the den, but they're not big at outdoor cooking." Their dog, a Boston terrier named Miss Kay, was fourteen years old and "getting feeble."

Downstairs the studio was "about 15 feet square inside with almost every inch lined with electrical amplifiers, tape players, recorders, earphones, knobs, buttons, wire, tools of every description, a set of drums and an antique Gramophone." The reporter noted that Chet "spends part of every day here when he's at home." He had about fifteen guitars. "Chester usually picks up the guitar while I fix breakfast, keeps it nearby and works on it some afterwards," said Leona, "and then when he gets home he usually practices three or four hours downstairs." The reporter noted that "a guitar can be found in just about every room of the house and when Chet's around one of them is usually in use."

There was also an exercise room downstairs and a "rumpus room" with a pool table. On the walls of the basement hung "a picture of Perry Como soaking his feet in a pail of water," pictures of Leona's golf wins, and a stack of pictures of almost every celebrity in the country music field. The reporter stated that on Sundays, Chet was usually "fiddling with his ham radio" and had "talked to people all over the world and keeps a log of each contact." He owned a replica of a Model A Ford.

The Atkins did not have domestic help; Leona maintained the house. She spent her time playing golf or bowling and had won the Women's City Golf Tournament and the Hillwood Country Club title three times, although she had been playing for only four or five years. Chet and Leona often played golf together at the Hillwood Country Club on the weekend. Chet also played a couple of rounds a week, usually with friends Jerry Reed, Archie Campbell, and Bob Jennings.

"I guess you could say my hobby is Chester," said Leona. "I stay on the phone half the time trying to help people reach him, or get his clothes ready for a trip. He packs for himself, though. Lays out everything he's going to take very carefully—he's particular about his dress." The article stated that Chet traveled a good deal but Leona rarely went with him.

Leona noted that "it's fun to meet the celebrities who are in town and we often have them out to the house. I'm not a good cook [Chet said she "passes"]. Usually I fix things like fried chicken, green beans and corn bread—typical southern food." However, most of the time they took their celebrity guests out to dinner.

The article concluded that "Chet's life is unbelievably busy and Leona's is often one of being the patient [often waiting] wife. But she never suffers from the tired housewife syndrome!"[4]

The Chet Atkins Guitar Festival was moved to Knoxville in 1971. Like the festival in Nashville, there were two guitar divisions, electric and classical. Chet cited his East Tennessee heritage for the move: "I'm sentimental about this area. In fact, I frequently refer to myself as I travel throughout the country as 'just a hump-backed guitar player from East Tennessee.'"

The festival was held at Knoxville's Civic Coliseum in conjunction with the Chet Atkins Celebrity Golf Tournament, held that same weekend at Knoxville's Deane Country Club. Invited golfers included Perry Como, Glen Campbell, Dean Martin, and Roy Rogers. The fact that he could combine his golf tournament with the festival was a major reason for the move; another was the high cost of renting Nashville's Municipal Auditorium. Like the first festival, this one awarded cash prizes to the winners: $1,000 for first, $500 for second, and $250 for third, with the winner of first prize also receiving a guitar. The competition was open to those aged fourteen to twenty-three. "This festival is designed to give anyone who aspires to be a guitarist the opportunity to obtain advanced training and develop their natural talents," said Chet.

Discussing his own guitar playing, Chet said, "If you don't practice for three days and pick up a guitar it doesn't know you," adding that "I guess I practice three or four hours a day. I always carry a guitar with me, wherever I am. Sometimes I play to soothe my nerves or just to work out an idea before I forget it. I look forward to the end of the day so I can go home and grab a guitar and start picking. I'll be playing for people until I'm 70—if I live that long."[5]

Chet was involved in the formation of FAME (Famous American Musicians and Educators), which offered "guitar training in schools by means of a special 'laboratory' which included a tape player synchronized with a 16 millimeter movie projector." Chet filmed instructions for the program, which included thirty-two lessons over the nine months of a school year. Students who took the lessons purchased a guitar "specially designed for the course" by the General Music Corporation, in addition to instruction books and records for home use.

Chet was chairman of the board of directors for FAME. It was reported that the FAME organization had been capitalized at over $500,000. Chet's brother Jim served as vice president and his accountant, Joe Kraft, was another founder.

Plans called for the company to expand from schools to a home study division with instructions designed and implemented by professional Nashville musicians. The "institutional division would be directed towards churches, camps and other private organizations interested in the development of music as an outlet for recreation." Chet and Jim were responsible for the content and quality of the guitar course. Chet was described as "very excited" about the undertaking and felt "a course of this nature is a much-needed instructional program" that would "provide professional guitar instruction to students from every walk of life as part of their normal education."[6] For the project Chet recorded songs that were released on a two-album set titled *Chet Atkins Guitar Method.*

In July, Chet was in the studio and recorded six more songs for his instrumental album *Pickin' My Way*. On the afternoon of the 14th he recorded "Troubles on My Mind," "Black Mountain Rag," and "When You Wish Upon a Star" (from the Disney film *Pinocchio*). The next morning he recorded a Paul McCartney song "Junk," the Simon & Garfunkel song "The Boxer," and "Hellacious," the latter accompanied only by Larrie Londin. Two of the songs, "Lover Come Back to Me" and "Black Mountain Rag," were new versions of songs first recorded on his 1953 *Gallopin' Guitar* album. On his earlier album Chet played both numbers on his electric guitar unaccompanied; this time he played classical guitar with Henry Strzelecki on bass and Larrie Londin on drums.

On "Black Mountain Rag" Chet played in open G tuning—the low E lowered to D, the low A lowered to G and the high E lowered to D. "It was always one of my favorite fiddle tunes," said Chet about "Black Mountain Rag." "I don't remember how it happened but back in the '50s I got to wonderin' what it would sound like on guitar and I found that I could play it more easily in the key of 'G' with that 'open G' tuning. It's one of the favorites of my fans; they always want to hear it." Chet first heard the song from fiddler Tommy Magness. It became popular as "Black Mountain Blues" during the 1930s, but Curly Fox renamed it "Black Mountain Rag" in 1947.[7]

"Lover Come Back to Me" came from the 1928 operetta *The New Moon*. Chet first recorded his version in May 1952 at Brown Radio Productions. On this version he was accompanied by Pete Wade, Henry Strzelecki, and Larrie Londin. "When You Wish Upon a Star" featured "cascading harmonics," produced by the thumb and first finger of the right hand playing a bell-like note, followed by a regular note played with the right hand third finger on an adjacent string. "I came up with that [technique] in 1961 [when] I played the intro to 'White Christmas' using that effect," stated Chet.

It was a devastating personal loss to Chet when Homer Haynes died of a heart attack on August 7 at just fifty-one. Chet had worked with Homer and Jethro from his days in Chicago and Knoxville during the 1940s. Homer and Jethro were working on *The World's Greatest Melodies* for the Nashville String Band series. Chet, Jethro, Johnny Gimble, and session musicians finished the album. Chet had produced a series of albums under the name Nashville String Band that featured him with Homer and Jethro performing mostly middle-of-the road songs, often from Chet's earliest recordings.[8]

"The Mad Russian" was written by Paul Yandell and Jerry Reed. Chet, Reed, and Yandell all played on it, accompanied by Stephen Schaffer on bass and Larrie Londin on drums, on a session for the second collaborative album of Chet and Reed. The song has a minor-key-based melody and is furiously paced like a Russian dance. Chet played his Gretsch electric, while Reed used a classical.[9]

Yandell had been working in Jerry Reed's band since 1970, and Chet was soon as impressed by Paul's talent as Jerry was. The recording of "The Mad Russian" was the start of Yandell regularly working with Chet. The bass player on the session, Stephen Schaffer, had been Bobby Goldsboro's guitarist, but Goldsboro was hot—he had a number-one hit with "Honey," a string of chart records, and a TV show—so Schaffer obtained a lot of studio work and left Goldsboro.[10]

Jerry Reed was losing interest in touring because he was busy making movies, said Yandell. "So I felt it was time to move on. I gave my notice and went straight to Chet's office and said, 'You know, I am not working for Jerry anymore. Do you need a guitar player?' So Chet called Jerry and said, 'Do you mind if I hire Paul?' Jerry said, 'No, I don't care.' The next week we were playing a symphony date in Jackson, Mississippi. Chet rented a tux for me. That was the first date I played with Chet."

Yandell soon became Chet's right-hand man musically and one of his closest personal friends. "I was so blessed to work with Jerry and Chet," said Yandell. "Had I not worked for Jerry I would not have been a good enough musician to work with Chet. Through Jerry, I learned how to play in a groove. Every time Chet played it was something special," said Yandell. "He amazed me all the time. Anybody who had the chance to watch Chet play would hear him play a tune like it had never been played before. I got a guitar lesson every night."[11]

During an afternoon session in November, backed by Bobby Dyson, Larrie Londin, James Isbell, Pig Robbins, and Pete Wade, Chet and Jerry recorded "American Melody," also known as "Red White and Blue Medley," an arrangement of "You're a Grand Ole Flag," "The Caissons Go Rolling Along," "Anchors Away," "Marines Hymn," and the "U.S. Air Force Song." On December 7 Chet was in the studio and recorded "Kentucky," "Mystery Train," and "Amos Moses" during a morning session with Jerry Reed, Paul Yandell, and Larrie Londin.

Chet and Reed continued recording their duet album into the next year. In February they recorded "Flying South," "Limehouse Blues," "All I Ever Need Is You," and "Good Stuff." In March they added "I Saw the Light," "Liebestraum," "Nashtown Ville," and "Serenade De Summertime."

During 1971 there was one studio album released by Chet, *For the Good Times*, and three compilation albums. *Country Pickin'* was released on Pickwick, while Camden released *Mr. Atkins—Guitar Picker* and *This Is Chet Atkins*. There were two Nashville String Band albums released in 1971, *Strung Up* and *Identified!* Although Chet had cut back on his producing, he was still in charge of RCA's Nashville division and oversaw single and album releases.

CHAPTER 41

Chet lost two guitars—a Gretsch electric and a Barbero classical—on a trip to Canada in early April. Leaving Nashville Chet "checked them through to Calgary on the airlines, and when I got ready to do my concert in Calgary the Gretsch was gone." Coming back to Nashville "either in Toronto or Cleveland, the classical guitar disappeared."

He had a homeowner's insurance policy that covered the losses, but the Barbero was "irreplaceable, because there are only a very few of them in existence," said Chet. "I had one, and Jerry Reed has one, and a kid up in Syracuse, New York has one." He believed his mistake was carrying them in expensive cases. "The classic was in a fiberglass case that cost about $175. Lots of times I'd check it on the plane just as if it were another person occupying the seat next to me, but I didn't this time because I had to change planes three times and walk so far while I was changing." Chet didn't believe the instruments were stolen because they belonged to him. "I like to think that if I had had my name on the outside of the cases, they never would have been taken. I think I've got a lot of friends out there in radio land."[1]

In May Chet received an award from the National Conference of Christians and Jews. The presentation was emceed by Archie Campbell and the medallion was presented by Johnny Cash, who declared, "The downtrodden flock to him because he is a human anchor. He has been that kind of man for a long time. He has been a helper of the underdog, and I believe one reason he has been that is because he remembers what it was like to be in a cornfield on the side of a hill in Luttrell, Tennessee. He not only cares for his associates in the music business but for the guy on the street as well. He should get this award for this year because he has deserved it for many years." Accepting the award, Chet said, "I don't have any heavy things to say, because when I say heavy things I cry. I've been grateful for the things that have happened to me in this life. I don't think I deserve them, and I don't think I deserve this, but it will be great for my inferiority complex. I've got one and I'm sure I'll always have one." Reflecting on the tribute he was given by RCA on his twentieth anniversary, Chet said, "I told myself then to remember everything about that because things like that wouldn't happen more than once, and here it is happening again."[2]

During the afternoon of May 10, Chet recorded three songs: "Summer of '42," "Vincent," and "Love Theme from the Godfather." He was accompanied by Henry Strzelecki, James Isbell, Ray Edenton, Jerry Shook, and Ferrell Morris. Chet spent two full days recording current pop hits. On Thursday morning he recorded Paul Simon's "Me and Julio Down by the School Yard," "The Masterpiece," which was the theme song for *Masterpiece Theatre*, on PBS during the seventies and eighties, and Neil Diamond's "Song Sung Blue." That afternoon he recorded Diamond's "Sweet Caroline" and "I'd Like to Teach the World to Sing," a hit for the New Seekers that was used in a Coca-Cola commercial. On Friday morning Chet recorded "After Midnight," written by J. J. Cale, that had been Eric Clapton's first hit single as a solo artist in 1970, the gospel standard "Amazing Grace," and "Knee Action." That afternoon he recorded "Just an Old Fashioned Love Song," a hit for Three Dog Night. These sessions were for his album *Chet Atkins Picks on the Hits*; the tapes were shipped to New York, where strings were added.

Jerry Reed hosted Glen Campbell's summer replacement show. On the July 18 broadcast Reed and Chet performed a Beatles medley. The viewers at home were not aware but Chet was in pain; during rehearsal he had fallen from a six-foot-high riser and was forced to use crutches for the next several weeks.[3]

In 1972 Waylon's contract with RCA was set to expire. Jerry Bradley had gone to Waylon and promised him five thousand dollars if he agreed to a 5 percent royalty, a continuation of Waylon's royalty rate. Bradley brought Waylon's record royalty statements "to show me that this was all they could give me," said Waylon in his autobiography. Bradley stressed that RCA "loved me and thought of me as part of the RCA family." The negotiations were held in Chet's office, with executives from New York present. "New York could tell Nashville what to do, but Nashville couldn't tell New York: The power of attorney only flowed one way," said Waylon.

"When the smoke had cleared, I had gotten a recording contract I could live with," remembered Waylon. "My percentage was up close to eight. Chet was amazed; it was a better deal than he had. 'I didn't know they gave out big contracts like that,'" said Chet, whose RCA recording contact was at five percent. Waylon had formed his own production company, so he could make records on his own and then hand the completed masters to RCA. "Chet always worried that I was out to destroy something; he thought I was determined to ruin country music, that there would no longer be a reason for people like himself or Owen Bradley to produce records," wrote Jennings, who moved his sessions over to the Glasers' studio.

RCA executives had told Waylon they could not release the album that he recorded at the Glasers' studio because the label had a contract with the engineers union that stated all recording had to be done in-house with an RCA engineer. Jerry Bradley attempted to get a waiver, but the union was uncompromising. Finally, RCA shipped the record, violating their contract, and "that broke the whole system's back," wrote Waylon.[4]

Another side of the story came from Jerry Bradley, who claimed that Waylon hadn't been selling records—he was in the hole with the company. Mel Ilberman flew down from New York, and the executives withdrew to another room to discuss the signing. Ilberman asked Bradley, "Do you want him?" Bradley was hesitant but then confirmed he did want Waylon, and the deal was concluded.[5]

The Everly Brothers left Warner Brothers and signed with RCA in the summer of 1971. Their first recording sessions were in Los Angeles, but frustrated by their lack of success and the fact that it took six months to record *Stories We Could Tell* in LA, they decided to record again in Nashville. "We went back with Chet because everyone in LA said how difficult I had been in the studio," said Don Everly. "I said, 'Well, hell, I can cut a record in three days in Nashville.' So I called Chet up and said, 'Would you produce us?' He said, 'What are you going to do, rock'n'roll or country?' I said, 'We're probably gonna do that country stuff like we've always done.' He said okay and that was it. It took about four days and it's one of my favorite albums. It was fun."[6]

On Monday, July 24, the Everlys had their first Nashville recording session in seven years. During an afternoon in RCA Studio A, with Chet in the producer's chair and David Kershenbaum as associate producer, they recorded three songs, then four songs on Tuesday, four more on Wednesday, and five on Thursday to finish *Pass the Chicken and Listen*. Chet played on the sessions—just like in the early days.

During the sixth annual CMA Awards, broadcast on CBS in October, Chet and Minnie Pearl presented Loretta Lynn with the Entertainer of the Year honor. Chet left empty-handed; Charlie McCoy won the Best Instrumentalist award.

On October 19 Loretta Lynn, Conway Twitty, and Chet were on NBC's *Today Show*. During the show Chet admitted "a tinge of regret" because "maybe I tried to bring country music a little too far up town." Host Frank McGee gave Chet credit for helping save country music after rock and roll hit. "That ain't necessarily so. The only thing I did, I decided if we were gonna survive, we'd have to make good country records. I had fortunately been exposed to a lot of different kinds of music and I incorporated any new idea I came across into my recordings. Maybe I tried to bring country a little too far up town, with horns, and strings. I'm kind of ashamed of that now. But, you know, when you're trying to sell records you'll do anything."[7]

On Monday, November 27, Chet announced that Jerry Bradley, who had been his administrative assistant since 1970, was now director of RCA Records in Nashville, adding that he would remain with the label on a "reduced work basis." "I'm turning my office over to Jerry and I'm going to do less work and enjoy it more," stated Chet. "I'll be more or less on my own. I'll definitely be around to counsel with Jerry when he needs me. However, I don't intend to do much work during 1973. I suppose you might call me the 'chairman of the board emeritus.' I'll continue to be a part of RCA. My employment contract does not expire until next November and it is now being renegotiated. I have an artist contract with RCA that runs through 1991," adding that "I'll still be picking 19 years from now."

"I really need a rest," continued Chet. "The paper work and other work have worn me to a frazzle. I'm 48 and that is too young to die from tension. No, I'm not going to just sit around in a rocking chair. I have eight or nine appearances with symphony orchestras scheduled for next year. I want to work up some new arrangements on the guitar for those appearances. I may go on tours to Europe, England and Japan with some artists. RCA wants me to take some of our people over there to promote their records. I'll continue to do some producing. I'll supervise sessions for Jerry Reed, Perry Como and Hank Snow. I'll also be scouting around for new material [songs] and new artists. I think the discovery of new talent has been my biggest success at RCA. The company is going to fix me up an office to use when I feel like it and I have a feeling I'll be using it quite a lot as time goes by. Psychologically, I think I need to work."

Bradley stated that the promotion was "more a change of titles than of responsibilities." "When I came over here it was on the basis that Chet was going on the road more and would be playing and practicing more with his guitar," said Bradley. "When I was hired, it was with the understanding that, if things worked out, he would do less and I would do more. It's not really a change in my duties. It's more a change in Chet's."[8]

Chet added that he had decided to end his tours with the Masters Festival of Music to "take a good rest and make some good albums. I'll take off a year and see what it is like not to have to work so hard." The decision by Chet to quit the Masters Festival of Music meant that Danny Davis and the Nashville Brass would join that group. Jethro Burns and Charlie McCoy were also expected to be on several concert dates in the future with the Masters Festival. Chet's final show with the Masters was scheduled for December 2 in Knoxville.[9]

In 1972 RCA celebrated Chet's twenty-fifth year as an artist with the label by releasing the single "Chet's Tune, Part 2" (Cy Coben's penned sequel to 1967's "Chet's Tune) and a two-record set *Now and Then*. Packaged with a twenty-page illustrated booklet, it contained the previously unreleased "Bilbao Song" and a new track "Knee Action." Several of Chet's early recordings ("Canned Heat," "Gallopin' on the Guitar," and "Sweet Bunch of Daisies") made their LP debut on that compilation.

During 1972, Chet released one studio album, *Picks on the Hits*, and three compilation albums, *Now and . . . Then*, *Finger Pickin' Good*, and *Nashville Gold*. During the period 1969–1972 Chet recorded six albums as a member of the Nashville String Band. The artists were anonymous until their third release, *The Nashville String Band Identified*.

CHAPTER 42

During the Christmas season in 1972 Chet called Perry Como in Lake Tahoe, where he was playing a two-week stand, and told him he had a song that he should hear, "And I Love You So." Perry had not been in a recording studio in eighteen months. Chet had heard the debut album of a young singer-songwriter, Don McLean, and "And I Love You So" leapt out. McLean had written the song before another of his songs, "American Pie," catapulted him to stardom.

On January 17 Perry Como began recording twelve songs over five consecutive days in Nashville. The planned album was similar in concept to *The Scene Changes*, with many new and unfamiliar songs, although musically it lacked the simplicity that Atkins and Anita Kerr had brought to the 1965 LP. When the album did eventually appear, it was much different from what Atkins had in mind. The reason was that RCA quickly realized that "And I Love You So" was set to do what "It's Impossible" had done two years before. With the likelihood of another massive Como hit, their thinking changed and Como returned to Nashville in March to record six hits by other artists. By including them on the album, at the expense of some of the less familiar titles, RCA strengthened its mainstream pop credentials. It was the same formula that had worked so well with the *It's Impossible* album in 1971.[1]

"And I Love You So" entered the U.S. charts in May 1973 and became a worldwide hit, popular in England, Australia, France, Germany, and Japan, plus a specially recorded version in Spanish. The *And I Love You So* album appeared on the charts later in the year.

The Grammy Awards were held at the Tennessee Theater on Church Street in Nashville on Saturday, March 3, 1973, and created much controversy in the New York and Los Angeles musical communities. The idea had been floated to alternate the Grammys between the three recording centers, Los Angeles, New York, and Nashville, and since ceremonies had already been held in Los Angeles and New York, it fell in place for Nashville to host the awards in 1973.

Broadcasting the Grammys from Nashville created objections from the Los Angeles and New York chapters, which led ABC, which had broadcast the first two awards, to refuse to participate. NBC did not like the location either, so they passed. That left CBS, which bowed to NARAS pressure and reluctantly agreed to broadcast the show. After the show received a 53 share of the audience (over half the people watching TV that night were tuned into the ninety-minute Grammy telecast), ABC realized it had made a major mistake, while CBS had fallen into a gold mine and had a contract to continue to broadcast the show. Attempting to recover, ABC created the American Music Awards, produced by Dick Clark, who hosted *American Bandstand* on that network.

On Friday night, March 2, the Nashville Chamber of Commerce hosted a pre-Grammy party. Attending the party was Ringo Starr with his wife Maureen. He came to Nashville because an album he was on, *Concert for Bangladesh*, was nominated for Album of the Year. During the reception Ringo was asked, "Will the Beatles get back together as an act?" He answered, "Not a chance." Ringo did not linger in Nashville and soon returned to England.

Prior to the telecast an article in the *Nashville Banner* quoted Grammy producer Pierre Cossette: "The efficiency of the Nashville people is amazing. Everybody—the stage hands, musicians, technicians, citizens—has been cooperative. The theater is perfect for the show too." Cossette admitted that "I battled NARAS about having it here. I had nothing against Nashville. I just thought Los Angeles was the proper, logical place to have it. I didn't believe Nashville had the facilities or manpower to do such a show [but] I am now a believer. We have had absolutely no problems here." Cossette concluded, "I tell you how sold I am on Nashville. I wouldn't oppose having it originate from here next year or any year."

Actually, a major problem emerged on Sunday evening eight minutes before the show went on the air. The electrical power in the building was lost and things were jittery until the power returned one minute before airtime.

The fifteenth annual Grammy Awards were emceed by Andy Williams, who also performed. The big winner that evening was anticipated to be "American Pie" by Don McLean, but it won nothing; instead the Album award went to the three-LP set *Concert for Bangladesh*, the first rock concert organized as a benefit. That was the first Grammy win for George Harrison, Eric Clapton, Bob Dylan, Leon Russell, and Billy Preston, who were on the album; the award was accepted by Ringo Starr. Former Beatle Paul McCartney was invited to the Grammys but refused because of a pending lawsuit to dissolve the Beatles. Former Beatle John Lennon was invited but refused to come because the invitation excluded a performance by his wife, Yoko Ono.

There was controversy in Helen Reddy's acceptance speech when she was awarded the Grammy for Best Female Pop Vocal for her hit, "I Am Woman." Reddy said she wanted to thank God "because She makes everything possible," spurring a torrent of protest letters from religious fans.

There were a number of Nashville connections at the Grammys. The Blackwood Brothers picked up their fourth Grammy for "L-O-V-E," and Elvis won his second Grammy for *He Touched Me*, which was recorded in Nashville. Vibraphone player Gary Burton, a former Nashville resident, won for his *Alone at Last* LP. Charley Pride performed "Kiss an Angel Good Mornin'," and Donna Fargo performed her hit, "Happiest Girl in the Whole U.S.A." Nominated for Best R&B Vocal, Male was Joe Tex for "I Gotcha." Tex's label, Dial, was based in Nashville, where Tex recorded. The best country song award was given to Ben Peters for "Kiss an Angel Good Mornin'." Charley Pride won the Best Country Vocal, Male award. Best Country Vocal, Female went to Donna Fargo for "Happiest Girl in the U.S.A." Charlie McCoy won Best Country Instrumental for his album *The Real McCoy*. Chet Atkins was nominated twice in that category—for *Picks on the Hits* and for his *Me and Chet* album with Jerry Reed. That was the last live Grammy Awards broadcast from Nashville.[2]

Chet was never in robust health and had not felt "right" for years. His stomach bothered him and kept him awake at night. At the beginning of the year, as he was working on his album *Alone* in his basement studio, he felt dizzy and nauseous. The room was unventilated, so Chet thought that the cigar smoke had caused the problem. As he worked on Perry Como's *And I Love You So* album, Chet felt a slight pain under his belt on the right side. After the hurt persisted he called Dr. Joe Robertson, who examined Chet in the studio and thought it was colitis.

Things cleared up, and Chet did concerts in Denver and Oakland. Back home he played golf with Jerry Reed and ate "a bunch of junk." The pain became intense, so Chet looked up the symptoms of colitis in an encyclopedia. He didn't like what he read and called Dr. Robertson, who arranged for X-rays, which showed a malignancy. He left the hospital and drove home, where he and Lorena "had a good crying jab." A few days later Chet entered the hospital and kept his eyes closed "all the way to the operating room" and throughout the operation, to remove eighteen inches of his intestine. When he woke up he "felt as if a Volkswagen had run over me."[3]

Chet was scared, but the doctor assured him the cancer had not spread and he was "going to be all right." That news spread throughout the waiting room, where Leona, Merle, and friends Archie Campbell, Jerry Reed, and X. Cosse (among others) erupted in jubilation. Everyone was joyous except Chet, whose first thought was "I'm going to die in six months." Chet spent nine days in the hospital, with only his family allowed to visit.

Chet wanted his guitar because the calluses on his fingers were getting soft. But, after Leona brought it, he was in no mood to play. Also, he didn't want others in the hospital dropping in. After he returned home the guitar still held no appeal. "All I wanted to do was sit around and worry about myself."

During the month after the operation Chet suffered from depression. He was "afraid it had spread to my brain and other organs." The doctors checked on him regularly, and he began to feel better until one day Leona brough home a copy of *Esquire* magazine. Inside, there was an article that said "if you have cancer of the colon, you will live an average of two years." Leona had not been aware of the article.[4] It took a lot of effort from a lot of friends to calm Chet down after reading it. His son-in-law, a medical doctor, read the article and saw problems with the data, which was over ten years old. That revelation cheered him up a bit.

A month after the operation Chet and Dr. Robertson went to the golf course and hit a few balls, even though he wasn't supposed to play for another two weeks. Then a few weeks later he played in the annual Chet Atkins Celebrity Invitational Golf Tournament in Knoxville.[5]

Chet could not bring himself to practice on his guitar. He wanted it around but didn't want to play it. Then Jerry Reed came over to his house and told him he had written a song he wanted to record.

Chet told Jerry he'd listen to it later, but Reed insisted, "Hell no, we're gonna learn it right now. Now you listen." Chet "wasn't ready; I wanted to worry some more," but Reed got his guitar, handed Chet his, and said "Play!" Chet obeyed.[6]

Chet's album *Alone* was released and contained Jerry Reed's classic "The Claw" and "Take Five," released by the Dave Brubeck Quartet in 1959. On the album were "Smile," written by Charlie Chaplin, and "Over the Waves," a popular song with old-time fiddlers that was first published in 1888. "Me and Bobby McGee," written by Kris Kristofferson and Fred Foster, was a hit by Roger Miller and Janis Joplin, and the classic hymn "Just As I Am" was included. The other songs on the album were "Hawaiian Slack Key," "Spanish Fandango," "Flop Eared Mule and Other Classics," "Blue Finger," "Londonderry Air," and "The Watkins Man," which was arranged by Paul Yandell and Atkins. Photographer Jimmy Moore shot the cover of the album but thought the title was a misnomer: "It didn't seem like Chet was alone. He was talking to people a lot. A lot of times some of his best friends would be up there in his office playing. Jerry Reed would be up there a lot and they'd be having dueling guitars."

"Jerry Reed was just electric," said Moore. "You never knew what he was going to do. We were in a restaurant once just getting a Coke and the waitress said, 'I know who you are.' He said, 'You do?' She said, 'Yeah, I've seen you on TV' and Jerry says, 'Well, who am I?' She said, 'You're Chet Atkins.' He said, 'That's right!'"

Moore considered Chet a close friend. "If somebody in my family passed away, he'd call me and talk to me about it. He would write me notes. If I went by his office and missed him and I left a picture or something I thought he might like, he'd write me and thank me for it and say come back by. He did thoughtful things that I know he didn't have time to do for all his friends. He must have had a million friends."[7]

The annual CMA Awards were held on Monday night, October 15, at the Grand Ole Opry House in Opryland Park and broadcast on CBS. The show was emceed by Johnny Cash, and Roy Clark was Entertainer of the Year. It was a big night for Chet Atkins, although he did not win the CMA's Instrumentalist award. Instead he received a much greater honor—induction into the Country Music Hall of Fame.

Chet Atkins was forty-nine years old and had been in Nashville for twenty-three years. He had gone from being a struggling picker, playing whenever and wherever he could, to a world-renowned guitar player whose name was synonymous with the instrument. He had transformed from a session player to a session leader to a producer of hit records for numerous artists. He was also an executive who guided RCA Records in Nashville to a position of prominence to the point where when you said "Nashville" or "RCA," Chet's name was linked. But he was not well, and Chet joked later that he was voted into the Hall of Fame "because I had cancer and they thought I was going to die."[8]

After the CMA Awards Show a group of artists traveled to London for a Nashville Cavalcade tour. On the tour were Dottie West, Jim Ed Brown, Bobby Bare, Danny Davis and the Nashville Brass, and Chet Atkins. The tour included a stop in Oslo, Norway, where they recorded a show for Norwegian Television, before ending in Birmingham, England. During the tour Chet went to Paris, where he met Marcel Dadi, who had learned the fingerpicking style of guitar from Chet's records. This meeting led eventually to a concert by Chet and Dadi in Paris; Dadi also formed a Chet Atkins Appreciation Society in France, which furthered Chet Atkins's fame internationally.

CHAPTER 43

Chet and Merle Travis were in a studio in Hollywood in January 1974 for an historic recording session: the first time the two had recorded together. Chet went to Los Angeles for the recording. In LA "Merle was in bad shape," said Paul Yandell. "He had taken some pills that day. Chet would ask Merle a question and Merle was so tired he could barely respond. Merle didn't play well."[1]

Jerry Reed produced the sessions, and all three played acoustic guitars, although Reed played rhythm only on a few tracks. Chet played a Martin D-41.

There was an easy camaraderie in the studio, and Chet and Merle bantered, especially on the Shel Silverstein song, "Is Anything Better Than This?" Songs on the album included "Down South Blues" (written by Merle Travis and Chet Atkins), "Mutual Admiration" (Shel Silverstein), "Muskrat Ramble" (Kid Ory and Roy Gilbert), "If I Had You" (Campbell-Connelly-Shapiro), "Cannonball Rag" (Travis), "Boogie for Cecil" (Atkins and Travis), "Is Anything Better Than This?" (Silverstein), "Dance of the Golden Rod" (Travis), "Who's Sorry Now" (Snyder-Ruby-Kalmar), "Nine Pound Hammer" (Travis), and "I'll See You in My Dreams" (Isham Jones and Gus Kahn).

In 1939 Django Reinhardt released "I'll See You in My Dreams" and Travis performed Django's version as an instrumental during the 1950s and recorded it on *Strictly Guitar* in 1968. On their album Chet's guitar is mixed hard to the left while Merle's is mixed hard to the right, so the listener can easily decipher what each played.

The rock and pop worlds were back in their comfortable confines of Los Angeles for the Grammys in March 1974. Nominated for Best Pop Vocal was "And I Love You So" by Perry Como.

At the time controversy pervaded the country music community because many felt that the genre had gone "too far pop"; for many this was confirmed when Olivia Newton-John won the Best Country Vocal, Female award for "Let Me Be There." In the Best Country Vocal, Male category former R&B singer Charlie Rich won for his smooth "Behind Closed Doors." Chet was nominated in the Best Country Instrumental category for "Fiddlin' Around," a duet with Johnny Gimble, but Eric Weissberg and Steve Mandell won for "Dueling Banjos," a hit from the soundtrack to the film *Deliverance*.

Hascal Haile spent his early life making classic furniture and did not begin building guitars until he was almost sixty years old, but he eventually constructed some of the finest guitars ever made; Chet bought several. An article in the *Tennessean* in January spotlighted Haile's guitars he had built for Chet, John Johns, Porter Wagoner, Dolly Parton, Grady Martin, Hank Snow, and Tommy Jones. Chet's Haile guitars included a classical, a flamenco inlaid with abalone shells and ebony, and a folk model. Every guitar Haile made had "a personality of its own," said Haile. "You have to know something about music and mathematics and have a good knowledge of acoustics. Then all the strings have to be synchronized so that they harmonize. All must be at peace."

In February Lloyd Green and Tommy Cogbill were in the studio with Chet, who recorded "Dizzy Fingers" and "Ave Maria." A week later, Chet recorded "Down Home" with Larrie Londin, Pete Wade, and Henry Strzelecki. On the morning of March 7 Chet was in the studio with Londin, Henry Strzelecki, and Paul Yandell to record "Baby's Coming Home," "Jerry's Elegant Junk," and "East Wind."

Les Paul sought to construct a solid body guitar that would sustain better than a hollow body, but guitar manufacturers were skeptical. Merle Travis sketched out a solid body design in 1948 and brought it to Paul Bigsby, a woodworker. Bigsby carved the guitar out of maple and at Travis's request put all the tuning pegs on one side of the head. That guitar led Leo Fender to develop the first commercially successful, mass-produced solid body guitars. Bigsby developed a tail piece that allowed the strings to bend. In April Merle Travis presented that original solid body guitar, valued at over five thousand dollars at the time, to the Country Music Foundation. Chet and publisher Cecil Null joined Travis when he presented the guitar to Bill Ivey, executive director of the Hall of Fame. "Merle Travis was an artist and took it upon himself to design a new guitar which would have a strong, sustaining sound," said Chet. "It is the first solid body guitar ever made and played professionally and no doubt was responsible for revolutionizing the guitar and music industries."[2]

On April 2 Chet recorded "Mister Bojangles," "Just Another Rag," "Faded Love," and "Muskrat Ramble" during an afternoon session with Jerry Shook on harmonica.

Chet performed with the Nashville Symphony, conducted by Dr. Thor Johnson, for their Spring Pops Program on May 12 in Massey Auditorium at Belmont University, sponsored by Commerce Union Bank. A *Nashville Tennessean* review stated, "The audience responded quite as warmly to Atkins' completely genuine, quietly unassuming friendliness, and his dry, understated humor, as to his superior brand of 'guitar pickin'.' In most of his numbers (even Tarrega's famous tremolo study 'Memories of the Alhambra') he had his own rhythm section (piano, drums and guitar). But he also did some unaccompanied solos, and in all he played with such expressiveness and mostly with such a feeling of improvisational intimacy that the listener felt he was enjoying them in his own home." He played a medley of many of the hits associated with him, as well as a very effective medley of patriotic songs, Boots Randolph's 'Yakety Sax,' 'Wheels,' 'Time in a Bottle,' 'Yellow Bird,' 'Black Mountain Rag,' 'Snowbird' and others." Chet was accompanied by Henry Strezlecki and Paul Yandell.[3]

On May 28 Chet went to the Cokesbury Book Shop in Green Hills for a book signing of his autobiography, *Country Gentleman*, written with Bill Neely. Later, Red O'Donnell interviewed Chet in his office: "The people at the publisher's tell me the first printing already is a sellout. Yet, I don't know how many copies they printed. It could be only 10 or 12. I think Bill Neely did a good job. Everything he wrote is exactly how I told it to him." O'Donnell told Chet that his was a rags-to-riches story, but Chet countered that he didn't have everything. "I'd like to have a better education," said Chet. "What I know I learned from reading. . . . Yet, I wish I had a diploma, a graduation ring or something to show."

The book retailed for $7.95, and Chet opined, with a grin, "I never thought when I was growing up in East Tennessee, and struggling as a picker around the country, that one day a book would be written about me that would sell for almost eight dollars."[4] In his book Chet stated, "Country music is an attitude. If it's good it's completely lacking in pretense," continuing that "I think country music's strength is in its honesty and its sincerity, because nothing sells like the truth. . . . Country music is the story of people trying to get along as well as they can," said Chet. "It is basic music with a strong lyrical quality. The whole thing is geared to a guitar rather than a piano. It is rural, southern, conservative, blue-collar, patriotic, and fundamental. It doesn't trust city slickers but puts up with drinking and running around, so long as it's understood that those vices don't come without a price."[5] A month after the interview Chet turned fifty.

On June 6 Paul McCartney and his family arrived in Nashville to get his new band, Wings, ready to record and tour; they rented a farm from songwriter Curley Putnam in Lebanon, about thirty miles east of Nashville. McCartney visited Opryland Theme Park and the Grand Ole Opry and recorded in the Sound Shop studio. McCartney wrote two songs, "Sally G." and "Junior's Farm," while in town and recorded both in addition to adding overdubs on several other songs. McCartney had originally planned to record in Bradley's Barn, but Buddy Killen, who owned the Sound Shop studio—and who made arrangements for the visit—convinced McCartney to record there instead. That created a lifelong wedge between Jerry Bradley, whose father built the Barn, and Killen.

McCartney let it be known that he wanted to meet Chet, and one evening the McCartneys—Paul, his wife Linda, and their three daughters—visited Chet at his home. "Paul called me and he and Linda came out to the house," remembered Chet. "He wanted to meet Jerry Reed and I had Jerry here too. We all visited and talked about people I recorded and had hits with, like Elvis and Waylon Jennings, the Browns and Don Gibson and Paul knew all that stuff."

Chet and Leona took the McCartneys to dinner at the Loveless Café, a legendary "meat and three" restaurant on Highway 100, west of Nashville. McCartney remembered that during the dinner "this little kid came around" and "he got my autograph, and he got Linda's and he went round to get Chet's, but he kind of looked like he wasn't quite sure whether Chet was a celebrity or not, and he said, 'Can I have yours too?' and Chet said, 'Oh, no, you don't want mine. I'm just old folk!'" McCartney called Chet a "country gentleman, just such a lovely man, so unassuming."

Back at Chet's home McCartney played a song he had just written; Chet asked him, "Do you mind if I record that and play it for my daughter?" and so McCartney played the piano and recorded it for her. McCartney told Chet that his father had written "a song called 'Walking in the Park with Eliose' and it was kind of a 'Darktown Strutter's Ball' type of song." Chet shared, "The best gift you could ever give your father would be to record that." Chet then told McCartney that he "had recorded a tune my Dad wrote called 'Prancin' Filly' and my Dad made two or three hundred dollars from the publishing. He loved it!" McCartney loved that story.

Chet lent McCartney a book, *Secrets of the Pyramids*. After reading it McCartney wrote a song, "Spirits of Ancient Egypt," for his *Venus and Mars* album. Before he left Nashville McCartney returned the book, scribbling a note of thanks in the pages.

McCartney later asked Chet if he could set up a session to record "Walking in the Park with Eloise." Chet arranged for Floyd Cramer, guitarist and banjo player Bobby Thompson, fiddlers Vassar Clements and Johnny Gimble, and a horn section comprising George Tidwell on trumpet, Dennis Goode on trombone, Norm Ray on baritone saxophone, and Billy Pruett on clarinet to meet with McCartney at the Sound Shop on July 10.

McCartney played the song for the musicians; they ran it down a couple of times and then recorded it with him on bass and Geoff Britton, a member of Wings, on drums. The horn section, arranged by Tony Dorsey, doubled their parts, and McCartney added a washboard that he'd found in a local antique shop. The song was recorded straight through, but Chet, ever the perfectionist, insisted on playing his part again. McCartney arranged to have the song released on his record label, EMI, as "The Country Hams."

McCartney invited Chet, Jerry Reed, and Roy Orbison to his birthday party on June 18, but heavy storms postponed the celebration until the next day. Around sundown, Chet and Reed drove down the driveway to the farmhouse in Chet's white Cadillac. Orbison also came. The only others there for Paul's thirty-second birthday were his wife Linda, his three daughters, and his band members. It was a rather quiet, low-key birthday; Chet and Reed left fairly early.[6]

On Thursday morning, September 5, Chet recorded "Emily" and "Tara's Theme" from *Gone With the Wind*. Five days later he recorded "Paramount Theme" and "Everybody's Talkin'."

The eighth annual CMA Awards were held in October; Chet and

Roy Acuff presented the Female Vocalist award. Acuff announced the winner as "Oliver Newton-John." Her winning a Grammy and CMA Award for Best Female Vocalist was too much for some, who grumbled that country music had lost its way.[7]

Chet's final appearance on the *Porter Wagoner Show* came in December when he performed "Somewhere My Love" and a Bob Dylan medley that included "Blowin' in the Wind" and "Don't Think Twice, It's Alright." The show closed with Chet and Porter doing a snippet of "Nine Pound Hammer." TV fans of *Hee Haw* could see Chet on that program on December 7 when he performed a duet with Roy Clark on "Rainbow." The syndicated TV series *Dinah!*, starring Dinah Shore, featured Chet on December 12.[8]

On the afternoon of July 24 Chet recorded just one song, Scott Joplin's "The Entertainer," which was featured in the 1973 film *The Sting*. The song was written on piano in 1902, but John Knowles created a fingerpicking arrangement, recorded by Chet on his classical guitar. The first guitarist Knowles remembers was Les Paul, but around the time he was fourteen or fifteen, he bought a Chet Atkins album, *Finger Style Guitar*. John wanted to study the guitar in college, but the music department told him the guitar wasn't a "real instrument" and refused to accept him, so he majored in physics, eventually earning a doctorate and working in research for Texas Instruments in Dallas.

There's something about true musicians that won't let them live without music. Eight weeks after his son was born, Knowles quit his comfortable job at Texas Instruments and began teaching guitar at a music store in Dallas. During the early 1970s he saw an advertisement, "Sign up for Segovia's Master Class." John applied, was accepted, and went to Spain—but Segovia wasn't there; instead, his assistant, Jose Tomas was. When Knowles mentioned Chet Atkins, Tomas played "Mister Sandman" on his classical guitar.

In 1974 Knowles began transcribing Chet's recordings because one of his students, Dick Roby, was a big Chet fan. When news arrived that Chet would be in town to perform with the Dallas Symphony, Roby insisted on meeting Chet, so he and Knowles went to the rehearsal. When they met, Chet looked at Knowles and said, "I think I know your name from somewhere. Did you work out this arrangement?" and Chet played a Beatles tune Knowles had arranged, which had made its way around by photocopies. Knowles realized later that "from hanging around Chet, how often others tell him about guitar players he should hear. The first project we worked on together, Chet was going to do an album of movie themes, and *Guitar Player Magazine* wanted him to write a book, so Chet said, 'I'll do the movie album, get John to transcribe the tunes, and then we'll have a book.' I found out about the project when I got a call from the editor of *Guitar Player* magazine, who said, 'Chet wants you to write this book.' I couldn't breathe. I didn't know how hard it would be to write down a whole album," which meant he stayed up late for many nights in a row with a turntable and a fountain pen.

"Chet had sent me a test pressing, as the record wasn't out yet," remembered Knowles. "Of course, he had learned my arrangements from a cassette I had sent him. They didn't sound exactly the way I had played them, so I had to listen very carefully. That was the first time I tried to figure out how to play those harmonics like in 'Somewhere Over the Rainbow,'" said Knowles. "I was determined that I was going to get this whole thing written down, without having to ask Chet how to do it. But I finally called him and said, 'Man, I have no idea what you are doing.' He picked up his guitar over the phone and talked me through how to play the harmonics. I wrote down everything he said, and I still couldn't tell what he was doing. After sleeping on it, I picked up the guitar and realized what he was doing. Once I saw it, I knew I'd been hearing it on records for several years. It was flying right past me because I couldn't even relate to it."

Knowles had arranged "The Entertainer" but "didn't know it had been nominated for a Grammy for Country Instrumental of the Year." He was at Dick Roby's house, watching the Grammys on TV, when he saw a list of awards that were not shown on camera. That's when John Knowles knew Chet had won a Grammy with his arrangement. "So I called Chet the next morning and I said 'I saw this scroll by. Did that really happen?' and he said, 'Yeah, it did.' So I kinda had this impression, 'Well gee, write a book, win an award, this is an easy business," said Knowles. "That is not quite how it is, you know, but I had really, I think, stumbled into opportunities. I've realized over the years [that] Chet creates opportunities when he can tell that somebody loves something and that they might be good at it. He figures out a way to give them a shot at it. That is what he was doing. I asked myself later, 'How did he know that I would be able to write a whole book like that?' and the answer is, 'I bet he didn't but if I didn't write it, there just wouldn't be a book, that's all, and if I did, there would be a book.'"[9] Knowles observed that "when people knew that you knew Chet, it opened a lot of doors."[10]

In 1974 RCA released Chet's *Superpickers* album, which gathered a number of A Team musicians in the RCA studio with producers Bob Ferguson and Jerry Reed. In addition to Chet, musicians on the session included Johnny Gimble (fiddle), Buddy Spicher (fiddle), Buddy Harman (drums), Charlie McCoy (harmonica), Weldon Myrick (pedal steel guitar), Jerry Shook (guitar), Farrell Morris (percussion), Hargus "Pig" Robbins (piano), Larrie Londin (drums), Paul Yandell (guitar, ukulele), Henry Strzelecki (bass), and Bobby Thompson (banjo, guitar). The album included "Paramaribo" (written by John Loudermilk), "Fiddlin' Around" (Johnny Gimble), "Mr. Bojangles" (Jerry Jeff Walker), "Beef and Biscuits" (Mat Camison), "Sweet Dreams" (Don Gibson), "Just Another Rag" (Chet and Jerry Reed), "Canadian Pacific" (Ray Griff), "City of New Orleans" (Steve Goodman), "Bells of Saint Mary" (Doug Tringer), and "Are You From Dixie?" (George Cobb and Jack Yellen).

CHAPTER 44

Chet Atkins and Merle Travis took home a Grammy for their *Atkins-Travis Traveling Show* album at ceremonies in New York in March 1975. The controversy over country music being "too pop" continued when "Fairytale" by the Pointer Sisters won the Grammy for Best Country Vocal Duo or Group. That song was also nominated for Best Country Song, won by Charlie Rich's very pop sounding "A Very Special Love Song."

Chet's *The Night Atlanta Burned* album was released as the Atkins String Company and performed by a classical string quartet of Paul Yandell on guitar, Lisa Silver on violin and viola, Johnny Gimble on mandolin, and Chet on classical guitar. This was an example of Chet leaving the administrative duties at RCA behind and stretching as an artist. The song "The Night Atlanta Burned" was recorded on April 23 and referred to the night, captured in *Gone With the Wind*, when Union General Sherman and his troops torched Atlanta. The album showed Chet involved in a collaborative project, which would be a trend for the rest of his career as he sought to define himself as an "artist" instead of a producer and RCA executive. The adventuresome *Night Atlanta Burned* indicated where Chet was headed, collaborating and setting no boundaries.

The album had four songs written by John D. Loudermilk—the title track, "To Ann," "Sonora," and "Odd Folks of Okracoke." The album featured two traditional songs, "Bill Cheatham" and "The Women of Ireland," a Bill Monroe song, "Scotland," "San Antonio Stroll," and two classical pieces, "Mostly Mozart" and "Carnavalito."

Roy Horton was a trustee on the Country Music Hall of Fame Board of Directors and worked for Peer Southern Publishing, which had the Jimmie Rodgers and Carter Family catalogues of songs. Horton had been encouraging Chet to record an album with Les Paul; Chet finally agreed after Horton brought them together at Manhattan's Warwick Hotel for a jam session. Although Chet's brother Jimmy had worked with Paul for years, Chet had met Paul only once before that jam session—back in 1949 in the KWTO studio in Springfield when he saw someone walk in the door. Intending to impress the stranger, Chet remembered, "I thought, I'm gonna knock this guy out," so he "played a lot of fast runs and spun out a Les Paul chorus or two, pullin' the strings just like Les." When Chet finished, Les Paul walked into the studio and said, "I opened this goddam station fifteen years ago." Chet "almost fell over. I was embarrassed because I had played a few of his choruses," he remembered. "I guess he thought I was a thief."

Les Paul flew to Nashville with his son Bobby. Les arrived at the studio first, carrying his custom-built white flat top Gibson. At the studio he ran into songwriter Vic McAlpin, who shook his hand and said, "Hey, man—what are you doing in these parts?"

"I'm down her to make an album with Chet," said Paul.

"What are you going to record?"

"Oh, I don't know. We're just gonna wing it." McAlpin, a practical joker, leaned in to Paul and whispered, "You know what Chet will do to you? He'll get you in there and play all the songs he knows best. Why, he'll pick his ass off and make you sound like a goddam sharecropper!"

Chet and Les Paul, along with Paul Yandell, Ray Edenton, and Bobby Thompson (all playing guitar), Randy Goodrum (piano), Henry Strzelecki (bass), Bob Moore (bass), and Larrie Londin (drums) were in the studio for two days. The musicians recorded six instrumentals the first day and another seven the next; ten of those thirteen were included on the album. The sessions were informal; Yandell remembered that "Chet and Les would work out basic arrangements for the songs they were going to record, quickly run through them, and then commit them to tape." There was almost no overdubbing or rerecording.

"We were completely unprepared," remembered Chet, but he could not understand why Les rejected almost every song he suggested. "It's hard to nail Les down on what he wants to do," remembered Chet. "He just pointed to the mike and said, 'turn that son of a bitch on. We'll get it."[1] Most of the songs they recorded were those that Les had performed a week earlier at Carnegie Hall. Only "Lover Come Back to Me" and "Caravan" were not recorded live. Chet thought the songs could have used a bit more work, but Les insisted that he needed to get back to New Jersey.

"What'll we do about all those clams?" asked Chet.

"Leave 'em in," said Les. "Let people know we're human."

Les Paul "is a very funny fella," said Chet. "He can tell you a story and keep you laughin' all day. It wears me out to be around him because he's so funny. He was one of my heroes when I was a kid."[2]

Chet and Les had each previously recorded "Avalon," and during the middle of the song they start kidding each other with Chet telling Les they need to play the song faster—and then sets a blazing tempo, which Les picks up and carries. Another vocal banter follows where Chet tells of forgetting to zip up the pants of his tuxedo during a symphony performance before they end the song.[3]

Included on the *Chester and Lester* album were "It's Been a Long Time," "Medley: Moonglow/Picnic (Theme from *Picnic*)," "Caravan," "It Had to Be You," "Out of Nowhere," "Avalon," "Birth of the Blues," "Someday Sweetheart," the old Fred Rose song "Deed I Do," and "Lover Come Back to Me.

Anita Kerr flew into Nashville from her home in Switzerland for sessions that Chet produced for RCA. It would be a choral album, along the lines of the Ray Conniff Singers, that covered popular songs. She also hoped to record some "new" songs that could be released as singles. "I used to be with RCA years ago, and just re-signed with them about a month ago," said Kerr. "Chet felt that Victor should have someone on the label with a smoother sound. They had the country artists, and some rock, but not many along the lines of what Perry Como and the Ray Conniff Singers were doing."

Anita left Nashville in 1965, but "when I was here, Chet and I worked together all the time," she said. "The nicest thing about this album is that it's kind of a reunion in the studio." Three of the songs she wanted to record were Charlie Rich's "Every Time You Touch Me (I Get High)," the Seals and Crofts' song "I'll Play for You," and the Tom T. Hall song "I Love." Anita sang with a group of four or five singers. She was excited about the project and wanted to do future recordings in Nashville "as long as Chet wants to produce me."[4]

The ninth annual CMA Awards Show was held in October. It became an eternally memorable show when, after announcing that John Denver had won the Entertainer of the Year award, an inebriated Charlie Rich took the card that held the winner's name, lit it aflame, and watched it burn while the audience sat in stunned silence. Finally,

Charley Pride led him offstage. The next day the publicity department at his record label announced that Rich had experienced an allergic reaction to a bug bite.

Chet closed the show that evening with a bicentennial medley of "Dixie," "Battle Hymn of the Republic," and "America the Beautiful," performed on his Super Chet guitar.

Chet stopped producing Hank Snow in 1975 because "during the mid-1970s and into the 1980s, country music became more pop oriented, and I became frustrated," said Snow. "Chet was my producer at that time, and he always did a great job. However, as country music changed, he wanted me to change and be more contemporary. And since some of my records toward the end of the 1970s were not setting any woods afire, Chet felt that to be fair to the company he had to follow the trend and go more into the pop-oriented songs, with arrangements aimed toward the younger generation. I certainly didn't blame him for that, but I told him if I couldn't continue recording in the same way that had made me successful, I didn't have the heart to record anymore. If some of the artists wanted to sing pop, with all the musical gimmicks, that was perfectly okay with me. But I was a country singer, and as long as I was appearing before the faithful public who had stood by me all these years, I was going to keep it that way."[5]

The Outlaw Movement in country music began in 1975 when Waylon Jennings and Willie Nelson had a number-one hit for three weeks (reaching number 25 for pop) with "Good Hearted Woman." This was the beginning of the end of the Nashville Sound era. Session musicians with twenty to twenty-five years of experience were called less often and a new group of musicians—often the singer's band members—took their places. The major labels could no longer dictate to the singers where or what to record and a producer was not needed to find songs, although the next few years saw the "old way" still being used. But youth—and rock and roll—had gotten into country music.

Chet released three studio albums in 1975, *The Night Atlanta Burned*, *Chet Atkins Goes to the Movies*, and *Teen Scene*, and a compilation album, *The Golden Guitar of Chet Atkins*.

CHAPTER 45

The year 1976 marked America's bicentennial, and the two hundredth birthday was marked with patriotic events throughout the year. On the first day of the year, TV viewers could see Chet on the show *Dinah!* On January 2 PBS-TV aired a special, *Hill Country Sounds—History of Country Music*, hosted by Bill Anderson, that featured appearances by the Carter Family, Roger Miller, Earl Scruggs, and Chet.[1]

The generation of musicians responsible for the early years of the Nashville Sound and their audience came of age during the Great Depression and World War II. However, by the mid-seventies a new generation of musicians had arrived who came of age with rock and roll and the Vietnam War. A new group of producers replaced Chet, Owen Bradley, and others of that generation; the new producers wanted new, younger musicians they could relate to and connect with. Artists who came of age during the sixties had their own ideas of what they wanted, and they expected the studio musicians to listen and conform. Over several years the old A Team musicians were replaced with newer, younger musicians who formed a new A Team. When the old-line studio musicians—the former A Team—stopped being called for sessions, they were frustrated because they felt they could play anything quite competently.

The Nashville Sound, dominated by producers who usually picked the songs, hired the musicians, and called the shots, had become a very efficient factory that turned out great music for its time, but that time was passing. The young musicians wanted to write the songs, record with their band, and call the shots. Their influences included Bob Dylan and the Beatles as well as Hank Williams and Lefty Frizzell.

The old Nashville Sound also failed them in the political arena. This was a generation who saw injustice in race relations, frustrations with the draft, and failures of the Vietnam War and were much more open-minded about sex, drugs, and individualism than the previous generation. That first generation of studio musicians was growing older while the new artists were getting younger.

Nashville's music establishment and citizenry were conservative, but by the mid-seventies the counterculture was creeping into the mainstream. The older generation drank beer and whiskey; the new generation smoked pot. Country music was a counter to the counterculture during the turbulent sixties, but by the mid-seventies countercultural ideas had gradually become part of the mainstream.

Chet often said that he wanted to be remembered as someone who played in tune and well. He certainly achieved that, but by the mid-seventies his mastery of the guitar was technical; the emotions felt in Chet's playing were the emotional state of relaxing with soft music.

The cowboy came back into country music during the mid-seventies as part of the Outlaw Movement. Country music artists of the fifties generally wore Nudie suits full of rhinestones; during the Nashville Sound era they wore sport coats, suits, and even tuxedoes. It was a way of saying, "We are not the past, we are part of mainstream America, the middle class." During the sixties the youth wore torn jeans and T-shirts, a casual look of the working class. That wasn't the case in traditional country music; the act was always "dressier" than their audience. In some ways Chet couldn't relate to the new generation. He told John Knowles, "I had two pair of pants growing up, and if one had a hole in the knee, I would never wear it out in public."[2]

The "cowboys" of the mid-seventies, whom Willie Nelson and Waylon Jennings personified, never rode a horse but wore cowboy boots, drove a pickup truck, and sported a rebellious attitude. They rebelled against crowded cities and embraced the freedom of wide-open spaces.

Willie Nelson's home in Nashville had burned down so he needed a place to live until it could be rebuilt. He had an audience in Texas, so he moved to Austin, which had a burgeoning Redneck Rock movement. In 1973 he held his first Fourth of July picnic outside Austin, and in 1975 he enjoyed his first number-one hit, "Blue Eyes Crying in the Rain." That hit came from his album *Red Headed Stranger*, which was recorded in Texas and didn't sound anything like what was on country radio at the time. In 1975 Waylon had a hit with "Are You Sure Hank Done It This Way"; "Bob Wills Is Still the King" appeared on the flip side. It became known as the Outlaw Movement because the country artists weren't playing by Nashville's rules.

Nashville artists and the country music industry have never been as clean-cut as their image. This was a business full of the pills—uppers or "speed"—musicians and artists needed for those long road trips. The image of rock music and the counterculture of the sixties was "sex, drugs and rock and roll," but "sex, drugs and country music" arrived in the mid-seventies, when the Baby Boom generation discovered country music. That generation continued to smoke weed, but they also drank beer. The hippies cut their hair while the rednecks grew theirs long. Waylon, Willie, and those who followed were part of a revolution in country music that rebelled against the Nashville Sound. Waylon and Willie, who had deep roots in Nashville, were a bit conflicted about being outlaws, which they saw as a marketing tool. Both artists had been produced by Chet and both deeply loved and respected him. Waylon and Willie simply wanted to have control over their music and escape the domination that corporations such as RCA had over their lives and careers.

In the Bear Family collection of Waylon's recordings, writer Lenny Kaye noted, "It was a producer's town [but] the Nashville Sound at least had the virtue of being overseen by a master musician" at RCA. "The Nashville production line accented form, following function," continued Kaye. "Such a streamlined system doesn't take into account the wild card, or the weeds that are blown by the winds, and have their own beauty."[3]

Chet Atkins was out of touch with the Outlaw Movement; he was friends with Waylon and Willie, but it was a new day in country music and Chet was not part of that. And yet Chet, like Waylon and Willie, was blazing his own trail. Just like Waylon and Willie were rebelling against being just "singers" for a machine and wanted to be "artists," Chet was quietly pushing to be an "artist" rather than an executive and producer.

Chet's rebellion was more quiet and internal. First, he stepped away from his duties as head of RCA's Nashville office to spend more time playing guitar. Then he experimented with new songs and new lineups of musicians. Chet did not wear a black cowboy hat and call himself an "outlaw," but he was rebelling against the Nashville structure in his own quiet, subtle way.

Chet's initial recording contract with RCA had him as a singer, and he always admired Merle Travis, a top instrumentalist who sang. Chet knew he wasn't a great singer, but he also knew that singing was helpful for live performances. Also, by 1976 instrumentals had largely left the radio and the big stars were singers, not instrumentalists.

Chet looked for opportunities to sing, finding one with Buddy Kalb's "Frog Kissin'," published by his close friend, Ray Stevens. Chet and Stevens were in the studio on March 25 to lay down the tracks, with Ray producing and arranging. The song is based on the old tale of a princess kissing a frog, who turns into a handsome prince. The song was sung by Chet in a pleasant, laid-back voice, with Stevens providing harmony and electric keyboard parts that were "croaky." The recording was done in a studio; a laughter track was added so the recording would appear to be live, which is what that song needed. "Frog Kissin'" reached number 40 on the *Billboard* country singles chart.

It wasn't just Hank Snow who was frustrated with country music's direction. At the Grammy Awards, held on February 28 at the Hollywood Palladium, Linda Ronstadt's recording of the Hank Williams classic, "I Can't Help It (If I'm Still in Love With You)," won the Country Vocal Female award over Dolly Parton's "Jolene." For Country Vocal Performance by a Duo or Group the Pointer Sisters were nominated for *Live Your Life Before You Die*, and Best Country Song honors went to "(Hey Won't You Play) Another Somebody Done Somebody Wrong Song," recorded by B. J. Thomas. A number of people in the country music community insisted that those were not "real" country artists.

Chet won Best Country Instrumental for "The Entertainer." Chet and Jerry Reed were nominated in the Best Country Instrumental category for "Colonel Bogey."

Randy Goodrum went into the studio with Jerry Reed to record "Lightning Rod," and "I ended up writing and playing the bridge solo on the finished recording," said Goodrum. "They had the track cut and I went over to this little studio with Jerry and Paul Yandell and I told them I had an idea for a solo in one spot and they liked it and so I demoed it. Well, then they played it for Chet. After that they called me into the studio and I went in and sat down and played the piano part." That's how and where he met Chet.

"Jerry had told him that I was a jazz player and Chet liked that and, of course, in those days Jerry was all over the place," said Goodrum.

"I got a phone call from Chet's secretary one day and she said 'Are you booked at 2 o'clock on the 21st? Chet wants you over at Studio A at RCA.'"[4] Goodrum was in RCA's Studio A at two o'clock, but no one was there. After a while Chet walked in. "He was by himself and he sat down and took his guitar out of the case and had me sit down at the piano and I said, 'Are we going to do a session?'" Chet said, "No, I just want you to show me some things. I want to learn some new alternate chords and new things I can play." For two hours Goodrum showed Chet some voicings, alternate chords, different scales, and modal and diminished chords.

Chet and Goodrum "shared one thing in common," said Goodrum, "we worshipped the melody. I was in a car with him one day and on the radio there was a commercial and part of the music in it was the song 'Take Me Out to the Ballgame' and Chet made a comment about what a great melody it was and I thought maybe he was kidding. In my mind that song was kind of hokey and old fashioned, but then as I mentally stepped back and thought about it, it really is a good song, a remarkable, unforgettable and perfectly designed melody."

Goodrum began touring with Chet and noted that "Chet was the kind of person that made an impact because he was a southern man making real music. He wasn't the guy trying to stamp out cookie cutter records that would be called 'country.' He had the vision that he could cut anything and it would be a Nashville record. It would have that flavoring. He was willing to try anything; he just wanted to do good stuff." Goodrum said that Jerry Reed and Chet "were real renaissance men. They had no fear in producing. They wanted Nashville to truly be a Music City. When I played on the road with Chet, he played everything. I mean, he could play old standards, jazz, Appalachian things and all kinds of stuff," said Goodrum. "You just had to be able to play all of it."

A memory of Chet that stands out with Goodrum came after Goodrum's father died. "I was sitting at home a few weeks later and I heard a knock at the door and Chet was standing there and said, 'Hey Randy, you like video games don't you?' And I said 'Yeah' and he said, 'Let's go play some' and so we went to this place he had found and I played a couple games and he was just watching and finally I asked him, 'What are you gonna play?' And he said, 'Nothing—I just thought you might like to do this and get your mind off of things.'"[5]

Chet was in the studio on the evening of July 23 with Bob Moore, Paul Yandell, Mark Casstevens, Randy Goodrum, Pig Robbins, and Larrie Londin to record "Terry on the Turnpike," which would be released on *The Best of Chet Atkins and Friends*, and "Casacade," which would be on his *Me and My Guitar* album.

"Me and My Guitar" was written by pop singer/songwriter James Taylor, an excellent guitarist himself who wrote about the connection between a guitarist and his instrument. It was a perfect song for Chet to sing. Chet composed "Terry on the Turnpike" as a collaboration with saxophonist Boots Randolph. Chet laid down his part in July, while Boots recorded in September.

Lenny Breau was a guitar genius, blending country, jazz, classical, and flamenco. Impressed by Lenny's playing, Chet signed him to RCA; unfortunately, Lenny developed drug and alcohol problems. He recorded some albums, sometimes with Chet. They recorded "Sweet Georgia Brown" as a duet. Although Breau was much younger, he influenced Chet, in much the same way that Django Reinhardt, Les Paul, and Jerry Reed had.

After recording "Sweet Georgia Brown" with Breau, Chet accompanied Dolly Parton on a song she wrote, "Do I Ever Cross Your Mind?" She had written the song in 1973 but never recorded it. Chet and Dolly each played classical guitars, and Chet provided a harmony vocal to Dolly's lead vocal. For "Do I Ever Cross Your Mind?," Chet played in the key of "D" with "drop D" tuning. This recording was released on the *Best of Chet Atkins and Friends* album later that year.[6]

After the CMA Award for Entertainer of the Year went to John Denver the previous year, things seemed to settle down a bit in the country music community—Mel Tillis won Entertainer of the Year, Ronnie Milsap was Male Vocalist, Dolly Parton won Female Vocalist, and the Statler Brothers took Vocal Group. The only "outlier" was Song of the Year, awarded to "Rhinestone Cowboy," a country and pop hit in 1976 for Glen Campbell.

During 1976 *The Best of Chet Atkins and Friends* was released. A best-of album is generally not a greatest hits, which are composed of songs that have achieved success on the charts and in sales. Best-of albums are more subjective. *The Best of Chet Atkins and Friends* contained half previous collaborations and half new songs.

Jerry Reed landed his own TV show, and two days after Christmas TV watchers could see Chet on the show playing "The Night Atlanta Burned" on his Juan Estruch classical with a Prismatone pickup, accompanied by Lisa Silver, Mark Casstevens, and Kenny Penny. Chet played a Fender Telecaster when he and Jerry played "Baby's Coming Home." Chet also played snippets of "Oh, By Jingo" and "Chinatown, My Chinatown." The show closed with Chet, Reed, Lynn Anderson, and Jerry Clower singing "Thank God, I'm a Country Boy."[6]

CHAPTER 46

At the nineteenth annual Grammy Awards, held in February, Chet and Les Paul won Best Country Instrumental honors for their *Chester and Lester* album.

In April 1977 Chet was in Cookeville, Tennessee, about eighty miles east of Nashville, to perform with the Tennessee Tech University Symphony. Chet performed regularly with symphonies and usually brought along conductor Albert Coleman of the Atlanta Pops Orchestra. However, on this evening the symphony was conducted by James Wattenbarger. Dave Stewart wrote an article for *Mister Guitar* magazine where he captured the event.

There was a rehearsal that afternoon in the university's gymnasium. Chet brought along guitarist Paul Yandell (who played the Yairi classical that Chet had given him), bassist Henry Strzelecki, and drummer Randy Hauser. Chet performed that evening with two different guitars—his electric Gretsch Country Gentleman and Ramirez classical. In front of Chet was a microphone that was plugged into a small Music Man amplifier that was connected to four large Kustom speakers. During the rehearsal there were a number of interruptions and changes and it was not unusual for Chet "while in full step with the orchestra to stop playing, make note of something, and then jump back into the tune exactly on the beat as though he had never stopped." After the rehearsal Chet drove to the Holiday Inn in his brown Mercedes and rested until the concert began at eight o'clock that evening.

The concert began with the symphony performing "Sabre Dance," "Marriage of Figaro," and "Blue Danube," before Chet walked onstage in a dark gray, almost black tuxedo with an open-collar blue shirt. During his portion of the concert Chet performed "Recuerdos de la Alhambra," "Black Mountain Rag," "Alabama Jubilee," "Frog Kissin'," "Just Another Rag," "Wheels," "Yakety Axe," "Snowbird," and "Time in a Bottle." Stewart remembered that Chet "left fairly quickly" after the concert finished.[1]

During the summer of 1977 Gretsch released the Chet Atkins Super Axe guitar, designed by Chet for rock musicians; it retailed for eight hundred dollars. "They asked me a year ago to design a guitar for the rock people," said Chet. "This is it. They determined the company was missing the rock market so they asked for something different, an instrument which would produce a little different sound and at the same time be comfortable to play."

The Super Axe was a solid body guitar that was heavier and bigger in circumference than the standard Gretsch Country Gentleman. "This guitar sustains more than the others," said Chet. "By this, I mean the sound will carry longer. . . . It's also more comfortable . . . shaped so that the body will rest on the musician's knee."

Atkins said that rock stars became interested in the new instrument because of Randy Bachman of Bachman-Turner Overdrive. "I read where Randy's old guitar was stolen. I sent him one of these. Now they all want one. The Eagles just bought one. So did the Doobie Brothers."[2]

Chet's personal collection of guitars at that time included the Gibson L-10, built for Les Paul during the late 1930s, that his brother had given him and the D'Angelico that had been repaired by Randy Wood after the binding had crystalized and disintegrated. It was a rhythm guitar that he never used. Waylon Jennings had given him a twelve-string Martin a few years back, but someone had stolen it from the studio. Chet took the insurance money and bought a new twelve-string. He had a D-28 Martin that Harlan Howard used to have (and "wrote a lot of his hits with it"), which someone had stepped on with a cowboy boot. It was used "for rhythm, for the modern rhythm sounds," said Chet. He had a D-41 Martin that he'd loaned to Shel Silverstein and was "up in New England somewhere" because Shel "left it at somebody's house."

Chet had a Gretsch electric twelve-string that he'd had for years. He "kept thinking about using it on a record because that was a different sound" but he "waited too long. Glen Campbell finally did it on 'Southern Nights.'" There were three Del Vecchios, short-scale, like the ones Los Indios Tabajaras played; he had received one from them. He also had a full-size Del Vecchio, the same size as a dobro, which had a similar neck that he received from Charlie Callan, who bought it in San Paulo. The Del Vecchios were "pretty" but "you've got steel strings on them and the neck pulls." Chet used "classic strings on the basses, which helps." He was having Randy Wood put a rod in the neck "to see how that works." Chet continued to use the Gretsch Country Gentleman that he had used since 1959 as his main electric guitar. It was "a single cutaway that has a long scale on it that I like," said Chet. "It's easy to tune and plays in tune better than the short-scale."

Chet "had an awful lot" of input in designing most Gretsch models. "The first one, the 6120, when I first went with them, we all went to New York, and we decided to come out with something different like that. Then the Country Gentleman, I had a lot to do with that. But I had more to do, I guess, with the Super Chet and the Super Axe than any guitars because of the guy who used to be with Baldwin, who owns Gretsch, named Clyde Edwards. So I made notes of things I thought would be nice on that Super Chet. I went to Cincinnati and got with him. He's a great craftsman."

Chet always resented the fact that Les Paul only put his name on his signature guitar, while Chet actively worked on the Gretsch Chet Atkins signature models.

Chet disliked the Gibson Les Paul guitars "because they're so hard to play sitting down. So we made a solid that's bigger, kind of a lap guitar that you can play in reasonable comfort. Made it thinner than usual. It's kind of a hybrid Super Chet," adding that "it has all the phase-shifters and things like that. I use the Country Gentleman. That's what I've used on my records for years. It has a different sound than anything else. For sustaining things, I like some of the solid guitars, but for the style I play, the old one is better for me. You know, I've got to have a guitar that plays in tune. All these solid guitars with the unwound third, they won't stay in tune for four bars, so I'm in trouble when I try to play them."

Chet noted that he played the Martin D-41 on his album with Merle Travis. The classical guitar he played on that album was built by Hascal Haile. He planned to donate it to the Smithsonian. Haile's guitars "get better all the time," and now and then "he'll come up with a great one," said Chet. Haile's guitars are built "very good, as good as most any you can buy."

Chet kept most of his guitars in his basement. In his office he had "three of them behind the couch" that belonged to Shel because "this is his storage place, because he doesn't have a home," adding that "his only home is a boat." In his office, Chet kept an electric, an acoustic, "and I try to keep a classic in case any of my friends come by and want to play me a tune or something." He didn't have one at the present time because Lenny Breau borrowed it the previous week.

Chet practiced mostly at home, although "I don't practice as much as I should," before adding "I do practice quite a bit, especially if I'm going to do a show." For a show he tried "to work up some new things that they haven't heard in ten or fifteen years. For his upcoming concert in Dallas, I dug out my records and tried to rehearse a couple of tunes Jerry Reed wrote for me."

For his personal appearances Chet had two guitars, "a classic and an electric." He wanted to start taking a Del Vecchio "if I can get a case built for it that the airlines won't tear up." Chet resigned himself to the fact that the airlines "tear them all up eventually," although he thought he could "get one of those metal cases built, with the foam all inside" because "foam rubber will protect it." The Del Vecchio "is very fragile," said Chet, "because the resonator's built out of soft aluminum, and you just touch it and it'll collapse."

Chet admitted that he worked on all his guitars and "most of them before I play them. I soup them up, I call it." For the Gretsches, "I don't like the condensers they use to knock off the highs. I change those, and adjust the pickups. Once in a while, I'll get a pickup rewound with more wire, or less or whatever. Sometimes I change the pots because I don't like the taper they've got."[3]

On May 24 Chet spent all day in the studio—morning and afternoon sessions with Lenny Breau and an evening recording songs for his *Chet Atkins Workshop* album. The following two days Chet continued recording songs for *Workshop*. He recorded "Cascade," "West Memphis Serenade," "Long Long Ago," "All Thumbs," "Vincent," "Me and My Guitar," "Struttin'," "You'd Be So Nice to Come Home To," "David's Dance," "Song for Anna," and "My Little Waltz."

Fan Fair was an annual event held each year in Nashville during June when country artists performed for fans, who could watch them, meet them, and obtain autographs. During the 1977 Fan Fair Mose Rager came to perform on the *Reunion* show and visited with Chet. Chet and Merle Travis were at the bus station when Mose arrived. He had been a coal mine inspector but was now retired.

When he got off the bus, Rager quickly told two funny stories and then sat down in the middle of the station to play his guitar. "Give me a pick, Chet," he said. "Here, but don't lose it," replied Chet as he handed him a thumbpick. "I've got to do a show next year."

"Because of Mose, we learned to play the thumb and pick method," Chet told reporter Bill Hance. "Merle learned it from Mose as a boy, then Merle taught me. The thumb and pick method is picking the melody on the guitar with the fingers and playing rhythm at the same time with the thumb." Rager remembered the day he first heard the fingerpicking guitar style. "It was about 1925," he said. "My brother came home one day from nearby Cleaton, Kentucky, tellin' me he had just seen an old black man sittin' by the railroad tracks playin' some amazin' guitar. So I went up there. His name was Kennedy Jones. He taught me how to do it."[4]

On August 16, 1977, Elvis Presley died in Memphis. His death, at just forty-two, caught the world by surprise; an eleven-day tour was scheduled to begin that evening in Portland, Maine. On Thursday, August 18, a funeral service was held in the music room in Graceland, Presley's home. There were over six thousand people gathered outside the gates of Graceland for the funeral procession down Elvis Presley Boulevard to Forest Hills Cemetery. The graveside services were attended by two hundred family members, close friends, and entertainment business associates, including Chet.

On August 17, the day after Elvis died, RCA Studio B, where the singer had recorded over 260 songs, was shut down. Negotiations between RCA and the engineers union had broken down, and there would be no more contractual agreements requiring RCA artists to use the studio. Technology was improving for studio recording, but that meant dramatic investments in equipment; labels were reluctant to cut into their profits to upgrade their studios.

After it became known that RCA had to close their studios, Waylon approached Chet about buying one of RCA's studios. "Chet was standing there lighting a cigar," remembered Waylon when he asked, "Why don't you let me buy that?"

"You've got the nerve of Hitler," answered Chet. "You're the reason we're having to sell it." Then Chet started laughing, saying that RCA "would not allow Waylon to have the studio."[5] In fact RCA did not own its Studio B; Dan Maddox and family owned it and leased it to RCA. Studio A was owned by Chet and Owen and Harold Bradley.

For "My Little Waltz," Chet "had written the first half of that," said John Knowles. "I don't think he had written the introduction that ended up on it, but that kind of SINGS. And he had that nice little half step back, like using a D flat as if it were an A7. He taught that to me, and he said, 'I don't know how the rest of it goes.' So we fiddled around for a little bit and he said, 'Keep working on that. Let me know how the rest of it goes.' So I went home and a couple of days later came back. I put those open strings in there because I thought 'This is like Chet.' At the same time, I just listened to the first half of the piece, and that's where it felt like it went."

"I learned a lot about working with him," continued Knowles. "That's the first time he and I did something together. Then he recorded it and asked me to play some little fill things. I had my Kohno classical guitar with me and he said, 'No, it sounds too good' and he handed me a guitar that you would pass by in a pawn shop. It played like a dream but it was a clunker. He had a ton of those guitars around because they all had certain qualities when you miked them. We did that and then he said, 'Well, that's pretty good. How much of this recording stuff have you done?' I said, 'This is my first time.' and he said, 'Well, how come?' I just laughed and said, 'Well, I was just waiting for a chance to start at the top.'"[6] "My Little Waltz" appeared on Chet's *Me and My Guitar* album.

Chet taped an appearance on the PBS show *Austin City Limits* on September 28, playing "Autumn Leaves," "Black Mountain Rag," "Recuerdos de la Alhambra," "You'd Be So Nice to Come Home To," "Frog Kissin'," and nine more tunes. The performance aired the following year.

In October the eleventh annual CMA Awards Show on CBS was held with Chet as a presenter.[7]

The *Chester and Lester* album was successful, so a follow-up, *Guitar Monsters*, was planned. The first recording session occurred on November 15 and was an all-day affair, starting at ten o'clock and finishing at nine thirty that evening. With Chet and Paul in the studio were Joe Osborn, Paul Yandell, Buddy Harman, Randy Hauser, and Randy Goodrum, while Bob Ferguson produced. Only two songs were recorded on that first day; the next day they recorded four songs, and on November 18 they recorded six songs. Like with their earlier album, Chet and Les worked out the basic arrangements of the songs in the studio, did a practice run, then recorded them. On those sessions Chet played his 1959 Country Gentlemen.[8]

Progress was slow, frustrating Chet. The album remained incomplete in April. "It's all Les's fault," Chet grumbled as he took a slow drag off his cigar. "He's the reason I look so ragged. He's causing me to stay in the studio night and day." The album was originally scheduled to be released in a few weeks, but the deadline had passed. "Les and I cut the tapes several months ago and then I sent them to Les for him to over-dub some guitar licks on some of the tunes," said Chet. "He's lazy. He slept on the job. I called him, telling him to hurry up. He always had an excuse. First, he said his guitar was on the blink. Then he said he had to hurry and do a show. Next, he was working on his taxes. I know what it was. He wanted the time to run out so I wouldn't have time to do my part. He knew I'd outplay him."

Chet finally received the tapes with Les's part. "I've been in the studio night and day ever since the tapes arrived," he said. Songs on the *Guitar Monsters* album included "Limehouse Blues," "I Want to Be Happy," "Over the Rainbow," "Meditation," "Lazy River," "I'm Your Greatest Fan," "It Don't Mean a Thing (If It Ain't Got That Swing)," "I Surrender Dear," "Brazil," "Give My Love to Nell," and "Hot Toddy."

In December Chet and Paul Yandell went to France, where Chet recorded a live album on December 10 and 11 at the Olympia Theatre in Paris. On that concert was Marcel Dadi, whom Chet had met in 1973.

"We did this rehearsal tape of the tunes we were going to play," said Yandell. They did it on the back porch of Chet's office on Music Row and "Chet played like he never played." In Paris, "Marcel opened the show. He played Chet's complete show—played all his tunes," said Yandell. "It made me so mad. I went back into Chet's dressing room and said, 'Chet he played your show. That is the most unprofessional thing I had ever seen.' Chet said, 'Don't worry about it.'"[9]

During the concert Chet played almost thirty songs. "It was great," said Henry Strzelecki. "I did about thirty albums with Chet and this was the best." After they returned to Nashville "we went to Chet's home studio. We were listening to it on his 24 track recorder and he didn't like it. Chet and someone else were on the same track together so he wanted to overdub it. He wanted me to redo my part. I said, 'Chet, this won't work. This is live, not in a studio. I don't think I can do it.'

We tried and it didn't work. That was the only time in a twenty-year relationship that I told Chet what to do. I think he ended up using the original. I remember saying, 'Chet don't touch it.' And he would say, 'I can't get the guitar out enough.' I finally said, 'Chet it is so good the guitar doesn't need to come out more.'"[10]

Because that concert was successful Marcel convinced RCA France to release Chet's albums in France, which is how Chet became well-known there. Dadi formed the Atkins-Dadi Guitar Players Association, which further popularized the fingerpicking style.[11]

Chet released a studio album, *Me and My Guitar*, and two compilation albums, *Love Letters* on the Camden label and *A Legendary Performer* in 1977. He collaborated with Floyd Cramer and Danny Davis on *Chet, Floyd & Danny*.

CHAPTER 47

For the Grammys, held in February 1978, Chet was nominated twice in the Best Country Instrumental Performance, for his album *Me and My Guitar* and for *Chet, Floyd & Danny*, with Floyd Cramer and Danny Davis. Pig Robbins won the Grammy that year.

Steve Wariner's single "I'm Already Taken" entered the *Billboard* country singles chart on April 22. It was produced by Chet Atkins and had a long story behind it.

Steve's dad had a band and played guitar in the fingerpicking style, so Wariner was familiar with Chet from an early age. Bob Luman was recording some of Steve Wariner's songs, and Paul Yandell and Wariner played on the session. Paul told Wariner that "Chet might be interested in hearing some of your tunes." Wariner put a tape together, and Paul took it to Chet. That led to Chet and Wariner having lunch and Wariner insisting on paying, before he discovered that he'd left his wallet behind. "I was so embarrassed I could have died and Chet, of course, loved it and he picked up the lunch. He brought that up a bunch over the years."

Chet wanted to hear Wariner's voice on tape, so he gave him some songs to learn. They went into RCA Studio B and recorded some. Later, Chet invited Wariner to Studio B and, when he arrived, there was Jerry Reed, another hero of Wariner's. Chet told Steve to "grab Jerry's guitar and play him something." Warner played and sang a song, then handed Reed's guitar back to him. "Chester, sign this boy up to a contract," said Reed. "What do you want, Blood?"

A short while later Chet signed him.[1]

After "You Needed Me," written by Randy Goodrum for Ann Murray, there had been a string of hits from the songwriter, which put him in demand and caused conflicts in his schedule for touring with Chet, so Goodrum asked Tony Migliore to sub for him, which led to Migliore becoming Chet's regular piano player on the road.

Chet sent over some cassette tapes but "we had no rehearsal," said Migliore, who made some chord charts from the tapes. During the shows, Chet "did the stuff that he was most known for, like 'Windy and Warm' and 'Snowbird'—those things, plus he did what he called 'The Medley of My Hit,' which was a bunch of things that he produced on other artists. One was Perry Como's version of Don McLean's song, 'And I Love Her So.' Don Gibson's 'Oh Lonesome Me' and 'Dream' by the Everly Brothers. I remember also that Jim Reeves's 'He'll Have to Go' was in there too."

Chet "was on this lofty throne somewhere way up above the rest of us," said Migliore. "Come to know the man, and he was the most humble, self-deprecating person you'd ever meet. He couldn't believe people actually paid money to come hear him play."

When he began touring with Chet, Migliore "had a tendency to play a little busy. He would tell me, 'Play a little something but don't get carried away, just relax,'" said Migliore. "I realized I didn't have to run up and down the keyboard like Van Cliburn to make a statement . . . the saying was, 'Know when to lay out.'"

The band did a show at the Bottom Line in New York with Les Paul, "and here was Chet sitting on a stool with his legs crossed, just calmly playing as he did, and when it came Les Paul's turn he had every knob on the amp cranked up to 10 . . . the contrast between the two was incredible."

Chet was "kind of reticent around people," observed Migliore. "He was kind of shy but very, very intelligent and read people very well. He didn't always say much to them because you learn a lot more by listening than you do by talking." Musically, Chet was "a master of understatement," said Migliore.

After working with Chet for about a year Migliore began writing arrangements, then began conducting orchestras. Working up a new arrangement "we'd play it through," said Migliore. "If he didn't like something he'd never insult you. He'd be very subtle and say, 'Can we leave that part out?' and I'd say, 'Sure, no problem.' We can't have big egos. Chet might say, 'Maybe we can not do this part right here. Wait for this part.' That was his way of saying he didn't care for that particular part, or maybe say, 'Can we change that?'"

"He pretty much let me have my own thoughts about the arrangements," said Migliore. "If he had something specific he wanted, he'd say, 'I'd like you to do something with horns here' or 'Let's do something rhythmic here.' But, other than that, he kind of let you go," although "if Chet didn't like something, he just wouldn't perform the song. He really knew what to perform and when." Chet would "go in spurts," said Tony. "He'd play some of them for awhile and then put them up and play some other ones instead. Then he'd come back to something and say, 'We haven't played that in awhile. Let's do that one.'"[2]

To promote their second duet LP, *Guitar Monsters*, Chet and Les Paul, with Henry Strzelecki on bass and drummer Bob Sutton, were guests on NBC's *Today Show*; they performed "Avalon," "It Don't Mean a Thing," and "Limehouse Blues." Les dominated the interview, but when Chet finally found an opening he demonstrated the folding guitar (to fit in a suitcase) built for him by inventor Roger Field of Germany.[3]

During the 1977–1978 period Floyd Cramer recorded an album and wanted to release it with silver piano keys that would pop out from the album cover. Joe Galante was a numbers guy from New York in the Nashville office and made his decision to decline the idea by looking at sales of Cramer's albums and comparing them to the cost of artwork. Galante did not consult anyone else.

Defending Cramer's request, Chet first contacted Jerry Bradley, then had his assistant call Joe Galante and told him to come up to Chet's office on the third floor, where Chet was fuming and frustrated. He wanted to defend his longtime fellow musician. "I went in and he was sitting at his desk," said Galante. "I didn't even get to sit down. He pointed his finger at me and said, 'You're from the North, you're Eye-Tal-Yun, and *nobody* likes you. So watch yourself, boy.'"[4] Galante was "hurt" and went to see Jerry Bradley, who had his head in his hands when Galante walked in. In a way this marked the introduction of a new era at RCA that would see Chet and Bradley eventually leave the label and Galante emerge as the head of RCA's Nashville division.

Chet wasn't totally wrong when he told Galante that "nobody likes you." Galante did not have a musical background. The joke going around Music Row circles was "What has two arms, two legs and no ears? Answer: Joe Galante."[5]

The leaders of the Nashville labels had been music guys. Chet and Owen Bradley were musicians. Others, like Jim Fogelsong (a graduate of the Eastman School of Music), had a background in music or, like

Jerry Bradley, who was not a musician, had deep connections to those in the Nashville industry and had worked in publishing and as an engineer. What they all had in common was that they came from the creative side of the music industry. Galante did not. From the mid-1970s on the heads of music labels came from the business or legal side. It was an evolution that needed to happen as the music industry became increasingly corporate and complex.

Chet and Galante did not have an antagonistic relationship. There were weekly A&R meetings where Chet, Jerry Bradley, RCA staff producers Roy Dea and Bob Ferguson, and Galante sat around a table and discussed singles and album releases as well as new and potential signings. Chet and Galante would see each other in the studio when Waylon or Jerry Reed or other RCA acts were recording. They'd pass each other in the hallways at RCA and attended the same industry events. Their time together was always civil, polite, and professional.

Galante learned how to temper his "New York ways" and what it took to fit into southern culture. It was a steep learning curve that Galante climbed. Eventually he was so at home in Nashville that he was widely acclaimed as an innovator in marketing country music and was elected to the Country Music Hall of Fame in the "Non Performer" category.

When Chet and Les Paul released their *Guitar Monsters* album, Galante was with them at the Bottom Line in New York. "It was an incredible show," said Galante, "and such a strong contrast. Les was so overstated and bombastic while Chet was so understated, dry and witty." Chet had met Segovia and played before him at a luncheon in Nashville and observed that Segovia had "the biggest ego I ever met" until he worked with Les Paul. "Les Paul was the Ty Cobb of the guitar players," said Chet. "You'd get onstage with him and couldn't get a note in edgeways. He was raised to go into joints and play other guitarists off the stage."[6]

On the twelfth annual CMA Awards in October Chet performed "The South's Gonna Do It Again" with the Charlie Daniels Band. *Lynn Anderson's Country Welcome* was a special syndicated TV show, on which Chet and Paul Yandell performed a Beatles medley of "If I Fell," "For No One," "Something," and "Lady Madonna." Chet also sang "Frog Kissin'." Chet played "Lover Come Back to Me" on a Hascal

Haile guitar with animated dancing pigs and a donkey on *Hee Haw*'s tenth anniversary show. He went to Canada to appear on Liona Boyd's TV special *Supersession*. The show featured Chet and Liona playing "Recuerdoes de la Alhambra." On October 25 Chet was seen on NBC being interviewed about the death of Mother Maybelle Carter, who had passed two days earlier. On October 29 Chet was on the PBS program *Soundstage* that was taped at WTTW-TV in Chicago with George Benson and Earl Klugh. The trio performed "Cherokee," "Oh Lonesome Me," "A Day in the Life of a Fool," and "Bluesette." Chet performed "Cascade," "Kentucky," "Don't Think Twice, It's Alright," and "Stars & Stripes Forever" as solos.[7]

In January 1967 Earl Klugh first heard Chet Atkins on a Perry Como TV special. "He had that beautiful Gretsch Country Gentleman guitar and he was playing the theme from *Dr. Zhivago*," remembered Klugh. "When he came on and started playing, it was like the way a person plays a piano. Nobody was singing and he was playing all the parts on the guitar. Right from that moment I immediately knew that this was what I wanted to do . . . it changed the course of my life." For the next two years Klugh bought Chet Atkins records and learned to play by listening to them.

When Klugh first met Chet in 1978, it was after he "had made a few records that started selling well." Klugh called his manager, Fred Hewley, and told him he'd like to meet Chet. The meeting came while Klugh was in Nashville recording. "My manager set it up so I would call Chet, he came by and picked me up," said Klugh. "We went back to his house and played a little bit. He was such a wonderful person. I tried not to wear him out or go on and on about stuff, but I was a huge admirer. We developed a pretty good friendship."[8]

The Nashville Quartet, composed of John Knowles, Liona Boyd, John Pell, and Chet, "came together at the suggestion of Shel Silverstein," remembered John Knowles. As a songwriter, Silverstein had written "One's On the Way" for Loretta Lynn, "The Unicorn" for the Irish Rovers, "The Cover of the Rolling Stone" and "Sylvia's Mother" for Dr. Hook and the Medicine Show, "Queen of the Silver Dollar" for Dave and Sugar, and numerous others. He wrote the children's book *The Giving Tree* and was a popular cartoonist for *Playboy* magazine. Silverstein was "a very creative person and his idea, as he articulated it, was to put together four guitarists in the form of a string quartette," said Knowles. "He suggested this to Chet and Chet then spoke to me and later with Liona [Boyd] when she was in town." The album was similar in concept to *The Night Atlanta Burned.*

On Monday, November 10, the quartet began a series of recordings that lasted through Thursday. Chet was the producer of those recordings and seemed to have a vision from the first session. Liona Boyd was a classical guitarist from Canada who had studied under Andres Segovia and Julian Bream, the crème de la crème of classical guitarists. John Pell had been an award winner back when Chet held his guitar contests and then toured with Dolly Parton. The recordings were made in the former RCA Studio A, renamed Music City Music Hall after Owen Bradley purchased it, and in Chet's home studio, known as the CA Workshop.

"I was working with good musicians and, with the exception of Chet, each one had to learn to do what they do in a very different manner to what they had been used to," said Knowles. "For instance, in some cases, on some of the tracks on the recording Liona and I would play a duet to begin with and the other guys would add their parts. John Pell and I then played 'Carolina Shout' together and Chet and Liona would come back and add their parts. Then Chet and I would record a duet and add parts, but some of the pieces we would all play together. Overdubbing was new to us and we had a lot of laughs doing it, especially with Liona, who was only used to public performing. You see she had never been in the position of overdubbing before, so we each had to find ways to make all four of us feel at ease and it was very challenging, laughing and calling out the chords, and Liona saying, 'What the hell are you talking about, Chet?' She wasn't used to working like this. It was laughs all the way, especially after working everything out. Chet would say, 'Hey, I've got a better idea, let's do it this way' and the whole thing would change again. But looking back, we all thoroughly enjoyed ourselves making that album."[9]

On the album was "Bound for Boston," "an old Revolutionary War song," said Knowles. "Actually, my Dad found that tune. Chet said, 'Oh, this'd be great.' It was like a fife and drum kind of song so we worked it out for the guitars and decided that it would kind of enter and then leave, like it was marching through. That's the way we produced the track. And there's a little place in the middle where we left thirty-two bars. John Pell and Chet were going to do sixteen each. So John plays his sixteen and Chet's in there with him. And then Chet plays sixteen. Chet says, 'Well, let's do it again. I think I can do it better.' And I said, 'Do you want to keep that one?' And he said, 'Yeah, let's keep that one.' Well, we kept about two of them and then we quit keeping them. And at some point John says, 'I don't know if I'm going to get this any better.' Chet says, 'No. I need to play off of you. You can't just play yours and then I play mine. I'm listening to you.' So this is making life tough on John and John's just laughing, saying 'Oh, my goodness!'"

"What I heard Chet do was attempt to find what he was looking for," remembered Knowles. "It's almost like he went through a Rolodex of everything he had ever done—all the little pull-off tricks and great licks. It was just almost like an encyclopedia, you know? And like I said, if we'd kept the whole thing you'd have Chet in a nutshell. It was him going really deep into everything and I was the bad guy. I had to erase some of those tracks. That was part of the thrill of working with him because, with him, it wasn't about what he had done, it was about what he was trying to do."

As they prepared to do "Rings of Grass," they divided up the arrangement. "Chet says to me, 'Why don't you make up a little solo thing at the front? And then John Pell will do a little quartet thing in the middle. I'll arrange a solo part for Liona with a tremolo; this tune will be good for a tremolo,'" said Knowles. "So we did that and when you hear the recording, you'll hear those sections very clearly. What's not clear is that Liona was somebody who learned by reading. That was her main way of learning a piece. So Chet sat down and wrote out that entire solo. And it looks just like a handwritten classical guitar manuscript. Before he gave it to Liona, he showed it to me and he said, 'Now, am I doing this right?' and I said, 'Oh yeah, that's great.'"

"There was no engineer on a lot of it," continued Knowles. "He would put the amp in one room and put the microphone on it and then put a long cord on his guitar and sit at the console. So he's got this good sound in the other room. The other thing that he did was his net good sound, which is phenomenal. It's not just coming from him, it's coming from all the people he ever worked with. It's influencing the touch on the guitar. It's influencing the electronics. It's influencing the way the stuff is mixed and EQ'ed. If you listen to all of the sounds he's gotten over the years you notice that it's constantly in motion. It's him rediscovering having fun playing with the sound."[10] It is interesting that when painters talk they talk about light, but when musicians speak it is about sound.

Songs recorded for the album included "Carolina Shout," "Love Song of Pepe Sanchez," "Skirts of Mexico," "You Needed Me," "Bound for Boston," "Washington Post March," "Someday My Prince Will Come," and "Rings of Grass."

CHAPTER 48

In January 1979 *Nashville!* magazine published an article by Bob Allen titled "The Real Chet Atkins." Allen described Chet's office as an "ornate executive sanctum chock-full of easy chairs, a sofa and nearly a dozen guitars and guitar cases."

After the interview Chet's publicist, Susan Hackney, and Allen went with Chet for lunch; they rode over in Chet's Mercedes-Benz with the back seat "full of tape boxes and record albums." At the restaurant Chet had a lunch of fruit—a plate of apples, oranges, and grapes served with French bread and cream cheese—and a bottle of Perrier.

"Every second person who comes through the restaurant seems to know Chet," observed Allen, who stated that Chet greeted everyone with "Hi, how are you getting along?" and, after they left, asked Hackney and Allen, "Who was that, do you know?"

"Chet talks slowly, organizing his thoughts carefully and putting them into soft, short sentences," stated Allen. "He doesn't relish talking about himself, and often during an interview his mind seems to drift away to a better place and time, like perhaps a quiet afternoon on the golf course, for instance, or a quiet evening back home with his guitar."

"I appeal to all the old ladies," said Chet in his wry, sly, dry humor. "They almost fall out of their wheelchairs."

"I always loved the guitar," continued Chet. "The older folks were always playin' one and I loved it. I don't know why I love the guitar so. I still don't . . . I don't know where that sort of drive or inspiration comes from. I do think it's part of a person's chemistry though. You have to love the guitar with all your heart and soul—more than anything else. I don't think anybody excels who has to be forced to practice. It's all got to come from within them."

"I was introverted, backwards and shy," said Chet. "A lot of people thought I was stuck-up, when actually I was just scared to death. . . . I was afraid to express myself. I think it was more than shyness because I was from so far back in the mountains that I was afraid I'd make a mistake or mispronounce a word so I was quiet. But I think a lot of musicians are that way; they try to express themselves through music because they're backward in some other way."

Asked about the Nashville Sound Chet said it "was not something that Owen and I sat around and said we're gonna do this or that. We were trying to make a living, trying to make hit records, and it gradually grew into that. Like most things that happen, it was an accident. . . . If there was any secret to my success as a producer it was, I don't know, you just hear something you like and if you're halfway like the public, chances are they'll like it too. That's what I always went by."

"People tell me all the time that I helped build the music industry, but I really can't see it," said Chet. "I think I was just lucky. I don't have any ego about that at all. All I was trying to do was keep my job. I was just lucky that I had my job at RCA and had the privilege of being able to help some people."

"It sometimes seems like Chet Atkins is his own walking, talking disclaimer," noted Allen.

"I think Chet was born feeling sort of like, 'You should expect other people to take you seriously, but don't take yourself seriously,'" said Joe Talbot, who had known Chet "since 1951 or '52." "He's just not impressed with himself. It disturbs me in a way that he has no awareness of the love and respect and the fame and the stature he has earned, and it's too bad he can't enjoy some of it. But I don't think he believes any of it, or if he does, he's not impressed with it. Chet has met all his goals."

"I wanted to be a famous guitarist," confessed Chet. "I wanted to play on the network shows. I wanted to make records. Those were my goals, and I've done all those things. I can do anything I want to. The time flies by. It's always a case where you gain something and lose something. I've gained that respect, but I lost years to do it. I mean, . . . a lot of younger people don't understand the years it took to build the reputation that I've got. I think it was all kind of an accident. But whatever it was, it's there and it's nice. But the years run out on you. So you gain something and you lose something. But I've done all those things, and I want to continue if I can."

"Everything I did was all done out of a fear of becoming mediocre," said Chet. "That's the reason I still try and learn new things. I have a great fear of people saying 'Yeah, he's pretty good, but he's old-fashioned,' which happens. It's happening to me, but maybe it will happen a little slower. I'm still aware that I have to keep coming up with something different. I have to keep surprising people. You know, once you become predictable, they're not interested anymore."[1] Chet was fifty-four at the time of the interview.

In 1979 *Billboard* devoted a special section in tribute to the career of Anita Kerr. The editors asked Chet and Owen Bradley to write articles about Anita. Chet stated, "I've gotten an awful lot of credit for having created the Nashville Sound and I always say Owen Bradley and Anita Kerr are just as important in its development. They gave a sophistication and smoothness to country music that made it so much more palatable to audiences all over the world. Anita deserves much more credit than she gets." Chet and Bradley both credited her as being the "under appreciated third architect of the Nashville Sound."

In May Chet had recording sessions in the morning and afternoon for "March Right Back," "Silhouette," and "La Cadenza." In July he and Randy Goodrum recorded "Theme From an Unmade Movie," "Carolina Clog," and "Platform Princess."

Chet often told his friends that when John Knowles "comes by my office, we play the guitar, tell stories and fix things," said Knowles. "The 'fix things' is so funny because I swear that's thirty percent of what we did. I remember one time we went by the hardware store after lunch and bought light bulbs and went around to Music Row properties that he owned and changed light bulbs. I held the ladder while Chet climbed up and changed the light bulbs. We drove around and did that all afternoon. He hated to do stuff like that alone—he loved to have a tag-along."[2]

Chet was in the studio with flatpicking legend Doc Watson on the morning of September 12, when the duo recorded "Dance With Me" and "This String." After that session ended Chet recorded "Stars and Stripes Forever" (which he referred to as "The John Phillip Sousa March") with Randy Hauser on drums. Guy Van Duser, a finger-style guitarist and arranger, had arranged the song for solo guitar during the 1970s. Chet learned Van Duser's arrangement and played it at a number of concert appearances. On the recording he made Chet played a classical guitar until he finished the song by singing, "You may think that this is the end—well it is," which is how Mitch Miller ended his TV show.

For three days in September Chet was with flatpicking legend Doc Watson in Music City Music Hall to record more songs for an album titled *Reflections*. Producer for the album was John D. Loudermilk. On the afternoon of September 25, with Jerry Shook, Terry McMillan, and Thomas Coleman backing them, Chet and Watson recorded "I'm on My Way to Canaan's Land," "Dill Pickle Rag," and "You're Gonna Be Sorry." The next day they started in the afternoon and went through the evening; during those back-to-back sessions they recorded "You're Gonna Be Sorry," "Goodnight Waltz," "Old Joe Clark," "Texas Gales," and "Don't Monkey Round With My Widder." On the final afternoon, September 27, they recorded "Melody for Mr. Flatt," "Black and White Rag," and "Doc and Chet Made a Record."

Chet and Doc sang on "On My Way to Canaan's Land," an old traditional gospel spiritual; in the liner notes Chet claimed he first heard the song at the Copper Ridge Holiness Church in Luttrell, Tennessee, when he was about ten. As he and Doc sang, Chet threw in the names of Minnie Pearl, Porter Wagoner, and Dolly Parton during the verses.[3]

In 1979 Bill Piburn met Chet when he performed at the school where John Knowles was teaching. One day Knowles said, "Let's go see Chet." Chet wasn't in his office, but they ran into Lenny Breau in the parking lot. During that afternoon they played and Lenny drank. Chet finally showed up and called for them to come up to his office.

In his office Breau said, "Hey Chet, I want to introduce you to my good friend, Bill Piburn." As far as Chet knew, Lenny and Piburn were old school friends. They went into his office and Chet started joking around with Lenny, telling him that there was an article from the *Chicago Tribune* about the pitfalls of marijuana use. Lenny said to Chet, "Man, that's not true. I had a couple of joints on the way over here."

Chet asked Piburn where he was from and handed him the Hascal Haile classical with the "tree of life" inlay on the fingerboard and said, "Play something." Piburn played while sitting on a beanbag chair with "a guitar that is very confusing to play because of the inlay on the fingerboard," said Piburn. "I remember thinking as I was playing, 'I have lost my mind!' Chet was complimentary. We proceeded to pass the guitar around for a while."

Chet played a song, then Bill played "The Nearness of You." When he finished Chet said, "Right there, I think you need to play this note.

I think you have it wrong. Now this tune was a tune Chet's friend, Perry Como would always sing at all the golf tournaments they attended together," said Piburn. "So Chet felt like he really knew the song pretty well. So he is correcting little things here and there. He said, 'You know I am an old codger. I know all these old songs. If you have any questions about how a song goes, just call Uncle Chet.' He also told me if he didn't know a tune, he either had the record or he had the sheet music."[4] As Piburn and Lenny were leaving RCA, Piburn asked Breau if Chet liked his playing. Breau replied, "Oh yeah, man. If Chet didn't like your playing, he wouldn't have said anything to you."

Steve Wariner's early releases weren't getting much traction, so he was on the road with Chet, playing bass after Henry Strzelecki left. Wariner loved touring with Chet "because every now and then Chet would just hand me his guitar and say, 'Hey, do so-and-so, do this song,'" said Wariner, "and I would set my bass down and Paul would go over and play bass and I would play one of my new songs on Chet's guitar and he would feature me in the show. Sometimes we did 'Frog Kissing' in the show and I would sing harmony with Chet. Someone would tell him a good joke and he would pull out his little pad and write it down," said Wariner. "I mean, he was always working on his show so he would take out a pad and write it down and remember it for his show."[5]

During one show, as they were playing Chet walked over to Steve and said, "Anybody ever tell you that you're a great bass player?" Steve looked at him and said "No." Chet said, "Ever wonder why?"[6]

Three days after Christmas Chet was in the studio with John C. Williams, Kenny Malone, and Randy Goodrum to record "With a Guitar on My Knee" and "Gringo."

CHAPTER 49

Long car trips were a good way for Merle to get to know her dad better. On one car trip from Durham, North Carolina, where he had played in a golf tournament, to eastern North Carolina, where she lived, "Dance With Me" by Orleans came on the radio. "I said, 'I love that' and he said, 'I love that too. I'm going to record it.' 'You are not!'" said Merle. "'I am too,' he replied. . . . Well, we went on and on about that tune." Chet did record it. "Dance With Me" "became my tune, since Mom had already laid claim to 'Vincent' as her tune."[1]

On March 1 Chet's record of "Blind Willie," about blues singer Blind Willie McTell, written by Buddy Kalb, the same songwriter who wrote "Frog Kissin'," became the second song with Chet singing to chart as a single. On March 15 his album *The Best of Chet on the Road—Live* entered the *Billboard* country album chart. The album contained "The Stars and Stripes Forever," "Blind Willie," and "Dance With Me."

In 1980 Tony Brown joined RCA in the A&R department. Chet's office was on the third floor of the RCA building, while Jerry Bradley, Joe Galante, and the administrative staff were on the second floor. "I was the fresh A&R guy and Chet would have me come up to the top floor and give me a lot of shit about this and that," remembered Brown. "Being the new kid in the building, he sort of gave me a lot of grief that let me know he liked me. Sometimes I would go up to his office and he would have a new guitar to show me." They became friends because of their mutual friendships with Ray Stevens, Don Light, and Harry Warner, who were close to Chet. "Chet was the Elvis of record executives," said Brown. "As a musician, he was a star. He was and is the guitar player. He was a bigger than life person. When Chet walked into a room, you knew it. Owen Bradley was very much a southern man, easy going in a southern kind of way," continued Brown. "And even though Chet was from the South, he came off as a well-educated person schooled in the Northeast. He was really classy, in the way he dressed, the way he carried himself, and the way he spoke. I always thought he was the perfect representative for Nashville. He showed that not all of us are 'Country bumpkins!'"

"Chet never took himself as serious as the rest of us did," noted Brown. "All of us had him up on a big pedestal. He was definitely not into that! He lived modestly. He owned a lot of property here in Nashville."[2]

A gala fundraiser for the American Cancer Society was held on May 14 at the Grand Ole Opry House. The show, *A Tribute to Chet Atkins From His Friends*, was taped for TV. The show saluted Chet "for his accomplishments as a guitarist, composer, producer, discoverer of talent, executive, sportsman and innovator in musical electronics." Artists appearing on the show, shortened to two hours for TV viewers, included a who's who of country greats—over twenty in all. Chet opened the show with a medley of "Battle of New Orleans" and "Sugarfoot Rag," then did his "Producer's Medley" before he performed a duet with Earl Klugh on "Good Time Charlie's Got the Blues." Chet also did duets with the Everly Brothers and Ray Stevens, who sang "Night Games." Don Gibson sang "Oh Lonesome Me," and Jim Stafford performed "Mama Knows."[3]

In August TV viewers could see Chet on *Hee Haw* as part of the Million Dollar Band, which included Boots Randolph, Roy Clark, Floyd Cramer, Charlie McCoy, Danny Davis, Jethro Burns, and Johnny Gimble.[4] The Million Dollar Band was a popular segment on *Hee Haw* that producer Sam Lovullo had dreamed up, but Chet almost wasn't on it. He had initially agreed to do the show but shortly before the taping band leader Charlie McCoy received a call from Chet, who said, "You know that 'Million Dollar Band' segment that Sam wants to do? Well, I don't think I want to do it." "I knew that Sam would be devastated if this segment fell through," said McCoy, so he asked Chet, "Are you in your office?" Chet replied that he was so McCoy told him, "Don't move! I'm coming right over." McCoy "sprinted down the alley to the RCA studios" and "for Sam's sake, I swallowed my pride and begged Chet to reconsider. After some time, Chet agreed to try it."[5]

Tommy Emmanuel was born in New South Wales, Australia, and received his first guitar when he was four. He became part of the family band called the Emmanuel Quartet; his sister played Hawaiian lap steel, his brother played drums, his father emceed their shows, and his mother sold tickets.

Tommy first heard Chet in 1962 or 1963; “I can’t remember the tune, but I remember the feeling that came over me,” said Emmanuel. “I got butterflies, and my heart was thumping, and I wanted to tear my teeth out. I didn’t know how to express it, but I knew that I loved it and knew that it was really special and I said, ‘I want to be able to do that.’”

“Then I got *The Best of Chet Atkins* album and *Reminiscing* with Hank Snow, and I wore them out, then I went and found other albums. In the outback and in small country towns, you’ve got to order a record and wait six months for it to come through.”

Emmanuel was completely self-taught. “When you’re a dedicated Chet fan, you go out and buy that new album [because] with every album he does something that will totally blow your mind,” said Emmanuel. “There are always great tunes and great playing but there’s definitely something new and totally mind boggling on every one of his albums.”

When Tommy was eleven he wrote a letter to Chet: “’Dear Chet, I’m a kid from Australia. You may not have heard of my country, but I’m a fan’ and Chet wrote back! I got home from school and my mother said there’s an envelope here for you.” In it was “a signed photo and a letter which I still have.”

Sometime around 1978 a friend of Tommy’s sent a tape to Chet that was recorded while Tommy sat in his friend’s house and played “and Chet wrote my friend a letter saying ‘Tell Tommy I listened to his tape and I hope to meet him one day.’”

In 1980 Tommy thought it was time to leave Australia for a trip to Nashville to meet Chet. He flew over, checked into a Holiday Inn, and called Chet’s office, but he was out playing golf. “I was so excited I didn’t sleep for three days,” remembered Emmanuel. “I played every day and I would go play in the park and the fourth day I called again and Chet answered. ‘It’s Tommy Emmanuel from Australia.’ Chet said, ‘Oh, Hi Tommy. I’ve got your tape. I’ve just been playing it.’ So I went over and showed him my photo album of me with his records, and stuff like that. And he says, ‘You want to pick a little?’ So I started playing ‘Me and Bobby McGee.’ By the time I got to the chorus he joined in and we were locked in.”

“Then he said ‘Come upstairs, I want to you to meet someone’ and there was Lenny Breau. The three of us played for three hours without hardly taking a breath. Can you imagine a kid from the sticks coming here and playing with them? And then I took Lenny to his gig that night."[6]

On Friday, September 19, Chet was in Washington, D.C., to present one of his guitars to the Smithsonian Institute. He also visited with President Jimmy Carter in the Oval Office.

RCA released *Reflections*, the album by Chet and Doc Watson, and the two appeared on several television shows to promote it. They played a medley of "Tennessee Rag" and "Beaumont Rag" on Johnny Carson's *Tonight Show* and then did "On My Way to Canaan Land." The next evening they played the same set on the *Toni Tennille Show*. On December 11 they performed "On My Way to Canaan's Land" on the *John Davidson Show*.[7]

CHAPTER 50

In 1967 Fred Gretsch sold his company to Baldwin, a musical instrument company based in Ohio that specialized in pianos and organs. The primary reason Gretsch sold was because he did not have a family member interested in taking it over.

The deal was completed on July 31, 1967; the unofficial figure for the sale was four million dollars, and Fred remained as president. Baldwin wanted assurance that Gretsch's chief asset remained with the company because "I was important to that sale," said Atkins. "Mr. Gretsch came to me, said he was gonna sell to Baldwin and asked me if I would sign a contract for so many years. I said, 'Why don't I get some stock?' And he wouldn't do it. I was real busy at the time and I didn't have an attorney or anything so I went ahead and signed it."

There were problems from the start. The Baldwin engineers and salesman were inexperienced with manufacturing guitars, which is very different from building pianos and organs. Then an economic downturn struck.

In September 1970 Baldwin moved the Gretsch factory to Booneville, Arkansas; very few Gretsch employees made the move. Jimmy Webster had drifted away from the company; he died in 1978. "They just couldn't build Gretsch guitars in Booneville," said Chet. "I complained and they hired a man called Dean Porter. He moved to Arkansas and got the guitars so they would play. But the quality never was like it was in Brooklyn."[1]

Chet was fed up with Gretsch by the time he was approached by Gibson for an endorsement agreement. In May 1981 the official announcement came that Chet would serve as a "consultant in new product development for Gibson."[2] Chet appeared on the *Mike Douglas Show* to promote his *Country After All These Years* album and made the round of talk shows to debut his new Gibson "signature" guitar, a custom-built 350X-T model.[3]

Roger Whittaker grew up in Nairobi, Kenya, and began singing while a student. In 1970 he released the album *New World in the Morning*, which contained his biggest hit, "The Last Farewell." Whittaker toured extensively, especially in Europe, where he acquired a large following. Chet produced the album *Changes*, on him, which had several songs from Nashville songwriters, including "When I Dream" by Sandy Mason, "So Good, So Bad, So Soon" by Shel Silverstein, and two Felice and Boudleaux Bryant songs, "I Can Hear Kentucky Calling Me" and "Rocky Top."

Atkins had never received producer royalties for the RCA acts he produced but did from Whittaker 's album, and those payments proved substantial since Whittaker had a worldwide following. The two appeared on the *Nashville on the Road* program where Chet played "Ready for the Times to Get Better" and accompanied Whittaker on "Smooth Sailing" and "Rocky Top."[4]

On March 12 TV viewers could see Chet on the CBS TV special *Country Comes Home*, where he did a Bob Wills medley of "Maiden's Prayer," "Faded Love" (featuring a vocal by Steve Wariner), and "San Antonio Rose." That may have been the last TV appearance where Chet played his classic 1959 Country Gentleman guitar.[5]

Chet's contract with RCA was up at the end of July, and Jerry Bradley had been to New York to discuss the renewal. "He's our Nipper," Bradley told the New York executives, advocating for Chet, who was not selling enough records to pay for what it cost to make them. His sales had slipped to the point where he was only selling five to seven thousand copies of each release. The New York executives saw Jerry Bradley and Joe Galante regularly, but they didn't see Chet, who hated to travel to New York. As a result, the New York office of RCA "didn't think Chet was doing anything," said Bradley. "They thought we [he and Galante] were doing everything." That meant that Chet's value to RCA had declined in terms of promoting and marketing their current roster.

One day Chet called Jerry and asked him to come up to his office, where Chet "talked about everything under the sun" before he got to the point where he told Jerry "I really want to leave." "That's the way Chet was," said Bradley. "He'd talk about everything under the sun before he got to the point he wanted to make or the question he wanted answered." Jerry agreed to support Chet leaving and went back to New York and relayed that message.

The New York executives liked the idea of having the money they were paying Chet go into their budget and not having an unprofitable artist on the label. Chet was a legend, an iconic artist on RCA, and Bob Summers, the label's president, knew that he had to come to Nashville to discuss the issue. Jerry Bradley picked Summers up at the airport. "Summers was nervous," said Bradley. "He kept asking, 'What am I going to say?'" and Bradley didn't have an answer.

The meeting was set for four thirty in the afternoon and that's when Bob Summers went into Chet's office. He did not emerge quickly. "It was 5:30, then 6:30, then 7:30," said Bradley. "I wasn't in the room and don't know what they talked about but Summers came out smiling and happy" and said that he and Chet had "a wonderful conversation" and "mainly talked about the old times."

During his conversation with Summers Chet agreed to remain with RCA until May 1982, his thirty-fifth anniversary with the company. That meeting laid the groundwork for Chet leaving RCA amicably.[6]

"I've been thinking about this for some time," said Chet. "I told the bosses four or five months ago that I didn't want to renew." He planned to move into an office in a house on Seventeenth Avenue South, about two blocks south of the RCA Building that he owned. "Once I'm settled there I just may open a mini-museum, put my wife Leona in charge—she needs the work—and promote it as a tourist attraction. Tell the friends and neighbors, ole Chester thanks the songwriters, singers, pickers and all others who have helped through the years, and that he'll still be around—probably more visible—but not in an executive suite."

He would not be "totally severing ties," said Chet. "I'll still turn out a few albums annually and produce studio sessions for Perry Como, Roger Whittaker, and help develop new artists." This decision was a "phase two" of a decision he made ten years previously to ease out of management responsibilities and devote more time to the creative side of the music business.

"Ten years ago I hired Jerry Bradley as a future replacement and through the years he has, to my great pleasure, taken over all my duties, allowing me to become more involved in my own recording career," said Chet.[7] Later, when asked why he left RCA, Chet told Ralph Emery that "I went to work one day and looked down and my shoes didn't match. Both were black but one wasn't a wing tip. I thought, 'You've been on the job too damn long,' so I started quitting and turning the artists over to other people."[8]

At the CMA Awards in 1981 Chet was awarded the Instrumentalist award, marking the first of five straight CMA Awards shows where he won that award. Chet had "quit goin' for a while" to the CMA Awards. He had won the award from 1967 to 1969 but did not win the award again until 1981. "I said, 'Hell, I'm tired of going down there and not winning. I've lost long enough,'" said Chet. "They put the cameras on you and you lose. For ten damn years—that's too long."[9]

In late 1981 RCA released *Standard Brands*, an album that Chet recorded with Lenny Breau over a two-year period. Chet had signed Lenny to RCA, and the songs for the album were recorded in 1979, 1980, and 1981 because of Breau's drug and alcohol problems. RCA did little to promote the record, which became another reason for Chet's increasing frustration with the label.

During the recording of *Standard Brands* Lenny "kept a bottle of alcohol hidden in Chet's garage," said Paul Yandell. "In between takes he'd go out to take a drink. Chet didn't know about it."[10]

"He wouldn't take care of himself but Lord did he take care of his talent," said John Knowles about Breau. "I don't know anybody that worked and worked and worked to deliver the music like he did. I always felt like it was like knowing Vincent van Gogh to know Lenny. Somebody that is tortured and beautiful all in one. And I knew that some day I'd get a phone call saying that he was gone."[11]

During 1981 Chet released a studio album, *Country After All These Years*, the compilation album *Country Music*, and his collaboration with Lenny Breau, *Standard Brands*.

CHAPTER 51

Chet continued to make a number of TV appearances during 1982, including *Austin City Limits* on January 20; it had been taped the previous year. On March 1 Chet was seen on the NBC special *50 Years the King of Country Music*, a tribute to Roy Acuff. Chet endorsed the mail-order album *Greatest Country Music Recordings of All Time* and became a spokesman for the company, the Franklin Mint Record Society. He appeared on the TV special *Country Comes Home* hosted by Glen Campbell and broadcast on April 10. During the World's Fair held in Knoxville, Chet was interviewed by Jane Pauley for the *Today Show* and talked about working on the "Midday Merry-Go-Round" on WNOX in 1942. Tom T. Hall replaced Ralph Emery as host of *Pop Goes the Country* for its final season in 1982. Chet made his last appearance on that show on July 16 and performed "Sukiyaki" and "Me and Bobby McGee" in addition to doing comedy sketches with actor/comedian Jim Varney. In December Chet was on the CBS TV show *Nightwatch* with Jim Crockett, editor of *Guitar Player* magazine, in December where Chet performed "Vincent" and a brief excerpt of "This Can't Be Love" and then accompanied B. B. King on "The Thrill Is Gone." Chet also performed on the *Nashville Alive* program on WTBS.[1]

In 1974 "Hello Love" by Hank Snow entered the *Billboard* country chart. This song was sung by Snow during the last performance of the Grand Ole Opry at the Ryman Auditorium before they moved to the new Opryland facility. Garrison Keillor heard the song while he sat in one of the Ryman's pews on assignment for the *New Yorker*; that performance gave birth to the idea for the *Prairie Home Companion*, which became a popular show on National Public Radio, with "Hello Love" as its initial theme song.

On May 15, 1982, Chet made his first appearance on the *Prairie Home Companion*. Chet's office had received calls from Keillor to appear on the popular show but had declined because he wasn't familiar with Keillor or the show. However, his daughter Merle was a fan of the show and sent him newspaper clippings. Chet spoke with Guy Van Duser, who had appeared on Keillor's show and Duser recommended that he do the show. According to Chet, he "put a note in among his thumbpicks" as a reminder to listen to the show; when he did he became a loyal listener, "sometimes postponing Saturday night chores and obligations to listen to the radio show." That led Chet to call Garrison Keillor and leave a message saying, "I want to do your show." Keillor called him back, and an immediate personal friendship and professional relationship developed. On his first appearance on the show he and Keillor did a skit advertising the "Chet Atkins Player Guitar" that allegedly came equipped with tiny fingers and a music roll.

An article by Walter Carter about Chet's appearance on the show in the *Nashville Tennessean* followed. The article spotlighted the satirical ad for the "Chet Atkins Player Guitar" where Keillor stated, "A guitarist is a popular person who has a lot of friends and is the center of attention at a party. Now you can play guitar instantly with the Chet Atkins Player Guitar—the guitar that lets technology take over the tedious part." The "player guitar" came with six little plastic pluckers to play the strings. "Turn the lights down and nobody will know the difference." Keillor then called out tunes for a demonstration—without letting Chet know them ahead of time—and Chet played "She'll Be Comin' Round the Mountain," "Aunt Rhodie," "Maleguena," and "Beer Barrel Polka," but when Keillor said "Misty" there was silence, followed by laughter. "I guess it doesn't work on that one," said Keillor. During an interview with the reporter back in Nashville, Atkins said he didn't know which songs Keillor was going to call "and he was just trying to figure out what key to do 'Misty' in."

"Talking to Atkins last week was like talking to a single-minded promotion man for Keillor's show," said Carter. Chet was "producing a movie soundtrack with Roger Whittaker, working on a new album for RCA, playing in a pro-celebrity golf tournament (12 handicap), preparing for a concert with the Nashville Symphony at the World's Fair, and bringing out in a few weeks a new, solid body classical guitar model."

"My ambition is to get everybody to listen to the 'Prairie Home Companion,'" said Chet. "There are people out there who are missing this wonderful show." The show only paid union scale ($125), but "I'm glad I did it. Minnie Pearl said, 'I want to go work it for nothing, just to see what is this mousetrap he's built.' It's a very different show. His audience—they get every joke no matter how clever, how cerebral. If there's a Mark Twain today, I think he's it."[2]

"Chet Atkins' new instrument looks like a classical guitar from the front—nylon strings and spruce top—but from the side view it is thin. Actually, it was a solid body electric classical guitar designed by Chet and guitar maker Hascal Haile for Gibson," reported the *Nashville Tennessean* in June. The first thousand models were made not at the Gibson factory in Nashville but in Kalamazoo, Michigan. "It sustains a lot more than an acoustic-electric," said Chet. "It just goes on and on." The development of the guitar was "kind of an accident," said Chet. "I had this piezo electric pickup I was experimenting with. I took it to Mr. Haile and he just made me a neck and a slab of wood. I said, 'Take it and put some sides on it so I can play it' and he said, 'I'm not going to do that. That'd be ugly.' So this is just what he built."[3]

The "Country Gentleman" and "Tennessean" brands were owned by Chet, and Gretsch had stopped manufacturing guitars so Gibson could use them. There were actually two new guitars Chet endorsed for Gibson. The Gibson Chet Atkins CE had a narrow neck, while the CEC had a classic neck. Both were solid body nylon electric guitars.

Fred Kewley was a well-known and respected manager who had managed and produced Harry Chapin. He had also managed Buffy Sainte-Marie and Michael Johnson and was managing Earl Kluge. Kewley was based in New York in 1982, and on a visit to Nashville Bob Beckham "asked me to go over to RCA and sit with Chet Atkins. Beckham thought there might be something I could do with Chet and his career," said Kewley. "Beckham is known for his crazy genius—most of his ideas work because he insists on it." Beckham had a habit of saying "Son" to someone before or after delivering his message, and he told Kewley, "Son, even if you don't end up working with Chet, you should meet the man, get to know him. Your career as a manager will be better for it. You will learn what the definition of a 'class' artist is and can use that as a measure of others you may be thinking of signing."

Kewley took Beckham's advice and met with Chet, eventually becoming his manager. "We had fun at those first meetings," remembered Kewley, "unlike any experience I've had before or since. Chet spent most of the time telling stories and having a lot of laughs."

Chet had decided to leave RCA, so Kewley told him, "If you want to quit as an executive at RCA, you should quit as an artist as well. Let's go to another label where you haven't released more than 100 albums and let's make some records for the big city markets—jazz, urban-contemporary, fusion music. You can play anything you want on that guitar but I'll guarantee you that if you were in New York, Detroit or Baltimore, no one would recognize you and ask for your autograph."

It was at that point that a couple came to their table and asked for Chet's autograph. When the couple left, Kewley said, "In two years, I'd like to see that happen in a major Northern City." The two laughed and had some more drinks. "We knew what we wanted to do."[4]

Kewley contacted Rick Blackburn, head of the Nashville office for CBS Records, who began drawing up a contract. On October 1, 1982, the announcement came that Chet was joining the label. "Chet Atkins is my idol," said Blackburn. "I have every LP Chet ever made, and I'm a real fan. He is simply the best guitar player in the world." When asked about contract details, Blackburn said, "Nothing is firm yet."

Blackburn stated that he wanted to make producing records an "option available to him. If he wants to produce, he can. He'll get as much space as he needs here. When you get right down to it, country music has had a lot of success in the past five or six years, but those of us who are taking the credit now are really just the interior decorators. It's people like Chet Atkins that built this thing."[5]

After the rumor of Chet joining CBS as an artist became fact, Chet stated, "I never enjoyed or liked being an executive. It was stressful for me because I never learned to say 'no' to songwriters pitching their songs or to artists who wanted to record for me. Now, my main interest is in being an artist, although I don't want to rule out the possibility of producing while at CBS. I have spent half my life developing other artists' careers, and now it's time to perpetuate my own. I've got some new and fresh ideas, and CBS has some too."

Chet said the reason for the switch was "enthusiasm. At CBS they still feel that there's life after 30 in the recording business—that one can still sell records after 30. Besides, they sell more records than anybody in the whole business. Now I have the opportunity to see why and how."[6]

For Blackburn and CBS Records president Tommy Mottola, signing Chet Atkins to RCA's biggest rival was a great poke in the eye to RCA that they relished.

Later, Chet told author Alanna Nash, "The last three or four years I was with RCA, I just had an office over there. They paid me a salary . . . [but] I got to feeling kinda guilty taking the company's money and not doing anything for it. But they used to tell me, 'Well, consider it pay for years gone by when we didn't pay you enough money.' And I said okay, and I accepted it for quite a few years. But then I looked around and I had so much junk and I didn't have any place for my awards. I'd always kept them down in the basement hidden away. So I bought an old house just down the street from RCA and now I have room for all my junk and my guitars, my photographs and my awards."

Chet admitted that "there was a little lack of interest at RCA. You have regimes running most record companies that are youth-oriented, and they aren't interested in old artists, so they drop them. I saw what was happening and I felt I had to go where I could keep developing my career. I didn't have anything to do with the running of the operation at RCA for many years, but I didn't approve of them dropping a lot of the artists who'd been with the label a long time. I thought they should have kept people like Hank Snow."[7]

When Chet signed with CBS Blake Chancey, a twentysomething young man working in A&R, was assigned to Chet. His job was to stay in touch and ensure Chet was happy. Chancey made several calls to Chet's office but could not get him on the phone. Finally, Chet, in a sour mood, called Chancey: "Did you know that I produced Elvis?" Blake replied, "Yes, sir." "And I produced the Everly Brothers?" "Yes, sir." "And I produced Eddy Arnold." "Yes, sir." "He went down the whole line," said Chancey, and he finished with "so I don't need any dumb assholes over there to tell me what to do" and slammed down the phone.

Blake's dad is Ron Chancey, well-known producer of hits for the Oak Ridge Boys. Blake was friends with publisher Bob Beckham and told him about his experience with Chet. Beckham chuckled: "Let me help you on that, son." About three o'clock in the afternoon Blake received a phone call from Chet, who wanted to apologize. They chatted a bit, but Chet finished the conversation with "you're still a dumb ass" and slammed down the phone.

Blake remembered that one day he was on a conference call with Tommy Mottola, head of CBS Records. Blake's assistant came in and told him that Chet was on the phone and said to come immediately because it was an emergency. Blake drove to Chet's office, only a few blocks away, where Chet was sitting on the back porch. An attractive young woman, ex-wife of a recording artist, was sitting with him and Chet said, "Isn't she beautiful?" Blake said, "Chet, are you O.K.? Is something wrong?" Chet said, "I need an 'E' string for my gut string guitar." Blake said, "That's not an emergency, Chet," who replied, "It is if you're me."

On another occasion Chet called Chancey and told him they had to meet. Chancey went over to Chet's office, where Chet told him, "Never buy a new car because, as soon as the car drove off the lot, the value decreased by a third." He also told Chancey that he should "never drive a better car than the act you're producing. The artist should always drive a better car." Chancey pointed out that Chet drove a Mercedes-Benz. "I'm an artist now," replied Chet. "Chet had more confidence than any artist I'd ever worked with," said Chancey. "Chet knew that he could play."[8]

During the sixteenth annual CMA Awards Show in October, Chet sang "Picker of the Year" with nominees Floyd Cramer, Charlie McCoy, Johnny Gimble, and Hargus "Pig" Robbins. After the performance it was announced that Chet had won the Instrumentalist of the Year Award for the second year in a row. When he accepted the award Chet said, "Back in the 60s, I won this several times, then Jerry Reed won it and I took the award to the shop and smashed it with a claw hammer and beat the heck out of it. I didn't come last year, and I'm so glad I won this year. I may be making a comeback," and then he smiled.[9]

RCA's Studio B celebrated its twenty-fifth anniversary in 1982. The Country Music Hall of Fame and Museum acquired the studio in 1977 after RCA ceased recording there; Dan Maddox owned the land and building and donated them. During the celebration members of the Country Music Foundation's board of directors wore white roses on their lapels, and key figures in the studio's history received silver medallions from CMF executive director Bill Ivey and chairman Frank Jones. Receiving medallions were Dan Maddox and Jerry Bradley, who in 1977, after learning that RCA would no longer use the studio, presented to the CMA board the idea of operating the studio as a historic site.

The last RCA artist to record at the studio was Bobby Bare, who recorded "Auld Lang Syne" during a party that RCA threw in honor of the closing.

Although Chet had moved over to CBS, RCA still had his catalogue of recordings and wanted to use the publicity Chet's move generated and release albums to capture sales. In 1982 RCA released a Chet compilation album, *Solid Gold Guitar*.

CHAPTER 52

Chet's young ambition was to be famous. After years as a guitarist, producer, and executive at RCA his name was well-known, but his real fame came during the 1980s when he increased his personal appearance schedule. He was comfortable onstage and enjoyed increased exposure on TV. He reached a new, young audience by playing on the *Prairie Home Companion* with Garrison Keillor. The biggest negative was Chet's colon cancer, which returned, but he beat it, and exercise became an important part of his daily routine.

Jim Ferron worked for Magnavox and moved with the company from New York State to Knoxville in 1981. The year before Mark Pritchard had finished medical school and moved to Knoxville to begin his medical residency. The two met in a local music store and quickly discovered their common interest in Chet Atkins. Ferron had been a member of the original fan club started by Margaret Fields and had long wanted to start an "appreciation society" for Chet because he felt the term "fan club" had a negative connotation. Sometime around the end of 1981 Ferron contacted Chet's office and told him of their desire; Chet gave his blessing. That year Chet was the grand marshal of the Knoxville Dogwood Arts Parade, and the two met and discussed the endeavor after the event.

Ferron placed advertisements in *Frets* magazine and spoke about the society until a small group of Chet's admirers formed a nucleus and Ferron updated Chet on their progress. They published a newsletter, *Mister Guitar: The Journal of the Chet Atkins Appreciation Society*, in 1983, marking the official beginning of the society. There were only a few hundred members at the time. They decided to publish their journal three or four times a year, covering Chet's appearances, recordings, news, and whatever they felt would be of interest to the group. The newsletters were originally printed on a mimeograph machine—a labor of love completed in spare time. They held an annual gathering in Nashville, and at their first convention Chet performed with Mark Casstevens and Thom Bresh.

The Chet Atkins Appreciation Society, which began with about a hundred members, was an organization by thumbpickers for thumbpickers as well as for admirers of Chet. It became a way to promote Chet, who actively supported it. The journal evolved into a slick magazine, and the membership grew until there were over twelve hundred members across the globe. The organization survived and then thrived to become not only an "admiration society" for Chet but also the premier gathering of thumbpickers from all over the world.

Answering a question about guitar strings in the "Asking Chet" feature in the magazine, Chet said that to get a rich sound from his guitars "you've got to use the right strings on any guitar to get the tone like I try to get, something not too tight and something not too loose either, but something that will 'sing' when you play it. On that particular guitar, I use a .010" on the 1st and a .012" on the second, then I use a silk and steel 3rd, 4th, 5th and 6th that I order from the Casa de Musica in Sao Paulo. But I think most any silk and steel string would be pretty good. It's pretty hard to find gauges as small as these that I use; usually the gauges that you get in stores are a little too large."[1]

During the early 1980s plans were laid for the creation of a TV cable network based in Nashville consisting of country music programming. This network, to be financed originally by radio and television station WSM and its parent company, the National Life and Accident Insurance Company, would be headquartered at the Opryland complex, where the Opryland amusement park and the Grand Ole Opry House were located, about fifteen miles east of Music Row.[2]

The National Life and Accident Insurance Company, which owned WSM FM, AM, and TV, the Grand Ole Opry, Ryman Auditorium, and Opryland from their inceptions, became the victim of a hostile takeover by American General in 1982. American General was not interested in any of the non-insurance properties and put them up for sale. Many Nashvillians were worried, concerned about the future of the Grand Ole Opry, the radio and TV stations, the Ryman, and Opryland.

Ed Gaylord, head of Gaylord Entertainment in Oklahoma City and a fan of country music and the Grand Ole Opry, purchased the entire package in 1983 and grew the operation. The establishment of two television networks in Nashville—the Nashville Network (TNN) and Country Music Television (CMT)—provided a huge boost for country music in general and Chet Atkins in particular. No longer did Chet and other performers have to go to New York or Los Angeles for regular TV appearances—or wait until a network did a show from Nashville; now there was a regular outlet for TV exposure for Nashville artists. Ralph Emery's *Nashville Now* and other shows created a busy time for TV production in Nashville, which had to fill seven and a half hours of airtime each day.[3]

TNN's launch night was March 7, 1983: "We started at 8 p.m. and did five remote broadcasts as well as the studio portion from two Nashville locations—the Grand Ole Opry House and the Stage Door Lounge of the Opryland Hotel," said Emery. During its time on the air, "we broadcast from New York, Los Angeles, Austin, Denver and Chicago."[4]

During this kickoff for TNN and *Nashville Now*, Chet performed "Battle of New Orleans/Sugarfoot Rag," "If I Should Lose You," and "Dance With Me." On the next night of broadcasting "we cut the program to ninety minutes . . . and shelved our black ties and tuxedos," said Emery.[5]

Chet appeared on a number of TNN shows during 1983. On *Backstage at the Grand Ole Opry*, hosted by Bill Anderson, Chet performed "Yakety Axe," "Faded Love," and a brief version of "Wheels." He also did a card trick for Bill Anderson. On *Nashville Now* he did "Harlequin Romance" and "Rocky Top," then, with Doc Watson, performed "Don't Monkey 'Round Wid My Widder." On *Off Stage*, a show hosted by Teddy Bart, Chet did a candid interview for the release of his first CBS album, *Work It Out With Chet Atkins*. On TNN's *Yesteryear in Nashville* Chet played "Alabama Jubilee," "Wildwood Flower," and "Peanut Vendor" and was interviewed by Archie Campbell.[6]

Ralph Emery and Chet were friends, the appearances on *Nashville Now* led Emery to note that Chet "is more misunderstood than anyone in commercial music. He has the image of a shy and retiring genius, but he also has one of the most hilariously dry wits" that Emery ever encountered. "To his friends, he's a walking frolic factory, a slow-talking mischief maker," said Emery.[7]

Emery stated Chet also had "a serious side . . . devoted to what he believes is right." When Mickey Newbury arrived in Nashville during the sixties he was considered a "hippie." At that time a man was labeled a "hippie" if he had long hair and wore jeans. The owner of the

Pancake Pantry in Hillsboro Village, a popular place near Music Row that served breakfasts, barred Newbury from eating there because the owner didn't like the way Newbury looked. "Chet got wind of the edict and posted a note on the bulletin board at RCA, asking personnel not to patronize the restaurant," said Emery.

"Chet is among the most even-tempered artists in a temperamental business I ever met," wrote Emery in his book, *More Memories*. "He brings a low-stress presence to high-strung people."[8]

Chet's first album for CBS—the 115th of his career—was *Work It Out With Chet Atkins*, an "exercise" album on cassette. It was an opportune time for workout videos, as Jane Fonda was selling a lot of them. Chet's album was introduced by CBS with a debut party at the Country Music Hall of Fame. At the event CBS executive Rick Blackburn introduced Chet as "the best guitar player in the world." Chet took the mic and replied, "I didn't identify with that. I thought George Benson was, or Jerry Reed."

"I'm not gonna make a long speech because I'm incapable of it, don'tcha know?," said Chet. "But I appreciate this so much." (Chet had a habit of saying "don'tcha know" at the end of sentences.) In an article in the *Nashville Tennessean*, reporter Robert Oermann observed that "Chet spent much of the evening looking a trifle out of place, a little embarrassed, and a touch uncomfortable. He smiled shyly as compliments and praise were heaped upon him from all sides."

"I do have an ego," stated Chet. "I came to town with Red Foley and I was talking to these people about making my own records. He said, 'I want you to just work with me. I don't want you recording with anyone else.' I said, 'I don't want to be working in a band all my life. I want to be a star just like you, Red. I want to be famous like you.' Well, that kinda cooled things with him."

"Steve (Sholes) just went on faith for a long time, I guess," continued Chet, "because I didn't have any hits when he first put me in down here. I was afraid to spend any money; and I didn't do well at first. He was kind of disappointed in me. Steve Sholes told a friend of mine in the early 1950s, 'I don't know why I don't drop him from the label as an artist. He doesn't sell.' And it was true. For the first two or three years I didn't sell any records at all."

Things changed a lot from those early days, and by 1983 Chet spent a typical day rehearsing for his concert appearances, producing records for others, experimenting in his home studio, and conducting business at his antique-appointed Music Row office. Before he began work each day, "I get up early to exercise and run around in my basement," said Chet. "I put on records and exercise to 'em."

"I don't know why I didn't think of this album before," said Chet about his workout record. "For two or three years I've been exercising to records, and it's so hard to find something with the right tempo when you're working out. So I made this album for joggers with their Walkman's."[9]

Before he left RCA Chet recorded an album of hit songs that he had produced. *Great Hits of the Past* included "Sweet Dreams," "Amos Moses," "Abilene," "That's What I Get for Loving You," "Oh Baby Mine," "And I Love You So," "Java," "Detroit City," and "The Three Bells." Bergen White arranged the strings.

Chet had been using White to arrange strings and horns since around 1966. "It was always a puzzle to figure out if Chet liked what you did or hated it," said White, "but he kept using me, so I guess he liked it. After a recording I'd stand in the control room with him listening to a playback, watching him intently to try to see any expression that indicated whether he liked it or not. He would be drawing doodles on his pad and maybe, just maybe when the playback ended he'd say, 'Yeah, that'll be okay, I guess.'"

"Without-a-doubt Chet was the most laid-back human I ever met," said White. "Whatever reaction a normal person would have to a certain event, Chet's reaction would hardly register on the 'reaction meter.' To get any reaction at all was a milestone."[10]

The June issue of *Frets* magazine had a column by Chet that became a regular feature. It began with Chet talking to the editor but soon evolved to John Knowles talking to Chet and then putting his ideas into words. During the first column, Chet demonstrated how to play his "Superlick." The July issue discussed the basics of his style and offered exercises to help coordinate the thumb and fingers for fingerpicking. The following issue discussed "squeaks and scratches" and the care of fingernails; Chet stated that he used wet or dry sandpaper on his fingernails and that he lets his fingernails "grow out a bit" on his left hand. He also revealed that he "wipes his left fingers on the sides of his nose to pick up some natural oils and make his fingers slide easier."[11] Chet was also published in *Guitar Player* magazine.

An article by Robert Oermann in the *Tennessean* stated, "It has been said many times before that Chet is a fundamentally reclusive personality who has forced himself into the glare of public life. He is private and soft-spoken, but thoughtful and articulate in conversation. His high Indian cheekbones and clear-eyed gaze give him a dignified air, but he's quite witty when he relaxes. He thinks his withdrawn personality is partly because of his embarrassment about the poverty in his youth."

"I think all Depression-era kids had it rough," said Chet. "I came from a real poor background. My father left when I was six or seven. I'm just amazed at how well I've done. We were so far back in the sticks, I didn't know anything of the world. I didn't know how to dress. I didn't know if green went with blue. I didn't know how to order food in a restaurant. I used to talk just like Loretta Lynn."

"I'm a shy person, but I've learned to live with it and to capitalize on it and to use it," continued Chet. "I'm still very ignorant. I still learn things every day. When you're reading all the time and are self-educated like I am, that happens. I'd watch other people and did 'monkey-see, monkey-do.' The other musicians made fun of me." Their jeers made him determined to become as worldly-wise as they were.[12]

In October Chet won his third straight Instrumentalist of the Year award at the seventeenth annual Country Music Association Awards. The group Alabama presented him with the award as Chet received a standing ovation. Accepting the award, Chet said he was "the luckiest guy in the world" and it was "mighty nice of Leona to put up with my practicing all these years and not complain for letting me put the guitar first."[13]

That same month Chet went on a European tour. During his performance at the Wembley Conference Center in London, Chet was joined by Jorge Morel, Barney Kessel, Albert Lee, Pete Townsend, Paco Pena, and Big Jim Sullivan. Chet did a Christmas album for Columbia in 1983. It was primarily remakes of songs from RCA's *Christmas with Chet Atkins*, but there was one new song, "East Tennessee Christmas," written by John Knowles and Chet and recorded in the CA Workshop and at Sound Emporium studios. Chet sang on "East Tennessee Christmas," and it was one of his most autobiographical compositions. He was backed by keyboards, bass, and drums.

Mark O'Connor was a child prodigy, starting on the guitar when he was six, and as a teenager he won national championships on the guitar, mandolin, and fiddle, including the Grand Master's Fiddling Contest sponsored by WSM and the Grand Ole Opry. In 1978, when O'Connor was sixteen, he released *Markology*. Chet heard the album and about a year later sent O'Connor a letter: "I heard your album and I really loved it." He invited O'Connor to "come see him whenever I was in Nashville."

It was five years later, when O'Connor was twenty-two, that he "finally went to Nashville and met Chet in his office," said O'Connor. "I remember the conversation like it was yesterday. I was sitting in Chet's office and he said, 'You're a talented young man. Where are you living?' I said, 'Well, currently I'm living in Atlanta, Georgia' and he said, 'Well, you should be in Nashville' and I said 'Well, what would I do here?' and he said 'Anything you want to!'"

"Of course, I was completely blown away," said O'Connor. "He asked me again what I wanted to do and at that point I was kind of lost for words so I blurted out, 'Well, I guess be on television' and as soon as I said that, I felt kind of embarrassed because I really only said it because I didn't know what to say—I was young and awkward."

Chet replied, "Well, I think you can do that—I'll make a call."

Chet called Ralph Emery, spoke for a few minutes, then hung up. "What's your schedule the next couple of weeks?" asked Chet.

O'Connor and Chet were on Ralph Emery's *Nashville Now* show on October 21; Chet performed "Gallopin' on the Guitar," a medley of "House in New Orleans" and "Copper Kettle," and "Pickin' In The Wind."[14]

Pat Kirtley noted that Chet often said to a promising musician he met, "You oughta move to Nashville." Some did not take his suggestion, but Chet took those who did under his wing, meeting with them, introducing them to his friends, and helping them find work.[15]

When asked about the transition from Gretsch to Gibson, Chet replied, "I haven't had many problems. I had them make the neck the same width and everything and the same arch to the neck. With the bone nut I can use a plain third on it and stay in tune. I've never been able to do that before." Chet said he used strings that Gibson made for him, "starting at the first .010, .012, .015 I believe or .016 for the third, the others are about .028 .038 and .048/.049—something like that."

For his nylon string guitars Chet said he went "directly into the board because it's more mellow and I like it better. With the electric (steel string) I hardly ever go directly into the board; if I do go directly into the board, then later on when I mix it down, I run it out into an amp and a microphone and back into the board again." Chet revealed that he used a "large pick" when he played his classical guitar but "I cut it down on the end to make it shorter so it doesn't hit the top of the classic guitar. They're pretty thick; I guess they are nylon. I cut 'em off with the Dykes, you know, and then take an emery board and file them off smooth, and then take 600 sandpaper and try to get 'em slick and shiny." Chet said that when he played his nylon electric guitar "I turn the tone control down a little bit and I put echo on the amp when I use that, a little reverb and I boost the lows quite a bit [on the amp]. It tends to be a little too bright for me on the basses if I don't do that."

On December 17 Chet's single with Ray Charles and George Jones, "I Didn't See a Thing," entered the *Billboard* country singles chart and reached number six the next year. This was Chet's last single on the *Billboard* country chart.

CHAPTER 53

On August 12 Lenny Breau was found dead in his swimming pool in Los Angeles; an autopsy indicated he had been strangled.

After hearing of Lenny's death, Terry Wedding, a guitarist friend, drove to Chet's house. "I couldn't reach him on the phone," said Wedding. "I knocked on the door and a light comes on and I noticed someone looking at me through the window. Chet opened the door. He looked at me and I looked at him. I said, 'Is it true?' He said, 'Yes, come on in.'"

"Chet started crying," remembered Wedding. "Sat down at the kitchen table. Chet's wife, Leona was so sweet. She broke the mood by saying, 'Let me make you all some sandwiches. Terry do you want something to eat?' Leona was kind to me; I will never forget the love she showed to Chet that night and her compassion for me. He was completely broken hearted and she consoled him. Chet loved him like a son. He was crying."[1]

"Lenny burned too brightly," said Tommy Emmanuel. "His light burned out too quickly. Some people have a huge gift and let it go. They allow the gift to grow and be appreciated. In others, like with Lenny, the gift is a disturbance of the soul, a tormentor. Chet loved him. Chet was tough on Lenny when he needed to be. He understood him very well."[2]

"I always felt proud that I had some hand in helping Lennie because he was one of the greatest guitar players that ever lived," said Paul Yandell. "I've heard Chet say he was the greatest but I think Chet's the greatest. Lenny could play anything, just unbelievable, He had great hands, had the strongest little finger on his left hand that you ever saw. It was really sad that his life ended the way it did. There will never be another one, I will say that without reservation." A benefit concert was quickly organized for August 19 at the Bluebird Café in Nashville; Chet initially agreed to take part but then canceled, citing a previous commitment.[3]

The next day Chet performed in Orange, Texas, then on the following two days in Nacogdoches and Texarkana, Texas.

Chet was voted Instrumentalist of the Year again at the eighteenth annual CMA Awards in October.[4]

Chet Atkins's third album for CBS was a departure from his previous recordings—a smooth jazz collection recorded in Nashville at the CA Workshop and Sound Shop Studio and at Larry Carlton Studios in Los Angeles. Most recording was done during the fall of 1984. The recordings began with a "surprise" session for the engineer and drummer.

On a Sunday afternoon Chet called engineer Mike Poston and told him there'd be a session the next day at six o'clock and then hung up "before I could ask him who was recording—or anything else," said Poston. Poston arrived at the studio in the basement of Chet's home around five o'clock, shortly before drummer Larrie Londin arrived. Poston asked Londin, "Do you know what we're doing?" He said he didn't and told Poston that Chet had called and said to bring only a snare drum because they could use the drum set in the CA Workshop but Londin knew that the drum set in Chet's studio "should have been retired years ago." Poston set up some microphones while Londin set up his own drum set. Around six o'clock the door opened and Chet walked in with George Benson, followed by David Hungate, who would produce the session, keyboardist Clayton Ivey, and other musicians. Poston and Londin looked at each other incredulously.

George Benson was signed to Warner Brothers, Chet to CBS Records, but both labels had approved the collaboration. The plan at that time was to record a full album. Benson had a breakthrough number-one album, *Breezin'*, in 1976. He followed that with a string of top ten albums.

In the back of the small studio was a fireplace, where David Hungate sat. Poston put Benson's amplifier in front of Londin's drum set, about two and a half feet from Londin's hi-hat. Londin played the bass drum with a heavy foot, and Poston wondered how Benson would sound until the guitarist plugged in and "it was his signature sound." Chet was sitting beside the door leading to the studio, and "after about ten minutes of setting up, that's all I had to do," said Poston, who managed the control board.

Chet then looked at Benson and asked, "What are we going to do?" They had not even discussed any songs. They first recorded Roger Miller's "King of the Road," but "everybody was shooting from the hip," said Poston. Randy Goodrum had pitched to Chet "Sunrise," so they played the demo as the musicians made charts, and then they recorded it—the first song on what was to be their collaborative album. After they finished Benson wanted to replay a four-bar section, so Poston got Londin to play along, to keep the sound in sync; that four-bar punch was the only overdub on that session, the beginning of four consecutive days in the CA Workshop. After the first few songs, as musicians dropped in for the project, it was undecided what would happen next. Poston said to Chet and Chet's manager, Fred Kewley, "We'd better stay tuned for whatever happens." Chet and Kewley looked at each other and decided that might be a good name for the album.

"We recorded 11 or 12 cuts," said Poston. Randy Goodrum took the tapes to LA and recorded guitarist Steve Lukather and drummer Jeff Porcaro, both popular LA session players who were also in the pop group Toto.

Poston and the musicians were thrilled to be working with George Benson, whom none of them had met before the session, and learned that Benson was thrilled to be recording with Chet. It was a free-wheeling session where the musicians would noodle around and a song would emerge. Chet and Benson never planned ahead, never even discussed songs—just turned up and played.

After the sessions Bergen White arranged strings and then Mike Poston mixed the songs. That's when word came down that "a guy from Warner Brothers got cold feet" and would not approve the joint album. Instead, Benson would be allowed to appear only on two cuts, "Sunrise" and "A Mouse in the House," although "Dream," a Johnny Mercer song, was later included on Chet's *Read My Licks* album. A conflict with Earl Klugh was avoided by listing him as "Millard Greeb" as a guitarist on "Quiet Eyes." That meant that songs like "King of the Road," "Help Me Make It Through the Night," "Take Five," "Sails," and others would not be released. Although Benson has sought to make those songs available, they remain unreleased. With Warner Brothers allowing the release of only two cuts with Benson, Chet and producer David Hungate had to rethink the album.[5]

When Chet heard the Dire Strait's radio hit "Sultans of Swing" ("Money for Nothing" and "Walk of Life" had not hit yet), he thought that Mark Knopfler was fingerpicking and "I thought, 'I believe he's heard me a few times,'" said Chet. Looking for songs and collaborators, "Earl Klugh owed me one because I'd played on his record, and we were going to use Larry Carlton and several other people as guests," said Chet. "I told my manager, Fred Kewley, I'd like to have Mark on it, so he said, 'I know his manager, I'll call him.' . . . We had a good conversation and he told me he'd love to do it. So he came down and we got on the back porch here and we played a tune. And our friendship grew from that."[6] Mark Knopfler first "met" Chet Atkins when he picked up his phone "and the voice on the other end said, 'Mark, this is Chet Atkins.'"

"Yeah man," remembered Knopfler. "It is not every day that Chet Atkins calls you up and asks you to play guitar with him on a record, you know. That was a real thrill. I went straight over there and Chet met me at the airport and drove directly to the Gibson factory. Chet told me, 'You're okay for a British kid.'" They went to Chet's office "and when we started playing Chet said 'Hell, Paul, look at the length of that thumb' and I had not really looked at my thumbs before. So Chet made some comparison of the length of my thumb with another something else. It just went on from there really. It was always good fun."[7]

During the 1960s Knopfler formed several bands and in 1968 became friends with Steve Phillips, who loved country blues. Knopfler was exposed to a wide variety of music from Phillips's record collection—which included albums by Chet. The two formed a duo, the Duolian String Pickers, and performed locally. Knopfler moved to London, and one evening with friends he picked up an old acoustic guitar with a warped neck. It was impossible to play unless Knopfler fingerpicked it, and "That's where I found my 'voice' on guitar," he remembered.

In 1977 Knopfler's band evolved into Dire Straits, and they recorded their first five-song demo, including "Sultans of Swing." Ironically, Mark Knopfler was on Warner Brothers—the same label as Benson. On the *Stay Tuned* album Knopfler appeared on two cuts.

The final lineup for *Stay Tuned* featured Chet and Benson on "Sunrise." Chet and Steve Lukather shared the lead on "Please Stay

Tuned"; "Quiet Eyes" featured Chet and Larry Carlton, and "Millard Greer" joined them on solos; "A Mouse in the House" featured Chet and Benson, "Some Leather and Lace" featured Chet with Mark Knopfler and Brent Mason; "The Cricket Ballet" featured Chet with Earl Klugh. "Cosmic Square Dance" had Chet playing with Knopfler, "The Boot and the Stone" featured Chet with LA session guitarist Dean Parks, and on "Tap Room" Chet soloed. The final song on the album, "If I Should Lose You," was Bob Hope's theme song, which Chet dedicated to Lenny Breau. With those songs and arrangements, Chet took a big step into the jazz world.

"I knew Chet was respected by guitarists around the world," said Kewley, "but when we made the calls to Mark Knopfler, Steve Lukather, Larry Carlton, Brent Mason and Dean Parks, all of them responded with the similar attitude. They would go anywhere their busy schedule allowed them to play with Chet."[8]

In 1984 RCA continued to release Chet on compilation albums. The CD had been introduced the year before, and as it became a popular medium for recordings fans went out and replaced their old albums with the new format. Labels mined their catalogues, and by releasing "best-of" albums and other compilations their sales soared. Pair records, a low-budget label, released many double albums, pleasing labels like RCA, happy to have their old hits repackaged and receive royalties.

CHAPTER 54

In February the *Stay Tuned* album was released, and CBS rolled out the red carpet for Chet with a reception at the Vanderbilt Plaza Hotel ballroom. At this point Chet was a widely recognized "elder statesman" in the music world.

"Chet Atkins rarely laughs," stated Michael McCall in an article for the *Nashville Banner*. "At least not those loud, up-from-the-belly howls that can rattle a room. He doesn't even smile often. At least not those wide, scrunch-the-facial-skin mouth openers. Instead, he expresses pleasure much more modestly, almost inwardly. His eyes lighten and open slightly wider. One corner of his lip curls upward. It's a small gesture: warm but non-committal, strong but reserved. The smile is very much like the man."[1]

That smile was on display at the lavish listening party for the music business elite gathered to hear a who's who of great jazz artists perform with Chet. The Nashville Music Association sponsored a preceding champagne reception.

The party began with an opening set by Mark O'Connor and guitarist Brent Mason. It was announced that Chet's jazz fusion album would be released at the end of the month and would be a joint project between the New York, Los Angeles, and Nashville offices for CBS. Dr. George Butler, vice-president of jazz for CBS, took the stage: "These people are giants in their respective areas of music. Only a person like Chet Atkins could have pulled these musicians together. This is an album that crosses all musical boundaries." Dr. Butler then introduced Atkins, who received a standing ovation. Chet first played "Some Leather and Lace" with Brent Mason, then introduced Larry Carlton, "who burned up the room with blistering guitar licks."

"A show-off, that's what he is," said Chet as the audience laughed. Chet then played "Quiet Eyes," a duet with Carlton, before he introduced harmonica wizard Terry McMillan, whom Chet ran across seven years earlier (in 1978) walking down Music Row in a long navy coat with his pockets full of harmonicas. Chet announced that McMillan would play a hot solo "just in case any of you are getting sleepy out there"; McMillan performed "Freight Train Blues."

Chet introduced Earl Klugh: "I hear him all the time—on everything on TV, golf tournaments, 'Lifestyles of the Rich & Famous,' everything. And it should be that way: He's a great player." Klugh played a nylon-string Ovation guitar for his duet with Chet on "Good Time Charlie's Got the Blues." Chet introduced George Benson, who played "Misty" before he joined Chet for a duet on "Sunrise."

For the final number Chet played "Vincent" on his Gibson electric classical, which left the crowd wishing for more. "I've been wanting to do something more contemporary for a long time," said Chet. "Y'know I've always had kind of a complex about bein' a Southerner. I've never felt comfortable about recording in Los Angeles or New York. But I think I'm gettin' over it."

After the performances were over Chet told a reporter, "That was something, wasn't it? Had a lot of fun. I think we all did. Lotta talent there. Think we kept it short enough for the crowd not to get too bored too."[2]

Stay Tuned was planned as a first release for a series of albums that Chet recorded with top guitarists. "It's quite a departure for me," he said. "You got to try new directions. If you get predictable, folks aren't interested too much anymore. You got to keep surprising your friends and neighbors." Chet wanted to challenge himself as a guitarist. A reporter asked why. "I don't know, really," replied Chet. "It's hard to do it. But if you work at it a lot, you can come up with different ideas. I never have enjoyed listening to myself play. And another thing is that I've never gotten it right. Not from my way of thinking. So I keep trying to get it right, I guess. I keep striving for perfection. I'm kind of driven by some unknown force. I don't know what it is—a desire to be accepted, I guess."

"I think the person who excels is the person who does something for the pure love of it and doesn't think of the commercial consequences," said Chet. "If you do something and do it right, then the financial side will usually take care of itself. I've never been a big star, but I've become semi–well known, which I prefer really," said Chet. "I don't have to play big halls where the sound is bad. I like to play in a hall of a thousand or so people where you have good sound and an intimate rapport with the audience. So it's been a good life. I've fulfilled most of my goals. I always tell people to be careful where they aim because that might be where they end up."

"Chet would call me and say, 'Mark, why don't you come and visit me Thursday afternoon,'" said Mark O'Connor. "And so I would show up and when I got there he would say, 'Mark, I've got something I want you to hear' and I never knew what it was going to be. Sometimes he would play something that he'd been working on for a recording or a show or sometimes he would just get out the turntable—this was before CD's were popular—and he would play me obscure stuff that he knew about and it was like a music history lesson every time I showed up."

Every time he got with Chet it was "interesting," said O'Connor. "We worked on some things together. Once in awhile he'd say, 'Hey, I want you to play on a show with me, so let's work up a song' and it could be a Beatles tune, it could be an old fiddle tune. I never knew what he had in mind." Chet "would pick up the fiddle now and then because he loved it," said O'Connor. "It reminded him of his childhood and his forefathers and so that was another connection that he and I had." O'Connor found it "ironic" that Chet and Owen Bradley "deemed the fiddle not commercial or contemporary enough so they started making recordings with strings, what was later called 'The Nashville sound.' He loved the fiddle and was good friends with Johnny Gimble but ironically, he was kind of responsible for decreasing the amount of fiddling in country music for a long period of time. By the time I showed up in Nashville, the fiddle was pretty much out of favor."[3]

Darryl Dybka was a keyboardist in Earl Klugh's band and met Chet when Klugh, George Benson, and Chet played on a *Soundstage* show in Chicago. Dybka remembers first seeing Chet at the hotel wearing a "big belt buckle with a cigar in hand, and was wearing a leather glove. One thing I noticed about him was he was really cool. He was like, 'Yeah, I play guitar. Check it out.'"

Klugh knew that Dybka was a jazz composer and told him that Chet was looking for more jazz-oriented material. Dybka had "three to five songs that I thought would be good to send to Chet." Dybka sent them and was soaking in his bathtub when Chet called and left a message: "Hey, Darryl. This is Chet down in Nashville. I really like that song you sent me, 'The Cricket Ballet.' I want you to hold it for me because I want to put it on my new album." Dybka got out of the bathtub as quickly as possible and grabbed the phone, but Chet had already hung up.

It was sometime around late 1985 or early 1986 when Chet called again and invited Dybka to come to Nashville to record "The Cricket Ballet" with him. The next Dybka song that Chet recorded was "The Boot and the Stone."

In Nashville Dybka needed a place to live, so Chet said, "How about if I work something out for you. You keep an eye on my office and just make sure everything is okay there. For doing that, you can stay there as long as you want." Chet had a closet built for clothes. The bottom of the door was sawed off to allow it to open over the thick carpet, and a metal vent was added. Bobby Campbell did the work, and Dybka was surprised to find that the man helping was Eddy Arnold. (Arnold and Campbell were best friends who often had lunch together.)

Chet told Dybka that he would play on Dybka's album, and Dybka chose the song "Jimmy." "I thought this tune would be nice for him to play," said Dybka. "It wasn't too hard but it had a pretty melody. I figured Chet could just hear it, and then play it." However, "when we were over in the studio, in a way I felt like I wanted to stop. Chet wasn't feeling good at all, and it was hard for him to play. I was feeling very uncomfortable with this but we kept going until we got it. What I was impressed about him was how sick he must have felt but kept his perseverance during the recording," said Dybka, who added, "When Chet plays, a note means something. He sculpted each note. When that one note was done, he was sculpting the next one. That was his signature, the beauty of his sound." Chet's sense of melody and harmony "was really great," said Dybka. "When he put a harmony to a melody he had more than one choice. He would graph out whether to use a third, sixth, and knowing when to shift at the right time. . . . Chet believed in playing the melody exactly the way it was written. If he didn't do that, he would play the appropriate rhythm to get the idea across without having too much or too little." Chet's "knowledge of the lyrics of the pieces he played allowed him to impart a certain emotional intensity to his phrasing," said Dybka. "This worked because he was affected by the emotional content of the lyrics."

Dybka sometimes arrived at Chet's house early in the morning, and Chet would say, "Leona, why don't you make something for the boy to eat." Dybka also enjoyed several dinners in their home.[4]

By 1985 Chet had improved his home studio, the CA Workshop, which now featured a twenty-four-track board, a MCI JH100-24 recorder, and a Neotek twenty-eight-channel console as well as a full complement of microphones and outboard processing gear (including his own EMT plate reverb).

Stay Tuned enjoyed commercial and artistic success. In early July Dr. George Butler announced that "sales are triple what we expected of Chet. And we are picking up radio stations on the record every day. Needless to say, Chet's performance is a significant reason for that longevity." Butler believed "that there is a very large yuppie market out there that doesn't want rock & roll or country or many of the other pop music forms."[5]

The Chet Atkins Celebrity Golf Tournament was moved from April to Labor Day weekend. The golf tournament had started in Nashville but moved to Knoxville and then, in 1979, to Callaway Gardens in central Georgia, less than twenty miles from where Chet spent his teenage years. Chet stated that he began playing golf in the late 1950s "when Archie Campbell showed me the proper grip, which I've probably forgotten by now," adding, "For me, it's just a chance to get some friends together and have a good time. I've never become very good at it. But then, I'm still trying to learn to play the darn guitar."

"Golf is a camaraderie thing," said Chet, who noted that he plays once a week. "It's a chance to get together and tell a few lies and make a few bets. But every once in a while you hit a good one, and it feels real good. It makes you remember why you play."[6]

Bob Beckham was an artist who had one hit, "Just as Much as Ever," before he became a respected music publisher. Beckham organized golfing trips for a circle of friends that included Chet, Bergen White, Floyd Cramer, Ray Baker, Ron Chancey, Don Gant, Jim Isbell, Fred Kewley, Tony Joe White, and Joe Light. The trips were often for a week in Palm Springs, but the group also went to the Dominican Republic, Naples, Florida, and Michigan. Beckham had two rules concerning golf: "Everyone had to drink (whiskey), and there had to be money on the line. Chet didn't like to wager—the highest he'd bet was a dime but it was mostly pennies."[7]

CHAPTER 55

During the 1980s Chet Atkins extended his artistic boundaries as he delved further into jazz. He was confident that he could compete with the top jazz guitarists. He performed often on the road and frequently with symphonies. Clearly he saw himself as an *artist* and not someone who had to sneak in his practices between other diversions. He played golf regularly, which helped him relax. He went to lunch with friends and became attuned to new guitarists. It felt like a heavy yoke had lifted off his back when he gave up his executive duties, but he still kept a busy schedule, although the busyness was largely his own choosing. He had grown as an artist since he left RCA and wanted to continue that growth.

Because the Nashville Network was headquartered in town and featured a number of interview shows, Chet received national exposure regularly. When he produced a new record or had something to say, the doors of television were open for him.

For his next project Chet took a deeper dive into jazz. He traveled to Los Angeles to record in the Yamaha Research Development Studio in Glendale and the Galaxy Sound Studios in Hollywood, in addition to the CA Workshop. Chet liked Darryl Dybka's musicianship, songs, and talent with synthesizers and named him producer for the new project. Coproducing with Dybka was Ronnie Foster, who had worked with George Benson.

For the LA sessions Chet hired well-known jazz players like bassist Abe Laboriel, drummer Harvey Mason, saxophonist Jim Horn, horn player Tom Scott, guitarists Lee Ritenour and Bruce Bolen, and Brazilian percussionist Paulina De Costa. These were the crème de la crème of LA studio jazz musicians. Nashville musicians included Terry McMillan (percussion), Paul Yandell (guitar), and Mark O'Connor (fiddle).

The *Street Dreams* album began with "Spats 'N' Hats," written by Dybka, who played keyboard synthesizer. Next was "(Like a) Crystal in the Night," which featured guitarist Lee Ritenour; "The Official

Beach Music" featured Dybka on synthesizer and drum programming, "Street Dreams" had guitarist Bruce Bolen, "(If You'll) Stay a Little Longer" was written by Orleans member John Hall with Paul Yandell, "Classical Gas" was written by Mason Williams and had been a hit single for him in 1968, and "The Last Farewell" was a Roger Whittaker song. Dybka did drum programming and played keyboard on "Alisha" and "The Homecoming Anthem." The final song on the album, "Honolulu Blue," was written by Chet and John Knowles.

When Knowles stopped by Chet's office, Chet was often talking on the phone "and a lot of times when he would be on the phone he would say, 'I've got to make some calls. Play the guitar,'" said Knowles. "One time I was playing something and he said, 'Excuse me' and he put the caller on hold. He turned to me and said, 'Tune your fourth string down a half step. It'll make a ninth chord so it's like A ninth when you strum across it.'"

When Chet finished his phone call he told Knowles, "Lenny did that and said you could really play the blues that way." Knowles said, "You know, I remember being in a little Hawaiian band and our steel guitar player used some kind of ninth chord like that—I think it was a C ninth." Chet then picked up his guitar "and played this kind of bluesy lick, and ended it with this classic little Hawaiian tag." "Oh we've gotta do that," said Knowles. "We gotta write one like that."

That led to "Honolulu Blue."[1]

In an interview to promote his *Street Dreams* album, Chet declared, "I play about the same way I've always played, but with a more contemporary rhythm sound. Yuppie-type people love it. I wanted to do that; I wanted to reach younger people."

"There's improvisation on every track but there's a lot of melody too," continued Chet. "That's what people like. I love the kind of jazz where you take four or five choruses, but I learned years ago that people don't buy that. I used to see sales figures come in on great jazz artists who sold two or three thousand copies."

The launch party for *Street Dreams* was held in Hollywood and featured a concert and dinner. "CBS flew in a lot of folks—jazz promotion people from all over the country," said Chet. "Larry Carlton and Michael McDonald were there. And Sarah Vaughan was there—I've been a big fan of hers for I guess 30 years. I'd like to do a record with her sometime—maybe take a great country song and see what she could do with it. It'd be very interesting."

For the showcase Chet called Randy Goodrum, who had moved to Los Angeles, and asked him to play piano. "He hired a bunch of LA guys," said Goodrum. "He had Harvey Mason, Abe Laboriel, me and Darryl Dybka and I said 'Chet you have Darryl on piano, what do you need me for?' And he said 'Just come, I want you to come to the gig.'"

"So I go to the Hollywood Palace and about half way into the show he stops and says, 'We have a very special guest in the audience tonight—Ms. Sarah Vaughan!' Sarah comes up on the stage . . . turns to me and says: 'I Got It Bad and That Ain't Good.' Then I suddenly realized why he called me to be there, it was because I knew that song. So I played the intro and Sarah sang and after she was done, Chet's manager at the time, Fred Kewley came up to me and says, 'That was just about the coolest thing I've ever seen.' And I said 'For a jazzer it's a day-at-the-beach!'"

Chet had decided that he was "going to ride this horse, this contemporary thing, as long as it sells and it's selling a lot of records. And when it stops, I'll make my own albums and sell 'em out of the back of my car or something!"[2]

At the twenty-eighth annual Grammy Awards, held in Los Angeles, Chet and Mark Knopfler won the Grammy for Best Country Instrumental for "Cosmic Square Dance" from the *Stay Tuned* album.

On Monday, May 19, Chet was in the studio for four days of sessions with Garrison Keillor. Musicians included Paul Yandell on guitar, David Hungate on bass (who surprised Atkins by performing adeptly on trombone and trumpet), Darryl Dybka on keyboard, and Johnny Gimble on fiddle.

The album featured songs and talking, including some Lake Wobegon songs and stories Keillor featured on *Prairie Home Companion.* "It's not a country album, and it won't be directed toward a country audience," said Chet. "It'll be aimed at the yuppies and intelligentsia of the world that [Keillor] appeals to."[3]

Janis Ian had her first hit, "Society's Child," in 1967 when she was seventeen; in 1975 she hit with "At Seventeen." She moved to Nashville in 1986; when she first met Chet he handed her a guitar and said, "Play me something pretty." Ian replied that she was a songwriter, not a guitarist, but Chet countered, "Horse hockey. I've heard your records. Now, sit back and play something pretty." It was "not a request, but a command," said Ian. After she played they went to lunch.

Chet "was interested," remembered Ian. "Whether it was a guitar piece, a bad joke, a new piece of technological wizardry, he demanded you show it to him right now or pay the price." That price was usually lunch, "half a tuna sandwich with pickle on the side, dry bread." Chet "loved to hear a good player," said Ian, "and if it was something new to him, he'd make you repeat it until he had it down. We bonded over tuna fish."

Ian arrived in Nashville "with all the assumptions Northerners make about the South; that people here were more bigoted, more ignorant, and generally more foolish than their Northern counterparts," but as she got to know Chet she "learned just how wrong I was." Ian went to dinner with Chet and Leona at the Hillsboro Country Club, where Chet was a member, and they began discussing country clubs. Ian asked why they didn't belong to the most exclusive country club in Nashville, and Leona, "with a look of horror on her face," said, "Because those people still use the 'N' word there and then shook her head."

Chet "was known for walking the thin line between the good old boys and the liberal faction," said Ian, and it was understood that you didn't mess with those under his wings. She noted that when Charley Pride came to town Chet "made sure they were photographed together for the paper," and he took Pride to breakfast at the Pancake Pantry to "make sure Pride was treated with respect."

"There wasn't a bigoted bone in Chet's body and he defended the right of anyone with talent to enter the arena," said Ian. Ian "discovered how honorable he was, and how fiercely he defended 'his own'" in 1992 when she began releasing records again and the media "made a huge fuss over my being gay. I was worried about Chet," she said, because she didn't want that fact to change their relationship. Later, after they had spent more time together and had more lunches, she asked "whether it had bothered him." He replied, "with a glint in his eye, 'Well, I kinda thought you might be getting sweet on me, but I guess with all this, you weren't.'" She laughed and hugged him and he asked, "Haven't had any problems in town, have you?" Ian later discovered that when the press found out she was gay, "Chet had called a bunch of friends who might have a problem with it and told them that any problem they had with me, they would have with him," and then added, "She's mine, you know."

When Ian bought a house Chet and Leona came to her "moved but not unpacked" party; she was amazed when several friends told her later that "Chet never goes to parties." Ian asked her partner what she thought of Chet and Leona's visit: "Honey, he's just serving notice to the community that we're all right with him."

Chet "loved jokes" said Ian, and she has fond memories of sitting in a restaurant with Chet and his friends "listening while they told the worst dirty jokes in the world." Chet "loved to be around women, all women. Big, small, short, tall, he made polite passes at them all," said Ian, because she surmised "flirtation was considered the duty of a polite male." Chet's "passes were always subtle, no follow-up necessary, just a bit of gentlemanly flirting." When she told another singer, who found it flattering and amusing that Chet had made polite passes at her, the singer asked if Chet had ever flirted with Janis. When Janis answered "never," the singer declared, "Honey, you must be the only woman in Nashville he's never made a pass at!"[4]

Chet's success went beyond his albums. The solid body classical guitar he designed for Gibson was selling well. The thin, nylon-stringed instrument allowed players to produce the sound of a classical guitar with the stage and studio flexibility of an electric guitar. "The success of that exceeded all my expectations," said Chet. "Willie Nelson bought seven or eight of them; he played one for a while, but it was too heavy for him because of the trouble he'd been having with his back. And Sting used one on the Academy Awards. I thought it was a good idea, but I never expected the rockers to take to it like they have."[5]

The Chet Atkins Guitar Society was formed in England by Jim Beam and associates in 1979. The group published a journal four times a year and promoted concerts and workshops. The Chet Atkins Appreciation Society of Japan was formed in 1986 by Mr. Kujime and Mr. Ishikawa, who were both "terrific guitarists." It had about fifty members.

For the Christmas season Epic Records, a label under the CBS umbrella, released *Nashville Christmas Album*, which featured Chet accompanying Connie Smith and Willie Nelson on "Silent Night." RCA continued to release albums of Chet's recordings, including *Twenty of the Best* in 1986. Pair released Chet's *Pickin' on Country*.

CHAPTER 56

Mark O'Connor worked in the studio with Chet and opened shows on the road, but the most memorable times with Chet came hanging out in Chet's office.

"We would hang out and play and I would hear him try out new ideas and new things on the guitar," said O'Connor, "and honestly, I heard him play some of the coolest stuff in those private sessions. He often played an acoustic guitar in those settings and he would play a little differently than what he did in shows or in recordings. He would play some different kinds of repertoire that you would never really hear him play on albums or in his concerts."

During his concerts Chet "would play more of his country style and a little bit of jazz and in his albums, he would play a little bit more of a contemporary style, sometimes a soft jazz style," said O'Connor, "but around his office, he would play kind of eccentric, esoteric material, things that he would be listening to, say, on a record if you transcribed it, or he would work out arrangements or renditions of things. I remember a lot of Spanish stuff, things with a Latin influence, some classical-oriented stuff and really some of the most beautiful guitar work I've ever heard."

"A lot of times he would play something for me and then he would invariably want me to play. I got a sense that he was like a kid in a candy store because he wanted to play something for me that he'd been working on," said O'Connor. "He wanted to have an audience that really appreciated and understood what he was doing, even if it was just one person."[1]

Steve Wariner had similar experiences with Chet. One day he was in Chet's office trying to play "Blue Angel." "He always had a boom box in his office and we recorded tons of stuff on it . . . just sitting around his office." Showing Steve how to play the song "was a lesson really," said Wariner. "He was going like 'then you come up here' and you hear him playing, then he'd say, 'and then do this.'"

"I would walk in sometimes and he'd be recording something to send to Garrison Keillor," said Wariner. "I'd walk in and he'd say, 'Oh, I'm putting down this old song to send to Garrison'" and then tell Wariner "grab that bass over there" and the two would record the song on cassette.

"We'd put down four or five songs and he'd say, 'Here's another song' [and] he'd name a song that was like 150 years old and then he would be mad that I didn't know it! You know, and it's a song that was pre-Civil War or something. He knew every song in the history of time, I think . . . I mean old songs that you just never even heard of. They'd have tricky little things in them and he'd look at you funny like—sometimes he wouldn't say anything but you'd miss a note and he'd give you that look like 'You idiot—you don't know this!??!'"[2]

On May 7 Chet performed in Maryville, Tennessee, and the next day traveled to Saint Paul, Minnesota for a *Prairie Home Companion* show. *Nashville Now* host Ralph Emery had Chet on the program on May 22, when Chet performed with several other guests: "In the Good Old Summertime" with the Jordanaires from his *Hum and Strum Along* album, "Would Jesus Wear a Rolex," which he wrote with Margaret Archer, and "Vincent" with Don McLean.

Chet had produced "And I Love Her So" on *Perry Como* and recorded "Vincent," both written by Don McLean. "Chet was thought of with tremendous respect," said McLean. "There were other well known producers that people were afraid of . . . but Chet was loved and respected."

McLean went by Chet's office several times: "I used to have a lot of fun talking with him about the Delmore Brothers or Gene Autry. By the way, I think Gene Autry was a magnificent singer with a beautiful vibrato and Chet would say, 'Well, yeah—he always hit the notes. That was often a big problem for a lot of singers, but not Gene Autry.'"

"Chet was not a guy that just went along with things, you know?" said McLean. "I once asked him what he thought of Bruce Springsteen and he said, 'The biggest hype in show business.' That's what he said and it wasn't any punches pulled at all and I thought, 'Wow, here's a guy who's not afraid to say whatever he thinks.'"

"'Vincent' was the follow up to 'American Pie' and 'Vincent' was so different from 'American Pie,'" said McLean. "'American Pie' was a phenomenon . . . then 'Vincent' came out and we just had terrible times with the record company"

"Chet was always into those kinds of songs," said McLean, "ones with an identifiable beautiful melody, a really nice chorus, a good story. Chet latched on to a few of my songs that he liked. I know he liked 'Vincent' but I'm not sure 'Vincent' is all that great a melody."[3]

The third annual Chet Atkins Appreciation Society Convention was held in Nashville on Friday and Saturday, August 21 and 22, and over 250 attended. On Friday Chet arrived, preceded by Paul Yandell and Darrell Dybka, and received a standing ovation. Chet picked up his Gibson classic electric and went straight into "Mr. Bojangles," followed by "San Antonio Stroll," with Paul Yandell providing harmony parts on his guitar. Chet then played the John Lennon tune "Watching the Wheels."[4] The CAAS Convention was followed by the Chet Atkins Golf Tournament.

The Cinemax special *A Session with Chet Atkins, Certified Guitar Player* was broadcast first on September 5. The audience was packed with music industry heavyweights. The show had been whittled down to an hour for the TV broadcast and featured Chet playing "Waltz for the Lonely" alone, duets with Mark Knopfler on "Imagine" and "I'll See You in My Dreams," and duets with guitarist David Pack on "Sunrise" and "Waltz for the Blues." The backup band consisted of A Team musicians Larrie Londin on drums, David Hungate on bass, keyboard players Darryl Dybka and Clayton Ivey, percussionist Terry McMillan, and guitarists David Pack and Paul Yandell.

Performers on the program included the Everly Brothers, Waylon Jennings, Willie Nelson, Emmylou Harris, and Ray Stevens, whose "Would Jesus Wear a Rolex?" was written by Chet and Margaret Archer.

The event was taped in the Neely Auditorium on the Vanderbilt campus. Chet looked into the camera at the beginning of the show and said, "My name is Chet Atkins . . . and has been for quite a while. I'm a guitar player and I've never wanted to be anything else." The Everlys sang Mark Knopfler's "Why Worry." Emmylou Harris performed "Precious Memories," backed by Chet on mandolin and Knopfler on guitar. Michael McDonald did "I Keep Forgetting," Waylon did "Rose in Paradise," Waylon and Willie performed "Good Hearted Woman," and Willie did "Island in the Sea." Chet performed "I Still Can't Say Goodbye," a tribute to his dad.[5]

Chet and Garrison Keillor cohosted *Nashville Now* on December 16. Chet accompanied Garrison on "Ain't That Good News" and "Slow Days of Summer," then Chet presented "Birth of the Blues" and "Avalon" with Les Paul—the first time the pair had performed together in almost a decade. Duane Eddy joined the duo to close the show with "White Christmas."[6]

Chet's *Sails* was released in 1987 and featured "Sails," "Why Worry," "Sometime, Someplace," "Up in My Treehouse," "Waltz for the Lonely," "Laffin' at Life," "On a Roll," "My Song," "Love Letter," and "Wobegon (The Way It Used to Be)." The sessions were recorded in the CA Workshop and at Sound Emporium. John Hall and Johanna Hall wrote the title track, originally a vocal number that Hall recorded with his band Orleans in 1970. It was originally scheduled to be on the *Stay Tuned* album. Chet played a Hascal Haile classical outfitted with a Baggs pickup; he played his Del Vecchio Dinamico on the solo guitar track in the middle of the song.[7]

Sails featured more fingerpicking by Chet than on his previous album. He wrote four of the songs, covered Dire Straits on "Why Worry" (which ran six minutes!), and did "My Song" by jazz keyboardist Keith Jarrett. Synthesizers and heavy drum tracks backed Chet throughout.

CHAPTER 57

Chet had decided to quit writing his column in *Frets* magazine. "I got busy and ran out of something to say and I thought 'Well, what the hell, I'll stop it for a while and write down some ideas and maybe do a column later on.'"

After Garrison Keillor ended his *Prairie Home Companion* show in 1987 and moved to Copenhagen, the home of his new wife, Chet wrote the humorist a couple of two-page letters because "I figured he was kind of lonely over there and didn't know the language too well and had nobody to talk to too much." Keillor responded with a "couple of four-pagers." The two had been friends for six years.

Here is one of the letters Chet wrote to Keillor: "I went up home to East Tennessee the other day. I was invited, went and saw a dozen folks that I hadn't seen in 45 or 50 years. Every damn one of them said, 'I'll bet you don't know who I am,' etc. I admitted I didn't and they seemed disappointed. I left there when I had just turned 11. I received an award for just growing up there, I suppose, and I couldn't think of one nice thing to say. Those were some of the worst years of the old man's life, don't'cha know. But even the bad ones are good now that I think about it.

"Back to the sunny side of life, I played New Bedford, Mass. last Saturday and did very well. I am warmer in the provinces, don'tcha know. I had a screamer in the audience. Saw her later and she wasn't all that bad, about thirty-five, a feller could run some of that weight off of her and maybe fall in love.

"Some of the folks had been to my other shows, though, because when I went into my ad libs, it seemed like they had heard it all before. Anyway I got some bifocal contact lenses the other day for when performing. This morning I got the left one in in about ten seconds, the other one took thirty minutes. I kept jabbing it in my eye and the damn thing kept sticking to my finger. I expect the people to audibly say, 'Who is that young cock up there?' Or I may hear them say, 'How does a man his age see to play without specs?' Anyway, when I got on the plane in Boston, I went to the toilet to get some Kleenex. Well, I opened the door and there sat a lady on the john. I took the time to say, 'Oh, excuse me' (why, I don't know) and got the hell out of there. I'm still embarrassed and it wasn't my fault. This has happened to me three times since 1942 and every time it has been a lady. Well, I probably have walked in on men but that is so uneventful.

"Anyway, I went back to my seat and composed a personals ad: 'Former star with youthful body and only slight loss of hair, is athletic and enjoys listening to country music, especially his own recordings, desires to meet young beautiful twenty-year-old star. Females only please.' Maybe you could use it on your show.

"As ever, Chet."

Keillor declared that Chet is "a man with a tremendous gift for friendship that I don't think I have. I don't think I'm that good a friend. But Chet really is. He's a great letter writer. He's a person who stays in touch. And he's a great person to be around. He's a great storyteller. The thing is that he knows so many wonderful, magnificent stories about all the Nashville stars. He knows all these wonderfully ribald, semi-scandalous and inspiring stories about the great and the near great and their sheer humanity. It's not that stories about these people are scandalous. They're just so human. He is an amazing mimic. He can do these people's voices and he has a tremendous ear. He's a funny, funny man. He's a lifelong reader and admirer of Mark Twain. He reads Mark Twain over and over. And I think from reading the letters he sent me, especially in Denmark, the man has a gift as a writer that I don't know that he'll ever develop. He's very happy playing the guitar."[1]

Alanna Nash authored *Behind Closed Doors: Talking with the Legends of Country Music* in 1988. In her interview with Chet she asked about the Nashville Sound; he replied, "That's just a sales tag . . . I did an interview with a German the other day and he said, 'Do you know the Nashville Sound, what it is?' and I said, 'No,' and he rattled some coins in his hand and he said, 'That is the Nashville sound.' . . . I've always just thought it was sort of a sales tag and didn't amount to much. If there was a Nashville Sound, it had to be, of course, Floyd Cramer, who played a different piano style that changed the whole world, and the Anita Kerr Singers, who were one of the greatest vocal groups of all time. She was a great, great woman, and had more to do with bringing great artists to town, I think, than anyone. Because she was such a great background singer and arranger, and people loved her because she was such a beautiful and nice woman. But as I say, though, it's just a sales tag and doesn't mean much to me."

Asked about his apology for changing the sound of country music, Chet stated, "I'm not apologizing anymore. It's gone so far pop now, that anything I did was very minuscule—very insignificant. But we had to do that because when you're making records, you try to keep your job. And the way you keep your job is to sell records. And the way to sell records is give those friends and neighbors something different all the time. They demand it. Anytime you put out a record, it's gotta have a hook in it—some little surprise that they didn't expect. And the way you do that is maybe put strings on a record, and if that sells real well, then you do that again. And then you try some other background—voices or harmonica, electric guitars in harmony, and you experiment around. And whatever sells, that's what you use. So maybe once in a while you'll use horns in the background, and if that sells, you do that again. Just trying to make hits for the artist, and trying to make yourself secure in a job with a company, and of course, the DJs are doing the same thing—they're playing records that they think will get listeners for them, so all the music takes a certain direction. Maybe it's uptown. Maybe it's back to the country, we hope."

"I like the melody," said Chet. "I can play you the melody on the guitar, I'll bet, fifteen different damn ways. And I used to sit around when I was a kid and figure out how to do that . . . I learned to play the melody all kinds of different ways, and I learned to phrase in many different ways, which has always been an advantage to me."

"The guitar has always been with me everywhere I go," said Chet. "It's my security thing. I hardly ever take a trip without it and a lot of time, I'll take it and won't even play it. But I feel very uncomfortable when I don't have it with me. It's like I left home without my shorts on."

Questioned about how people viewed him, Chet said, "Being around a long time, and being known a long time, you kind of become a legend in your spare time." He downplayed his influence and achievements. "I told somebody the other day that I didn't think I'd contributed a hell of a lot. I knew a good song when I heard it and knew when to keep my mouth shut and let the artists and musicians come up with a good arrangement and occasionally I made a suggestion or two. But I think just about any good musician could have done that. I was just lucky. I was in the right place at the right time and I was fortunate enough to be Mr. Sholes's friend."[2]

Chet's *C.G.P.* was his fourth straight smooth jazz album for Columbia in as many years. The title originally stood for "Country Guitar Picker," but Garrison Keillor revised it to "Certified Guitar Player." Since he never received a diploma, Chet gave himself this designation because he wanted some initials after his name.

The album, all instrumentals except for the last one, was produced by Chet and Darryl Dybka. "I Still Can't Say Goodbye," which Chet sang, was written by Robert Blinn and James Moore and reminded him of his late father. Chet wore a white fedora, like the hat his father wore, whenever he performed the song. His relationship with his father was often difficult, he admitted, but the song reminisced about his dad in warm and loving terms. In the song's introduction Chet made it clear that he really loved his dad and missed him; he even dedicated the album to him. On the album were the songs "Chinook Winds" (written by Chet and Darryl Dybka), "Put Your Clothes On" (Chet and Johnny Gimble), "Imagine" (John Lennon), "Light-Hearted Lisa" (Tony Joe White), "Knucklebusters" (Chet and John Knowles), "Jethreaux" (Jethro Burns, Chet, and Dybka), "Which Way Del Vecchio?" (Dybka), "Daydream" (John Sebastian, who recorded it with the Loving Spoonful), and "Mockingbird Variations" (Chet and Shel Silverstein). An applause track was added to "I Still Can't Say Goodbye" to make it sound like a live performance.

Chet won the CMA Award for Instrumentalist of the Year in 1988—after two years of not winning—but he was angry at the association for not presenting the award during the telecast in October. Chet won the award—his ninth—but did not attend the show "because he was told beforehand that the presentation would not be made during the broadcast." Chet said he learned that he won the award "by reading about it next day in the newspaper."

"I think it was very tacky and disrespectful to the musicians of the world," said Chet. "I think that they forgot what the initial 'M' stands for in CMA. If it weren't for the musicians and the melody writers, it would be the 'CPA'—Country Poets Association."[3] Chet threatened to resign from the CMA but decided against it after meeting with executive director Jo Walker-Meador.

Chet was involved in an attempt to enter the *Guinness Book of World Records* for the World's Largest Guitar Pickin' in the summer of 1988. Chet and Vince Gill were at Hickory Hollow Mall while Harold Bradley was at the Rivergate Mall in Nashville to lead a group of assembled guitar players in "Wildwood Flower." The event, broadcast live on WSM-AM radio, occurred during Fan Fair in Nashville.

During the time of the CAAS convention Chet appeared on the Crook and Chase TV show on TNN and told the hosts, "When I'm gone, they'll play a record or two and say, 'Boy he was good, wasn't he?' And then they'll move on to somebody else, and that's the way it's gotta be and the way it should be. But I enjoy it while I'm here and I hope it continues for a long time."[4]

The 1989 three-day CAAS featured performances by Earl Klugh, Marcel Dadi, John Knowles, Muriel Anderson, Eric Schoenberg, Jean Felix Lalanne, Paul Yandell, Guy Van Duser, Terry Wedding, Thom Bresh, Tommy Jones, Brad Jones, Eddie Pennington, and Tommy Flint. On Saturday afternoon it was Chet Atkins and Friends performing.[5] The convention had become a way to not only honor Chet and perpetuate his legacy but also showcase fingerpicking guitarists from around the world.

The Nashville Symphony honored Chet with the prestigious Harmony Award, "presented to an individual who has demonstrated continued interest and support of classical music in Music City and publicly exemplifies the unique harmony between the many worlds of music that exist only in Nashville." Accepting the award Chet said, "It's always nice to get awards. I've always felt I should get an award for being lucky. Anybody could have done what I've done if they'd been in the right place."[6]

Chet and his manager, Fred Kewley, worked well together; Kewley had a way of guiding Chet's career but let Chet take the lead. "There is none to compare with Chet Atkins," said Kewley. "He is supposed to be my 'client' and, in many ways, he is. But 'clients' don't normally take the time to call and ask 'How are you doing?' 'Clients' don't usually dig into my problems and problems of other clients and help me analyze and solve them. 'Clients' don't usually offer advice and consolation to me and my friends, as Chet has done on several occasions.

Here is a man born in poverty who lifted himself to near perfection at his trade, who created the possibility for so many others to find their success, who is an absolute pillar in Nashville who had created his wealth and place in history long before I met him."

"Out at Chet's house, in the control room of his studio," continued Kewley, "there is a glass window looking over the room where musicians toil with their craft, making records. Pasted high on the glass is a plaque inscribed with these words: 'It's nice to be important, but it's more important to be nice.'"[7]

There were big changes with major labels through sales and mergers during the eighties and nineties. In 1984 RCA was acquired by General Electric, which sold the label to the German firm Bertelsmann to create the Bertelsmann Music Group (BMG). In 1988 the Japanese firm Sony acquired CBS Records. The album *Chet Atkins C.G.P.* was released on Columbia, now part of Sony Music. RCA released two albums by Chet in 1989, *Masters of the Guitar Together*, a double CD release of the two albums Chet recorded with Les Paul, and *Pickin' the Hits*. Heartland released *The Magic of Chet Atkins*, the last Chet album released in LP vinyl format, which contained several songs from his Columbia albums and rerecordings of "Somewhere My Love," "Mister Sandman," "The Entertainer," and "For the Good Times."

CHAPTER 58

By 1990 Chet's company, CGP Enterprises, had their offices at 1013 Seventeenth Avenue South, on Music Row in Nashville. Chet had moved in during the late seventies. In 1981 Chet renovated the building, built in 1910, building a two-story addition to the back that came to be known as the back porch. Chet's formal office was on the first floor, but he seldom used it. There was also an office for his assistant, a bathroom, and a kitchen. The real action was on the second floor, with walls of exposed brick and the original oak floor. A credenza held his awards. Chet stored his guitars in the basement.[1]

It was difficult to obtain Chet's older albums by the nineties, when the music industry was dominated by physical product—LPs and CDs—and labels discontinued albums that were not selling sufficiently. Retailers could not stock everything from an artist with a large catalogue, so as the music industry phased out LPs and CDs began to dominate, labels repackaged older releases or leased songs to companies that specialized in repackaged releases. There were also labels, such as Heartwarming Records, that specialized in TV and mail-order sales. Heartwarming released *The Magic of Chet Atkins*, a double album that featured some old recordings and some Chet rerecordings.

A Tribute to Chet Atkins occurred in Nashville, but Chet observed "I wish these tributes could happen to everybody because it's a nice thing to have people's approval, but I also find it a little embarrassing. . . . I never was good at accepting compliments."

"In people's eyes, somebody always has to be the best," reflected Chet. "Luckily, I don't think there are enough people who feel that way about me to cause me any ego problems. I think I may have been one of the best-known guitarists around for a while, but I'm certainly not the best." Guitar continued to be his passion, "the thing you love so much you can't keep your hands off it." Atkins shared with reporter Laura Eipper, "I think my greatest ability, if I have any, was being able to see the ability in others. To be able to sift the wheat from the chaff. And Nashville has been a great place for that."[2]

After the release of *Stay Tuned* in 1984, Mark Knopfler returned to Dire Straits, who in 1985 released their fifth album, *Brothers in Arms*, selling over thirty million copies worldwide. In 1986 Knopfler formed the Notting Hillbillies, who in 1990 released their only album, *Missing . . . Presumed Having a Good Time*. During that period Chet and Knopfler stayed in touch and decided to record an album. In the summer of 1989 they began working in Chet's basement studio with Knopfler producing. "I was interested in Chet's country roots much more than his jazz thing," said Knopfler. "I'm going to tell him what I think, and I just really thought that he should get away from that easy listening jazz music stuff. I couldn't stand it then and I can't stand it now."

"Chet Atkins is inspirational because he will write you a letter or call you up on the phone talking about a new tune that he has discovered or some of the things that I would never bother with, and he is a reminder about staying in touch and serving your talent and your gift and respecting it," said Knopfler. "The thing with Chet and music is that he is always melodic . . . which is really essentially why Chet is not a jazz guitarist. He will always have interesting chords, but he is not really a jazzer. Chet loves the melodic and the emotional music. So, I think that's just it, that his love for music is so great, his love for the guitar is so great."

"He is full of jokes, you know, and every time on the telephone, he will always tell me a joke," said Knopfler. "I remember when we did this thing where we played 'Imagine' on this Cinemax thing and he came off [stage] and went back to the dressing room and said, 'Well, I fooled them again.'"[3]

On October 9 Columbia released *Neck and Neck* by Chet and Knopfler. A video for "Poor Boy Blues," Chet's first music video, was filmed to promote the song. In addition to Chet and Knopfler, other musicians on the album included Paul Franklin (steel), Guy Fletcher (bass), Edgar Meyer (bass), Steve Wariner (guitar), and Larrie Londin (drums). The album was recorded in CA Workshop, Sound Emporium, and Knopfler's studio, Hillbilly Heaven in London.

Chet borrowed a Maccaferri guitar from Don Gibson for the song "Tears," written by Django Reinhardt and Stephane Grappelli. Gibson's "got a Maccaferri that he found in Scotland and Django's supposed to have played it," said Chet. "It has that 'sound' and Mark played it on the record. But I borrow it now and then when I need to get that sound. It's a little guitar with kind of a short scale, but it's got all those high frequencies which was great in Django's time."

"Mark is madly in love with Don Gibson and I was just singing some of his hits for him," said Chet. "I came up with different chords to 'Sweet Dreams'—kind of like I thought Lenny [Breau] would have played it." (Chet started the song with a minor instead of major chord.) "I like the substitution of chords when you're playing a well known song—it's a lot more exciting."

"Next Time I'm in Town" was written by Knopfler, who "said he wrote that about me once when he was going back to England," said Chet. "It doesn't mention a girl although it could be—it's just talking about friends. I hadn't heard one that good in a long time for closing shows."[4] Vince Gill sang harmony on that song. Other songs on the album were "There'll Be Some Changes Made," "Just One Time" by Don Gibson, "So Soft, Your Goodbye" by Randy Goodrum, "Yakety Axe" by Boots Randolph and James Rich, "Tahitian Skies" by Ray Flacke, and "I'll See You in My Dreams" by Isham Jones and Gus Kahn.

When *Neck and Neck* was released, Nashville *Tennessean* reporter Thomas Goldsmith interviewed Chet in his office, where he first played "Danny Boy" on a classical guitar, introducing a few changes in the arrangement. "I've been needing so long some way of sustaining [notes] when you're playing fingerpicking," said Chet. "It's good isn't it? It's really nice to discover something different once in a while." Chet was sixty-six, still discovering new things on the guitar.

"It's more country than I expected it to be, but that's all right, I guess," said Chet of the new album. "That's how Mark wanted to do it. He wanted to get me away from that easy-listening jazz stuff I had been doing for the last four or five years. It was fine with me. I had been wanting to get back, although I don't think country radio will play it. They don't play instrumentals anymore."

"I want to appeal to somebody—I don't care who it is—and sell enough records to stay on a major label," continued Chet. "It would be nice if the country folks continued to buy my records. It would be nice, too, if the radio stations and record companies would break out of their conformity and promote an instrumental out there."[5]

Knopfler spent a good deal of time with Chet and saw him in a variety of settings. He was an astute observer and gained insight into the essence of Chet Atkins. "Chet was very proud of being Chet Atkins," said Knopfler. "Proud of what he achieved and very conscious of what he sacrificed in order to be able to learn to play. Chet would never say that; he never said it. He was very proud of it. He didn't like it belittled in any way."

"Chet was so deep," said Knopfler. "It didn't matter what it was. Chet loved classical guitar playing, he loved country guitar playing and Hawaiian guitar playing, he loved rhythm and blues guitar playing, he loved jazz guitar playing. He loved simple things. Nothing made him happier than to sit for an hour with me and repeat over and over again a simple phrase or a tune like 'Kentucky,' which only has two chords."

"Chet never expressed regret about anything except about his upbringing as a child," said Knopfler. "He was scarred his entire life over his early relationship with his Dad. When his Dad left Chet and his family when Chet was a little boy and eventually made it back, he did not bring Chet a gift when he returned. I think it was very hard for Chet to accept over the course of his entire life."

"He was a very sensitive guy," continued Knopfler. "He didn't have a hard heart at all; he had a very soft heart. He was very affected by the ebb and flow of other people's lives. One of the reasons he left the RCA situation was that he was in charge of people's lives and he was finding it hard to be the pivotal point for so many people's futures. People were depending on him."[6]

Chet loved to sing and "was always tickled by the little bit of lyric writing that he would do," remembered Knopfler. "He would often run it by me, you know. I remember he would sing unaccompanied. I remember Chet being quite pleased with 'Would Jesus Wear a Rolex.' Sometimes he would rewrite the lyrics to a popular song in a humorous way. That was the lovely thing about him, a kind of innocence that never really went away."

Another side of Chet surprised Knopfler. "Chet always watched his pennies," said Knopfler. "Whenever we went to breakfast he would dig out a tip. I would say, 'Hey Chet, you've got to leave a little more than that, mate.' Then he would throw down a few more bucks. He would look at me and say, 'What do you mean?' It was perfectly understandable because he came from grinding poverty; it just left its mark on him. He used to walk to school in the bitter cold without a coat. Having said all that, he was very generous to me and to many other people. He gave me guitars, a Gibson Country Gentleman and a nylon string Gibson (CE model). Chet suffered in his life and because of this was careful with his money. However, he was always generous when people were in need."[7] Chet's penny-pinching was legendary. On the golf course he would walk around hunting for tees so he wouldn't have to buy any.

In the nineties Chet became a spokesperson for Cracker Barrel restaurants and either appeared in or provided the narration for nearly a dozen commercials that aired throughout the decade. Chet enjoyed eating at Cracker Barrel for free because of his endorsement and once insisted on driving forty miles out of the way to find a Cracker Barrel. Chet always enjoyed free things.

CHAPTER 59

At the thirty-third annual Grammys, held in February 1991 in New York, Chet and Mark Knopfler won Best Country Vocal Collaboration for "Poor Boy Blues" and Best Country Instrumental for "So Soft Your Goodbye."

Nashville wanted to honor some of its musical legends and honored sixty-six-year-old Chet on Wednesday, May 8, by naming a street after him. Chet Atkins Place, originally South Street, is a four-block-long street between Sixteenth and Twentieth Streets South. Speakers at the event included Ray Stevens, Minnie Pearl, Owen Bradley, Eddy Arnold, and Billy Edd Wheeler. Chet thanked the city and the hundreds of guests gathered. At that time there were thirty-one celebrities who had their names on theaters in Branson, Missouri, that attracted over six million tourists, many of whom once came to Nashville. Accepting the honor, Chet, in mock seriousness, said that he was using this occasion "to announce the move of Chet Atkins Enterprises to Branson, Missouri."[1] Years later he complained privately that they should have named Hawkins Street, which ran beside RCA Studio B, after him instead of naming it Roy Acuff Place.

Later that day a dance troupe staged a performance that Chet had composed. Members of the Tennessee Dance Theatre heard Chet's album, *The Night Atlanta Burned*, and wanted him to compose music for a dance performance. John Knowles "had worked with them because my daughter was really into dance and I had played some music with them," said Knowles. "They had asked me, 'Do you think that you and Chet could write some music for us?' I said, 'Well, I'll ask him.' So I did and he said, 'Didn't guys like Igor Stravinsky and Aaron Copeland do stuff like that?' And I said, 'Yeah, they did' and he said, 'Well, I should too.' And so we did."

"We wrote this piece—it was like a twenty-minute piece," said Knowles. "We prerecorded most of what we did so they could rehearse and there were some live parts. It had a lot of songs in it; we took things that he already knew. It's written around the theme of a circus:

how the mirrors change the faces, how things appear to change when you're at the circus. It's called 'Midways' and it had 'Over the Waves,' 'Mother of Ireland' and some original stuff we wrote. It was kind of like a suite the way we did it. It really intrigued him to go and watch the dancers work with what we had done."[2] The dance was performed one time only, on May 8 at the Tennessee Performing Arts Center, as a fundraiser for the Tennessee Dance Theatre.

In the June issue of *Mister Guitar* Mark Pritcher interviewed Chet, who said that he was "trying to get permission to use some of Reinhardt's recordings on one of my records. I wrote a song about Reinhardt and I want to use one of his records in the song and close with me playing a duet with Django and we'll either use 'Minor Swing' or 'Mystery Pacific.'"

Chet said that Reinhardt's repertoire had influenced the selection of songs he recorded during his career and added, "I'd like to record a lot of his tunes. There are some obscure things I don't know the titles of that are really good. There's one called 'Dinette' that's fine, but the good record of it I haven't heard since 1950. It's a great record where he plays a terrific chorus and he recorded it several times. I've got several versions, but I don't have the good version. There are a couple of other tunes I can hum and play, but I don't know the titles. Someday if I can find the titles, I might record them."[3]

In 1991 Chet's daughter Merle and his two grandchildren, Jonathan and Mandy, moved back to Nashville from North Carolina after her divorce. This allowed Chet and the grandchildren to spend time together regularly. Chet and Leona had gone to North Carolina to visit several times a year, but now there would be a constant presence.

In an interview with *Mister Guitar*, Chet stated that he used three main guitars: the Country Gentleman made by Gibson that was based on his original Gretsch Country Gentleman; a Gibson CE electric classic; and his Brazilian Del Vecchio resonator guitar. Chet also used an acoustic flattop, a steel-string version of the CE classic/electric (the Gibson SST), and a solid body electric Chet designed for Gibson that sounds much like a Fender Stratocaster.

Chet used a Music Man RC112 tube amp with a Neuman microphone when he recorded with his Country Gentleman. He plugged the CE classic and other classical guitars with a tube preamp directly into the console. Chet preferred the electric to the acoustic classics because, "to me, the sound of the CE classic is just a lot nicer than a true acoustic sound." The Del Vecchio is the only completely acoustic that Chet recorded with. "I don't even think of it as an acoustic guitar," said Chet. "It has a metal resonator, and it has a very penetrating sound. I used it on a couple of cuts on the *C.G.P.* [album]. I usually just lay a 414 on the console and listen to myself play it through headphones. It's real quiet in the control room, and I turn everything off except the tape machine."

With his own records "I'm not a good mixer," said Chet. "I let the engineers do it, and I tell them whether I like the sound or not, but I don't really pay attention to what they're doing as far as the EQ and all." Chet revealed that he had lost some of his hearing over the years. "My high end isn't what it should be," said Chet. "I can hear some highs if I put pressure on my ear drums, I can hear them for a few seconds, and then it's back to no-man's land again."

Chet's CA Workshop studio control room had two Tannoy SRM 10B monitors, which Chet preferred over large enclosures or small Auratone-type speakers. He believed that low-level monitoring was better. Chet relied on engineers Mike Poston, Joe Bogan, and David Palmer to mix his records.[4]

"The *C.G.P.* album was mixed by Joe Bogan and Mike Poston at the Nightingale Studios. It's a nice studio with a lot of good outboard equipment that Mike likes and knows. I'm usually there when he mixes, or I'm somewhere nearby. I just check it and make suggestions. Dave Palmer is another great mixer because he listens to everything on a recording and then decides what he likes or finds what he can enhance," continued Chet. "I've used him a lot and he's real slow. He'll take a day and a half or longer to mix one song. But he does one hell of a job."

Poston began working on Chet's records during Chet's final years with RCA. He engineered the *Standard Brands* album and *Still Country . . . After All These Years* as well as projects with Perry Como and Roger Whittaker that Chet produced. He engineered and did some mixing on Atkins's CBS/Columbia records since *Stay Tuned*, including *Neck and Neck*. Poston said that "one of the reasons he gave up other engineering offers to work with Chet more or less exclusively was because they shared an understanding of how his records should 'feel.'"

"I remember Chet's commenting about the fact that I could not only hear frequencies and things that he no longer could, but that I had a 'feel' for his music," said Poston. "He plays on feel, even though technically he's a perfectionist, he also appreciates what 'feel' is all about on the overall record. You know the take is right when you're sitting there in the control room and you have goose bumps running up and down your arm, even though it may not be technically perfect, maybe somebody blew it if you're doing a live date, but if you got the goose bumps, you know it's right."

The CA Workshop is "not what one would call state-of-the-art by today's standards," said Poston. "It's adequate, and it fulfills most of our needs, except for mixing because Chet doesn't have an automated console, which we've needed on the last couple of albums where the tracks get fairly complex and there are guests playing with Chet."

John Knowles believed that a major reason Chet consistently turned out high-quality performances on records was because he'd always had a home studio where he could record whenever and as often as he wanted to.

"It's true," agreed Chet. "If I had to go into a commercial studio to record my things, the expense would just make it impossible. I record a tune and think 'Why did I play it like that?' and I'll record it all over again. So recording at home is a great help to me. It's also a hobby I've always had. I bought my first recorder, a Wilcox Gay disc recorder in 1947 from a music store in Denver on time payments. . . . It's a very expensive hobby because equipment is so expensive, but it's worth it when you compare what I've spent on equipment with what I would've spent on studio time somewhere else."

Chet estimated how much time he spent recording in his home studio and then billed CBS for the recording time and musicians against his budget for the album. Chet's albums thus cost much less than if he had recorded in a commercial studio. Additionally, "the quality wouldn't be there in my records," said Chet. "The way it is, I can record any time I want to. I can work down at my office and come home and record a little."[5]

Chet and Jerry Reed reunited in 1991 to record *Sneakin' Around*, their third duet album. Chet had lost touch with Reed both personally and professionally during the seventies and most of the eighties because Reed was focused on his singing and acting career. *Sneakin' Around* was produced by Chet; additional musicians on the album were Pat Bergeson on guitar, Darryl Dybka on keyboard, Terry McMillan on harmonica, David Hungate on bass, and Larrie Londin on drums. The album was recorded at the CA Workshop and featured country- as well as jazz-flavored guitar instrumentals that neither had recorded previously, except for "The Claw," written by Reed, which each had recorded separately.

The song "Sneakin' Around" is the reason Pat Bergeson plays on the album. At the National Guitar Summer Workshop in Connecticut, Chet's manager, Fred Kewley, received a cassette from R. L. Kass (Robert Lee Castleman) with "Sneakin' Around" on it that featured Kass playing melody with Bergeson playing "licks and fills." Kewley arranged for Kass to go to Muscle Shoals for some demos and wanted Bergeson to go with him. After the sessions Bergeson came to Nashville: "Chet heard I was in town and asked Fred and R. L. to bring me over to his office," said Bergeson. "We probably hung out for six hours that first day, sitting there playing guitar."

Chet "just played a number of songs," said Bergeson. They were playing Bergeson's green Stratocaster and "it was so cool how he was so interested in the guitar and interested in what I was doing."

One of the first things Chet did with Bergeson was take him to the Musicians Union and pay for his membership, telling Bergeson that although Tennessee was a "right to work" state that did not require union membership, Chet supported the union and was a longtime member. Bergeson toured with Chet "playing harmonica a lot." When Bergeson played guitar, Chet "really didn't tell me what to play," said Bergeson. "He pretty much let me do what I wanted to do. He liked the fact that I was a rock'n'roll guy and I knew about rock'n'roll, jazz and other styles that he didn't do as much. He liked me to inject my own style into what he was doing as a contrast."

On the tours Paul Yandell helped and encouraged Bergeson with thumbpicking. If Bergeson asked Chet for advice for a part to play, Chet would sometimes say "play something that somebody else could whistle."

Chet loved to jam with other musicians. "He was way into just sitting there and noodling around on the guitar," said Bergeson. "We did that a lot over at his office. Many times I'd go to his house on Sundays around noon and spend the day. I wouldn't leave there until about eight o'clock at night. We'd spend the whole day over there just sitting around, fooling around on the guitars and just playing through stuff. He would play records of old fiddle players and sit there and tinker with his guitars, replacing pickups and stuff." At the end of the day, they would go upstairs from the basement and Leona would fix dinner "and we'd listen to the ham radio, and sometimes he and Paul Yandell would talk some on the ham radio."

Bergeson learned that Chet "was very generous . . . and also extremely funny. He was mischievous too, in a good way."[6] Chet always liked to have young guys around whom he could mentor as a guitarist but also for their energy, helping Chet stay young and current.

On "Sneakin' Around" Chet played his Gibson electric while Reed played a classical guitar with a pickup. This was Chet and Jerry's last recording together.

CHAPTER 60

On January 4, 1992, Columbia released Chet's album with Jerry Reed, *Sneakin' Around.* Four days later Chet appeared on *Nashville Now* and played "Main Street Breakdown" and Hoagy Carmichael's classic song, "Stardust." On March 13 Chet and Jerry Reed were on the *Crook and Chase Show* on TNN, and three days later they performed "Sneakin' Around," "Summertime," and "The Claw" on *Nashville Now.*[1]

On August 29 Chet appeared on *Nashville Now* with President George H. W. Bush, who was running for reelection. Chet presented a medley of "America the Beautiful," "Battle Hymn of the Republic," "Dixie," "Yankee Doodle," and then "Yankee Doodle Dixie" "together and at the same time," as Chet joked.[2]

On October 2 Chet performed with the New York Symphony in Carnegie Hall and one week later performed at the Great Outhouse Blowout in Gravel Switch, Kentucky. Penn's Store in Gravel Switch was getting a new outhouse, so the owners decided to build a concert around the event. Billy Edd Wheeler sang "Ode to the Little Brown Shack Out Back" before he and Chet cut the ribbon on the outhouse door.[3]

RCA released a double CD album, *The RCA Years: 1947–1981*, covering Chet's entire career. There were performances with Les Paul ("Avalon"), the Boston Pops ("Country Gentleman"), Jerry Reed ("Good Stuff"), Lenny Breau ("Sweet Georgia Brown"), Boots Randolph ("Terry on the Turnpike"), Dolly Parton ("Do I Ever Cross Your Mind?"), and Merle Travis ("Nine Pound Hammer") as well as favorites such as "Yakety Axe," "Mister Sandman," and "Windy and Warm." Bear Family Records, based in Germany, issued *Galloping Guitar: The Early Years*, which contained every song that Chet recorded from 1946 to 1954.[4]

Chet Atkins was inducted into the East Tennessee Hall of Fame in February. Before the ceremony there was a banquet with the presentation of a plaque and oil painting to hang in the lobby of the Bijou

Theatre Centre. A video overview of Chet's career was shown, then Chet took the podium: "Daniel Boone was mentioned in the opening remarks by the governor, and I'm gonna start using this line when people ask me if I ever get lost on the guitar. Daniel Boone one time was asked if he ever got lost when he was exploring the west and he said 'No,' but 'I was once bewildered for three days!'"

"Boy this [ceremony] has been great," continued Chet. "The video presentation tonight brought back so many memories to me. I didn't realize I did all that stuff! So maybe I'll get a little more self-esteem after this. I'm very fond of Knoxville and all the people and of course all my kin folk are here and my sister and my friend Buster. So thank you very much, it's a very nice honor and I'll always treasure it and remember it and I hope I'll be remembering it for a long time."

In his closing remarks Governor Lamar Alexander, who emceed the show, shared, "There was a fellow in Nashville one time watching Chet play and he turned around to me and said, 'You know, he's so good most of us don't have any idea what he's doing!'"[5]

During the 1993 Grammy Awards, held in Los Angeles in February, Chet was given a Lifetime Achievement award and also won a Grammy with Jerry Reed for "Sneakin' Around." Chet did not attend the event in Los Angeles because the award was not shown on camera. On March 18 his secretary organized a surprise party, at the offices of BMI, where Chet was presented with the actual award by Dolly Parton, who said, "If anybody in this whole world is deserving of [this award] you are. You have created this Nashville sound. You have done more things for more people like me, who have ridden on your coattails for years."

In response Chet demurred, "Damn, I hate inconveniencing all you people. Coming out in the cold for this, I appreciate it so very much."

"I've been so lucky in my life; I've had several of these parties," said Chet. "It's so wonderful. It makes me feel like I did something right along the way. It's not over yet. I'll keep picking and recording long as I can, as long as it's fun for me and as long as people want to listen." In addition to the award, Ralph Emery presented Chet with photos from *Nashville Now* when he was a guest with President Bush.[6]

Gibson continued developing and marketing new guitars with Chet; the Gibson Chet Atkins Studio Classic made its debut in May 1993. Kirk Sand of Laguna Beach, California, created the "hollowed

Honduras Mahogany body with a specially braced Sitka Spruce soundboard resulting in a unique combination of a fine classical guitar and an advanced electric masterpiece." John Knowles introduced them when Sand was at Knowles's house installing a Baggs pickup on his Kohno guitar. Knowles asked Chet to come by to hear the new pickup. Chet arrived and asked Sand to install a Baggs on his Hascal Haile guitar. Sand left one of his guitars with him and "when I got back to California Chet called and said, 'I like this guitar. It's better than mine. Make me one.'"[7]

During the nineties Chet appeared on the records of a number of performers as a "special guest." He played "Heartbreak Hotel" on an album by the Chieftains, "Turn Around" on Nanci Griffith's *Other Voices, Other Rooms*, and "Grandfather's Greatest Hits" by David Holt. Chet played his Del Vecchio on "Darlin'" for a CD by Brendan Croker, Mark Knopfler's colleague. On the British CD *Carl Perkins: Friends, Family and Legends*, Chet played a solo on "Birth of Rock and Roll." He also produced and appeared on the *Garrison Keillor and the Hopeful Gospel Quartet* album.

During June Chet was on *Nashville Now* on a show hosted by Carlene Carter and premiered a song he had written for Carlene's grandmother, Mother Maybelle Carter. Chet played "Maybelle" on his Del Vecchio.[8]

Claes Neeb saw Chet in 1990 in Cannes at the Atkins-Dadi Guitar Pickers Association meeting. "I had met Chet before during his tours in Norway and we had corresponded when I was a teenager," said Neeb. "I asked Chet if he would like to hear some of my compositions. He said he would and I played them for him." Neeb really wanted Chet to hear a song he had adapted from some Norwegian fiddle music and "made a blues out of it."

After Neeb played "Norwegian Mountain Song," Chet asked him to play the piece several more times. "I pointed out its scale in the Lydian mode and showed him the fingerings," said Neeb. "He loved the strange notes and commented on the 'musical tension' they created. 'Do you have a tape of it?' he asked. I had a studio demo of it with full backing. 'Would it be too much trouble for you to mail me a copy when you get back home?' I told him it would be a pleasure and an honor. 'Well,' he said, 'I would very much like to learn it.'"

Neeb did not hear from Chet until early 1991, when Chet wrote that "he would be ready to record my tune in a few months and mentioned that he was considering having me come to Nashville to help him 'get it right.'"

"Some people from the NRK, Norway's oldest broadcasting company, discussed sending a film crew with me on my trip to Nashville," said Neeb. "I was thrilled when Chet gave this idea the go-ahead, saying 'It will give you some well-deserved publicity in Norway and it might be good for the record sales.'"

Neeb arrived in Nashville in June 1993, presented Chet with a handcrafted gift, and showed him a special Norwegian fiddle that had four extra resonating strings. Chet "tuned it up and played a tune. In his Nashville office he showed us many items that I had seen on albums, like the 12-string Country Gentleman from the cover of his Beatles album," said Neeb, "and pictures of Ray Stevens, Boots Randolph and Floyd Cramer. Chet and I had a nice jam session for the camera. We started with 'Vaudeville Daze' from his new album with Jerry Reed. He taught me his new tune 'Young Thing' written in honor of his friend Bill Young. With cameras running he took us to the old RCA Studio B museum, and told us about Elvis and Jim Reeves and the rest of the RCA family from the great days of country music. Next we went to the Country Music Hall of Fame and had a great time. Chet was nice enough to brag on me when fans came up to talk to him, and I got to share a few handshakes with the public myself."

Chet took them to lunch at the Loveless Café, then back to their hotel. The next day they were at Chet's home, where the temperature was in the mid-nineties, and went downstairs into the CA Workshop. Once inside, Chet said, "Let's get to work. Show me how you play the song." Neeb played it, and Chet "kept mentioning how he liked my slurs, hammer-ons and pull-offs." Chet told Neeb that he would learn the song but it might take him several days. Meanwhile, Terry McMillan came over and laid down some percussion tracks; Chet and Darryl Dybka had already recorded the basic tracks of bass, keyboard, and sampled drums and strings.

"The cameras were filming Terry in the studio and Chet and me in the control room," said Neeb. "Chet was telling stories about life on the road with Terry and the atmosphere was really relaxed and full of joy. I could see what made Chet such a great producer. He made people around him feel appreciated, comfortable and happy and brought out the best in them. Chet had laid down a guitar track to work with earlier, and the TV people wanted him to use that as a playback to get some live shots of him 'recording' the tune. He picked up his beautiful Gibson Studio Classic with the 'fleur de lis' and the abalone around the edge. He played along with the backing tracks several times so the crew could get their shots. By late afternoon, we were done. While the TV crew was packing up their gear, I talked with Chet and Leona. His birthday was fast approaching and he talked a bit about his career. He felt a lot of gratitude for the life he had lived."

"I have been so fortunate to be able to make a good living by doing what I love the most," said Chet. "There are a lot of players out there, a lot better than me, who never made it."

"I thought to myself that nobody else was as good as Chet at communicating important emotions through playing the guitar," said Neeb. "Many players, of course, express emotion and feeling through their playing, but most of them channel their talents into a more narrow vein, like blues, jazz or classical music. Chet had covered all possible directions and genres, and had done it in such a way that his audience, even if not well versed in his techniques, could appreciate his music. Trying to express this to Chet with my English was not easy, but he was touched and thanked me for my admiration."[9]

In 1993—thirteen years after they first met—Tommy Emmanuel called and left a message for Chet, who called back and said, in his short, staccato sentences, "Remember that day we played. Like it was yesterday." Tommy told him he was making an album, and Chet offered to play on a track. So Tommy came to Nashville, where they recorded "Villa Anita" for Tommy's album *The Journey*.

In an interview with Mark Prichard for *Mister Guitar*, Tommy said, "I revere a great melody. I think it's something that has been instilled in me, through listening to him. And as much as he would encourage me to listen to as many players as possible, it's still like you hear players but then you go back and listen to a great Chet Atkins album, and there is no comparison. He stands alone."[10]

About a month before their recording, Chet wrote to Tommy because he was "concerned that he might sound a little old fashioned and he had been listening to my stuff that was electric and acoustic and it was much more pop and rock oriented. 'You have to remember that I'm a dotted eighth note kid from the '30s and '40s so you'll have to bend back a little.'"

When they went to Chet's basement studio Tommy played him the track for "Villa Anita." "When he heard the track, he listened to it and said 'This sounds a bit modern for the old guy,'" said Emmanuel, who replied, "We'll see how it goes."

"Of course, the first solo he played was a gem," said Emmanuel, "and then he played two more really good solos. I ended up going with his first take because it was so damn good. Yet he was like, 'I don't know whether it's any good.' He was not sure but it was beautiful. He was actually a lot better than he thought he was!" laughed Tommy.[11]

A TV show, *Christmas With Vince Gill*, was taped at Vanderbilt University on November 20 and 30. Chet helped make the season bright by playing "Jingle Bell Rock" and then a guitar duet with Vince on "Santa Claus Is Coming to Town." Chet and Vince also sang "The Chipmunk Song," chiming in together on "Me, I want a hula hoop."[12]

Ralph Emery left *Nashville Now* in 1993, after ten years as "the spokesman for country music." That show was then combined with *Crook and Chase* to create *Music City Tonight* and then *Prime Time Country*, first hosted by Tom Wopat and then Gary Chapman. During 1993 Chet released an album with Christian star Amy Grant, *The Gingham Dog and the Calico Cat*.

CHAPTER 61

At the Grammys in March in New York Chet and six other musicians—Asleep at the Wheel, Eldon Shamblin, Johnny Gimble, Marty Stuart, Ruben "Lucky Oceans" Gosfield, and Vince Gill—received the Best Country Instrumental award for their rendition of "Red Wing."

Chet had lost interest in the smooth jazz he had recorded and in the early nineties began featuring a wide variety of tunes. On *Read My Licks* Chet featured Steve Wariner's vocal on the title track. He recorded a vocal duet with Suzy Bogguss on "After You've Gone," Chet and Eric Johnson did a duet on the jazzy "Somebody Loves Me Now," while Chet performed "Dream," a Johnny Mercer song, with George Benson. Chet and Mark Knopfler performed "Around the Bend," a song written by Chet and Jerry Reed. "Young Thing" was written by Chet in honor of longtime friend Bill Young. The song had the throwback feel of fifties rock and roll inspired by boogie-woogie piano.

Chet first recorded "Vincent" for his 1977 album *Me and My Guitar*, playing it on a nylon-string guitar. His recording for the *Read My Licks* album was just Chet, unaccompanied on his Gibson Chet Atkins Studio Classic. He played "Vincent" as a regular feature on his TV and concert appearances, and through the years a new arrangement had evolved.

The tenth annual Chet Atkins Appreciation Society Convention was held in July. On opening day Chet and Steve Wariner played "Read My Licks" for the TV show *Music City Tonight*. The Saturday night concert was the final event of the CAAS Convention, with over eight hundred audience members cheering in an uninhibited frenzy when emcee Bill Spann announced, "Ladies and Gentlemen—Mr. Chet Atkins." Chet played "Wheels," "Vincent," "Imagine," and "Sweet Alalee" with Paul Yandell. After he'd been onstage for about an hour Chet put on his hat and began "I Still Can't Say Goodbye," then began jamming with other guitarists on "Sweet Georgia Brown." Chet tried to leave after almost two hours, but the crowd refused. He then performed three more songs, finally wrapping up the show.[1]

Chet continued to perform on compilation albums during 1994. On *Rhythm Country & Blues*, country artists were paired with R&B singers; Chet performed "Southern Nights" with Allen Toussaint, who wrote the song. On *Come Together: America Salutes the Beatles*, Chet and Suzy Bogguss performed "All My Loving." Chet shared, "I find just complete perfection when I listen to their records. The bass lines just couldn't be better; the melodies could not be better. It's just the most wonderful era that we went through with The Beatles."

On Wednesday evening, August 31, the National Academy of Recording Arts and Sciences (NARAS) honored Chet and Owen Bradley with the Governor's Award. Over six hundred music industry executives and others with connections attended the hundred-dollar-a-plate event that honored Chet and Owen as the "Architects of the Nashville Sound." "Owen really deserves it," said Chet to an interviewer. "Owen was more of a perfectionist. I depended more on the engineer. I didn't mind a mistake or two if the record had a great feel and I suppose you could hear that in our records. I went for a lot of spontaneity."

"I do convey emotion through my records," continued Chet. "I just try to play what I feel in my heart. I wish I did show my emotions more. I wish I smiled more. I wish I was more of a Roy Clark type personality. But I'm not. I'm a shy, quiet kind of guy. I just try to play what's in my heart."

"Jazz, to me, meant Louis Armstrong, Django Reinhardt—those guys that would state the melody just for a few bars, then play beyond that," said Chet. "Now jazz is like Earl Klugh; stating the melody, a little improvisation in the middle, and re-stating the melody all over. They call it jazz. That's fine with me, 'cause that's what I play."[2]

In 1994 Nicholas Dawidoff interviewed Chet for *In the Country of Country: People and Places in American Music*. When Dawidoff arrived the front door of Chet's office building was locked; outside a plaque declared "By Appointment Only."

Dawidoff stated that Chet was "in a rocking chair behind a desk that was covered with so many music cassettes that there was no room for his size nine-and-a-half brown loafers. They were propped on a desk drawer." Chet did not want to produce any more, although people still brought him tapes. "I usually don't see 'em unless it's a shapely girl," said Chet. Scattered around the room "was an assortment of guitars" consisting of Gretsches, Ramirez Classics, Gibsons, and "some Japanese guitars with nylon strings and a twelve-string Martin." There were also "guitar fetishes: a guitar clock, a guitar frog, and a picture wire guitar."

Chet picked up a guitar and, settling back in his chair, "slouching over the fretboard with his shoulders curved, his head cocked left, his brows drawn together, and his eyes looking off at terrain somewhere in the distance beyond the knuckles of his left hand, he played a few bars of a melody straight with his ring finger. 'Pure tone' he said. Then he began to work again, adding his thumb to make a syncopated rhythm and his fore and middle fingers to create a harmonic progression. The melody was still there, but sprinkled all around it now were supplementary noises. It nodded a greeting, said something cheerful, and finally it winked."

"Chet Atkins can make a guitar chortle, and he can make it wince," wrote Dawidoff. "He can pick out a waltz, a jitterbug, or a jitterbug waltz. He can use it to banter like a butcher or brag like a senator" but "if things weren't going his way, he could summon up some devastating blues."

After Chet put the guitar down, he put his feet back up on his desk drawer and drank some black tea from an Elvis Presley mug. Dawidoff "could see his beautifully smoothed and rounded fingernails. The moment Atkins notices that he has developed a nick or rough spot on a nail, he files it down. Sometimes, when he is caught with a shaggy nail and no emery board, Atkins will reach out and manicure himself on the side of a brick building or even stoop and use the sidewalk."

Chet was wearing red socks, a habit he picked up from Garrison Keillor because with a drawer full of red socks you can just pull out two socks and don't have to worry if they match. "His clothing is natty—he has a penchant for checks," said Dawidoff. On the day they met Chet was "wearing a solid smart-blue silk necktie over a checked shirt that had come untucked from his trousers."

Talking about his speech at the NARAS Governor's Award the day before, Chet said, "I killed them. I told them how I remembered when I was born, my cradle wasn't painted, I had no clothes, no teeth, and no hair but I did have a pick on my thumb. I told them about playing my ukulele and how when a string broke, I ripped wire off the screen door. That's true. There was always one loose because a dog or a pig had run through and torn a hole. I told them when I got rich and successful, I got a swimming pool shaped like a guitar amplifier." That last line was stolen from Garrison Keillor.

Chet's conversation reflected a "passion for lascivious badinage. He can work something mildly salacious into conversations with the same fluidity that this fingers climb over the hill in 'Black Mountain Rag'" and was "an incorrigible connoisseur of profanity." Archie Campbell had worked up routines like "Beeping Sleuty" and "Pee Little Thrigs," where he altered "Sleeping Beauty" and "Three Little Pigs" by changing the letters of phrases. Chet often did that because "you can cuss and everything! I'll meet a new girl or something and say 'Do you live in a hood wouse or a hick brouse.'" Chet added that Dolly Parton "grabbed me by the ass three times last year. I was gonna sue her for sexual harassment, but only for fifty dollars 'cause I kind of enjoyed it."

During Dawidoff's next visit Chet wore "a well-tailored summer-weight gray suit." Discussing country music in Nashville, Chet said the city "was a terrible place for musicians until they allowed whiskey." (Nashville did not legalize liquor by the drink until the end of 1967.) "Nashville was ashamed of the country boys," claimed Chet. "Some of the people at National Life, which owned The Grand Ole Opry, were ashamed of it" until they discovered that their insurance salesmen found that doors opened when they mentioned the Opry. Speaking of the Nashville Sound, Chet declared, "I don't know if there is such a thing" but that he and Owen Bradley "took the twang out of it" by eliminating the steel guitar and fiddle when they produced records. "We polished it," said Atkins.

"I've said a lot of stuff, but we almost do lose our identity sometimes," said Chet. "We get so pop [that] fans turn away. . . . To young folks right now, country music just means some guy with a tight ass and a white hat. Right now we're in a curve with everything sounding alike, but somebody'll come along and get us back where we need to be."[3]

Chet Atkins and Suzy Bogguss collaborated on *Simpatico*, produced by Doug Crider (Bogguss's husband) and John Guess. Chet played guitar, with Matt Rollings on piano and Pat Bergeson on harmonica. "One More for the Road," written by Chet, Bogguss, and Crider, was chosen as the single and a video was produced with the band in a forties-style hotel. In October Chet and Bogguss promoted their album and performed "One More for the Road" on the *Tonight Show* and "Wives Don't Like Old Girlfriends" on *Live with Regis and Kathie Lee.* Asked about the current state of country music, Chet replied, "It's become a visual business. Its cowboy hats and you've got to look good in jeans and be young. [Fans] used to buy sounds, now they buy looks."

In November Chet and Suzy were on the *Today Show* where Chet played his Gibson L-200 flattop while they performed "In the Jailhouse Now." They performed "Wives Don't Like Old Girlfriends" and Elton John's "Sorry Seems to Be the Hardest Word," while Chet played "Vincent" alone on *Music City Tonight.*[4]

On Christmas Day 1994 *Nightside,* a new TV show on NBC, reported that Chet Atkins had died that year. In fact it was actor Claude Akins who had died. When Chet received the news he went to his office and placed a Mark Twain message on his answering machine: "The reports of my passing have been highly exaggerated."

An article in the next day's *Tennessean* featured an interview with Chet about the newscast: "You know, I wish I'd have seen that, and I'd have known what it would be like when I kick the bucket." Chet was seventy at the time.

"It's a terrible, terrible thing," continued Chet. "I may not get booked this year because people will think I'm gone and mark me off of their list of artists who book with symphonies and so on. I don't know where they got their information or anything. People used to get me and Claude Akins confused. We used to go to golf tournaments and I'd get his calls and he'd get mine."

On Christmas Day Chet said he "had my grandkids over and my daughter and people like that. It beats what it would have been if NBC was right. Considering that I may have one foot in the grave, I'm doing pretty good."[5]

During the Grammy Awards, held in March in Los Angeles, Chet won Best Country Instrumental for "Young Thing."

Chet played on a Billy Edd Wheeler album, *Songs I Have Written with Chet,* in March. The album included "Hormones" (with the hook line supplied by Paul Yandell), "Working for the Minimum Wage," and "I Still Write Your Name in the Snow." On "Django" Chet tells of the admiration he had for Django Reinhardt. After the vocal, the original recording of Django playing "I'll See You in My Dreams" comes on and Chet plays along with him, overdubbing from the original.

The Case knife company created the Chet Atkins Pocket Knife, available from Smoky Mountain Knife Works. The company gave Chet a number of the knives, which he gifted to relatives and others as a good way to save money.

Chet spent a day in May taping an instructional video, *The Guitar of Chet Atkins*, where he played nine songs, including "When You Wish upon a Star" and "Young Thing," in tempo and then slowly while explaining them. During a short monologue Chet reflected on his career.

Chet met Kevin King in 1981 when King, a magician, performed magic tricks after a celebrity golf tournament in Paducah, Kentucky. Chet loved magic tricks and sometimes tried to include them in his show, but "he didn't practice enough," said King, who taught Chet some tricks of the trade. After King performed his magic tricks at the golf tournament, Chet and other celebrities wanted him to perform at their golf tournaments. King thus moved to Nashville, where he and Chet became fast friends. During the mid- to late eighties and nineties, King and his wife had a standing Wednesday night dinner with Chet and Leona at the Hillwood Country Club.

In the summer of 1995 Gibson presented Chet with a Super 4000 guitar as part of Gibson recognizing and honoring the top three endorsers of custom-built instruments: Bill Monroe for mandolins, Earl Scruggs for banjos, and Chet for the Super 4000 guitar. Paul Yandell made several design suggestions, including extending the frets all the way to the edge of the bound fretboard, and chose the finish color, a rose-to-cream yellow sunburst.

The BBC ran an interview with Chet and Mark Knopfler hosted by Pete Frame and Devin Hubert in 1995. Asked about his style of guitar playing, Chet explained, "It is really a pseudo-classic style, it's like—play a little rhythm with your thumb and then you start adding tones, and I had my own little orchestra after awhile and I could play and get into more intricate things."

Knopfler shared, "The first time I heard Chet Atkins, I was probably about 14 or 15 and I just assumed it was multi-tracking and that it was impossible to play all those notes at one time on a guitar. So, I just didn't think it was possible."

"I remember some guy said something about how Chet had obviously multi-tracked all this stuff, you know, and it is the only time I have ever known Chet to be upset," said Knopfler, "and he actually wrote into this particular publication to whoever it was and said, 'so and so should understand that there was no double tracking and with practice, it is perfectly possible to [do this].'" Asked about his influence on British guitarists, Chet said, "The big influence was on George Harrison, I suppose, because he played my guitar and he wrote a liner for one of my albums once, and you couldn't have anyone better than that as an admirer because he was so very popular all over the world."

Chet was a known hypochondriac and scared of dying. He wanted to always be able to contact a doctor, to the point of carrying a short wave radio on the golf course. However, he had a reason to suspect something was wrong in 1995, when he was diagnosed with cancer and his doctors could only slow it. A hip fracture also set him back. He still tried to play when he could, but it became clear to him that he was fading. He poured out his thoughts in a letter to Garrison Keillor and painfully confessed that "my passion for the guitar and for fame is slowly dying and it makes me sad. I never thought my love for the guitar would fade. There are a lot of reasons, as we get older the high frequencies go, music doesn't sound so good. And for some damn reason after hearing so many great players, I lose the competitive desire."

Anxious to tell more while he still could, he collaborated with Missouri publisher Russ Cochran, a longtime Chet fan and guitar collector, on *Me and My Guitars*. It was a lavish work of new photos of important guitars in his career, starting with the Silvertone he'd gotten in Luttrell along with many new reminiscences. He was more reflective as he told these new tales and reiterated his joyful rediscovery of the early records he once dismissed as rough and sloppy.[6]

CHAPTER 62

“Spanish Fandango” was published in sheet music with what became known as “Spanish tuning” or “open G.” In this tuning the strings are, from low to high, D-G-D-G-B-D, stated Pat Kirtley in an article, “Chet’s Alternate Tunings.” Many early guitarists played in “open” tunings, especially those who played slide or steel guitar.

Chet’s two most often used alternate tunings were drop D and Spanish tuning. These tunings don’t require a drastic relearning of the instrument, but they offer interesting advantages. A normally tuned guitar naturally favors music in the keys of E, A, and, to some degree, C. Go to drop D, where the low E string is tuned down to D, and the guitar opens up arrangements in the key of D, and D-G-D-G-B-E makes the guitar more friendly to tunes in the key of G. Songs that Chet recorded in drop D include “David’s Dance,” “El Condor Pasa,” “Georgy Girl,” “Estrellita,” and “The Entertainer.” Songs in D tuning (D-G-D-G-B-E) include “Vincent,” “Both Sides Now,” “Kentucky,” “Wheels,” and “Yellow Bird.” Chet used open G tuning on “Black Mountain Rag,” “Cloudy and Cool,” “Spanish Fandango,” and “Old Double Shuffle.” Chet also used unique tunings or alternate tunings on “Steeplechase Lane,” “Honolulu Blue,” “Waiting for Susie B,” “Flop Eared Mule,” and “Black Jack.” *Solo Flights, Alone, Class Guitar,* and *Almost Alone* favored alternated tunings.[1]

Chet’s *Almost Alone* saw him recording an album almost alone at home in his CA Workshop. Many of the songs were personal; “A Little Mark Musik” was written for Mark Knopfler, “Waiting for Suzy B” for Suzy Bogguss, and “Maybelle” for Maybelle Carter. Chet brought in the Nashville String Machine, a group of session violinists, for some songs, pianist Randy Goodrum played on “A Little Mark Musik” and “I Still Write Your Name in the Snow,” Darryl Dybka played keyboards on “Pu, Wana Hulu,” Randy Howard added fiddle on “Sweet Alla Lee,” and Paul Yandell played acoustic guitar on “Maybelle.” Bergen White did the string arrangements.

Chet said that when he was learning to play people advised him to "stomp your foot" to keep time: "One of my greatest musical thrills happened many years ago when I first heard John Lee Hooker singing the blues, playing his guitar and stomping his foot on a piece of plywood," said Chet. That led Chet to place a microphone by his foot so listeners could "hear my big foot patting" on the song "Big Foot." "Jam Man" was written by Chet and featured him alone on guitar playing a minor-key-based melody. For that song Chet used "an audio looping device called the Jam Man manufactured by the Lexicon company in order to record it. That allowed Chet to layer a number of guitar parts over the recording's initial guitar part." "Happy Again," written by Chet, was inspired by his successfully surviving a serious health scare. This album was his last work as a solo artist; his cancer and declining health made him increasingly weak.[2]

One day Randy Goodrum and his wife Gail were sitting on their porch at home when Chet drove up. He got out of his car and, helped by a cane, brought a cassette player over, "put a cassette in and played this beautiful song and I thought it was great and asked him what he wanted to do with it," said Goodrum. Chet replied, "Nothing. I just wanted to share it with you. I thought this was something Randy and Gail Goodrum would like." Chet then got back in his car and drove off.[3]

Tennessee celebrated its two hundredth birthday in 1996; Chet performed for the Bicentennial Concert at the Ryman Auditorium on May 12. During an interview with reporter Tom Roland of the *Nashville Tennessean* Chet dryly commented on his street: "I'm always careful not to get hurt on that street. It'd be terrible if I got killed on Chet Atkins Place. But whenever I drive by there, I think, 'That's nice—somebody remembers I used to do some things that were important for the growth of the music industry.'"[4]

The theme of the Ryman concert was "Guitar Town Come Alive"; Chet was joined by Steve Wariner, Larry Carlton, and Leo Kottke. "I play better musically than I ever did, but I think I don't have the energy I used to," said Chet. "I don't play with the energy and ignorance and abandon I used to. . . . I play with better taste now—I hope."

At the Ryman concert Chet, with Paul Yandell, Randy Houser, Johnny Johnson, and Randy Goodrum, used Chet's "Jam Man" machine to do a new version of "Stompin' at the Savoy." At the end of the show all the performers returned to the stage and Chet led them in "Does Anybody Here Play the . . . We Need a Player in the Band." Each musician took a turn on the tune before Chet finished it off with a hot jazzy fiddle break.[5]

In the June issue of *Mister Guitar* Garrison Keillor wrote an article titled "A Few Thoughts about Chet." "I am awfully fond of Chet. He is always good company. He is full of jokes and is an accomplished storyteller way beyond me and a gifted mimic, a real student of human nature. I forgave him long ago for being a Republican. I wasn't always a big fan of his music—like most northern folkies, I tended to look down on the 'Nashville Sound' as somehow inauthentic—but Chet is completely authentic, and doesn't have to try to be. It's there."

"It's amazing to me that a man can love his instrument so much after all these years the way Chet does. But he does. Chet picks up a guitar the way other people pick up a phone or turn on the TV or pop open a beer on a hot day. Once I was at his house and we were watching a golf tournament on television and Leona was talking about seeing Bill Monroe on an awards show a few nights before and Chet reached over for his guitar and picked out a Monroe tune and went into a long stream-of-consciousness medley of country songs. It was the prettiest thing.

"Leona turned down the sound and Chet played this amazing string of old tear-jerker ballads (which he dearly loves, things like 'Pictures on the Wall' and 'Mother dear, come bathe my forehead') and Hank Williams and Lefty Frizzell and a little Django and Carter Family and a Bach chorale and the Beatles' 'Lady Madonna' and 'The Old Oaken Bucket' and so forth. I wished I had a tape recorder. What a gifted and good man."[6]

The twelfth annual Chet Atkins Appreciation Society Convention was held in July and featured performances by over forty of the world's greatest guitarists, with Chet and his group headlining the event on their Saturday night concert. A highlight for members was "A Session with Chet," where Chet spent about forty-five minutes with a small group talking and answering questions. He told the group that the *Almost Alone* album was something he had been wanting to do for a long time. The record label did not want to release the album, but Chet overruled them and intended to do his next album in the same solo style. He also revealed that pianist Frankie Carle was one of his early influences.

In a moving exchange Chet gave Paul Yandell his 1950 repertoire book. In that little book Chet kept track of all the songs that he knew and played.

The concert began with Chet performing "Gallopin' on the Guitar," with Paul Yandell on guitar, Pat Bergeson on guitar and harmonica, bassist Johnny Johnson, drummer Randy Hauser, and dancer Ted Walters. At the end of his set he told the CAAS audience that he was lucky to make a living by doing what he enjoyed so much and thanked the CAAS membership for helping to support his habit. Chet finished his set with "The Next Time I'm in Town." A standing ovation and ongoing applause called him back onstage, where he offered a solo rendition of "Vincent."[7]

After the concert Marcel Dadi and Bob Saxton went to the Kentucky Thumbpickers and Fingerstyle Guitar Room and joined a jam session, where they played for over an hour. After he stopped playing Marcel stayed into the early morning hours of Sunday, talking and entertaining "with his sparkling personality and off-the-wall sense of humor." It had been a memorable convention for Dadi; he had been inducted into the Walkway of Stars at the Country Music Hall of Fame, visited the NAMM (National Association of Music Merchandisers) convention, and arranged to have Taylor guitars introduced to France.

On Wednesday evening Marcel Dadi and Guy Dupont boarded TWA Flight 800 at Kennedy International Airport that was headed to Paris and then on to Rome. Twelve minutes after takeoff the plane exploded over the Atlantic Ocean.

Clarissa Cater, Chet's assistant, called Chet and Leona on Thursday morning. "It was one of the hardest things I ever had to do," she said, "to tell them the possibility of Marcel and Guy being on that TWA 800 flight." After speaking with Chet she telephoned Mark Pritcher, who came to Nashville to be with Chet, Leona, and Merle. "On that day, I don't know what we would have done without him," said Clarissa. Chet had been the best man at Dadi's wedding and stated, "I have lost one of my best friends. Sometimes I think he loved me as if I were one of his family. I feel the same way about him."

Les Paul had a regular Monday night gig at the Old Iridium Restaurant and Jazz Club in New York. On Memorial Day, Monday, May 27, Chet dropped by and sat at a table near the stage while Les and his trio played some opening numbers. Chet had his Gibson "Fleur De Lis" Studio Classic with him and joined Les onstage for "Stompin' at the Savoy," "It's Been a Long, Long Time," and "Avalon" from their *Chester and Lester* album and "Limehouse Blues" from *Guitar Monsters*. Chet then returned to his seat while Paul played a half dozen more songs until the first show ended. Chet left the club, signing autographs as he made his way out.[8]

Inspired by Les Paul's weekly gig, Chet began a series of Monday night concerts at the Caffe Milano. Chet had booked eight consecutive Monday nights for two 90-minute sets in the 250-seat listening room. On that first evening Allison Krauss attended and sang the Lefty Frizzell hit "That's the Way Love Goes." Suzy Bogguss performed "After You've Gone," Billy Edd Wheeler did a duet with Chet on "I Still Write Your Name in the Snow," and Mark O'Connor played a couple of fiddle tunes. Chet's band included guitarist Paul Yandell, guitarist and harmonica player Pat Bergeson, bassist Johnny Johnson, and drummer Randy Hauser. During the evening they performed "The Lion Sleeps Tonight," "I Got a Woman," "Tennessee Waltz," and "Vincent."

Chet ended his shows with some fancy fingerpicking, then in the middle of the song he took off his guitar and left the stage as the fingerpicking continued without interruption. Paul Yandell knew every lick that Chet played. It was a novel and dramatic ending.[9]

The first annual Chet Atkins CGP Festival was held in September in Mountain Hill, Georgia, where Chet spent his teen years. On Friday Chet attended a ceremony at the auditorium where Chet had performed as a student and talked about his school days. That evening a fundraising dinner included the auctioning of a Gibson ST. On Saturday Chet was scheduled to perform but a heavy rain fell, so the concert was moved to Sunday, when Chet and his band performed under beautiful skies.[10]

Following renovations, a historical marker was erected outside the school: "The school had 9 classrooms and a 436 seat auditorium to serve both elementary and high school students. In this auditorium Chet Atkins, member of the Country Music Hall of Fame and a student at Mountain Hill School during the 1930s perfected his distinctive guitar style."

Chet had been in Paris during Musicians Days (Fete De La Musique) where "people bring their instruments and play," said Chet. "They have bands playing on the street, and it's just a great day over there." That event inspired Chet to approach Tom Morales and Moose Moore of TomKats Catering, who had organized and promoted the Dancin' in the District series of concerts in Nashville and suggested they stage a music festival similar to the annual event in Paris. "I think the musicians, too many times, are overlooked," said Chet. "Without them, records wouldn't be much. What's responsible for the Nashville Sound and everything that's happened here is the quality of musicians in town, and I think they should be honored. Of course, we'll have some singers around to draw in the people in case the instrumentalists don't."

Plans called for mostly free concerts, workshops by and for musicians, night club performances, educational outreach programs, and informal musical events throughout the city. Chet declared a threefold purpose: "to honor the musicians," to "raise money to teach our youngsters music," and to provide an excuse for musicians to "get together and play music." Chet did not want his name attached to the festival but finally relented after he was persuaded that his name made it easier to land corporate sponsors and attract musicians. "I don't want it to look like I'm blowing my horn," said Chet. "I didn't have that idea at all." Chet hoped that city, state, and federal legislators would declare June 20, 1997—his seventy-third birthday—National Musicians Day.[11]

Morales agreed with Chet's vision, and in November it was announced that Chet Atkins' Musician Days would be held in Nashville next June with hopes that it would become an annual event. It would be held three days after Fan Fair and three weeks after Summer Lights, a popular series of concerts in Nashville.[12]

Chet was not well; cancer had returned, this time in his brain. Chet contacted Blake Chancey, his A&R representative with Sony, and told him to keep the news of his cancer secret because people would "write him off" if they knew.

Tommy Emmanuel came to Nashville in 1996 for Fan Fair and to record his album *Midnight Drive*; and Chet played on "How Many Sleeps." The executives at CBS Records, led by Chet, heard Emmanuel play during Fan Fair and "got excited and suggested that we do something together," said Emmanuel. "So Chet called me in Australia, and casually asked if we might do something."

That call came because the label knew that he would not be able to finish the solo album he was working on. "He started sending me tapes and I sent him tapes and we started piecing together our ideas and then I came back over and recorded," said Tommy.

Chet canceled his Caffe Milano dates in December, lamenting that his schedule was just "too hectic." The truth was that Chet's health was in serious decline. Although it was announced that Chet would return to his Caffe Milano shows in January, those shows had taken their toll. Chet thought he could follow Les Paul's lead but discovered that organizing and performing the concerts drained him. They had become more trouble than they were worth.

During that downtime Chet was in his studio with Tommy Emmanuel recording *The Day Finger Pickers Took Over the World.* Recording with Chet "is a good experience," said Emmanuel. "He's very open to suggestions and very forward with his ideas as well. He's always full of good ideas and always wants to try something different, to make a tune more interesting. Always ideas, ideas. . . . He has his way of doing things. He always puts a guide down, and he would re-do his part at his leisure with no one around. He likes to do that. But he's one of those guys who's so good that if we have to sit down and do something he'll get it the first time."[13]

The way the album got its title song goes back to a TV taping for TNN in Austin to promote *Read My Licks.* David Hungate, Chet's producer and bass player on that album, had fallen while mowing his yard and broken his ankle, so he couldn't make the Austin date. Dave Pomeroy had never played with Chet, but Hungate and Fred Kewley knew him and recommended him for the TV taping.

"The Day That Bass Players Took Over the World" was originally performed by Emily Kaitz at the Kerrville Folk Festival in Texas, where Guy Clark heard it and brought it back to Nashville. Dave Pomeroy heard it, added a second bridge, and rearranged the harmonies and received songwriter credit with Kaitz. Chet was looking for a place to play on Monday nights, and Pomeroy had a regular Monday night gig at the Exit/In. One night Chet dropped by unannounced and watched Dave's show, which featured him doing "The Day Bass Players Took Over the World." The next day Chet's secretary called Pomeroy and said that Chet wanted to speak to him. Pomeroy was flabbergasted. Chet asked for the lyrics to the song, which he referred to as "the funny song," to be sent to him typed and double spaced. He told Dave he might record it. Dave dropped off the lyrics and a copy of the song to Chet's office.

Then—silence. Dave never heard anything until he received a call one day from the record label wanting to know about the publishing and songwriter credits for "The Day Finger Pickers Took Over the World." Pomeroy gave them the information and then asked, "What's the name of the album?" "You don't know?" the woman replied before she informed him that he had the title song. Chet and Tommy Emmanuel had changed the song quite a bit but never requested songwriting or publishing credit.[14]

Chet was in poor health during the recording of the album, weakened by his brain cancer, so the fact that he could record in his home studio was a great help. Chet rested and worked on the album when health allowed.

Chet wanted to write a song in the key of B to be called "To B or Not to B" and enlisted the help of Randy Goodrum. "I hated playing in the key of B," said Goodrum. "We came up with this cool little melody then tried to find some subtle things we could weave in to make it more interesting." During the recording, Tommy Emmanuel "struggled." "I had a few passes at getting my solo and I wanted it to be really spontaneous but yet very memorable and all the things you look for in a good solo," said Emmanuel. "I was hoping for all those things and I struggled a little while he just walked in the control room. I said, 'Hey, Chief' to ask his advice but before I could ask him anything, he just turned around and said, 'Well, you can't beat the melody' and he walked away. So I started my solo by quoting the melody and I got it on the next take."

The last song on the album, "Smokey Mountain Lullaby," was written by Chet and had originally been released on Amy Grant's *The Gingham Dog and the Calico Cat*. They needed one more song for the album, so Chet suggested a duet on "Smokey Mountain Lullaby," but his health had taken a serious downturn and he was scheduled for brain surgery the next day.

Tommy Emmanuel was staying at Chet's home. Chet woke him up at three in the morning and asked if they could record the song right then and there. Chet and Tommy walked downstairs to the studio in their pajamas and sat down for their final number. "We sat down and worked it out and on the first take, there it was," said Emmanuel. Chet played his Ramirez classical, but the guitar was tuned with the low E dropped to D and the low A to G, while the remaining strings, D-G-B-E, were left in standard turning but every string was tuned a step down. The song was actually in the key of F, but the fingering was in G.[15]

A few hours later, Chet underwent surgery that left him unable to play at the level he was accustomed to for the rest of his life. Although his musical abilities were diminished, Chet continued to practice.

Songs on the album *The Day That Finger Pickers Took Over the World* include "Borsalino," "To 'B' or Not to 'B,'" "The Day Fingerpickers Took Over the World," "Tip Toe Through the Bluegrass," "News from the Outback," "Ode to Mel Bay," "Dixie McGuire," "Saltwater," "Mr. Guitar," "Road to Gundaghi/Waltzing Matilda," and "Smokey Mountain Lullaby."

The film *Michael*, starring John Travolta, premiered on Christmas Day. Music in the film included several numbers by Chet: "Young Thing," "Ave Maria," "Sweet Dreams" (with Mark Knopfler), and "Dream" (with George Benson). The songs were heard throughout the movie, exposing Chet Atkins to a new audience.

CHAPTER 63

In January Chet returned to Caffe Milano on Monday nights. He told a reporter that he "took off the middle of November to do an album, and then I got a little physical problem and had a little trouble getting my strength back." The truth was not revealed to the public.

Chet was interviewed on two of TNN's *Life and Times* series, one for Eddy Arnold, broadcast in January, and the other for Willie Nelson, broadcast in March.[1]

Chet Atkins won his last Grammy at the fortieth annual Grammy Awards held on February 26, 1997, at Madison Square Garden in New York. "Jam Man," from his *Almost Alone* album, won Best Country Instrumental that year. In March *The Day That Finger Pickers Took Over the World* was released; this was the last album of new music that Chet released during his lifetime.

The February 1997 issue of *Guitar World* magazine listed the "100 greatest guitarists of all time." The list appeared in alphabetical order, so Chet's name was on top, spotlighting him and his contributions to the guitar. "Merle Travis and I taught this country to play finger-style guitar, and I want credit for that sometime," said Chet; increasingly, people became aware. Asked what makes a great guitarist, Chet responded, "Obviously, it takes a little talent and a hell of a lot of practice. Everyone has limitations, so one should work with them. It is fine to imitate, but eventually you must express your own voice. Also, listen to a lot of folks on the way up. I don't believe there are many times when I haven't learned something after watching great players and, sometimes, mediocre ones."

"To my way of thinking, there is not a great musician alive who hasn't practically slept with an instrument for years while learning," said Chet. "There are no short cuts! Learn the fretboard from stem to stern and practice scales for every known chord. Play for the love of it. Forget about monetary success and play what touches your ear. If financial success doesn't come, at least you have had a blast."[2]

In late March Chet suffered another bout with cancer, this time in his colon. He did not attend the news conference that announced the Chet Atkins Musicians Days scheduled for June in Nashville. He had canceled several of his Monday night concerts at the Caffe Milano for "minor surgery." The surgery was to remove a "low malignancy" tumor from his colon.[3]

Chet Atkins Musicians Day was a dream of Chet's. A press conference on June 9 about the event announced the artist lineup. Chet was questionable to attend the Musicians Days, although it was announced that his cancer was "in remission." He had been out of the public eye since late March, when the seventy-three-year-old canceled several of his Monday night concerts at Caffe Milano.

On Wednesday evening, June 25, the Ryman hosted a tribute to Chet, "Witness History," with over twenty artists participating. During the tribute an "ailing, but smiling, humble Chet" did appear. During the four-hour show Chet, wearing a white fedora, sat in the front row beside Leona. He smiled and nodded as he received numerous compliments.

Garrison Keillor was scheduled to host the tribute but canceled at the last minute, so Chet called Ray Stevens to host. Stevens argued that he could not host a show like that at the last minute, "but Chet had a way of convincing you," said Stevens.[4]

Artists were backed by an all-star band that included guitarists Jimmy Capps and Jerry Kennedy, drummer Buddy Harman, and bass player Roy Huskey Jr. They opened the show by playing "Crazy" and "Last Date." Drummer D. J. Fontana, guitarist Scotty Moore, and keyboardist David Briggs performed a medley of Elvis's tunes, and Steve Wariner played a neoclassical acoustic solo, "For Chester B," that fit the New Age sound.

Chet asked Janis Ian to be on the concert, but she was concerned that her guitar playing was not at the level of the other musicians on the bill. During her part of the concert she said that several years earlier Chet had asked her "why I didn't take guitar solos." I replied, "I can't play as fast as those guys do, Chet." He considered this for a moment, then said, "Heck, if you can't play a whole lot faster, play a whole lot slower." That led to her guitar solo on "Welcome to Acousticville," which Ian played "winking at Chet on the end chord. He rose slightly, tipped his hat at me, and winked back."[5]

The climax of the evening came when Mark Knopfler took the stage and said, "This is the proudest moment of my whole life," before presenting Atkins with a special Chettie award.

Accepting the Chettie, Chet said, "First thing, I'm just so sick of hearing how great I am. What burns me up, I haven't heard Owen Bradley's name mentioned one damn time," then went on to salute Owen Bradley, Ken Nelson, and Anita Kerr and thanked a long line of people and organizations who made the inaugural Chet Atkins Musicians Days a reality. Chet was unable to play guitar but sang harmony with Knopfler on "Next Time I'm in Town."[6]

The thirteenth annual Convention of the Chet Atkins Appreciation Society began on Wednesday, July 9. On Saturday evening there was a "Special Concert for Chet," who attended with Leona and Merle. Chet did not play but was in a good mood. Before the concert began he was onstage accepting awards, drawing winners for various contests, and joking around. The concert began with Paul Yandell playing a medley of Chet's hits. Tommy Emmanuel closed the show with songs from *The Day Finger Pickers Took Over the World*.[7]

There were stories that, after his brain surgery, Chet would never play again, but he worked and practiced until he could play—although not at the level he was accustomed to. On September 20 Chet performed in Madisonville, Kentucky, with the Nashville Symphony. Accompanying Chet on the trip were road manager George Lunn and his band, Paul Yandell, Johnny Johnson, Pat Bergeson, and percussionist Tom Roady. Chet was escorted onstage by his daughter Merle as he received a standing ovation. During the concert Chet played "A Little Mark Musik," "I Still Can't Say Goodbye," "Vincent," and "There'll Be Some Changes Made," at which point Chet donned his latest wild wig and sunglasses.[8]

Three days later, at Planet Hollywood in downtown Nashville, the Nordoff-Robbins Music Therapy Foundation presented Chet with the inaugural Chet Atkins Humanitarian Award. It was announced that Paul McCartney had funded two Chet Atkins music scholarships to be given every year in conjunction with his Liverpool Foundation for underprivileged children in the United Kingdom.[9] On September 26 Chet, Duane Eddy, Scotty Moore, and James Burton were inducted into the Hollywood RockWalk. During the event the inductees placed their hand prints and signatures in concrete slabs, which were shipped back to Los Angeles.[10]

At the end of October Chet saw a section of Interstate 185, which runs through two west Georgia counties north of Columbus, named after him. Present at the event was Chet's stepmother, Tommie Swigart. The event began at the Mountain Hill Schoolhouse; Chet thanked the group and talked about leaving Luttrell for Hamilton, Georgia, when he was a child. Mike Voltz, representing Gibson, presented Chet with a new Chet Atkins model guitar.[11]

Chet continued to receive awards; on November 21 the Nashville Community Foundation presented Chet and Owen Bradley with the Joe Kraft Humanitarian Award in honor of their community service. There were over five hundred music industry figures, business leaders, and philanthropists at the event. In early December *Billboard* magazine honored Chet with its Century Award, "the highest honor for distinguished creative achievement." He appeared on the cover of the December 6 issue announcing that award, which was presented while Chet was at home. He prerecorded a video to be played for the event, describing leaving his position at RCA: "It just became difficult to work there because, in the end, I was always seen as an old-timer, the old guard, and I understood that."[12]

Nashville's entertainment industry was facing sweeping changes. In 1995 Westinghouse Electric purchased CBS and in 1997 bought the Nashville Network and CMT from Gaylord Entertainment. The Opryland Theme Park, built in 1972, was closed in 1997. On the last day of 1997 Floyd Cramer died of cancer at the age of sixty-four.

Health problems continued to plague Chet; in February 1998 he broke his hip. In March it was announced that Chet Atkins Musicians Days in Nashville would be held in June with Mark Knopfler headlining a show at the Ryman.

On April 11 Chet was inducted into the Thumbpickers Hall of Fame along with Merle Travis, Ike Everly, Kennedy Jones, Mose Rager, Arnold Schultz, and Grandpa Jones. The event was held in conjunction with the fifth annual Mose Rager Day. The Thumbpickers Hall of Fame is in Drakesboro, Muhlenberg County, Kentucky. Chet came but was unable to stay for the evening ceremony. John Knowles accepted his award.[13]

Chet was interviewed for *Interview* magazine around his birthday (he turned seventy-four) and was asked what he was doing for his birthday. "Trying to forget it, I guess," said Chet. "And to remember when I was younger."

Chet was pleased that the Musicians Day Festival was being held in Nashville again, but "the only thing I disliked about it is that they put my name on it. I didn't want it that way at all when I pitched it to the people. I just wanted it to be Nashville Musicians Days, and it will be that way eventually when I'm gone. They'll take my name off it; they say they will, anyway."

"I'm doing pretty good," said Chet when asked about his health. "I feel good and everything but I have a little trouble staying vertical. It's very easy for me to fall. I can play single string guitar pretty well now. Fingerpicking gives me a little challenge because I had a brain tumor, you know. When you have that, it bothers the use you need to have of your little finger and the finger next to it on your left hand. I've got to get over that with therapy and so on, and hope to play somewhat in the manner that I used to play years ago. Actually, that'll never happen, but maybe I'll play something that will be different and prettier."

"I think country music is as good as ever," answered Chet when asked about the state of the industry. "I think it's different in that it's more pop than it used to be. That's fine. You've got to give the young folks what they desire. Tastes keep changing, and, if they don't, music dies."

"I'm a golfer," said Chet, who paused and then corrected himself. "Actually, I was a golfer, but not anymore. . . . I try to not get sidetracked and get into too many things that take me away from the guitar."

When asked who he would like to record with Chet replied, "I'd like some time to do something with Paul McCartney because I admire him and his songwriting so much. We've done some things together, but not an album or anything. I did record with Paul once. We recorded a song his father wrote."[14]

The Chet Atkins Musicians Days festival was followed by the Chet Atkins Appreciation Society Convention from July 29 to August 1. The 1998 convention was the fourteenth, and it had certainly grown from its earliest days with forty-eight workshops or close-up concerts and twenty-eight manufacturers, luthiers, publishers, record dealers, suppliers, booths, and exhibits. The Saturday night concert was so big that overflow rooms were needed in a nearby hotel. Tommy Emmanuel played "I'll See You in My Dreams," before Chet took the stage and performed a few song excerpts. He finished his short set with "Next Time I'm in Town." Tommy Emmanuel then took over and closed the show.[15]

On November 28 the "CMA's 40th Anniversary Celebration" was shown on TV with Chet as part of Randy Scruggs's "Crown Jewels All Star Band," which included Earl Scruggs, Vince Gill, Duane Eddy, Steve Wariner, Anita Cochran, Leon Russell, Chad Cromwell, and Don Was. The ensemble performed "Lonesome Reuben."

CHAPTER 64

In January 1999 *Nashville Life* magazine published a profile of Chet, written by Beverly Keel.

The article began by noting that Chet was seventy-four and walked with a cane. He'd had an operation to remove a malignant brain tumor, followed by twenty-five radiation treatments that had left him unable to control his fretting hand. He had been practicing until he fell into a column in his house, jamming his thumb and hurting his finger. "It will heal up in a month or so and I can play some jobs around town," said Chet. "I would like to play Café Milano if I get into shape. I'm just getting the strength back in my hands. I try to play a little at home to keep my callouses up," said Chet. "They go away like ice cream in the summer if you don't use them enough."

The interview took place in Chet's office, which had tan walls with almost no pictures or awards. On his assistant's desk was one of his fourteen Grammys, while another Grammy and awards from BMI and *Country Weekly* stood on the mantel. The *Billboard* issue honoring Atkins sat on a cardboard box in the corner.

Chet was wearing jeans, a blue blazer, a blue-and-white striped shirt, and an unbuttoned, mismatched black-and-gold vest. A red bandana was tied around his neck, and a black fedora hid his thinning hair. Keel noted that Atkins "exudes a timeless dignity and majesty" and quoted June Carter: "He is a very private guy and a very classy guy. I've always felt Chet is a cut above the rest. He's a man's man."

There were some platinum albums on the wall and an autographed Bettie Page photo. Page was a famous pin-up girl during the fifties and appeared in a number of men's magazines. Chet had corresponded with her. There was also a framed picture of Atkins with Jimmy Carter, and tucked into that picture frame was a photograph of Carl Perkins, taken by Second Lady Tipper Gore and inscribed "To Chet, with love, Tipper Gore." Obviously, she had confused the two guitar players.

"I don't do much," said Chet when asked about his activities, although the reporter noted that he was "apparently forgetting he recently produced songs on Alison Krauss and Mary Chapin Carpenter on Sony's *Tribute to Tradition* and has another TV album coming out soon." "I come here and sign some checks and say hello and go upstairs to my office and return some calls," said Chet. "I try to think of somebody to go to lunch with who might be interesting and who will pick up the check," with the journalist noting that "self-deprecation is an Atkins trademark."

"I was a Depression child, and I never forget that," said Chet. "I don't even know how much money I have. My accountant started telling me one day and I said I didn't want to know." Keel noted that "the frequent firings early in his career, coupled with a longing for his father's acceptance and love, caused Atkins to be insecure about his abilities as a guitar player throughout most of his career, even after he became internationally famous."

"I used to be a hell of a player and really didn't know it," remarked Chet. "I think I was playing my best about 20 or 25 years ago. When I listen to those old records I think, 'Boy, I was good then. No wonder so many people copied me.' But I never thought so then. I always thought I was inadequate and always worked to try to get better. I never felt, 'This is great.' I worked so hard to get away from mediocrity. Once in awhile I would succeed, and you hear that stuff on my albums."

"I just love what I do and I love people," said Chet. "Whatever I want to do, I do. I don't ever fulfill all my goals, but I try. About the time I think I've accomplished something, I hear somebody else who is way ahead of me, so I work harder to be different. I think what has gotten me so much attention is that I have done what I've wanted to do and I had an undying love for the guitar and what I could make out of it. I try to record something the public will like, and they are naturally tunes that I like or I wouldn't record them. I don't ever want to be hungry again."

Chet admitted to another reporter, "The isolation, the poverty—that's what I came from. That's what makes you fight. That's what makes you learn. That's what makes you develop your talent, if you have any, to try and get out of that damned place. I 'picked' my way out of East Tennessee." About dying, Chet shared, "I haven't been maudlin about it. I don't worry much about it. Well, if I die, maybe it will be sudden and I won't care. But you can't predict that. You can't work out your own destiny; somebody else does it for you." Asked about his parents' divorce, Chet said, "It happened when I was so young. My dad just went down to the spring house where I was playing and said, 'Well, kiddies, goodbye. I'm leaving.' And I thought he would come back as he always did, but he didn't come back for a year. He came back about once a year, and he would bring presents for my sister and brother, but he never brought me anything" (a lone tear slowly falls along the right cheek; he fights to get the words out). "Stuff like that will make you tough. But I loved him. I was good to him until he died and I'm proud of that. I took better care of him than any of his kids."

"I never could be mean to people because I know how it is when you are raised up like that, without any love or compassion," continued Chet. "He never thought I would amount to anything."

After Chet became well-known, his father "would stop people in restaurants and say, 'Do you know my son Chet Atkins?' and they would say 'No, I don't,'" said Chet. "I would say, 'Dad, don't do that, damn it. I don't want to hear that stuff.'" Chet was secretly pleased when his father did that but always thought, "Why didn't he give me some encouragement years ago when I needed it so badly? But I'm glad. I wouldn't change a damn thing, I really wouldn't."

"I used to get blamed a lot for taking [country music] uptown too much, and I apologized for it," said Chet. "I guess I had a guilt complex that day, but I didn't deserve to have one. I finally got into a position as a producer where I could tell people what to do and change the direction of the music and hopefully make it better. I kind of took the public along with me."

Chet had been fighting various cancers for twenty-five years. The first was when he had a tumor removed from his colon. "I was voted in the Country Music Hall of Fame that year because everybody thought I would be dead in a few months," he said. He was forty-nine at the time. Prostate cancer followed, then lung cancer, then a brain tumor.

"I learned I'm a cry baby," said Chet. "I learned that I'm a coward, that I don't want to die. I want to keep on playing music. But I realize that as you get older, you may have four or five more years to live and you've got to use your time as intelligently as you can. I do it by being nice to my family and learning to play the guitar again."

As for his legacy, Chet said he hopes people will remember "that I was a nice fellow and that I helped a lot of artists get over the humps. I just hope it continues after I'm gone. I think of things like, how long is it going to last? I think, will they know me after I'm gone? Will they remember what I've contributed to the art of playing guitar? I don't think they will and I don't think they should, but I wish they would."[1]

On January 12 Chet appeared on the *Crook and Chase Show* and played "Stompin' at the Savoy." Asked about his health after his surgery, he shared, "It's difficult to converse with people and think of the words I want to use." He then spoke about the time his father left home and promised all the children he'd bring them back a gift: he did for all but Chet. He said a young reporter had asked, "You've had cancer five times in the last 25 years. In an odd way, are you almost getting used to it?" Chet replied, "No, it always scares the hell out of me."[2]

In March Belmont University honored Chet with their Applause Award for his "artistic significance and his encouragement of excellence in music education around the world."[3]

Groundbreaking for the new Country Music Hall of Fame, which was moving from Music Row to a downtown location south of Broadway, occurred in June during Fan Fair. A marching band was supposed to be part of the festivities, but John Knowles said that "didn't sound like country music to me." Soon he and some friends arrived at the idea of an all-guitar marching band. "When I told Chet about it, he liked the idea so I asked him to be 'Honorary Strum Major,'" said Knowles. Chet agreed, so Knowles gathered a marching guitar band that played and sang "You Are My Sunshine" and "Wildwood Flower." The band marched three blocks, from the Ryman Auditorium to the site of the new Hall of Fame with Chet leading the way in a golf cart.[4]

On September 23 Chet gave the keynote address to the Audio Engineering Society in New York; he was accompanied by his grandson, Jonathan Russell, who was a mastering engineer, and Denny Purcell, owner of Georgetown Mastering. A Chet Atkins Country Gentleman guitar that was twenty-eight feet long and weighed three thousand pounds was installed over the Hard Rock Café in downtown Nashville. Chet was on hand to flip the switch to light it up.[5]

In November RCA Studio B was closed. It was owned by the Country Music Foundation and had been refurbished in 1996. Since the new Hall of Fame would be located downtown, the Country Music Foundation had to reassess its connection with the property. Mike Curb purchased the studio, took care of the upkeep, and created an arrangement where the Hall of Fame could conduct tours.

Chet Atkins's last recorded performance probably occurred in December 1999 when he played "Alabama Jubilee" with Roy Clark and accompanied Barbara Fairchild on "Vincent" during TNN's *Ryman Country Homecoming*.[6]

CHAPTER 65

On January 2, 2000, a statue of Chet was unveiled at the corner of Fifth Avenue North and Union Street. The bronze statue had an empty stool next to Chet playing so anyone could sit and "pick with Chet." The statue was commissioned by the Bank of America, and the sculptor, Russell Faxon, had visited Chet's office to get his measurements. Chet had only one request: "Put my left hand in the middle of the neck so I'll look like a professional," said Chet. "If you put it too low, I'll look like a songwriter. Too high and I'll look like a show-off. Right around the fifth fret would be good."[1]

The day before the unveiling Blake Chancey picked up Chet from his office and they went to lunch. It was a rainy, chilly day, but after lunch Chet wanted Blake to drive by the statue so he could see it. A guard protecting the statue was there, and Chet lowered his window and requested the covering of the statue be removed. The guard did not want to do it, but Chet informed him the statue was "me," so the guard relented. Chet took it in and said, "It doesn't look like me at all." He rolled up his window and they drove off. Privately, Chet fumed because the statue was downtown "where nobody will see it" when it should have been on Music Row. But since the bank paid for the statue, they placed it in front of their offices.[2] At the unveiling ceremony the next day Chet declared, "This is a wonderful statue. It looks a lot like me, too."

The unveiling followed an hour-long reception at the bank for invited guests. Chet was "rather frail" but "nattily dressed in a black jacket and brightly colored scarf." The event was hosted by Vince Gill and attended by approximately 150 people. The program featured classic tunes and Chet's collaborators Suzy Bogguss, Charley Pride, Bobby Bare, and Eddy Arnold, who joked that he first met Atkins "in 1896." Each of the artists performed a song for Chet.[3] (In 2023 the statue was moved to the Musicians Hall of Fame.)

On January 27 Neil Strauss published an article in the *New York Times*, "The Pop Life: A Guitarist Synonymous with a City and a

Sound." The reporter quoted Chet as saying, "I have been real sick" as he went into his office, leaning on the arm of his grandson. "I've had three strokes in the past year. And the city wanted to build a statue" (paused to lean against his cluttered desk) "so, yeah, they thought I was going to bite the dust." The reporter noted that Chet's mother lived to be ninety-two.

The article stated that Chet had "had strokes, a brain tumor and three bouts with cancer," but he "still goes to the office every day he can and is considering recording a new album. On most Saturday mornings he has breakfast with a group." That breakfast group had been formed by Ray Stevens, Ralph Emery, and others "to cheer up Chet."

As he sat at his desk, flipping through phone messages, Chet said, "I was always nice to people but I could have been nicer. I also could have learned more about the guitar. I could have studied it more. I should practice more and I get requests all the time to record from this one and that one. But I don't do it. It's just not productive or fair to the people I work for to do that because I'm not in good shape." When asked about contemporary country music, he sidestepped the question by saying it was not the same country music he grew up with.

The reporter noted that Atkins's voice sometimes trailed off as he talked, that he forgot the question he was asked or started to go through his desk drawers as if he was alone in his office. But overall, said the reporter, "he was as sharp as legend has him being, his mind a treasure chest of information that no book can tell you."

Chet talked to the reporter about Ralph Peer and Steve Sholes and Hank Snow ("a little bitty guy") and Elvis ("a flashy dresser") and Charline Arthur. However, he mostly talked about his childhood in East Tennessee. John Knowles once said that when Chet talked about his childhood and young days he spoke in the present tense.[4]

The third annual Musicians Days was held in April. During a show at the Ryman called "Witness History III: The Twang Years," Duane Eddy was honored and received the Chettie award, named after Chet Atkins. The award was presented to Eddy by John Fogerty. "I always wanted to sing like Hank Williams and play like Chet Atkins," said Eddy. "Unfortunately, I wasn't able to do either."

Chet was at the concert and was helped onstage by Fogerty. He spoke to the crowd briefly, said he was unable to drive, and didn't know if he would need his twenty-year-old Cadillac any more. After the show Marty Stuart said, "My favorite thing was Chet trying to sell a car from the stage. That was the sneakiest, slickest way to sell a Cadillac I've ever seen."[5]

The first full-fledged documentary on Chet, *Chet Atkins: A Life in Music*, was broadcast on September 5.

Steve Wariner had finished his *Holes in the Floor of Heaven* album, so "I called Chet and said, 'Man I got my album done!'" said Wariner. "He goes, 'Bring it over!' This was so unlike him. He said, 'Bring it over, I want to hear it!' So we sat at his kitchen table. I played two or three tracks, then 'Holes' came on. I was thinking, 'I'm boring him.' I stopped the tape, and he grabbed my hand and said, 'What are you doing? I want to hear every bit of this album!' That shocked me. I figured he would want to go about his plans for the day. He listened to the entire record. I could see something was turning in his head, so when the whole album finished playing . . . I don't think he had a tear in his eye, but he almost did. He smiled and said, 'Man, I'm really proud of you!' He said, 'I guess I did alright when I signed you.'"[6]

Chet had stopped playing in public, and Janis Ian asked him why he refused to play for an audience any more. He replied, "Maybe they can't tell, but I can. I can't play as fast any more, and I know I'll never play the same."

"One of the things I learned from Chet toward the end of his life was how to behave like an honest star," said Ian. "Unfailingly courteous and cordial to his fans, he was conscious of their love for him, concerned that they'd worry over his health. As his strength declined, it became more difficult for him to go for lunch; he had trouble walking and it was hard to get in and out of a car. He'd shuffle around the office in slippers, but he still loved company."

Ian stopped by Chet's office one day and found his doctor showing him a new walker. "It was three-wheeled and seemed to give him an easier time balancing than the old one," said Ian. "He practiced up and down the hall, then said, 'All right, let's go get lunch.' We opened the door and handed him the walker. Chet looked at both of us in annoyance and said, 'Heck, I'm a star! I'm not going out with that thing in public!'"

The last time she visited Chet at his home, she brought tuna fish sandwiches. "He was thinner than ever, so frail the whites of his bones seemed to show through the skin," she remembered. She was set to go on a long tour the next week and had "always kept up with him by sending postcards of large-breasted women from around the world." She had a bundle of them packed in her suitcase, ready to send to him.[7]

Boots Randolph "asked Kevin King to set up a little lunch get together because I hadn't seen Chet since he went through all his surgeries," said Randolph. "On our way we stopped to pick up some sandwiches—I think we stopped at Burger King. We sat and talked for awhile. Chet spoke some, but not a lot. We spoke mostly about the past. I felt it was a very important thing for me to do for him because we had been close for years, and he had done so many things over the years to help me. I appreciated it so much. It was getting close to time for me to leave. We hugged and he said, 'Cock, I love you!' Within our circle of friends we called each other 'cock.'"[8]

Chet's old friends would drop by his house. Bob Beckham remembered that "Harry Warner and I used to go out to Chet's house about once a week. We would stop and get some barbecue sandwiches and some sweet tea in those glass jars. Chet would sit on his couch out in the living room and we would eat together. He was going down, you could tell it."

"I called Dolly Parton one day," continued Beckham. "I said, 'Dolly, Chester is not doing too well, it might be a good idea to come out to see him.' Harry and I went into the house to eat with Chet. Chet's sitting on the couch and he said, softly 'Hello Bob, Hello Harry.' I said 'Chester how are you doing?' 'Oh, I'm doing alright I guess.' About ten minutes later, Dolly pulls up, comes into the house wearing a low-cut top and a little short skirt. She walked in there and Chet said loudly 'Dolly! How are you?' I thought, 'Well, you old dog.' They sat there on that couch, Dolly and Chet laughing. She brought some real stuff into his life."[9]

"When Chet was done, he was done," said Steve Wariner. "I used to take him lunch when he was really sick. Sometimes I would go by myself; usually Paul and I would go. A lot of times Chet would point to the guitar and say, 'Play something for me.' He always had a guitar leaning in the corner of the room. I would play for a little while and then I would kind of look at him and try to offer him the guitar. He wouldn't say anything, he got to where he would just look at me and shake his head no. When it came to that point, I knew he wouldn't be around much longer. The guitar was his whole life. You just can't suddenly say, 'That's it.' That was his whole world."[10]

"The last day that I went out to be with him, he was in his wheelchair and was pretty frail but he was in a good mood," said Tommy Emmanuel. "I played for him for quite a while. When it was time to leave, he wanted to go have a nap. I got down on my knees and held him in my arms. He was one of those guys who didn't like you touching him. He held me, put his hand on my face and looked up at the nurse and said, 'There is real affection here.' I told him how much I loved him. I said, 'As long as I live, I will always tell people about you. I will do everything I can in my life to honor you and to show people what you have done for me and hand it on to them.' He said, 'I know you will.' I told him again how much I loved him and he said the same thing to me."

"You know, he was very different that day," stated Emmanuel. "He was very affectionate and sweet, loving like a daddy. I left and arrived back here and the phone rang. It was his nurse and she said, 'I wanted to let you know when you left, Mr. Atkins cried and he said, "I'll never see him again."'"[11]

CHAPTER 66

On May 17, 2001, the new Country Music Hall of Fame, built at a cost of $37 million, opened. Soon after the opening it was announced that Chet was lending a number of his guitars to the Hall of Fame. Paul Yandell brought in the guitars, accepted by John Knowles, deputy director for educational outreach. "Chet and I sat down and talked about his guitars," said Knowles. "These are the ones that Chet played on all his records. When you look at these guitars, you're seeing a workingman's tools for a lifetime of music."

Included were his Gretsch 6120 1954 prototype—orange hollow body—that Chet recorded with and used on the Grand Ole Opry TV shows, a Gretsch Country Gentleman, a Gibson electric classic prototype, and a Gibson Country Gentleman.[1]

In the June issue of *Mister Guitar* magazine Mark Pritcher wrote an article, "Chet in Print: A Survey of Books, Albums, and Videos Featuring Transcriptions of the Music of Chet Atkins," that cited the first books of Chet's playing—a series of guitar sheet music known as the *Chet Atkins Autograph Series* that Chet had published in 1954 through his company, Athens Music. Included in that book were "Wildwood Flower," "Trambone," "Hidden Charm," and "Hot Mockingbird."

Chet's *Picks on the Beatles* "came very close to being note-accurate transcriptions," and Pritcher noted that "the availability of Chet's music took a quantum leap when Tommy Flint and John Knowles had ground breaking books in the late 1970s." Marcel Dadi then followed with his albums containing tablature.[2]

By June Chet spent most of his time in bed. He used a cane or walker, sometimes a wheelchair, to get around. He was quite weak and was in hospice care. Chet had given Harry Warner some cash and told him to buy cemetery plots at Harpeth Hills Memorial Garden for both of them so they could be buried beside each other. On June 20 Chet turned seventy-seven.

Ten days later, on Saturday, June 30, Chet slipped away peacefully, surrounded by his family with his grandson Jonathan holding his hand. That evening Garrison Keillor announced Chet's passing during the broadcast of *Prairie Home Companion* from the Tanglewood Music Center in western Massachusetts. That evening and the next day his death was national and international news.

Backstage at the Grand Ole Opry there was a sadness that covered the performers and audience like a heavy blanket. The show went on, including the televised portion where artists paid tributes to Chet.

Backstage in Helena, Montana, Janis Ian received a call from her partner telling her the news. "It hit me harder than I'd expected," said Ian. "I couldn't imagine he'd die. Nashville without Chet was unthinkable; he'd been there for me almost from the week I arrived. I could count on him to explain why certain people didn't invite me to write with them, or ask me to their homes for dinner. I could count on him to make it all right, or make me not care."[3]

The day after Chet died Steve Wariner called Jerry Reed. "When he answered the phone all I said was 'Hey Jerry. It's Steve Wariner.' One of us said, 'We lost our Chief.' Jerry just broke down; we talked for a good 45 minutes to an hour. He said, 'Let me tell you something' and he just started pouring his heart out to me."[4]

On July 3 a "Celebration of the Life of Chester Burton Atkins" was held at the Ryman Auditorium, with Chet's casket down in front onstage. In the center of the stage was Chet's orange Gibson electric guitar, next to his trademark hat.

The service began with "Farther Along" by Connie Smith, accompanied by Marty Stuart, Mark Casstevens, bassist David Hungate, and fiddler Stuart Duncan. Eddy Arnold then shared his thoughts. "I don't know if I can get through this," he said as his eyes filled with tears. "If you ever heard of any one man who had it all in talent, it was this man. If you can love another man in a gentlemanly way, I loved Chet Atkins. We won't ever see the like, the talent, in one man again. If you ever heard of any man—anywhere—who had it all, it was this man. When you talk about guitar players, you don't include him with the others. You set Chet aside. He was in a category of his own."

Indeed that was true. Nobody played Chet Atkins style before Chet created it.

Paul Yandell, Vince Gill, and Steve Wariner played a medley of four songs, "Mister Sandman," "Windy and Warm," "Sails," and "Wildwood Flower," each of which featured Chet's signature fingerpicking style. Garrison Keillor's eulogy was especially poignant and moving in light of their close friendship and work together on NPR's *Prairie Home Companion.*

Keillor offered a recap of Chet's career, starting with his first appearance at the Ryman as part of Red Foley's band in 1946. "He played guitar in a style that hadn't been seen before, with a thumbpick for the bass note and two fingers to play the contrapuntal melody and, at a time when guitarists were expected to be flashy and play 'Under the Double Eagle' with the guitar up behind their head, this one hunched down over the guitar and made it sing, made a melody line that was beautiful and legato."

Chet remembered old hymns and sentimental songs that his father sang and "he could sing you several verses of 'In the Gloaming' or 'Seeing Nellie Home,' whether you asked for them or not," said Keillor, who noted that Chet knew old fiddle tunes and "mountain music that he picked up trying to play the fiddle," but it was "on the radio he heard music that really entranced him, that was freer and looser and more jangly and elegant and attitudinous."

"Chet tried to get the Merle Travis sound and, in the process, he came up with his own and then, he discovered Django Reinhardt and that set something loose in him." He continued, "You might be shy and homely and puny and from the sticks and feel looked down upon, but if you could play the guitar like that, you would be aristocracy and never have to point it out, anybody with sense would know it and the others don't matter anyway."

"He knew so many giants," said Keillor. "This man was a giant himself. He was the guitar player of the 20th century. He was the model of who you should be and what you should look like. You could tell it whenever he picked up a guitar, the way it fit him. His upper body was shaped to it, from a lifetime of playing: his back was slightly hunched, his shoulders rounded, and the guitar was the missing piece. He was an artist and there was no pretense in him; he never waved the flag or held up the cross or traded on his own sorrows. He was the guitarist. His humor was self-deprecating; he was his own best critic. He inspired all sorts of players who never played anything like him. He was generous and admired other players' work and he told them so. He had a natural reserve to him, but when he admired people, he went all out to tell them about it. And because there was no deception in him, his praise meant more than just about anything else. If Chet was a fan of yours, you never needed another one."

Chet "loved doing shows," said Keillor. "He never had a bad night. He played some notes he didn't mean to play but they never were bad notes. They were simply other notes. He was such a professional it was hard to bug him but I succeeded when we did a show together and at the end I took his hand and we took a bow together. The next night, he said to me before the show, 'Don't take my hand onstage that way, you know what people will think, you being a northern liberal and all.' I found that during the bow I could make him flinch just by gesturing toward him."

"God looks on the heart and is a God of mercy and loving kindness beyond our comprehension," concluded Keillor, "and in that faith let us commend his spirit to the Everlasting, may the angels bear him up, and may eternal light shine upon him, and may he run into a lot of his old friends."

The ceremony ended with Kevin King quoting Atkins's own words from his book, *Just Me and My Guitars*: "The players come and go, but the music lives on, and eternity will take care of the rest."

Pallbearers were Gary Atkins, Ray Stevens, Vince Gill, David Conrad, Steve Wariner, Jonathan Russell, Dr. Will Russell, Chad Sawyer, Paul Yandell, and Harry Warner. He was interred in Harpeth Hills Memory Gardens on Highway 100.[5]

On the day of the funeral the *Nashville Tennessean* ran an editorial declaring, "The death of Mr. Chet Atkins last weekend was far more than the loss of a famous musician. It caused people to reflect on the very history of Nashville music and its influence on the world because Mr. Atkins was so influential on the music. . . . In Nashville music circles, the giants of the industry generally fall into two categories—the artists whose talent and fame are recognized by the public and the business types who have the vision to record those talents and build a thriving industry. Mr. Atkins was at the top in both categories. Few music legends will ever come close to that. . . . Many music figures may be as famous as Mr. Atkins. None will ever be more respected."[6]

Less than two weeks after Chet's death, the Chet Atkins Appreciation Society was held with almost six hundred attendees. It was an emotional time, and many of the performers spoke of their memories of Chet and played tunes in his honor. At the Saturday night concert

Michael Cochran read from the book he wrote with Chet, *Me and My Guitars*. Bill Spann recited "Chet, You're a Legend in Your Time" to the melody of "I'd Be a Legend in My Time."

The music played on and on, with audience members not ready to give up Chet or the convention. The evening finished with Guy Van Duser leading the audience in singing "We Love You, Chet."[7]

Chet's legacy continued the year after his death when the Rock and Roll Hall of Fame inducted him as a "Sideman" on March 28, 2002, in a ceremony in New York.

In 2003 an album titled *Solo Sessions* was released that contained songs that Chet had been periodically recording at his home studio. No one knew of their existence until Mike Poston found them in Chet's studio. Some were newly arranged songs; some had never been recorded or released. It was just Chet, unaccompanied. The album was assembled by engineer Mike Poston, mastered by Jonathan Russell, with Paul Yandell as the album's creative consultant.

No one knew why or when he had recorded those twenty-eight songs. Maybe he was just practicing.

Acknowledgments

I want to thank Mike Curb and the Mike Curb Foundation for establishing a Professorship for me at Belmont University, which makes it possible to do research for articles and books like this one. I also want to thank the Atkins family—Merle Russell, Chad and Mandy Sawyer, Chris and Meagan Anderson, and Jonathan Russell for sharing their trove of pictures.

A Note on Sources

I began my career in Nashville in 1973 with the Country Music Association, and since that time I have interviewed and/or had conversations with a number of people about Chet Atkins (I interviewed Chet twice, but they were not extensive interviews). The following is list of people (some deceased) I interviewed or spoke with about Chet Atkins: Eddy Arnold, Chet Atkins, Jerry Bailey, Bobby Bare, Shannon Bare, Dave Barnes, Bob Beckham, Harold Bradley, Jerry Bradley, Owen Bradley, Erika Brady, Jim Ed Brown, Maxine Brown, Tony Brown, Del Bryant, Pat Burgeson, Bobby Campbell, Walter Carter, Blake Chancey, Jack Clement, Tom Collins, David Conrad, Peter Cooper, Ralph Emery, Tommy Emmanuel, Joe Galante, Vince Gill, Thomas Goldsmith, Michael Gray, Douglas Green, Peter Guralnick, Susan Hackey, Bill Hance, Martin Hawkins, Buddy Kalb, Beverly Keel, Jerry Kennedy, Anita Kerr, Kevin King, Millie Kirkham, Pat Kirtley, Otto Kitsinger, John Knowles, Michael Kosser, Charlie Lamb, Don Light, John D. Loudermilk, Jim Malloy, Bill C. Malone, Bobbie Malone, Michael McCall, John McClellan, Charlie McCoy, Bob Moore, Alanna Nash, Red O'Donnell, Robert Oermann, Jay Orr, Bill Piburn, Dave Pomeroy, Mike Poston, Frances Preston, Charley Pride, Mark Pritcher, Norbert Putnam, Tom Roland, Wesley Rose, John Rumble, Jonathan Russell, Merle Russell, Kenny Sears, Billie Rose Shockley, Dave Sichak, Jack Stapp, Jim Stephonay, Ray Stevens, Travis Stimelin, Michael Streissguth, Eddie Stubbs, Billy Swan, Walt

Trott, Steve Wariner, Richard Weize, Billy Ed Wheeler, Mac Wiseman, Charles K. Wolfe, and Chip Young.

The Frist Library and Archive of the Country Music Hall of Fame and Museum has a number of interviews that I consulted while working on this book. They were an invaluable source. The interviews I consulted were those on Chet Atkins, Jim Atkins, Owen Bradley, Boudleaux Bryant, Jerry Byrd, Archie Campbell, the Carlisle Brothers, Cliff Carlisle, Lightnin' Chance, Jack Clement, Danny Davis, Don Davis, Karl Davis, Pete Drake, Red Foley, Frank Fontaine, Mel Foree, Don Gibson, Lloyd Green, John D. Loudermilk, Ernie Newton, Bill Porter, Wesley Rose, Steve Sholes, Jack Shook, and Henry Strzelecki.

The Bear Family in Germany has compiled a number of boxed sets that include a comprehensive set of recordings and liner notes, often in a booklet, that are invaluable for information about artists and recordings, including the sessionographies, many compiled by Richard Weize, that give names of musicians, studios, and recordings. Boxed sets (sometimes multiple boxed sets) I consulted were those done on the following artists: Janis Martin, Hank Locklin, George Hamilton IV, Hank Snow, Connie Smith, Dave Rich, Waylon Jennings, Chet Atkins, Willie Nelson, Anita Carter, Porter Wagoner, Sonny James, The Browns, Eddy Arnold, Louvin Brothers, and Bobby Bare.

The Belmont University Library has all of these boxed set—and many more—and I must thank Belmont librarians Claire Wiley and Jenny Mills for their help.

Dave Barnes and the British Archive of Country Music provided important information, and the annual International Country Music Conference, held annually at Belmont University and cohosted by James Akenson, Greg Reish, Olivia Beaudry, and me, always provides good information as well as fellowship with other country music historians.

I'd like to especially thank Olivia Beaudry for her help with pictures.

The Chet Atkins Appreciation Society, particularly Mark Pritcher and Pat Kirtley, were a great help (Mark Pritcher took me to the Atkins old home place). Their publication, *Mister Guitar*, has insightful articles about Chet Atkins and his career.

NOTE: All references to charts and/or chart numbers can be found in these books

Whitburn, Joel. *The Billboard Albums*. 6th ed. Menomonee Falls, Wisc.: Record Research, 2006.

Whitburn, Joel. *Hot Country Singles: 1944–2017*. Menomonee Falls, Wisc.: Record Research, 2018.

Whitburn, Joel. *Pop Memories: 1890–1954*. Menomonee Falls, Wisc.: Record Research, 1986.

Whitburn, Joel. *Top Pop Singles: 1955–2017*. Menomonee Falls, Wisc.: Record Research, 2019.

Information on Chet Atkins's sessions through 1960 was found in discographies compiled by Richard Weize in two boxed sets, *Chet Atkins: Galloping Guitar: The Early Years* and *Chet Atkins: Mr. Guitar. The Complete Recordings 1955–1960*, both for Bear Family Records. Other documentation of Chet Atkins's sessions was found on the website Praguefrank's Country Discographies, at Praguefrank@seznam.cz.

Chet Atkins Selected Discography

Chet Atkins' Gallopin' Guitar (RCA Victor, 1953)
String Dustin' (with the Country All-Stars) (RCA Victor, 1953)
Stringin' Along with Chet Atkins (RCA Victor, 1953)
A Session with Chet Atkins (RCA Victor, 1954)
Chet Atkins in Three Dimensions (RCA Victor, 1955)
Stringin' Along with Chet Atkins (RCA Victor, 1955)
Finger-Style Guitar (RCA Victor, 1956)
Chet Atkins at Home (RCA Victor, 1957)
Hi-Fi in Focus (RCA Victor, 1957)
Chet Atkins in Hollywood (RCA Victor, 1959)
Hum & Strum Along with Chet Atkins (RCA Victor, 1959)
Mister Guitar (RCA Victor, 1959)
After the Riot at Newport (RCA Victor, 1960)
Chet Atkins' Workshop (RCA Victor, 1960)
The Other Chet Atkins (RCA Victor, 1960)
Teensville (RCA Victor, 1960)
Chet Atkins Plays Great Movie Themes (RCA Victor, 1961)
Christmas with Chet Atkins (RCA Victor, 1961)
The Most Popular Guitar (RCA Victor, 1961)
Caribbean Guitar (RCA Victor, 1962)
Chet Atkins Plays Back Home Hymns (RCA Victor, 1962)
Down Home (RCA Victor, 1962)
Our Man in Nashville (RCA Victor, 1962)
The Guitar Genius (RCA Victor, 1963)
Teen Scene (RCA Victor, 1963)
Travelin' (RCA Victor, 1963)
The Best of Chet Atkins RCA (Victor, 1964)
The Early Years of Chet Atkins & His Guitar RCA (Camden, 1964)
Guitar Country (RCA Victor, 1964)
My Favorite Guitars (RCA Victor, 1964)
Progressive Pickin' (RCA Victor, 1964)
Reminiscing (with Hank Snow) (RCA, 1964)
More of That Guitar Country (RCA Victor, 1965)
The Best of Chet Atkins, vol. 2 (RCA Victor, 1966)

Chet Atkins Picks on the Beatles (RCA Victor, 1966)
From Nashville with Love (RCA Victor, 1966)
Music from Nashville, My Home Town (RCA Camden, 1966)
Play Guitar with Chet Atkins (Dolton, 1966)
The Pops Goes Country (with Arthur Fiedler and the Boston Pops) (RCA, 1966)
Class Guitar (RCA Victor, 1967)
It's a Guitar World (RCA Victor, 1967)
Chet All the Way (RCA Victor, 1968)
Hometown Guitar (RCA Victor, 1968)
Solid Gold '68 (RCA Victor, 1968)
Solo Flights (RCA Victor, 1968)
Chet Atkins Picks on the Pops (with Arthur Fiedler and the Boston Pops) (RCA, 1969)
Lover's Guitar(RCA Victor, 1969)
The Nashville String Band (RCA Victor, 1969)
Relaxin' with Chet (RCA Camden, 1969)
Solid Gold '69 (RCA Victor, 1969)
C. B. Atkins & C. E. Snow by Special Request (with C. E. [Hank] Snow) (RCA, 1970)
Down Home (RCA Victor, 1970)
Me and Jerry (with Jerry Reed) (RCA, 1970)
Pickin' My Way (RCA Victor, 1970)
Solid Gold '70 (RCA Victor, 1970)
Yestergroovin' (RCA Victor, 1970)
Chet Atkins Guitar Method, vols. 1–2 (F.A.M.E., 1971)
For the Good Times (RCA Victor, 1971)
Identified! (with the Country All-Stars) (RCA Victor, 1971)
Me and Chet (with Jerry Reed) (RCA, 1971)
Strung Up (with the Country All-Stars) (RCA Victor, 1971)
American Salute (with Arthur Fiedler and the Boston Pops) (RCA, 1972)
The Bandit (with the Country All-Stars) (RCA Victor, 1972)
Chet, Floyd & Boots (with Floyd Cramer and Boots Randolph) (RCA Camden, 1972)
Picks on the Hits (RCA Victor, 1972)
World's Greatest Melodies (RCA Victor, 1972)
The Atkins-Travis Traveling Show (with Merle Travis) (RCA, 1974)
Chet Atkins Picks on Jerry Reed (RCA Victor, 1974)
Superpickers (RCA, 1974)
Chet Atkins Goes to the Movies (RCA Victor, 1975)
Chester & Lester (with Les Paul) (RCA Victor, 1976)

Chet, Floyd & Danny (with Floyd Cramer and Danny Davis) (RCA Victor, 1977)
A Legendary Performer (RCA Victor, 1977)
Me and My Guitar (RCA Victor, 1977)
Guitar Monsters (with Les Paul) (RCA Records, 1978)
And Then Came Chet Atkins (RCA Victor, 1979)
First Nashville Guitar Quartet (with Liona Boyd, John Knowles, and John Pell) (RCA Victor, 1979)
The Best of Chet on the Road—Live (with the Country All-Stars) (RCA Victor, 1980)
Reflections (with Doc Watson) (RCA Victor, 1980)
Country After All These Years (RCA Victor, 1981)
Standard Brands (with Lenny Breau)(RCA Victor, 1981)
East Tennessee Christmas (Columbia, 1983)
Work It Out with Chet Atkins C.G.P. (Columbia, 1983)
Stay Tuned (Columbia, 1985)
Street Dreams (Columbia, 1986)
Sails (Columbia, 1987)
Neck and Neck (with Mark Knopfler) (Columbia, 1990)
Sneakin' Around (with Jerry Reed) (Columbia, 1992)
Galloping Guitar: The Early Years (Bear Family, 1993)
The Gingham Dog and the Calico Cat (with Amy Grant) (Madacy Entertainment, 1993)
Read My Licks (Columbia, 1994)
Simpatico (with Suzy Bogguss) (Liberty, 1994)
Almost Alone (Columbia, 1996)
The Day Finger Pickers Took Over the World (with Tommy Emmanuel) (Sony Music, 1997)
The Guitar Genius / Relaxin' with Chet: Nashville Gold (RCA Camden, 2000)
Guitar Legend: The RCA *Years* (Buddah Records, 2000)
Guitar Man (RCA Camden, 2000)
The Master and His Music (Buddah Records, 2001)
RCA *Country Legends: Chet Atkins* (Buddah Records, 2001)
Chet Picks on the Grammys (Columbia, 2002)
The Best of Chet Atkins (BMG International, 2003)
Legendary (BMG International, 2003)
Solo Sessions (CGP, 2003)
Early Chet Atkins (Country Routes, 2004)
The Essential Chet Atkins: The Columbia Years (Columbia, 2004)
High Rockin' Swing (Universe, 2004)

I've Been Working on the Guitar: The Legend Begins (Country Stars, 2004)
Mr. Guitar: The Complete Recordings 1955–1960 (Bear Family Records, 2004)
Carter Sisters and Mother Maybelle with Chet Atkins (Country Routes, 2005)
Chet Atkins with the Carter Sisters and Mother Maybelle 1949 (Country Routes, 2005)
The Early Years 1946–1957 (JSP Records, 2007)
The Essential Chet Atkins (Legacy Recordings, 2007)

Notes

CHAPTER 1

1. Atkins with Neely, *Country Gentleman*, 9.

2. Atkins with Neely, *Country Gentleman*, 5, 6.

3. Timothy White, "Chet Atkins: A Portrait of the Artist," *Billboard*, December 6, 1997, 18.

4. Atkins with Neely, *Country Gentleman*, 10.

5. Atkins with Neely, *Country Gentleman*, 18.

6. Atkins with Neely, *Country Gentleman*, 6.

7. White, "Chet Atkins," 18; Atkins with Neely, *Country Gentleman*, 10.

8. Atkins and Cochran, *Me and My Guitars*, 15.

9. Conversation with John Knowles, June 20, 2023.

10. Atkins with Neely, *Country Gentleman*, 6.

11. Atkins and Cochran, *Me and My Guitars*, 15.

12. Atkins with Neely, *Country Gentleman*, 18–19.

13. Atkins with Neely, *Country Gentleman*, 19.

14. Atkins and Cochran, *Me and My Guitars*, 15.

15. Atkins with Neely, *Country Gentleman*, 19.

16. Mark Pritcher, "An Old Friend from East Tennessee," interview with Buster Devault, Chet's boyhood friend, *Mister Guitar*, no. 44 (June 1998).

17. Atkins with Neely, *Country Gentleman*, 24.

18. Atkins with Neely, *Country Gentleman*, 16.

19. White, "Chet Atkins," 18.

20. Dawidoff, *In the Country of Country*, 46.

21. Dawidoff, *In the Country of Country*, 46.

22. Atkins with Neely, *Country Gentleman*, 46, 47.

23. Atkins and Cochran, *Me and My Guitars*, 18.

CHAPTER 2

1. Ernie Newton, Frist Library and Archive of the Country Music Hall of Fame and Museum, oral history, interview by Douglas Green, September 24, 1974.

2. Shaughnessy, *Les Paul*, 67.

3. Atkins and Cochran, *Me and My Guitars*, 37.

4. Atkins with Neely, *Country Gentleman*, 56.

5. Erika Brady, "Contested Origins: Arnold Shultz and the Music of Western Kentucky," in *Hidden in the Mix: The African American Presence in Country Music*, ed. Diane Pecknold (Durham, N.C.: Duke University Press, 2013), 104.
6. Brady, "Contested Origins," 105.
7. Atkins and Cochran, *Me and My Guitars*, 18.
8. Atkins with Neely, *Country Gentleman*, 56–57.
9. Timothy White, "Chet Atkins: A Portrait of the Artist," *Billboard*, December 6, 1997," 19.
10. Tony Bacon Reverb.com, Bacon's archive.
11. Atkins with Neely, *Country Gentleman*, 58–59.

CHAPTER 3

1. Atkins with Neely, *Country Gentleman*, 61.
2. Atkins with Neely, *Country Gentleman*, 64.
3. Atkins with Neely, *Country Gentleman*, 70, 74.
4. Atkins with Neely, *Country Gentleman*, 75–76.
5. Atkins and Cochran, *Me and My Guitars*, 20.
6. Atkins and Cochran, *Me and My Guitars*, 19.
7. Mark Pritcher, "Fiddlin' Chet," *Mister Guitar*, no. 57 (June 2003).
8. Mark Pritcher, "An Interview with Chet," *Mister Guitar*, no. 25 (June 1991).
9. Timothy White, "Chet Atkins: A Portrait of the Artist," *Billboard*, December 6, 1997," 19.
10. Pritcher, "Interview with Chet."
11. Pritcher, "Interview with Chet."
12. Pat Kirtley, "Home & Jethro: All Kidding Aside," *Mister Guitar*, no. 80 (December 2012).
13. Atkins with Neely, *Country Gentleman*, 108.
14. Atkins with Neely, *Country Gentleman*, 109.
15. Atkins with Neely, *Country Gentleman*, 110.
16. Atkins with Neely, *Country Gentleman*, 111.

CHAPTER 4

1. Walt Trott and Eddie Stubbs, liner notes, *Johnny & Jack* (Bear Family Records, 1992).
2. Atkins with Neely, *Country Gentleman*, 113.
3. Cusic, *Eddy Arnold*, 88.
4. Atkins with Neely, *Country Gentleman*, 114.
5. Atkins with Neely, *Country Gentleman*, 121.
6. Atkins with Neely, *Country Gentleman*, 122, 126.
7. Hawkins, *Shot in the Dark*, 24–31.

8. Harold Bradley, interview in McClellan and Bratic, *Chet Atkins in Three Dimensions*, vol. 2. Also see personal interview, January 13, 2017.

9. Atkins with Neely, *Country Gentleman*, 126.

10. Atkins with Neely, *Country Gentleman*, 127; Dave Sichak, "WRVA Old Dominion Barn Dance: The History of a Radio Station, Sunshine Sue, a Program and the Promotion of Hillbilly Music," *International Country Music Journal* (2019): 9–102.

11. Karl Davis, Country Music Foundation Oral History Project, interview by Douglas B. Green, Chicago, June 8 and 9, 1974.

12. Mark Pritcher, "An Interview with Chet," *Mister Guitar*, no. 25 (June 1991).

CHAPTER 5

1. Eng, *Satisfied Mind*, 74–75.

2. Atkins with Neely, *Country Gentleman*, 132.

3. Steve Sholes, Country Music Foundation Oral History Project, interview by Tandy Rice, Nashville, February 8, 1968.

4. Biszick-Lockwood, *Restless Giant*, 115.

5. Biszick-Lockwood, *Restless Giant*, 116.

6. Sholes, Country Music Foundation Oral History Project.

7. Bradley Wayne Carson, interview in McClellan and Bratic, *Chet Atkins in Three Dimensions*, 2:227.

8. Atkins with Neely, *Country Gentleman*, 134–135.

9. Carson interview, 2:227.

10. Cy Coben, interview in McClellan and Bratic, *Chet Atkins in Three Dimensions*, 1:47.

11. Atkins with Neely, *Country Gentleman*, 135.

12. Atkins with Neely, *Country Gentleman*, 135–136.

13. Harold Bradley, personal interview, January 13, 2017.

14. Atkins with Neely, *Country Gentleman*, 137.

15. Reinhart, *Chet Atkins*, 31–32.

16. Coben interview, 1:47.

17. Atkins with Neely, *Country Gentleman*, 138.

18. Atkins with Neely, *Country Gentleman*, 142.

CHAPTER 6

1. Zwonitzer with Hirshberg, *Will You Miss Me When I'm Gone?*, 222.

2. Zwonitzer with Hirshberg, *Will You Miss Me When I'm Gone?*, 262.

3. Zwonitzer with Hirshberg, *Will You Miss Me When I'm Gone?*, 266.

4. Atkins with Neely, *Country Gentleman*, 148–149.

5. Zwonitzer with Hirshberg, *Will You Miss Me When I'm Gone?*, 269.

6. Zwonitzer with Hirshberg, *Will You Miss Me When I'm Gone?*, 272.
7. Atkins with Neely, *Country Gentleman*, 150.
8. Atkins with Neely, *Country Gentleman*, 150–151.
9. Zwonitzer with Hirshberg, *Will You Miss Me When I'm Gone?*, 279.
10. Zwonitzer with Hirshberg, *Will You Miss Me When I'm Gone?*, 280.
11. Atkins with Neely, *Country Gentleman*, 154.
12. Atkins with Neely, *Country Gentleman*, 157.
13. Zwonitzer with Hirshberg, *Will You Miss Me When I'm Gone?*, 286.
14. Atkins with Neely, *Country Gentleman*, 155.

CHAPTER 7

1. "Victor Considers Him 'Greatest Guitarist,'" "The Spotlight," RCA press release, early 1950.
2. Chet Atkins, Country Music Foundation Oral History Project, interview by John Rumble and John Knowles, September 18, 1992.
3. Atkins with Neely, *Country Gentleman*, 158.
4. Pat Kirtley, "Anita Kerr, Musical Architect," *Mister Guitar*, no. 79 (July 2012).
5. Atkins with Neely, *Country Gentleman*, 159.
6. Atkins and Cochran, *Me and My Guitars*, 47.
7. Atkins and Cochran, *Me and My Guitars*, 48.
8. Atkins and Cochran, *Me and My Guitars*, 52.
9. Atkins and Cochran, *Me and My Guitars*, 56.
10. Atkins and Cochran, *Me and My Guitars*, 58.

CHAPTER 8

1. Malone and Malone, *Nashville's Songwriting*. Also see Lee Wilson, *All I Have to Do Is Dream: The Boudleaux and Felice Bryant Story* (Nashville: House of Bryant, 2011), 52.
2. Malone and Malone, *Nashville's Songwriting*, 53.
3. Atkins with Neely, *Country Gentleman*,169.
4. Atkins with Neely, *Country Gentleman*, 169.
5. Atkins with Neely, Country Gentleman, 170.

CHAPTER 9

1. Atkins with Neely, *Country Gentleman*, 165.
2. Atkins with Neely, *Country Gentleman*, 168.
3. Atkins with Neely, *Country Gentleman*, 172.
4. Eddie Stubbs, Richard Weize, and Charles Wolfe, discography, *The Louvin Brothers: Close Harmony* (Bear Family, BCD 15561 BA, 2011).
5. Emery with Cox, *View from Nashville*, 46.
6. Nash, *Behind Closed Doors*, 45.

7. Emery with Cox, *View from Nashville*, 46.
8. Nash, *Behind Closed Doors*, 45.
9. Emery with Cox, *View from Nashville*, 45.
10. Cusic, *Hank Williams*, 107–108.
11. Cusic, *Hank Williams*, 108–109.
12. Nash, *Behind Closed Doors*, 45.
13. Reinhart, *Chet Atkins*, 43–44.

CHAPTER 10

1. Pat Kirtley, "Home & Jethro: All Kidding Aside," *Mister Guitar*, no. 80 (December 2012).
2. Jerry Byrd, interview in McClellan and Bratic, *Chet Atkins in Three Dimensions*, 2:11.
3. Dale Vicur, liner notes, *Porter Wagoner* (Bear Family Records). See also Eng, *Satisfied Mind.*
4. Hank Davis, liner notes, *On the Trail of the Lonesome Pine: Hal Lone Pine & Beddy Cody* (Bear Family BCD 16787 AH).
5. Reinhart, *Chet Atkins*, 45–46.
6. Timothy White, "Chet Atkins: A Portrait of the Artist," *Billboard*, December 6, 1997, 18.
7. Bob Allen, liner notes, *The Davis Sisters* (Bear Family Records). See also Skeeter, *Bus Fare to Kentucky*, and Richard Weize, discography, *The Davis Sisters* (Bear Family Records).
8. Chet Flippo, "Chet Atkins," *Rolling Stone*, February 12, 1976.
9. Personal conversation with Bill Ivey.
10. Colin Escott, liner notes, Charline Arthur, *Welcome to the Club*, and Richard Weize, discography, Charlie Arthur, *Welcome to the Club* (Bear Family Records, LC 5197, 1998).
11. Reinhart, *Chet Atkins*, 49–50.
12. Warren Denny, "Wayne Moss: A Cinderella Story," *Nashville Musician*, April–June 2021, 15.

CHAPTER 11

1. Margaret Fields, "My Story: The Tale of the Original Chet Atkins Fan Club, from Beginning to End," *Mister Guitar*, no. 82 (2013); and Mark Pritcher, "The Original Chet Atkins Fan Club," *Mister Guitar*, no. 59 (March 2004).
2. Fields, "My Story."
3. *Gallopin' Guitar News*, no. 7 (June 1954).
4. *Gallopin' Guitar News*, no. 7 (June 1954).
5. "Top Guitarist to Share Park Concert Spotlight with Duke of Paducah," *Nashville Tennessean*, June 2, 1954.

6. Pat Kirtley, "Chet Atkins: Electronic Innovator," *Mister Guitar*, no 67 (April 2007).

CHAPTER 12

1. Pat Kirtley, "Ray Butts: An Inventor and a Gentleman: Part Two," *Mister Guitar*, no. 43 (April 1998).

2. Bacon, *50 Years of Gretsch Electrics*, 28.

3. Bacon, *50 Years of Gretsch Electrics*, 28.

4. Pat Kirtley, "Chet Atkins: Electronic Innovator," *Mister Guitar*, no. 67 (April 2007).

5. Kirtley, "Ray Butts."

6. James Carty, "Methodist Radio, Film, RCA Plan New Location Here," *Nashville Tennessean*, June 20, 1954.

7. Reinhart, *Chet Atkins*, 56–58.

CHAPTER 13

1. John Chintala, "Chet Atkins as Seen on TV: 1943–1969: Part One of a Multipart Series," *Mister Guitar*, no. 78 (May 2012).

2. Dale Vinicur, liner notes, *Porter Wagoner*; Brooks and Marsh, *Complete Directory*.

3. *Gallopin' Guitar News*, no. 9 (July 1955).

4. Colin Escott, liner notes, Charline Arthur; Richard Weize, discography, Charlie Arthur, *Welcome to the Club* (Bear Family, LC 5197, 1998); Emily C. Neely, "Charline Arthur: The (Un)Making of a Honky-Tonk Star," in McCusker and Peckinold, *Boy Named Sue*.

CHAPTER 14

1. *Gallopin' Guitar News*, no. 11 (October 3, 1955).

2. *Gallopin' Guitar News*, no. 11 (October 3, 1955); Bob Guest, "Here's Paul Yandell," *Mister Guitar*, no. 2 (November 1989).

3. *Gallopin' Guitar News*, no. 12 (July 1955).

CHAPTER 15

1. Emery with Carter, *More Memories*, 190.

2. Guralnick, *Last Train to Memphis*, 238.

3. Emery with Carter, *More Memories*, 190.

4. Ernst Jorgensen, *Elvis Presley: A Life in Music: The Complete Recording Sessions* (New York: St. Martin's, 1998), 36.

5. Emery with Carter, *More Memories*, 190.

6. Colin Escott, liner notes, *Jim Reeves* (Bear Family, 1994).

7. Bob Allen, liner notes, and Richard Weize, discography, *Janis Martin:*

The Female Elvis: Complete Recordings, 1956–1960 (Bear Family Records, May 1987).

8. Sanjek, *American Popular Music*; Marmorstein, *The Label.*

9. Charles Wolfe, Hank Snow, *The Singing Ranger*, vol. 2 (Bear Family Records).

10. "Sholes Has Last Laugh as Presley Rings Up Sales," *Billboard*, April 21, 1956.

11. *Gallopin' Guitar News*, no. 15 (June 1956).

CHAPTER 16

1. "Chet Atkins to Entertain Advertisers," *Nashville Banner*, August 17, 1956; "Chet Pleasing Guitar Await You at Park," *Nashville Tennessean*, August 16, 1956; "Atkins, Young, Opry Stars To Shine At Ball," *Nashville Banner*, August 21, 1956.

2. John Chintala, "Chet Atkins as Seen on TV: 1943–1969: Part One of a Multipart Series," *Mister Guitar*, no. 78 (May 2012).

3. "Jim Denny Exits Opry," *Country Music Reporter*, September 24, 1956.

4. Reinhart, *Chet Atkins*, 66–67.

5. Reinhart, *Chet Atkins*, 67–68.

CHAPTER 17

1. Bacon, *50 Years of Gretsch Electrics*, 49; and Mark Pritcher, "The *Country Gentleman* Comes Home to Gretsch," *Mister Guitar*, no. 67 (April 2007).

2. Pat Kirtley, "Ray Butts: An Inventor and a Gentleman, Part One of Two Parts," *Mister Guitar*, no. 41 (June 1997); and Kirtley, "Chet Atkins: Electronic Innovator, Part Three," *Mister Guitar*, no. 67 (April 2007).

3. Streissguth, *Like a Moth to a Flame*, 131.

4. Colin Escott, liner notes, *Jim Reeves* (Bear Family, 1994), 41–42.

5. Escott, *Jim Reeves.*

6. Escott, *Jim Reeves.*

CHAPTER 18

1. Andrew Sandoval, liner notes, *A Brief Chronology of the Everly Brothers from 1937–1960* (Bear Family Records).

2. Sandoval, liner notes.

3. John Chintala, "Chet Atkins as Seen on TV: 1943–1969: Part One of a Multipart Series," *Mister Guitar*, no. 78 (May 2012).

4. Full page ad from RCA Victor, "Gallery of Hitmakers—Moneymakers for You," *Music Reporter*, April 27, 1957.

5. Double page spread ad, "The Cream of the Crop Is on RCA Victor," *Music Reporter*, May 25, 1957.

6. Dale Vinicur, liner notes, and Richard Weize, discography, Don Gibson, *Don Gibson: The Singer—The Songwriter: 1949–1960* (Bear Family Records).

7. Otto Kitsinger, liner notes, and Richard Weise, discography, Hank Locklin, *Please Help Me I'm Falling* (Bear Family Records BCD 15730–Dt).

8. Otto Kitsinger, liner notes, Hank Locklin.

9. Reinhart, *Chet Atkins*, 73–74.

CHAPTER 19

1. Andrew Sandoval, liner notes, *A Brief Chronology of the Everly Brothers from 1937–1960* (Bear Family Records).

2. "New RCA Studios to Tap All Fields," *Music Reporter*, August 17, 1957.

3. "Sholes RCA's New Pop-CW A&R Chief," *Music Reporter*, August 3, 1957.

4. "Chet Atkins Receiving a Gold Plaque Commemorating His Tenth Anniversary with the Company" (picture), *Music Reporter*, November 25, 1957.

5. Streeter, *Jimmy Driftwood Story*, 45.

6. Streeter, *Jimmy Driftwood Story*, 46.

7. Streeter, *Jimmy Driftwood Story*, 46.

8. Bill Porter, Country Music Foundation Oral History Project, interview by John Rumble, Fisherville, Ky., November 13, 1994; Dale Vinicur, liner notes, Don Gibson, *Don Gibson: The Singer—The Songwriter: 1949–1960* (Bear Family Records).

9. Walt Trott and Eddie Stubbs, liner notes, *Johnny & Jack* (Bear Family Records, 1992).

CHAPTER 20

1. Reinhart, *Chet Atkins*, 77.

2. Pinckney Keel, "Teenagers Make Up Half of Record Sales Market," *Nashville Banner*, March 20, 1958; "Cohen to Direct Coral, Brunswick A&R," *Music Reporter*, March 31, 1958.

3. "Cohen to Direct Coral, Brunswick A&R," *Music Reporter*, March 31, 1958.

4. Reinhart, *Chet Atkins*, 79–80.

5. Cusic, *Elvis in Nashville*, 56, 59–60.

6. "CMA Formed at Miami Confab," *Music Reporter*, July 7, 1958.

7. Richard Weize, discography, Janis Martin, *The Female Elvis: Complete Recordings, 1956–1960* (Bear Family BCD 15406).

8. Andrew Sandoval, liner notes, *A Brief Chronology of the Everly Brothers from 1937–1960* (Bear Family Records).

9. Pat Kirtley, "The Strange Tale of My Brother Sings," *Mister Guitar*, no. 81 (March 2013).

CHAPTER 21

1. Pat Kirtley, "Chet Atkins & Printer's Alley," *Mister Guitar*, no. 85 (June 2015): 4, 5, 9.

2. Smith, *Sideman*, 246.

3. Smith, *Sideman*, 209.

4. Smith, *Sideman*, 246.

5. Smith, *Sideman*, 247.

6. Smith, *Sideman*, 249.

7. Smith, *Sideman*, 250.

8. Boots Randolph, interview in McClellan and Bratic, *Chet Atkins in Three Dimensions*, 2:74.

9. John Chintala, "Chet Atkins as Seen on TV: 1943–1969: Part One of a Multipart Series," *Mister Guitar*, no. 78 (May 2012).

10. Stimeling, *Nashville Cats*, 133.

11. "Country Music Is Here to Stay," *Music Reporter*, November 17, 1958.

12. "Nashville Booms as Music Mecca," *Country Music Reporter*, November 17, 1958.

CHAPTER 21

1. Pat Kirtley, "Chet Atkins & Printer's Alley," *Mister Guitar*, no. 85 (June 2015): 4, 5, 9.

2. Smith, *Sideman*, 246.

3. Smith, *Sideman*, 209.

4. Smith, *Sideman*, 246.

5. Smith, *Sideman*, 247.

6. Smith, *Sideman*, 249.

7. Smith, *Sideman*, 250.

8. Boots Randolph, interview in McClellan and Bratic, *Chet Atkins in Three Dimensions*, 2:74.

9. John Chintala, "Chet Atkins as Seen on TV: 1943–1969: Part One of a Multipart Series," *Mister Guitar*, no. 78 (May 2012).

10. Stimeling, *Nashville Cats*, 133.

11. "Country Music Is Here to Stay," *Music Reporter*, November 17, 1958.

12. "Nashville Booms as Music Mecca," *Country Music Reporter*, November 17, 1958.

CHAPTER 22

1. Bill Porter, Country Music Foundation Oral History Project, interview by John Rumble, April 6, 1995.

2. Porter, interview in McClellan and Bratic, *Chet Atkins in Three Dimensions*, 2:149–150.

3. John D. Loudermilk, interview in McClellan and Bratic, *Chet Atkins in Three Dimensions*, 2:305, 306

CHAPTER 23

1. Bill Porter, Country Music Foundation Oral History Project, interview by John Rumble, November 13, 1994.

2. Bill Porter, Country Music Foundation Oral History Project, interview by John Rumble, April 6, 1995.

3. Streeter, *Jimmy Driftwood Story*, 48.

4. Reinhart, *Chet Atkins*, 88–89.

5. Brown, *Looking Back to See*, 117.

6. Brown, *Looking Back to See*, 144–145.

7. Brown, *Looking Back to See*, 146.

8. Porter, interview in McClellan and Bratic, *Chet Atkins in Three Dimensions*, 2:150.

9. Bill Porter, Country Music Foundation Oral History Project, interview by John Rumble, June 8, 1994.

10. Porter, Country Music Foundation Oral History Project, April 6, 1995.

11. Margaret Fields, "My Story: The Tale of the Original Chet Atkins Fan Club, from Beginning to End," *Mister Guitar*, no. 82 (2013).

12. Brown, *Looking Back to See*, 167; and Jim Ed Brown, personal interview.

CHAPTER 24

1. Reinhart, *Chet Atkins*, 92–93.

2. Smith, *Sideman*, 245.

3. Pat Kirtley, "Anita Kerr, Musical Architect," *Mister Guitar*, no. 79 (July 2012).

4. Thomas O'Neil, *The Grammys for the Record: The Ultimate, Unofficial Guide to America's Top Music Awards* (New York: Penguin 1993), 22.

5. O'Neil, *Grammys for the Record*, 25.

6. Reinhart, *Chet Atkins*, 93–94.

CHAPTER 25

1. Malloy, *Playback*, 100.

2. Hank Kitsinger, liner notes, Hank Locklin, and Otto Kitsinger and Richard Weize, discographer, *Hank Locklin: The* RCA *Victor Discography 1955–Mid 1964*.

3. Cusic, *Elvis in Nashville*, 77, 78.

4. Colin Escott, liner notes, *Jim Reeves* (Bear Family, 1994), 52.

5. Stimeling, *Nashville Cats*, 104.

6. Bill Porter, Country Music Foundation Oral History Project, interview by John Rumble, June 8, 1994.

7. Stimeling, *Nashville Cats.*

8. Marc Myers, "Riot in Newport, 1960," *Wall Street Journal*, July 2, 1960.

9. Pat Anderson, "Country Music Stars Plan Knox Festival," *Nashville Tennessean*, August 23, 1960.

10. "Step Up Hero with New Name for Country Music," *Music Reporter*, October 31, 1960.

11. Emery with Carter, *More Memories*, 194.

12. Emery with Cox, *View from Nashville*, 144.

CHAPTER 26

1. Dale Vinicur, liner notes, and Richard Weize, discography, *George Hamilton IV* (Bear Family Records).

2. Henry Strzelecki, Country Music Foundation Oral History Project, interview by John Rumble, March 14, 1990.

3. Eddy Arnold, interview in McClellan and Bratic, *Chet Atkins in Three Dimensions*, 1:37.

4. Ray Edenton, interview in McClellan and Bratic, *Chet Atkins in Three Dimensions*, 2:291.

5. Buddy Harman, interview in McClellan and Bratic, *Chet Atkins in Three Dimensions*, 2:341.

6. Ralph Emery, personal conversation.

7. Emery with Cox, *View from Nashville*, 144.

8. Buddy Harman, interview in McClellan and Bratic, *Chet Atkins in Three Dimensions*, 2:341.

9. Billy Edd Wheeler, interview in McClellan and Bratic, *Chet Atkins in Three Dimensions*, 2:350, 351.

10. Wayne Carson, interview in McClellan and Bratic, *Chet Atkins in Three Dimensions*, 2:232.

11. Dan Daley, *Inside the Business of Country Music* (New York: Overlook Press, 1998), 55.

12. Emery with Cox, *View from Nashville*, 144.

13. Henry Strzelecki, Country Music Foundation Oral History Project, interview by John Rumble, March 14, 1990.

14. Bill Porter, interview in McClellan and Bratic, *Chet Atkins in Three Dimensions*, 2:151.

15. Bacon Reverb News.

CHAPTER 27

1. John Loudermilk, interview in McClellan and Bratic, *Chet Atkins in Three Dimensions*, 2:306, 307.

2. Dale Vinicur, liner notes, Don Gibson, *Don Gibson: The Singer—The Songwriter: 1949–1960* (Bear Family Records).

3. Richard Weize, discography, *Rosemary Clooney* (Bear Family Records).

4. Harry Pearson, "Yeah! Let's Get a Swinging Beat!," *Nashville Tennessean*, May 10, 1961.

5. Harry Pearson, "Ann-Margret Records Here; Budding Star," *Nashville Tennessean*, May 9, 1961.

6. Charlie McCoy with Travis D. Stimeling, *50 Cents and a Box Top: The Creative Life of Nashville Session Musician Charlie McCoy* (Morgantown: West Virginia University Press, 2017), 51.

7. McCoy with Stimeling, *50 Cents and a Box Top*, 55.

8. Smith, *Sideman*, 245.

9. Reinhart, *Chet Atkins*, 99.

10. Emery with Cox, *View from Nashville*, 142.

11. Henry Strzeleki, interview in McClellan and Bratic, *Chet Atkins in Three Dimensions*, 2:261, 262.

12. Pat Kirtley, personal interview.

CHAPTER 28

1. Henry Strzelecki, interview in McClellan and Bratic, *Chet Atkins in Three Dimensions*, 2:263.

2. Dale Vinicur, liner notes, *Bobby Bare* (Bear Family Records).

3. Wayne Carson, interview in McClellan and Bratic, *Chet Atkins in Three Dimensions*, 2:230.

4. Streissguth, *Like a Moth to a Flame*, 169.

5. Colin Escott, liner notes, *Jim Reeves* (Bear Family, 1994).

6. Streissguth, *Like a Moth to a Flame*, 169–170.

7. Streissguth, *Like a Moth to a Flame*, 170–171.

CHAPTER 29

1. Dale Vinicur, liner notes, *George Hamilton IV* (Bear Family Records).

2. Bill Porter, "CMF," *Rumble*, June 8, 1994.

3. "Chet Atkins Music City's Mr. RCA Victor," *Music Reporter*, June 29, 1963.

4. Emmie Caldwell, "She's the New Hillwood Champ," *Nashville Tennessean*, July 7, 1963.

CHAPTER 30

1. John Chintala, "Chet Atkins as Seen on TV: 1943–1969: Part One of a Multipart Series," *Mister Guitar*, no. 78 (May 2012).

2. Streissguth, *Like a Moth to a Flame*, 197; "Music City Exports Depart for Europe," *Billboard*, April 3, 1964.

3. Henry Strzeleki, interview in McClellan and Bratic, *Chet Atkins in Three Dimensions*, 2:265.

4. Streissguth, *Like a Moth to a Flame*, 200.
5. Colin Escott, liner notes, *Jim Reeves* (Bear Family, 1994).
6. Streissguth, *Like a Moth to a Flame*, 199.
7. Streissguth, *Like a Moth to a Flame*, 151–152.
8. Streissguth, *Like a Moth to a Flame*, 203–204.
9. Streissguth, *Like a Moth to a Flame*, 206.
10. Escott, liner notes, *Jim Reeves*, 77–78.

CHAPTER 31

1. Malloy, *Playback*, 76–77.
2. Bob Beckham, interview in McClellan and Bratic, *Chet Atkins in Three Dimensions*, 2:73.
3. "Como Cuts Record Despite Cold," *Nashville Tennessean*, February 10, 1965.
4. Macfarlane and Crossland, *Perry Como*, 127–129.
5. Jennings with Kaye, *Waylon*, 99; Waylon Jennings, *The Journey: Destiny's Child* by Lenny Kaye (Bear Family Records).
6. Jennings with Kaye, *Waylon*, 104.
7. Rob Elder, "RCA Opens $1 Million Center Here," *Nashville Tennessean*, March 30, 1965.
8. Reinhart, *Chet Atkins*, 115–116.
9. Atkins and Cochran, *Me and My Guitars*, 128, 130.
10. Mark Pritcher, "An Interview with Nato Lima: Part One," *Mister Guitar*, no. 27 (June 1992).
11. David Conrad, interview in McClellan and Bratic, *Chet Atkins in Three Dimensions*, 1:14–15.
12. Brown, *Looking Back to See*, 226.
13. Noboru Komaki, "It's a Guitar World," *Mister Guitar*, no. 39 (October 1996).
14. Jack Hurst, "Country Stars Back from Europe," *Nashville Tennessean*, November 19, 1965.
15. Reinhart, *Chet Atkins*, 118–119.

CHAPTER 32

1. Dale Vinicur, liner notes, and Richard Weize, discography, Don Gibson, *Don Gibson: The Singer—The Songwriter: 1949–1960* (Bear Family Records).
2. Malloy, *Playback*, 98.
3. Malloy, *Playback*, 92.
4. Jack Clement, personal conversation.
5. Pride with Henderson, *Pride*, 143.
6. Pat Anderson, "Patti Page Joins Folk Artists," *Nashville Tennessean*, November 19, 1961, 68.

7. Sanders, *That Thin, Wild Mercury Sound*, 153–154.

8. Jennings with Kaye, *Waylon*, 131.

CHAPTER 33

1. Thomas O'Neil, *The Grammys for the Record: The Ultimate, Unofficial Guide to America's Top Music Awards* (New York: Penguin 1993), 99.

2. "Man Faces Trial in Threat to Atkins," *Nashville Tennessean*, April 3, 1966.

3. George Harrison, liner notes, *Picks on the Beatles*.

4. Cusic, *Elvis in Nashville*, 118, 119.

5. Malloy, *Playback*, 97.

6. Lee Callaway, "Building to Start on Villager East," *Nashville Tennessean*, August 10, 1966; "Zoning Board to Study Variances on 4 Projects," *Nashville Banner*, August 13, 1966.

CHAPTER 34

1. Brown, *Looking Back to See*, 203–204; and Jennings with Kaye, *Waylon*, 134.

2. Jennings with Kaye, *Waylon*, 134.

3. John Chintala, "Chet Atkins as Seen on TV: 1943–1969: Part One of a Multipart Series," *Mister Guitar*, no. 78 (May 2012).

4. Tom Redmond, interview with Jimmy Moore, www.misterguitar.com.

5. Jim Ohlschmidt, "Reed Rides Again," *Mister Guitar*, no. 46 (April 1999).

6. Red O'Donnell, *Chet Atkins* (Nashville: Athens Music Company, 1967), 1.

7. O'Donnell, *Chet Atkins*, 5.

8. O'Donnell, *Chet Atkins*, 22–24.

9. O'Donnell, *Chet Atkins*, 25–27.

10. O'Donnell, *Chet Atkins*, 27–28.

11. O'Donnell, *Chet Atkins*, 30–31.

12. O'Donnell, *Chet Atkins*, 32–33.

13. O'Donnell, *Chet Atkins*, 35.

14. Howell Pearre, "Red Writes Chet's Story," *Nashville Banner*, May 2, 1967; and Red Donnell, "Atkins Book Party Bombed, but the Bahamas Were Great," *Nashville Banner*, August 11, 1983.

CHAPTER 35

1. Howell Pearre, "Carters Recall Hiring 'Unknown' Chet," *Nashville Banner*, May 26, 1967.

2. Geoffrey Cooper, "Jimmy Dean Arrives for Show," *Nashville Tennessean*, May 27, 1967.

3. Geoffrey Cooper, "Fiedler, Page Tune Up for String-Along Man," *Nashville Tennessean*, May 29, 1967.

4. Pearre Howell, "8,000 Give Chet 'Greatest Dad-Burned Day,'" *Nashville Banner*, May 29, 1967.

5. Geoffrey Cooper, "Nashville Sound Rings the Bell," *Nashville Tennessean*, May 28, 1967.

6. Howell, "8,000 Give Chet 'Greatest Dad-Burned Day.'" Also see "Chet Atkins Show Ticket Sale Nears," *Nashville Tennessean*, May 11, 1967; "Special Tribute to Atkins Set for May 28 at Auditorium," *Nashville Tennessean*, April 18, 1967; "Fitting Honor for Mr. Atkins," *Nashville Banner*, April 18, 1967; "Music Fans to Honor Guitar King," *Nashville Tennessean*, May 24, 1967; "Warm Tribute for Warm Person," *Nashville Banner*, May 30, 1967.

7. Reinhart, *Chet Atkins*, 125–127.

8. Paul Yandell, interview in McClellan and Bratic, *Chet Atkins in Three Dimensions*, 2:122.

9. Reinhart, *Chet Atkins*, 128.

CHAPTER 36

1. "Now 'Veep" (picture), *Nashville Tennessean*, March 11, 1968.

2. Jack Hurst, "A Song for Dad," *Chicago Tribute*, June 19, 1988.

3. "Father Gave the Desire: Chet Atkins," *Nashville Tennessean*, March 13, 1968.

4. "Chet Atkins Gets Executive Post: RCA in Nashville," *Nashville Tennessean*, n.d.

5. Emery with Cox, *View from Nashville*, 141.

6. Reinhart, *Chet Atkins*, 129–130.

7. Charles Wolfe, Hank Snow, *The Singing Ranger*, vol. 2 (Bear Family Records).

8. "Third Minnie Pearl's Nashville Outlet Set," *Nashville Banner*, March 20, 1968.

9. Ray Stevens, personal interview.

10. David Conrad, interview in McClellan and Bratic, *Chet Atkins in Three Dimensions*, 1:13–14.

11. Nash, *Behind Closed Doors*, 41.

CHAPTER 37

1. Howell Pearre, "Boots, Floyd and Chet Delight Fans," *Nashville Banner*, September 16, 1968.

2. John Johns, interview in McClellan and Bratic, *Chet Atkins in Three Dimensions*, 2:251.

3. "New Note for 'Mr. Guitar'" (picture), *Nashville Banner*, October 14, 1968.

4. John Chintala, "Chet Atkins as Seen on TV: 1943–1969: Part One of a Multipart Series," *Mister Guitar*, no. 78 (May 2012).

5. Chintala, "Chet Atkins as Seen on TV."

6. Tom Redmond, interview with Jimmy Moore, www.misterguitar.com.

7. Hemphill, *Nashville Sound*, 48–49, 50.

8. Hemphill, *Nashville Sound*, 51.

9. Hemphill, *Nashville Sound*, 52–53.

10. Hemphill, *Nashville Sound*, 53–54.

11. Jennings with Kaye, *Waylon*, 127–136.

12. Emery with Carter, *More Memories*, 188.

13. Jennings with Kaye, *Waylon*, 127–136.

14. Chintala, "Chet Atkins as Seen on TV."

CHAPTER 38

1. Putnam, *Music Lessons*, 70–74, 78–79.

2. Millie Kirkham, personal interview.

3. Putnam, *Music Lessons*, 79–82.

4. "Facility Gets Executive OK," *Nashville Tennessean*, May 29, 1969; "Tudor Inns Adds 3 Board Members," *Nashville Banner*, May 29, 1969.

5. "RCA Nashville Mounts 600G Renovation Plan," *Billboard*, July 12, 1969, 57.

6. Emery with Carter, *More Memories*, 194–195.

7. Reinhart, *Chet Atkins*, 131–132.

8. Jerry Thompson, "Atkins Named to Aurora Board," *Nashville Tennessean*, October 14, 1969.

CHAPTER 39

1. "Chet Atkins Plans Scholarship Fund for Music Students," *Nashville Banner*, January 14, 1970; "New Talent, Music Set for Festival," *Nashville Tennessean*, January 15, 1970; "Planning Addition to the Nashville Sound" (picture), *Nashville Banner*, January 15, 1970.

2. John Chintala, "Chet Atkins as Seen on TV: 1970–1979: Part Two of a Multipart Series," *Mister Guitar*, no. 79 (July 2012).

3. Reinhart, *Chet Atkins*, 135–137.

4. Kosser, *How Nashville Became Music City U.S.A.*, 194–195.

5. Red O'Donnell, "Bradley Named RCA Executive," *Nashville Banner*, June 9, 1970.

6. Clara Hieronymus, "Chet Atkins Guitar, Song Festival Slated in August," *Nashville Tennessean*, March 18, 1970.

7. Millie Milam Murphy, "Stars to Light," *Nashville Tennessean*, July 24, 1970; "Pickin' Singin': The Chet Atkins Guitar Festival Comes to Municipal

Auditorium Aug 7 and 8," *Nashville Tennessean*, August 1, 1970; Hance Bill, "St. Louis Performer Takes Top Honors," *Nashville Banner*, August 8, 1970.

CHAPTER 40

1. Merle Russell, personal conversation.

2. Merle Russell, interview in McClellan and Bratic, *Chet Atkins in Three Dimensions*, 1:111, 112.

3. Russell interview, 1:160.

4. Norma Condra, "At Home with the Chet Atkins," *Nashville Banner*, June 18, 1971.

5. "Chet Moves His Festival to Knoxville," *Nashville Tennessean*, March 19, 1971; Weldon Grimsley, "Chet Atkins Guitar Festival Slated for Knoxville in June," *Nashville Banner*, March 19, 1970; George Ene, "Chet Atkins Guitar Festival Not Easy?," *Nashville Banner*, May 29, 1971.

6. "Recently Formed FAME Inc. (Famous American Musicians and Educators) Headed by Guitarist Chet Atkins and Jerome Glaser," *Nashville Tennessean*, May 27, 1971; Elmer Stewart, "Atkins, Glaser to Market Music Teaching Concept," *Nashville Banner*, July 13, 1971.

7. Reinhart, *Chet Atkins*, 141–142.

8. Pat Kirtley, "Home & Jethro: All Kidding Aside," *Mister Guitar*, no. 80 (December 2012).

9. Reinhart, *Chet Atkins*, 144.

10. Jim Stephany, personal conversation.

11. Paul Yandell, interview in McClellan and Bratic, *Chet Atkins in Three Dimensions*, 2:120, 122; and Bob Guest, "Here's Paul Yandell," *Mister Guitar*, no. 22 (November 1989).

CHAPTER 41

1. Jack Hurst, "Chet Atkins 'Picked' on Tour," *Nashville Tennessean*, April 4, 1972.

2. "Chet Atkins Recognition Dinner Set," *Nashville Banner*, May 9, 1972; "Cash to Present Medallion in Tribute to Chet Atkins," *Nashville Tennessean*, May 4, 1972; "Atkins Gets NCCJ Humanities Award," *Nashville Banner*, April 6, 1972; "Planning for Presentation: For National Humanitarian Award," *Nashville Tennessean*, April 10, 1972; "Atkins Given Christians, Jews Brotherhood Honor," *Nashville Banner*, May 10, 1972; Jack Hurst, "Modest Mr. Guitar Accepts Honor," *Nashville Tennessean*, May 10, 1972.

3. John Chintala, "Chet Atkins as Seen on TV: 1970–1979: Part Two of a Multipart Series," *Mister Guitar*, no. 79 (July 2012).

4. Jennings with Kaye, *Waylon*, 177–182.

5. Jerry Bradley, personal conversation.

6. Andrew Sandoval, *Chained to a Memory: The Everly Brothers: The Recordings 1966–1972* (Bear Family Records).

7. Chintala, "Chet Atkins as Seen on TV"; "Maybe Too Uptown, Chet Tells 'Today,'" *Nashville Tennessean*, October 20, 1972.

8. Red O'Donnell, "Bradley Named Director of RCA Records Here," *Nashville Banner*, November 28, 1972; Jerry Bailey, "Bradley Sways Switch Primarily Only Title," *Nashville Tennessean*, November 9, 1972; "Atkins Says He Will Not Quit as VP," *Nashville Banner*, November 9, 1972; "Chet Atkins to Quit RCA Post," *Nashville Banner*, November 23, 1972.

9. Jerry Bailey, "Chet Won't Tour in '73 Festival," *Nashville Tennessean*, November 23, 1972.

CHAPTER 42

1. Macfarlane and Crossland, *Perry Como*, 140.

2. Bill Hance, "Robert Flack Takes Top Grammy Prize," *Nashville Banner*, March 5, 1973; Red O'Donnell, "Grammy Show Producer Impressed by Nashville," *Nashville Banner*, March 3, 1973; Hance, "Move Over Opry, It's Grammy Time," *Nashville Banner*, March 3, 1973; O'Donnell, "This Probably Galls Them a Lot," *Nashville Banner*, March 3, 1973; Hance, "Roberta Flack Takes Top Grammy Prize," *Nashville Banner*, March 5, 1973; Tom Flake, "Guy Lombardo Style Remains Entrancing," *Nashville Banner*, March 5, 1973; O'Donnell, "Hot Hands Slowed Awards," *Nashville Banner*, March 5, 1973; Hance, "Music City Lives Up to Title with Grammy Awards Show," *Nashville Banner*, March 5, 1973.

3. Atkins and Neely, *Country Gentleman*, 216.

4. Atkins and Neely, *Country Gentleman*, 217.

5. Atkins and Neely, *Country Gentleman*, 218.

6. Atkins and Neely, *Country Gentleman*, 219.

7. Tom Redmond, interview with Jimmy Moore, www.misterguitar.com.

8. Emery with Carter, *More Memories*, 182.

CHAPTER 43

1. Paul Yandell, interview in McClellan and Bratic, *Chet Atkins in Three Dimensions*, 2:122.

2. Bill Hance, "Hall of Fame Displays 1st Solid Body Guitar," *Nashville Banner*, April, 1974.

3. "Kollar, Robert. A Man of Guitars," *Nashville Tennessean*, January 25, 1974.

4. Louis Nicholas, "Symphony, Chet Spring Pops Program Pleasant, Relaxing," *Nashville Tennessean*, May 13, 1974; "Chet Atkins to Perform in Spring Pops May 10–12," *Nashville Banner*, May 2, 1974; "Mr. Guitar' Solos

with Symphony," *Nashville Tennessean*, May 5, 1974; "Chet Appears with Nashville Symphony Orchestra Today at 3 p.m. in Belmont College's Massey Auditorium" (picture), *Nashville Tennessean*, May 12, 1974; "Pondering Picking Points" (picture), *Nashville Banner*, May 11, 1974.

5. Red O'Donnell, "Chet Chats about Biog, Age, Education, Etc.," *Nashville Banner*, May 27, 1974.

6. Atkins with Neely, *Country Gentleman*, 209.

7. Cusic, *Beatles*, 163–166, 182.

8. John Chintala, "Chet Atkins as Seen on TV: 1970–1979: Part Two of a Multipart Series," *Mister Guitar*, no. 79 (July 2012).

9. Mark Pritcher, "John Knowles C.G.P.," *Mister Guitar*, no. 44 (June 1998).

10. John Knowles, personal interview, June 16, 2023.

CHAPTER 44

1. Shaughnessy, *Les Paul*, 272–274.

2. Reinhart, *Chet Atkins*, 154–156.

3. Reinhart, *Chet Atkins*, 156–157.

4. Eve Zibart, "Anita Kerr Back for Disc Session: With Chet Atkins," *Nashville Tennessean*, June 14, 1975.

5. Snow with Ownbey and Burris, *Hank Snow Story*, 477–478.

CHAPTER 45

1. John Chintala, "Chet Atkins as Seen on TV: 1970–1979: Part Two of a Multipart Series," *Mister Guitar*, no. 79 (July 2012).

2. John Knowles, personal interview, June 16, 2023.

3. Lenny Kaye, *Waylon Jennings: The Journey: Destiny's Child* (Bear Family Records), 3, 5.

4. Tom Redmond, interview with Randy Goodrum, www.misterguitar.com.

5. Reinhart, *Chet Atkins*, 157–158.

6. Chintala, "Chet Atkins as Seen on TV: 1970–1979: Part Two."

CHAPTER 46

1. Dave Stewart, "Reminiscing: Chet Atkins in Concert with the Symphony, 1977," *Mister Guitar*, no. 50 (June 2000).

2. Bill Hance, "Chet Atkins Involved in Rock Music: Designs 'Super Axe' Guitar," *Nashville Banner*, July 20, 1977.

3. Chet Atkins, Country Music Foundation Oral History Project, interview by Douglas B. Green, Nashville, 1977.

4. Bill Hance, "Atkins', Travis' Mentor Mose Rager at Fan Fair," *Nashville Banner*, June 11, 1977.

5. Jennings with Kaye, *Waylon*, 183.

6. Knowles, interview in McClellan and Bratic, *Chet Atkins in Three Dimensions*, 2:205.

7. John Chintala, "Chet Atkins as Seen on TV: 1970–1979: Part Two of a Multipart Series," *Mister Guitar*, no. 79 (July 2012).

8. Reinhart, *Chet Atkins*, 164–165.

9. Paul Yandell, interview in McClellan and Bratic, *Chet Atkins in Three Dimensions*, 2:121.

10. Henry Strzelecki, interview in McClellan and Bratic, *Chet Atkins in Three Dimensions*, 2:264.

11. Mark Pritcher, "The Musical Life of Marcel Dadi," *Mister Guitar*, no. 39 (October 1996).

CHAPTER 47

1. Mark Pritcher, "An Interview with Steve Wariner: No More Mister Nice Guy," *Mister Guitar*, no. 38 (June 1996).

2. Tom Redmond, interview with Tony Migliore, www.misterguitar.com.

3. John Chintala, "Chet Atkins as Seen on TV: 1970–1979: Part Two of a Multipart Series," *Mister Guitar*, no. 79 (July 2012).

4. Joe Galante, personal interview.

5. Kay West, "They Barked, He Bit Back: Joe Galante," *Nashville Scene*, November 6, 2003.

6. Galante, personal interview.

7. West, "They Barked, He Bit Back."

8. Jack Hurst, "The Accent's on Atkins," *Chicago Tribute*, July 8, 1999.

9. Chintala, "Chet Atkins as Seen on TV: 1970–1979: Part Two."

10. Tom Redmond, interview with Earl Klugh, www.misterguitar.com; "John Knowles: Nashville Guitarist," *Mister Guitar*, no. 15 (July 1987); Knowles, interview in McClellan and Bratic, *Chet Atkins in Three Dimensions*, 2:196.

CHAPTER 48

1. Bob Allen, "The Real Chet Atkins," *Nashville!*, January 1979.

2. John Knowles, interview in McClellan and Bratic, *Chet Atkins in Three Dimensions*, 2:201.

3. Reinhart, *Chet Atkins*, 168–169.

4. Bill Piburn, interview in McClellan and Bratic, *Chet Atkins in Three Dimensions*, 2:35.

5. Tom Redmond, interview with Steve Wariner, www.misterguitar.com.

6. Steve Wariner, personal conversation.

CHAPTER 49

1. Merle Russell, interview in McClellan and Bratic, *Chet Atkins in Three Dimensions*, 1:110.

2. Tony Brown, interview in McClellan and Bratic, *Chet Atkins in Three Dimensions*, 1:53.

3. Laura Eipper, "'Tribute to Chet Atkins' Presents a Rare View," *Nashville Tennessean*, November 30, 1980.

4. John Chintala, "Chet Atkins as Seen on TV: 1980–1989: Part Three of a Multipart Series," *Mister Guitar*, no. 81 (March 2013).

5. Charlie McCoy with Travis D. Stimeling, *50 Cents and a Box Top: The Creative Life of Nashville Session Musician Charlie McCoy* (Morgantown: West Virginia University Press, 2017).

6. Mark Pritcher, "Tommy Emmanuel: A Great Guitarist Comes Up from Down Under," *Mister Guitar*, no. 40 (January 1997).

7. Chintala, "Chet Atkins as Seen on TV: 1980–1989: Part Three."

CHAPTER 50

1. Bacon, *50 Years of Gretsch Electrics*, 73, 76–77.

2. "Prime Picker Picked for Instrumental Role" (picture), *Nashville Tennessean*, May 29, 1981.

3. John Chintala, "Chet Atkins as Seen on TV: 1980–1989: Part Three of a Multipart Series," *Mister Guitar*, no. 81 (March 2013).

4. Chintala, "Chet Atkins as Seen on TV: 1980–1989: Part Three."

5. Chintala, "Chet Atkins as Seen on TV: 1980–1989: Part Three."

6. Jerry Bradley, personal interview.

7. Red O'Donnell, "Atkins Not Renewing Contract as RCA VP," *Nashville Banner*, July 27, 1981; "Chet Atkins to Leave RCA Executive Post," *Nashville Tennessean*, July 28, 1981.

8. Ralph Emery, personal conversation.

9. Nash, *Behind Closed Doors*, 43.

10. Paul Yandell, interview in McClellan and Bratic, *Chet Atkins in Three Dimensions*, 2:123.

11. John Knowles, interview in McClellan and Bratic, *Chet Atkins in Three Dimensions*, 2:198.

CHAPTER 51

1. John Chintala, "Chet Atkins as Seen on TV: 1980–1989: Part Three of a Multipart Series," *Mister Guitar*, no. 81 (March 2013).

2. Walter Carter, "'Player Guitar' Turns Any Picker into Chet Atkins," *Nashville Tennessean*, May 22, 1982.

3. Walter Carter, "Thin Guitar Gives Chet New Sound," *Nashville Tennessean*, June 19, 1982.

4. Tom Redmond, interview with Fred Kewley, www.misterguitar.com.

5. Robert K. Oermann and Sandy Neese, "'Mr. RCA' Chet Atkins Ready to Sign with CBS," *Nashville Tennessean*, October 2, 1982.

6. "It's Official. Chet Atkins Has Signed with CBS as a Columbia Act," *Mister Guitar*, no. 1 (January 1983).

7. Nash, *Behind Closed Doors*, 41–42.

8. Blake Chancey, personal conversation.

9. Chintala, "Chet Atkins as Seen on TV: 1980–1989: Part Three."

CHAPTER 52

1. *Mister Guitar*, no. 1 (January 1983).

2. Cusic, *Randy Travis*, 45.

3. Emery with Carter, *Memories*, 176.

4. Emery with Carter, *Memories*, 180–181.

5. Emery with Carter, *Memories*, 183.

6. John Chintala, "Chet Atkins as Seen on TV: 1980–1989: Part Three of a Multipart Series," *Mister Guitar*, no. 81 (March 2013).

7. Emery with Carter, *More Memories*, 182.

8. Emery with Carter, *More Memories*, 185.

9. Robert K. Oermann, "CBS Helps Chet Atkins Celebrate Release of His 115th Album," *Nashville Tennessean*, April 28, 1983.

10. Bergen White with Mitchell B. White, *Right Place at the Write Time: A Colorful and Candid Behind-the-Scenes Look at My 60 years in the Recording Industry: A Memoir* (D. Bergen White, 2022), 53–54.

11. *Mister Guitar*, no. 2 (July 1983).

12. Robert K. Oermann, "'Mr. Guitar' Keeps Low Profile," *Nashville Tennessean*, July 10, 1983.

13. Chintala, "Chet Atkins as Seen on TV: 1980–1989: Part Three."

14. Tom Redmond, interview with Mark O'Connor, www.misterguitar.com.

15. Pat Kirtley, personal interview.

CHAPTER 53

1. Terry Wedding, interview in McClellan and Deyan Bratic, *Chet Atkins in Three Dimensions*, 2:175.

2. Tommy Emmanuel, interview in McClellan and Bratic, *Chet Atkins in Three Dimensions*, 2:285.

3. Bob Guest, "Here's Paul Yandell," *Mister Guitar*, no. 22 (November 1989).

4. Atkins Can't Play at Breau Benefit," *Nashville Tennessean*, August 19, 1984.

5. Mike Poston, personal interview.

6. Thomas Goldsmith, "Mr. Guitar Strikes Again: Chet Atkins Makes More Music with Mark Knopfler," *Nashville Tennessean*, October 27, 1990.

7. Mark Knopfler, interview in McClellan and Bratic, *Chet Atkins in Three Dimensions*, 2:356.

8. Tom Redmond, interview with Fred Kewley, www.misterguitar.com.

CHAPTER 53

1. Terry Wedding, interview in McClellan and Deyan Bratic, *Chet Atkins in Three Dimensions*, 2:175.

2. Tommy Emmanuel, interview in McClellan and Bratic, *Chet Atkins in Three Dimensions*, 2:285.

3. Bob Guest, "Here's Paul Yandell," *Mister Guitar*, no. 22 (November 1989).

4. Atkins Can't Play at Breau Benefit," *Nashville Tennessean*, August 19, 1984.

5. Mike Poston, personal interview.

6. Thomas Goldsmith, "Mr. Guitar Strikes Again: Chet Atkins Makes More Music with Mark Knopfler," *Nashville Tennessean*, October 27, 1990.

7. Mark Knopfler, interview in McClellan and Bratic, *Chet Atkins in Three Dimensions*, 2:356.

8. Tom Redmond, interview with Fred Kewley, www.misterguitar.com.

CHAPTER 55

1. John Knowles, interview in McClellan and Bratic, *Chet Atkins in Three Dimensions*, 2:197–198.

2. Tom Redmond, interview with Randy Goodrum, www.misterguitar.com.

3. Thomas Goldsmith, "Garrison Keillor Hits Town to Record with Chet Atkins," *Nashville Tennessean*, May 23, 1986; "Atkins, Keillor Produce Album Aimed at Yuppies," *Nashville Banner*, May 24, 1986.

4. Janis Ian, "In Memoriam: Chet Atkins," *Performing Songwriter*, no. 57 (August 2001).

5. Thomas Goldsmith, "Music Row Monarch Chet Atkins Reigns as Jack of All Guitar Trades," *Nashville Tennessean*, June 1, 1986.

CHAPTER 56

1. Tom Redmond, interview with Mark O'Connor, www.misterguitar.com.

2. Tom Redmond, interview with Steve Wariner, www.misterguitar.com.

3. Tom Redmond, interview with Don McLean, www.misterguitar.com.

4. "Convention News," *Mister Guitar*, no. 14 (May 1987).

5. Greg Bailey, "Chet, Friends Make Cable Special Sing," *Nashville Banner*, September 5, 1987.

6. John Chintala, "Chet Atkins as Seen on TV: 1980–1989: Part Three of a Multipart Series," *Mister Guitar*, no. 81 (March 2013).

7. Reinhart, *Chet Atkins*, 178–179.

CHAPTER 57

1. Tom Rogers, "Atkins, Keillor Together Again at Langford," *Nashville Tennessean*, May 6, 1988.

2. Nash, *Behind Closed Doors*, 46–50.

3. "Angered Atkins Blasts 'Tacky' CMA," Associated Press, November 2, 1988; Joe Edwards, "Chet Atkins Still Miffed by CMA Show," *Nashville Tennessean*, November 2, 1988.

4. Thomas Goldsmith, "Famed Guitarists to Host Pickin,'" *Nashville Tennessean*, May 31, 1989.

5. *Mister Guitar*, no. 22 (November 1989).

6. Sandy Smith, "Symphony Ball Presentation to Pay Tribute to Chet Atkins," *Nashville Tennessean*, November 23, 1989; "Will Receive Harmony Award at the Symphony Ball on Dec 9," *Nashville Tennessean*, November 23, 1989.

7. Tom Redmond, interview with Fred Kewley, www.misterguitar.com.

CHAPTER 58

1. Pat Kirtley, "Chet's House on Music Row," *Mister Guitar*, no. 92 (June 2019).

2. Laura Eipper, "Chet Find Compliments Are Hard to Handle," *Nashville Tennessean*, May 11, 1990.

3. Mark Knopfler, interview in McClellan and Bratic, *Chet Atkins in Three Dimensions*, 2:356.

4. Mark Pritcher, "An Interview With Chet," *Mister Guitar*, no. 25 (June 1991).

5. Thomas Goldsmith, "Mr. Guitar Strikes Again: Chet Atkins Makes More Music with Mark Knopfler," *Nashville Tennessean*, October 27, 1990; Thomas Goldsmith, "Mr. Guitar Strikes Again," *Nashville Tennessean*, October 27, 1990.

6. Knopfler interview, 2:350, 355.

7. Knopfler interview, 2:357–358, 356, 357, 358, 359 356.

CHAPTER 59

1. "Chet Atkins: 'Mr. Guitar' Has Street Named After Him," *Nashville Banner*, May 9, 1991; "Chet's New Place. Street Named for Him" (picture), *Nashville Tennessean*, May 9, 1991; "An Instrumental Legend: Chet Atkins Place in Nashville—Four-Block Stretch of Famed Music Row," *Nashville Tennessean*, May 10, 1991.

2. John Knowles, interview in McClellan and Bratic, *Chet Atkins in Three Dimensions*, 2:206.

3. Mark Pritcher, "An Interview with Chet," *Mister Guitar*, no. 25 (June 1991).

4. Jim Ohlschmidt, "The Basement Tapes," *Mister Guitar*, no. 26 (December 1991).

5. Ohlschmidt, "The Basement Tapes" *Mister Guitar*, no. 26 (December 1991).

6. Tom Redmond, interview with Pat Bergeson, www.misterguitar.com.

CHAPTER 60

1. John Chintala, "Chet Atkins as Seen on TV: 1990–1995: Part Four of a Multipart Series," *Mister Guitar*, no. 83 (March 2014).

2. Chintala, "Chet Atkins as Seen on TV: 1990–1995: Part Four."

3. *Mister Guitar*, no. 43 (April 1998).

4. John Chintala, "Chet Atkins: A Half Century of Excellence," *Mister Guitar*, no. 48 (December 1999).

5. Mark Pritcher, "Hall of Fame," *Mister Guitar*, no. 29 (May 1993).

6. Mark Pritcher, "Grammy," *Mister Guitar*, no. 29 (May 1993); Jay Orr, "Chet Atkins Is Lauded by Friends," *Nashville Banner*, March 19, 1993.

7. Stan Surman, "An Interview with Kirk Sand," *Mister Guitar*, no. 29 (May 1993).

8. Mark Pritcher, "Grab Bag," *Mister Guitar*, no. 29 (May 1993).

9. Claes Neeb, "Norwegian Mountain Song: How One Small Guitar Lick Made a Difference!," *Mister Guitar*, no. 64 (April 2006).

10. Mark Pritcher, "Tommy Emmanuel: A Great Guitarist Comes Up from Down Under," *Mister Guitar*, no. 40 (January 1997).

11. Tom Redmond, interview with Tommy Emmanuel, www.misterguitar.com.

12. Chintala, "Chet Atkins as Seen on TV: 1990–1995: Part Four."

CHAPTER 61

1. John Chintala, "Chet Atkins as Seen on TV: 1990–1995: Part Four of a Multipart Series," *Mister Guitar*, no. 83 (March 2014).

2. Chintala, "Chet Atkins as Seen on TV: 1990–1995: Part Four."

3. *Mister Guitar*, no. 43 (April 1998).

4. John Chintala, "Chet Atkins: A Half Century of Excellence," *Mister Guitar*, no. 48 (December 1999).

5. Mark Pritcher, "Hall of Fame," *Mister Guitar*, no. 29 (May 1993).

6. Mark Pritcher, "Grammy," *Mister Guitar*, no. 29 (May 1993); Jay Orr, "Chet Atkins Is Lauded by Friends," *Nashville Banner*, March 19, 1993.

7. Stan Surman, "An Interview with Kirk Sand," *Mister Guitar*, no. 29 (May 1993).

8. Mark Pritcher, "Grab Bag," *Mister Guitar*, no. 29 (May 1993).

9. Claes Neeb, "Norwegian Mountain Song: How One Small Guitar Lick Made a Difference!," *Mister Guitar*, no. 64 (April 2006).

10. Mark Pritcher, "Tommy Emmanuel: A Great Guitarist Comes Up from Down Under," *Mister Guitar*, no. 40 (January 1997).

11. Tom Redmond, interview with Tommy Emmanuel, www.misterguitar.com.

12. Chintala, "Chet Atkins as Seen on TV: 1990–1995: Part Four."

CHAPTER 62

1. Pat Kirtley, "Chet's Alternate Tunings," *Mister Guitar*, no. 38 (June 1996).

2. "Chet Atkins Almost Alone," *Mister Guitar*, no. 37 (February 1996).

3. Tom Redmond, interview with Randy Goodrum, www.misterguitar.com.

4. Tom Roland, "The Atkins Sound: Chet Atkins Shares Guitar Licks to Celebrate Tennessee's Birthday," *Nashville Tennessean*, May 12, 1996.

5. "Chet at Ryman Auditorium with Steve Wariner, Larry Carlton and Leo Kottke," *Mister Guitar*, no. 38 (June 1996).

6. Garrison Keillor, "A Few Thoughts about Chet," *Mister Guitar*, no. 38 (June 1996); Mark Pritcher, "Chet's 'Radio Days' with Garrison Keillor," *Mister Guitar*, no. 37 (February 1996).

7. *Mister Guitar*, no. 39 (October 1996).

8. Bernard Laux, "Marcel Dadi," *Mister Guitar*, no. 39 (October 1996); Mark Pritcher, "The Musical Life of Marcel Dadi," *Mister Guitar*, no. 39 (October 1996).

9. Mark Pritcher, "Grab Bag," *Mister Guitar*, no. 29 (May 1993).

10. I was at that Café Milano show.

11. *Mister Guitar*, no. 39 (October 1996).

12. Jay Orr, "Major Citywide Music Festival to Honor Chet," *Nashville Banner*, November 1, 1996; Tom Roland, "Add Chet to Festival Mix: Atkins' 'Musician Days' Part of Busy Summer," *Nashville Tennessean*, November 2, 1996.

13. Mark Pritcher, "Tommy Emmanuel: A Great Guitarist Comes Up from Down Under," *Mister Guitar*, no. 40 (January 1997).

14. David Pomeroy, personal interview.

15. Reinhart, *Chet Atkins*, 195–196.

CHAPTER 63

1. John Chintala, "Chet Atkins as Seen on TV: 1996–2001: Part Five of a Multipart Series," *Mister Guitar*, no. 84 (June 2014).

2. Mark Pritcher, "Guitar World Picks the 100 Greatest Guitarists of All Time," *Mister Guitar*, no. 41 (January 1997): 3; Tom Roland, "Atkins' Cancer in Remission: Mr. Guitar Hopes to Be at Festival," *Nashville Tennessean*, June 11, 1997.

3. Ray Stevens, personal conversation.

4. Janis Ian, "In Memoriam: Chet Atkins," *Performing Songwriter*, no. 57 (August 2001); Jay Orr and Michael Gray, "Ailing, but Smiling, Humble Chet Turns the Spotlight on Others," *Nashville Banner*, June 26, 1997; Tom Roland, "Concert Honors 'Mr. Guitar': Atkins' Work, Influence Echo during Tribute," *Nashville Tennessean*, June 11, 1997; Tom Roland, "Atkins' Cancer in Remission: Mr. Guitar Hopes to Be at Festival," *Nashville Tennessean*, June 11, 1997; Tom Roland, "Musicians in the Spotlight: Chet Atkins Musician Days Turns Stages over to the Musicians behind the Stars," *Nashville Tennessean*, June 24, 1997; Michael Gray, "Chet's Pals Hop Aboard for Salute at Ryman," *Nashville Banner*, June 10, 1997; Tom Roland, "Concert Honors 'Mr. Guitar': Atkins' Work, Influence Echo during Tribute," *Nashville Tennessean*, June 26, 1997; John Chintala, "Chet Atkins: A Half Century of Excellence," *Mister Guitar*, no. 48 (December 1999).

5. Bob Guest, "Convention '97: The 13th Annual Convention," *Mister Guitar*, no. 42 (December 1997).

6. Joanne Henry, "Chet Performs in Madisonville Kentucky," *Mister Guitar*, no. 42 (December 1997).

7. *Mister Guitar*, no. 42 (December 1997).

8. "Chet Inducted to the Hollywood Rockwalk," *Mister Guitar*, no. 42 (December 1997); James Childer, "Chet's Highway Is Dedicated in Georgia," *Mister Guitar*, no. 42 (December 1997).

9. "Music City: This Year's 'Billboard' Century Award Pick Is Mr. Guitar," *Billboard*, December 6, 1997.

10. Mark Pritcher, "Chet Inducted to Thumbpickers Hall of Fame," *Mister Guitar*, no. 43 (April 1998).

11. "Interview," *In Review*, June 23, 1998.

12. Bob Guest and Mark Pritcher, "Convention 98! Master of Ceremonies Bill Spann, 14th Annual Convention," *Mister Guitar*, no. 43 (January 1999).

13. Mark Pritcher, "Chet Inducted to Thumbpickers Hall of Fame," *Mister Guitar*, no. 43 (April 1998).

14. "Interview," *In Review*, June 23, 1998.

15. Bob Guest and Mark Pritcher, "Convention 98! Master of Ceremonies Bill Spann, 14th Annual Convention," *Mister Guitar*, no. 43 (January 1999).

CHAPTER 64

1. Beverly Keel, "A Nashville Life: Mr. Guitar: Chet Atkins Is Perhaps the Most Influential Man to Ever Walk Down Music Row," *Nashville Life*, December 1998–January 1999.

2. John Chintala, "Chet Atkins as Seen on TV: 1996–2001: Part Five of a Multipart Series," *Mister Guitar*, no. 84 (June 2014).

3. *Mister Guitar*, no. 46 (April 1999).

4. "Cheers for Chet" (picture), *Nashville Tennessean*, July 10, 1999.

5. "Hard Rock Sign Puts Chet Atkins' Guitar Up in Lights" (picture), *Nashville Tennessean*, October 29, 1999.

6. Chintala, "Chet Atkins as Seen on TV: 1996–2001: Part Five."

CHAPTER 65

1. Pat Kirtley, "Chet's Home on Music Row," *Mister Guitar*, no. 92 (June 2019).

2. Blake Chancey, personal conversation.

3. Alan Bostick, "Grab a Seat Next to Chet," *Mister Guitar*, no. 49 (March 2000); Mark Pritcher, "New Nashville Landmark Looks a Lot Like Chet Atkins," *Mister Guitar*, no. 49 (March 2000).

4. Neil Strauss, "The Pop Life: A Guitarist Synonymous with a City and a Sound," *Mister Guitar*, no. 49 (March 2000).

5. Mark Pritcher, *Mister Guitar*, no. 50 (June 2000).

6. Steve Wariner, interview in McClellan and Bratic, *Chet Atkins in Three Dimensions*, 2:50.

7. Janis Ian, "In Memoriam: Chet Atkins," *Performing Songwriter*, no. 57 (August 2001).

8. Boots Randolph, interview in McClellan and Bratic, *Chet Atkins in Three Dimensions*, 2:75.

9. Bob Beckham, interview in McClellan and Bratic, *Chet Atkins in Three Dimensions*, 1:75.

10. Steve Wariner, interview in McClellan and Bratic, *Chet Atkins in Three Dimensions*, 2:49.

11. Tommy Emmanuel, interview in McClellan and Bratic, *Chet Atkins in Three Dimensions*, 2:287–288.

CHAPTER 66

1. "Chet Atkins Loans Priceless Guitars to the CMF Hall of Fame," *Mister Guitar*, no. 52 (June 2001).

2. Mark Pritcher, "Chet in Print: A Survey of Books, Albums, and Videos Featuring Transcriptions of the Music of Chet Atkins," *Mister Guitar*, no. 52 (June 2001).

3. Janis Ian, "In Memoriam: Chet Atkins," *Performing Songwriter*, no. 57 (August 2001).

4. Steve Wariner, interview in McClellan and Bratic, *Chet Atkins in Three Dimensions*, 2:49.

5. Peter Cooper, "Friends, Fans Celebrate Atkins' Life and Music," *Nashville Tennessean*, July 1, 2021.

6. Editorial, *Nashville Tennessean*, July 3, 2010.

7. Mark Pritcher, "CAAS Convention 2001," *Mister Guitar*, no. 53 (February 2002).

Selected Bibliography

Anderson, Bill. *A Life of Music, Love, Tragedy & Triumph. An Autobiography.* Atlanta: Longstreet, 1989.

Atkins, Chet, and Michael Cochran. *Me and My Guitars.* Milwaukee, Wisc.: Hal Leonard, Russ Cochran, 2001, 2003.

Atkins, Chet, with Bill Neely. *Country Gentleman.* Chicago: Henry Regnery, 1974.

Bacon, Tony. *50 Years of Gretsch Electrics: Half a Century of White Falcons, Gents, Jets & Other Great Guitars.* San Francisco: Backbeat, 2005.

Biszick-Lockwood, Bar. *Restless Giant: The Life and Times of Jean Aberbach & Hill and Range Songs.* Urbana: University of Illinois Press, 2010.

Brooks, Tim, and Earle Marsh. *The Complete Directory to Prime Time Network and Cable TV Shows 1946–Present.* 8th ed. New York: Ballantine, 2003.

Brown, Maxine. *Looking Back to See: A Country Music Memoir.* Little Rock: University of Arkansas Press, 2005.

Bufwack, Mary A., and Robert K. Oermann. *Finding Her Voice: The Saga of Women in Country Music.* New York: Crown, 1993.

Byrd, Jerry. *It Was a Trip: On Wings of Music.* Anaheim Hills, Ca.: Centerstream, 2003.

Cusic, Don. *The Beatles and Country Music.* Nashville: Brackish, 2015.

———. *Discovering Country Music.* Westport, Conn.: Praeger, 2008.

———. *Eddy Arnold: His Life and Times.* Nashville: Brackish, 2016.

———. *Elvis in Nashville.* Nashville: Brackish, 2012.

———. *Hank Williams: The Singer and the Songs.* Nashville: Brackish, 2016.

———. *The Nashville Sound: An Illustrated Timeline.* St. Louis: Reedy, 2018.

———. *Randy Travis: King of the New Traditionalists.* New York: St. Martin's, 1990.

———. *Roger Miller: Dang Him!* Nashville: Brackish, 2012.

Davis, Don, as told to Ruth B. White. *Nashville Steeler: My Life in Country Music.* Atglen, Pa.: Schiffer, 2012.

Davis, Skeeter. *Bus Fare to Kentucky: The Autobiography of Skeeter Davis.* Secaucus, N.J.: Birch Lane, 1993.

Dawidoff, Nicholas. *In the Country of Country: People and Places in American Music.* New York: Pantheon, 1997.

Dean, Jimmy, and Donna Meade Dean. *Thirty Years of Sausage, Fifty Years of Ham: Jimmy Dean's Own Story.* New York: Berkley, 2004.

Duncan, Dayton, and Ken Burns. *Country Music: An Illustrated History.* New York: Knopf, 2019.

Emery, Ralph, with Tom Carter. *Memories: The Autobiography of Ralph Emery.* New York: Macmillan, 1991.

———. *More Memories.* New York: Putnam, 1993.

Emery, Ralph, with Patsi Bale Cox. *50 Years Down a Country Road.* New York: William Morrow, 2000.

———. *The View from Nashville: On the Record with Country Music's Greatest Stars.* New York: William Morrow, 1998.

Eng, Steve. *A Satisfied Mind: The Country Music Life of Porter Wagoner.* Nashville: Rutledge Hill, 1992.

Escott, Colin, with George Merritt and William MacEwen. *Hank Williams: The Biography.* Boston: Little, Brown, 1994.

Freda, Michael. *Eddy Arnold Discography 1944–1996.* Westport, Conn.: Greenwood, 1977.

Guralnick, Peter. *Last Train to Memphis: The Rise of Elvis Presley.* Boston: Little, Brown, 1994.

Havighurst, Craig. *Air Castle of the South: WSM and the Making of Music City.* Urbana: University of Illinois Press, 2007.

Hawkins, Martin. *A Shot in the Dark: Making Records in Nashville, 1946–1955.* Nashville: Vanderbilt University Press & Country Music Foundation, 2006.

Hemphill, Paul. *The Nashville Sound: Bright Lights and Country Music.* New York: Simon & Schuster, 1970. Reprint, Athens: University of Georgia Press, 2015.

Jackson, Carlton, and Nancy Richey. *Mose Rager: Kentucky's Incomparable Guitar Master.* Morley, Mo.: Acclaim, 2016.

Jennings, Waylon, with Lenny Kaye. *Waylon: An Autobiography.* New York: Warner, 1996.

Kingsbury, Paul, ed. *The Encyclopedia of Country Music.* New York: Oxford University Press, 1998.

Kosser, Michael. *How Nashville Became Music City U.S.A.* Milwaukee: Hal Leonard, 2006.

Maastricht, Norm. *Paul Yandell: Second to the Best: A Sideman's Chronical.* Anglen, Pa.: Schiffer, 2016.

Macfarlane, Malcolm, and Ken Crossland. *Perry Como: A Biography and Complete Career Record.* Jefferson, N.C.: McFarland, 2009.

Malloy, Jim. *Playback: A Collection of Stories and Musical Memories*. n.p.: Createspace, 2005.
Malone, Bobbie, and Bill C. Malone. *Nashville's Songwriting Sweethearts: The Boudleaux and Felice Bryant Story*. Norman: University of Oklahoma Press, 2020.
Marmorstein, Gary. *The Label: The Story of Columbia Records*. New York: Thunder's Mouth, 2007.
McClellan, John, and Deyan Bratic. *Chet Atkins in Three Dimensions: 50 Years of Legendary Guitar*. Vol. 2. Pacific, Mo.: Mel Bay, 2004.
McCusker, Kristine, and Diane Peckinold, eds. *A Boy Named Sue: Gender and Country Music*. Jackson: University Press of Mississippi, 2004.
Nash, Alanna. *Behind Closed Doors: Talking with the Legends of Country Music*. New York: Knopf, 1988.
Pecknold, Diane, ed. *Hidden in the Mix: The African American Presence in Country Music*. Durham, N.C.: Duke University Press, 2013.
Price, Deborah Evans. *The CMA Awards: Country Music's Biggest Night*. Atlanta: Whitman, 2010.
Pride, Charley, with Jim Henderson. *Pride: The Charley Pride Story*. New York: William Morrow, 1994.
Putnam, Norbert. *Music Lessons: A Musical Memoir*. Nashville: Thimbleton House Media, 2017.
Reinhart, Mark S. *Chet Atkins: The Greatest Songs of Mister Guitar*. Jefferson, N.C.: McFarland, 2014.
Sanders, Daryl. *That Thin, Wild Mercury Sound: Dylan, Nashville and the Making of Blonde on Blonde*. Chicago: Chicago Review, 2019.
Sanjek, Russell. *American Popular Music and Its Business: The First Four Hundred Years*, vol. 3: *From 1900 to 1984*. New York: Oxford University Press, 1988.
Shaughnessy, Mary Alice. *Les Paul: An American Original*. New York: William Morrow, 1993.
Shockley, Billie Rose. *From the Hills of East Tennessee: As I Remember It*. Privately published, 2011.
Smith, W. O. *Sideman: The Long Gig of W. O. Smith: A Memoir*. Nashville: Rutledge Hill, 1991.
Snow, Hank, with Jack Ownbey and Bob Burris. *The Hank Snow Story*. Urbana: University of Illinois Press, 1994.
Stevens, Ray, with C. W. "Buddy" Kalb. *Ray Stevens' Nashville*. Nashville: Clyde, 2014.
Stimeling, Travis. *Nashville Cats: Record Production in Music City*. Oxford: Oxford University Press, 2020.

Streeter, Richard Kent. *The Jimmy Driftwood Story.* Chattanooga, Tenn.: 2003, 2007.
Streissguth, Michael. *Eddy Arnold: Pioneer of the Nashville Sound.* New York: Schirmer, 1997.
———. *Like a Moth to a Flame: The Jim Reeves Story.* Nashville: Rutledge Hill, 1998.
Whitburn, Joel. *The Billboard Albums.* 6th ed. Menomonee Falls, Wisc.: Record Research, 2006.
———. *Hot Country Singles: 1944–2017.* Menomonee Falls, Wisc.: Record Research, 2018.
———. *Pop Memories: 1890–1954.* Menomonee Falls, Wisc.: Record Research, 1986.
———. *Top Pop Singles: 1955–2017.* Menomonee Falls, Wisc.: Record Research, 2019.
Williams, Roger M. *Sing a Sad Song: The Life of Hank Williams.* Urbana: University of Illinois Press.
Wolfe, Charles. *Tennessee Strings: The Story of Country Music in Tennessee.* Knoxville: University of Tennessee Press, 1977.
Zwonitzer, Mark, with Charles Hirshberg. *Will You Miss Me When I'm Gone? The Carter Family and Their Legacy in American Music.* New York: Simon & Schuster, 2002.

Index

Music of the American South

Whisperin' Bill Anderson: An Unprecedented Life in Country Music
by Bill Anderson, with Peter Cooper

Party Out of Bounds: The B-52's, R.E.M., and the Kids Who Rocked Athens, Georgia
by Rodger Lyle Brown

Widespread Panic in the Streets of Athens, Georgia
by Gordon Lamb

The Philosopher King: T Bone Burnett and the Ethic of a Southern Cultural Renaissance
by Heath Carpenter

The Music and Mythocracy of Col. Bruce Hampton: A Basically True Biography
by Jerry Grillo

An OutKast Reader: Essays on Race, Gender, and the Postmodern South
edited by Regina N. Bradley

Straight Into Darkness: Tom Petty as Rock Mystic
by Megan Volpert

Kill Your Masters: Run the Jewels and the World That Made Them
by Jaap van der Doelen

Chet Atkins: Mr. Guitar
by Don Cusic